TABLE OF CONTENTS

Vol. II Nature and Rites

Chapter 1 Venerating Nature 5

Chapter 2 Sacred Stones 22

Chapter 3 Flora 31

Chapter 4 Animals 53

Chapter 5 Elements and Celestial Bodies 73

Chapter 6 The Wheel of the Year 102

Chapter 7 Beliefs and Rites of the Life Cycle 156

Chapter 8 Healing, Divination, and Magic 175

Notes 212

Index 219

Copyright © Randy P Conner 2019
First paperback Edition

All rights reserved. No part of this work may be reproduced or utilized in any form by any means electronic or mechanical, including *xerography, photocopying, microfilm,* and *recording,* or by any information storage system without permission in writing from the publishers.

Published by
Mandrake of Oxford
PO Box 250
OXFORD
OX1 1AP (UK)

Vol. 1: Deities and Kindred Beings
Vol. 2: Nature and Rites
Vol. 3: Ritual Specialists
Vol. 4: Christianization
Vol. 5: The Arts and Philosophy

Chapter 1
Venerating Nature

A part of thee on the grey stones,
A part of thee on the steep mountains,
A part of thee on the swift cascades,
A part of thee on the gleaming clouds, ...
A part of thee on the great surging sea...

from a Gaelic "Charm for Chest Seizure"[1]

Such touches as these...redeem the subject from...the domain of the Devil [and "lift it"] into the brighter and lovelier world of the Spirits of Nature.

Elizabeth Lynn Linton, *Witch Stories* (1861)[2]

The Church's opponent was Mother Nature herself.

Wilhelm Holmqvist, *Swedish Vikings on Helgö and Birka* (1979)[3]

In *The Balts* (1963), archaeologist Marija Gimbutas describes her Lithuanian ancestors as believing that trees, "flowers, groves and forests, stones and hillocks, and waters were endowed with miraculous life-giving forces. They were thought to bring blessings upon human beings by healing diseases, safeguarding them against misfortunes, and assuring health and fertility." In regard to the proto-environmentalist ethics of these ancient peoples, she asserts that "[a]ll manifestations of the earth's fecundity were lovingly cared for and protected; the written records from the eleventh through the fifteenth centuries" – prior to that time, Lithuanians possessed a non-literate, oral culture – "repeatedly mention a profound respect for groves, trees and springs." Sharing this worldview in common with other ancient and indigenous cultures, in ancient Lithuania, "no one was permitted to cut trees in sacred forests, to fish in sacred springs, or to plough in sacred fields, which were referred to variously as *Alka*, *Alkas* or *Elkas*, and were guarded by 'tabu.'" According to Gimbutas, names like alka and elkas indicate, by way of being related to "Gothic *alhs*, Old English *ealh*, [and] Old Saxon *alah*, a "protected" status.

Gimbutas' description very succinctly depicts the earth-centered, indigenous worldview of the ancient Balts. "Nature," Alfred Biese (1856-1930) observes in *The Development of the Feeling for Nature in the Middle Ages and Modern Times* (1905), "in her ever-constant, ever-changing phases is indispensable to man, his whole existence depends upon her, and she influences him in manifold ways, in mind as well as in body." Indigenous deities and kindred beings, Biese relates, "dwelt in mountain tops, holes in the rocks, and rivers, and especially in dark forests and in the leafy boughs of sacred trees; and the howling of the wind, the rustle of leaves, the soughing in the tree tops, were sounds of their presence." Morris Berman echoes Gimbutas and Biese in describing the "enchanted" worldview of the ancient and some places in the medieval West in *The Reenchantment of the World* (1981, 1984): "The view of nature which predominated in the West down to the eve of the Scientific Revolution was that of an enchanted world. Rocks, trees, rivers, and clouds were all seen as wondrous, alive, and human beings felt at home in this environment. The cosmos...was a place of *belonging*." Berman explains that humans living in such cultures experienced neither a disengaged, alienated consciousness, nor a Humanist consciousness, with "man" at the center or zenith, nor a Transcendentalist consciousness, but rather one of participating *with*, and *in*, nature as a "member of the cosmos." He referred to this way of experiencing consciousness as a "participating consciousness," which "involves merger, or identification, with one's surroundings, and bespeaks a psychic wholeness." In other words, an *embodied* consciousness.

In *The Paganism Reader* (2004), Graham Harvey, for whose work I have great respect, praises Chas S. Clifton's article "Nature Religion for Real" for "its recognition that the definition of paganism as a 'nature religion' [cannot] be predicted with certainty from earlier sources." My research indicates, to the contrary, that one of the most basic and significant elements of the earth-centered pagan or indigenous European worldview is that which religious studies scholars traditionally refer to as "nature worship." I find Clifton's reasons for making this claim even somewhat troubling: "we do not own a single text written by a pagan Celt...no anthropologist ever sat down to interview a Druid," etc. Has he stopped to consider *why* these statements ring true? This rather sarcastic, cavalier response to the destruction of texts and religions/traditions frankly amazes me; I'm reminded of the notion of 'blaming the victim.' That we do not have "a single text written by a pagan Celt" or a Druid (not a present-day 'neo'-Druid) interview says much about Christianization but tells us little or nothing about nature worship, the earth-centered worldview, or paganism. My purpose herein is to demonstrate that ancient and indigenous sacred European traditions, generally termed "paganism," may indeed be considered earth-centered (or earth-based, nature-based) traditions.

Earth's Essence

The sacredness of nature described by Biese, Gimbutas, and Berman appears to have been rooted in a belief that all nature is imbued with sacred energy, force, or divinity. The world's religious and philosophical traditions and worldviews name diverse manifestations of this energy, force, or divinity, *mana* (Polynesian and Melanesian traditions/worldviews), *ase* (or, *aché*, *ashé*, *axê*, the Yorùbá religion of Nigeria and its branches in the Americas), *ch'i* (Daoism), *hey shae* (present-day Chinese rural tradition), *chi-sei* (*ki*, also possibly *kami*, Shinto), *teotl* (Nahuatl [Aztec]), *navala* (Hopi), and *élan vital* (philosophy of Henri Bergson). The Lithuanian term for this concept is *šventas*, which translates as "sacred" or the "power of life." A river imbued with this force is *šventa upe*; a tree, *šventas medis*; a stone, *šventas akmuo*. In ancient Germanic/Teutonic/Scandinavian tradition, it is probable that the word *aurr* was used by to indicate this energy/force/divine presence. Torun Zachrisson, in "The Holiness of Helgö" (2004) explains: "The word *aurr* means either "clay which clings to a bare foot," or the "fertile mud deposited when a river overflows its banks." In Old Norse mythological/religious vocabulary *aurr* means the life-giving powers of the earth itself."

In the context of Anglo-Saxon culture, Francis Peabody Magoun, Jr. suggests that the word "*máttr*," from which the English "matter" derives, as well as, or especially in combination with, the word "*megin (magen/mægen, moegen/mægen)*" may have signified the life force. He writes: "Everything can, and is likely to, have its mana [i.e., its *máttr*, its *megin*]: plants, parts of the human body, the earth itself (jarðar megin)." The possession of the life force causes something to become "*máttigr, máttugr*, 'potent,' 'powerful.'" Magoun, Jr. further suggests that other Anglo-Saxon terms including *croeft* and *miht* may have signified the life force or possession of it.

Åke Hultkrantz, in "Swedish Research on the Religion and Folklore of the Lapps," suggests that *seite*, a term which is frequently deployed to describe a sacred stone site, is often extended to include "tree, wooden figure, stone, rock, mountain, etc." In other words, *seite* may ultimately refer to that which houses the life-force, or that which divinity decides to embody. Hultkrantz argues that both Sámi shamans and Germanic heathens were intimately familiar with this concept; in regard to the latter, he suggests that the Germanic world-tree, one hypostasis of which is the Irminsul, represents an example of *seite*.

In Irish, the term *toradh*, which is typically translated today as "fruit," may have once referred to an "essence" akin to *mana*. In the early twentieth century it was defined as "the essence of milk or corn or of an animal," that which fairies traditionally deplete from food they are offered or take. *Toradh* derives from terms meaning "root," "to give," "gift," and "grace."

Many persons dwelling in medieval and post-medieval Europe continued to venerate stones, bodies of water, trees, animals, and other elements and/or beings of nature, as they had for millennia. These were sometimes referred to in Christian texts as *loci abhominati*, "abominable sites;" they included "trees, groves, woods and shrubs (*arbor, lucus, silva, locus silvestris, sentius*), bodies of water such as a spring, marsh, river, stream, sea, current or well (*fons, palus, flumen, rivus, mare, torrens, puteus*), stones (*lapis, saxum, petra*) and mountains (*montes*)." The use of the term *loci abhominati* is significant here. Regardless of the degree to which veneration of nature may have been appropriated by the Church, such concepts and practices as conceiving a stone or tree as ensouled or making offerings to these are *not* rooted in Christianity or in Biblical teaching; *they are rooted in indigenous spirituality, or the earth-centered worldview*. Indeed, such concepts and practices are frequently branded anathema by the Church. The practice of such traditions in a Christianized milieu, or their practice by populations who have been converted to Christianity under duress (as were many Celts, Germanics, Slavs, and Balts), does not mean, as some scholars have inferred, that the practices have miraculously become Christian ones; as we shall see, Church authorities who condemned and banned them were under no such illusion.

George P. Fedotov, in *The Russian Religious Mind: Kievan Christianity* (1946), asserts: "Nature, of course, is the necessary source of every primitive world view. It is commonly...accepted that paganism is identical with nature worship." Although I would replace "primitive" with "ancient" and/or "indigenous," and "identical" with "synonymous," I would agree with Fedotov that the veneration of nature holds a profoundly significant place in the earth-centered worldview. Fedotov insists that the "core of Russian paganism was not the belief in great gods but the religious veneration of nature."

The *First Novgorod Chronicle* reported that in the mid-tenth century, many inhabitants of Kiev and the surrounding area "continued to ma[ke] offerings to lakes, springs, and forests, like other pagans." In the late tenth century, Old Prussians venerated the "sun, moon and stars, as well as animals, birds and fire. They [held] certain woods, lakes and streams sacred, and in these no man [might] hunt, fish or cut timber." Eleventh-century Norwegians continued to venerate trees, hillocks, and bodies of water. In seventeenth-century Scotland, on the Isle of Skye, persons continued to venerate a "sanctified lake...surrounded by a fair wood, which none presumes to cut;" also at this time, a Jesuit priest, Stribing(ius) (fl. 1606), after interrogating a Lithuanian or East Prussian practitioner of indigenous spirituality/enspirited materiality, wrote in his report: "There are different gods, according to the diversity of places, persons, and needs. 'We have,' he [i.e., the pagan, possibly a pagan priest] said, 'a god who takes his place in the heavens, we have a god who governs the earth...we have a god who gives us fish.'" The pagan priest spoke to him of certain trees that were "deemed sacred" and that were not to be harmed."

When Lutheran Church 'Visitors' toured Estonia in 1667, they were extremely distraught on encountering peasants worshipping "at sacred groves and stones." almost three hundred years later, Conrad Arensberg (1910-1997), in *The Irish Countryman: An Anthropological Study* (1937), documented beliefs held by Irish farmers regarding nature. They told him that they were careful not to violate certain locations via such actions as cutting down trees or fouling the water; should they do so, they would be punished by the fairies. A decade later, Fedotov reported that in mid-twentieth-century "Russia, many relics of the cult of stones, trees, and wells [were] still partly preserved." Although many "sacred trees and stones" had "been Christianized," many others had "received no Christian sanctification at all," and, like the "sacred birches," continued to be associated with deities and similar beings. Incidentally, the term "cult," from the Latin *cultus*, is significant here; as Antal Bartha explains in "Myth and Reality in the Ancient Culture of the Northern Peoples": "The Latin word *cultus* is connected with the environment; it originally meant...the cultivation of the soil and reverence for the gods of agriculture."

Earth-centered Traditions

In no small part because the West has strayed so far from its ancient origins in a worldview that envisioned nature as sacred, I will speak very briefly of several present-day traditions, religions, and/or worldviews that venerate nature, so that we may more nearly approach what it must have been like to sense everything around us not only as alive but as sacred and as in constant and profound relationship with us, as we are with it, and as actively affecting the events occurring in our lives, the lives of other entities, and the life of the cosmos as a whole. Otherwise, I fear that when we read about the veneration of stones, trees, water, and other entities, we may register this data as little more than a menagerie of quaint trivia rather than recognizing it as signs of an ancient path of wisdom – one that might illuminate and perhaps assist in alleviating the current ecological/environmental crisis we are experiencing at present.

Indigenous American Ojibwe people believe that an encounter with nature "is not human performance towards an object upon which human-likeness is projected, but an encounter with persons who intentionally act towards and communicate with other persons." Similarly, Nahwiri Rafael Chanchari, a spokesperson for the Shawi people of the Amazon, relates that trees, stones, water, and other 'elements' and forces of nature are simultaneously comprised of both matter and spirit: "We Shawi think that all living beings have souls, which are their own spirits....Take a stone, for example.... [F]or the Shawi, a stone has its own soul, as does water. And earth also has its mother. For us, everything is alive."

Chancari's view is reiterated by present-day spiritual teacher Sobonfu E. Somé, whose *The Spirit of Intimacy: Ancient Teachings in the Ways of Relationships* (1997) illuminates the sacred concepts and practices of the Dagara of Burkina Faso, West Africa: "[T]here is such a thing as a pool of ancestors – it doesn't have to be a person...it can be a tree out there. It can be the cows out there, your dog or cat at home." In the religion of the Yorùbá of West Africa and its New World manifestations, including La Regla de Ocha (Lucumí, Santería) and Candomblé, everything is imbued with both *ashé* sacred energy or force, and *ori*, or consciousness. Humans share intimate relationships with both the deities and the natural forces they embody. Stones, trees (especially their often medicinal leaves), and bodies of water play very significant roles in worship.

In an enlightening essay on "Chinese Religion, 'Daoism,' and Deep Ecology" (2001), Jordan Paper, a professor of religious, Asian, environmental, and women's studies, explains that Western interpretations of Daoism have tended to be overly romantic and that Daoism is somewhat more anthropocentric and less animistic than Westerners have generally perceived or described it; among numerous examples from Daoist texts, he quotes one which, although acknowledging the need to love "mountains, rivers...birds, animals, and plants," explains that the *reason* humans should do so is "to realize [their] humanity" so that *they* will attain enlightenment. This is far from the worst way one might live, to say the least, but in terms of relationship to the pagan worldview, it is too focused on the human yearning for his or her own enlightenment rather than on profound and passionate relations with other sentient beings.

Paper, however, points toward a Chinese tradition that is linked more profoundly to Daoism and that resonates with the earth-centered European worldview: Rujia. He explains that many persons practice both Daoism and Rujia. Rujia, in accord with animism and with the earth-centered worldview, acknowledges that life feeds on life. Also, like animism and like the earth-based worldview, Rujia emphasizes the creation of "ritual ceremonies (*jiao*) that celebra[te] cosmic renewal and...that reinfor[ce] the connections between humans and the spirit realm, including Earth, Waters, and Sky." Rooted in an agriculture-based economy, Rujia rites have been performed for over 2,400 years. In earlier epochs, "the imperial couple sacrificed to Sky and Earth; regional governors, as well as the emperor, sacrificed at altars to Soil and Grain; and farming families...sacrifice[d] at small shrines in the farm fields to Grandmother and Grandfather Earth,"the last, a practice that Paper reports continues to be practiced today. Also resonant with animism and the earth-centered worldview, Rujia rites include those that honor ancestors. At present, Rujia rites are being interwoven with the expanding tradition of Fahui, which emphasizes "continual inspiration from the deities through spirit-possession," a practice also embraced by the pagan worldview.

I find it noteworthy that by the late seventeenth century (if not before), European scholars were comparing European earth-centered traditions to others, albeit primarily in a negative light. For example, Pierre Bayle, in *Pensées diverses sur la comète* (*Various Thoughts on the Occasion of a Comet*, 1682), in a section titled "On the Abominable Idolatry of Today's Pagans," harshly judges followers of Indian (e.g., Hindu and village traditions), Chinese (e.g., Daoism, and possibly Rujia-like practices), and Japanese (e.g., proto-Shinto) religions/traditions as well as Indigenous American traditions as he compares them to those of "ancient pagans." They find themselves," according to Bayle, "in the most frightful deviations that can be spoken of in the matter of religion; that they worship monkeys and cows; that they consult the demon in burning mountains."

The Renovation of Animism, and a word about Hylozoism

Believing that stones, trees, bodies of water, elements, celestial bodies, and animals are entities possessing souls, intellect and/or wisdom, and agency, that certain stones listen with empathy and keep secrets, that trees possess the power of speech or communication, that lakes moan, wail, and "move from place to place," all of which we will encounter, are considered attributes of "animism," especially as reclaimed, redefined, or reinvented by Graham Harvey in *Animism: Respecting the Living World* (2006). Harvey commences his book by defining "animists" as "people who recognize that the world is full of persons, only some of whom are human." Inspired by the work of anthropologist Alfred Irving Hallowell (1892-1974), Harvey refers to non-human entities, to animals, plants, stones, etc., as "other-than-human persons." It is important to note that Harvey's definition of animism does not infer, as earlier definitions of animism, such as those given by early anthropologist Edward Tylor (1832-1917) or as "some Christian missionizing discourses" were wont to do, that animism is in any way "primitive" or "childlike." Harvey also acknowledges and critiques as mistaken and Eurocentric the equation of animism, as in New Critical literary analysis, with the so-called "pathetic fallacy" (in my view, a "pathetic" attempt on the part of reactionary critics to deny consciousness and personhood to animals). Harvey goes on to define animists as people who understand "that life is always lived in relationship with others," those "others" including such "persons" as stones, trees, bodies of water, and other entities. He stresses that a significant aspect of such relationships is mutual, deep respect. Stones, trees, etc. are considered as sacred *per se* because they are embodied by sacred energy and also because they are often guarded by divinities. This double source of sacrality is reflected, for example, in the Maori understanding that "rocks and plants are alive" and ensouled and simultaneously "under relative degrees of control by their respective deities (of forest, field, storm and so on)." From the brief examples from Biese, Gimbutas, Berman, and Harvey, we can say that one of the significant elements of the earth-centered worldview is an animistic element.

Totemistic relationships of humans with plants and animals and other entities/other-than-human persons may include: kinship bonds manifesting as totem-like bonds, or bonds of clan; transmigration of human souls into other-than-human entities; and the existence of hybrid or were-creatures. Harvey explores these types of relationships as he takes a fresh look at "totemism." He observes that although many families and communities are related via blood, "some communities are comprised of a greater diversity;" "totemism is considered to be a mode of sociality and socializing that includes particular other-than-humans in kinship and affinity groupings and practices." In this type of relationship, "there is a clear recognition" – and here, Harvey is citing Debbie Rose's work with Aboriginal Australians – "that the lives of these beings are enmeshed in perduring relationships which bind people and certain animal or plant species together." Some say that totemistic relationships are also suggested by names such as Mac Cuill, "son of the hazel" and Macc Dara, "son of the oak." Totemistic relationships may also be reflected in special relationships shared between clans and serpents, horses, and bears, and in the form of a human soul's transmigration into "trees, flowers, animals, birds." Thus, another significant element of the pagan worldview, related to animism, is a totemistic element.

In the present academic environment, when we are obsessed with stressing differences at the expense of commonalities, I think it's important to acknowledge that animism shares a great deal with shamanism. As Stephen O. Glosecki puts it in *Shamanism and Old English Poetry*, "Animism underlies ...all shaman-ism." Although the Old English poem "The Seafarer" is a predominantly Christian text, it rather beautifully appropriates the notion of an animistic worldview and a concomitant shamanistic journey: "My soul with the sea flood/ Over the whale's country soars widely – / Over the surface of the earth – then comes back again to me."

Closely related to animism is hylozoism, which, according to Donald Gutierrez, refers to the "archaic pre-Socratic conception that all matter is alive, or that life and matter are indivisible." Hylozoism emphasizes the "interrelatedness or even interchangeability between the animate and inanimate," with stones being exemplary of the inanimate. Moreover, hylozoism does not tend to divide persons or things into subject and object, but is instead a form of what has been called "subject-subject consciousness."

From Sacred-Material Earth-Centered to Platonic, Transcendentalist Approaches

David Abram, in *The Spell of the Sensuous: Perception and Language in a More-Than-Human World* (1997), observes that in ancient Greek mythology or tradition, the "gods seem indistinguishable at times from the natural elements that display their power: Poseidon...is the very life and fury of the sea itself; Helios, 'lord of high noon,' is not distinct from the sun...even 'fair Dawn, with her spreading fingertips of rose,' is a living power."

Although many of us acknowledge the animistic and hylozoistic dimensions of ancient Greek mythology/religion, we do not tend to be cognizant of the profoundly animistic, hylozoistic, and pantheistic (-like) elements of ancient Greek philosophy. In my view, it may also assist us in processing the data and discussion that follows to briefly consider the role of nature in Western philosophy, including the treatment of nature in pagan- as well as Christian-based philosophy (and, by extension, Christian theology). This will permit us to see certain significant shifts in response to the pagan worldview.

In *Panpsychism in the West* (2005), David Skrbina observes that the "pre-Christian era acknowledged the presence of spirit and mind in nature." The pre-Socratic philosophers, to a large extent, envisioned the natural world as "inherently animated," insisting upon "the union of matter and spirit in a material substance." Thales (*c.* 636-*c.* 546 BCE) spoke of water, lodestone, and other entities as ensouled (he employed the term "psyche"), and of water in particular as the "cosmic *arche*, the fundamental principle underlying all material things;" indeed, he was of the opinion that "all things are full of gods." It is conceivable that Thales drew upon knowledge attained in Africa while sojourning among the Egyptians to arrive at these conclusions, as they believed that *ntr*, "divinity," was comprised of both spirit and matter, and that the 'water of life' evidenced the inextricable bond of matter and spirit (or consciousness). Théophile Obenga, in *La Philosophie Africaine de la période pharaonique: 2780-330 avant notre ère* (1990), suggests that Thales may have been familiar with a Pyramid text which reads: "She emerges from the living water that is in the heavens; she emerges from the living water that is on the earth." Anaximenes (fl. *c.* 544 BCE) put forth a similar argument, emphasizing *pneuma*, here, roughly, air, as the fundamental principle. This is sometimes called, in philosophical terms, the "argument by indwelling powers."

Pythagoras (fl. *c.* 530 BCE), who established a school of mysteries focusing on mathematics, music, and the immortality of the soul, venerated nature so profoundly that he believed in the transmigration of souls into animals and thus practiced vegetarianism. F. M. Cornford, in *From Religion to Philosophy*, describes Pythagorean philosophy as recognizing a kind of sacred "participation" in a web of interrelations of sentient beings, rooted in an acknowledgment of an "immanent collective soul." Moreover, the "Passage from the divine to the human, and from the human to the divine, remains permeable, and is perpetually traversed. The One can go out into the Many; and the Many can lose themselves in reunion with the one."

Whereas Thales conceived of water as the fundamental principle, and Anaximenes conceived of air as such, for Heraclitus (fl. *c.* 500 BCE), the fundamental animating, ensouled "life-energy" was fire. Empedocles added earth to the other three, speaking of the four elements working in "love" or "strife" in the cosmos. Obenga, in *Philosophie*, and Cheikh Anta Diop, in *Civilisation ou barbarie* (1981; translated as *Civilization or Barbarism: An Authentic Anthropology* (1991), suggest that this working in harmony of the four elements may have been influenced by traditional African beliefs such as those found among the ancient Egyptians, wherein earth (the god Geb), water (the goddess Tefnut), air (the god Shu), and fire (the goddess Nut) work together; or among the present-day Bambara, who believe that the spirit of creation, *yereyereti*, is comprised of the feminine elements of earth (*wali*) and water (*tali*) and the masculine elements of air (*miri*) and fire (*nati*).

Zeno of Citium (335-263 BCE), founder of Stoic philosophy, in a certain respect, echoing the pre-Socratic philosophers, "placed emphasis on the need to know the concrete universe" and taught that fire and air, when joined together, produce the *pneuma*, "the life energy of the universe," and that the divine "is not apart from the cosmos, but is in it." M. Tullius Cicero (106-43 BCE), while rejecting certain features of the pagan tradition, stated in *Of the Nature of the Gods*: "The world is a living and wise being, since it produces living and wise beings."

Other early Greek philosophers, however, commenced to divide the worldview of paganism into a dualism of matter vs. spirit, immanence vs. transcendence, science vs. spirituality or religion. As Tarnas puts it in *The Passion of the Western Mind* (1991): "The Greek mind now strove to discover a natural explanation for the cosmos by means of observation and reasoning, and these explanations soon began to shed their residual mythological components. It is worth noting that Tarnas uses the word "mythological," which signals a significant departure from viewing the earth-centered worldview as it is viewed herein, that is, as one possessing a profound religious or spiritual dimension, certainly as profound as that of Christianity. The use of the term "residual" is also somewhat jarring, suggesting a need for 'spring cleaning.' Yet Tarnas' observation is otherwise accurate. He points out that the philosopher-scientists Leucippus (fl. *c*. 440 BCE) and Democritus (*c*. 460-*c*. 370 BCE), in promoting atomic theory, led the ancients toward a materialistic worldview robbing matter of spirit, splitting the pagan worldview. Democritus, Tarnas reminds us, "considered that human belief in gods was no more than an attempt to explain extraordinary events like thunderstorms or earthquakes by means of imagined supernatural forces." The fifth century BCE also witnessed the rise of the Sophists, who taught a "flexible atheism or agnosticism in metaphysics and a situational morality in ethics," regarded nature as "an impersonal phenomenon whose laws of chance and necessity bore little concern for human affairs." He argues that "the general tenor of Greek intellectual evolution" led to an emergent "naturalistic science matur[ing] in step with an increasingly skeptical rationalism." It occurs to me that, although this is certainly a familiar narrative, we should perhaps pause to consider if this movement truly qualifies as "evolution' – "intellectual" or otherwise. How is it that we judge evolution of intellect? Simply by way of chronological movement? "Progress"? Is the desacralization of nature necessarily 'evolutionary' or 'progressive'? Does "skeptical rationalism" indicate greater wisdom than veneration of nature, reverence of the Divine? What are the origins of these standards of measurement, of judgment? Why do we continue to deploy them?

In this light, one might argue that "philosophy," from its inception, was a misnomer; it should have from the outset more accurately indicated its love of rationality and intellect, combined with a penchant for the scientific method, rather than a "love of wisdom," which, one might argue, embraces the deepest expressions of intuition, empathy, compassion, passion, the sacred.

To a limited extent, Socrates (*c*. 470-399 BCE) and Plato (*c*. 427-347 BCE) accepted the idea of an ensouled nature, describing it as an *anima mundi*, a World-Soul or "soul of the world." In *Timaeus*, he describes the world as "the fairest and most perfect of intelligible beings, framed like one visible animal comprehending within itself all other animals of a kindred *nature*." However, this *Anima Mundi* was to become increasingly divorced from the *tangible* natural world.

Plato departed from the earth-centeredness of Greek religion by way of valorizing archetypal entities inhabiting a realm of Ideas and in devaluing their tangible counterparts. Furthermore, he rejected the possibility that humans and other-than-humans might have empathic relationships. In *The Reenchantment of the World*, Morris Berman goes farther in critiquing Socrates and Plato: The "Homeric mentality," in which we experience the cosmos "through emotional identification with it," is "precisely what Socrates and Plato intended to destroy."

From Socrates and Plato until the emergence of Christianity, the struggle between an ensouled nature, on the one hand, and a desacralized nature and a privileged realm of Ideas and/or archetypes, on the other, intensified. With each movement away from the former, the earth-centered worldview lost ground. Aristotle (384-322 BCE), in accordance with pagan tradition, promoted the notion of a hierarchy of ensouled entities, but he departed from it in insisting upon an anthropocentric hierarchy with plants "as the lowest order of living things." Generally speaking, the Neoplatonists of Late Antiquity did not value the physical, tangible world of nature; rather, as Antoine Faivre observes: "[I]n Neoplatonism...[it is] the intelligible reality, the realm of the mind to which one strives to gain access [rather than]...the world of the senses. [Neoplatonism]...aids us in quitting this world in order to enter more easily into the pure region...[of] the world of ideas." Moreover, as Tarnas observes, in Neoplatonism "[t]he material world...is the level of reality furthest from unitary divinity. As the final limit of creation, it is characterized in negative terms...and as constituting the principle of evil." Late Antiquity also witnessed the rise of Hermeticism, with texts attributed to Hermes Trismegistus and others filled with contradictory statements of Platonic idealism and of coming to know the divine "through the contemplation of the world;" and Gnosticism, with many of its manifestations portraying "the world of the senses...[as] the work of an evil demiurge." Although to a certain extent Plato and numerous of those inspired by him continued to revere the ancient deities, in splitting the sacred from matter, in denigrating and in some cases even demonizing the natural world, they turned their backs on the pagan, earth-centered worldview.

In contrast to the main anti-nature thrust of medieval Christianity, some medieval Christians claimed nature as "God's Book;" however, in a move typical of this subset of anti-hegemonic Christians, the "twelfth-century Christian Cathedral School of Chartres...[while] personif[ying] Natura as a goddess," limited "the power attributed to her in pagan philosophies by emphasizing her subservience to God." In 1160, Alain de Lille (*c.* 1128-1203) portrayed Natura as God's "humble servant." Much more rarely, an earth-centered mysticism surfaced within a Christianity, as in the beautiful vision of St. Francis of Assisi (1181-1226): "[H]e would speak to [the flowers] and encourage them, as though they could understand, to praise the Lord. It was the same with the fields of corn and the vineyards, the stones in the earth and in the woods...earth, fire, air and wind...[H]e was wont to call all created things his brothers and sisters."

Francis' vision was shared by St. Clare (1194-1253), whose community adhered to "Franciscan ideals, including Francis' love of the world of nature, long after his death." Indeed, one might contend that St. Francis' and St. Clare's Christianity may have been informed in part by the earth-centered worldview and that their expression of faith spoke to a hybrid indigenous-Christian sensibility.

A mélange of Platonism, Jewish (in particular, Kabbalistic) mysticism, and other sacred elements, the alchemical tradition and related premodern philosophies represented "radical alternatives" to the prevailing Christian worldview of the Middle Ages and Renaissance: "Natura was...pictured as the mother goddess Isis;" marriage (*hieros gamos*) was celebrated between her, as an earthly and lunar principle, and a male solar and celestial principle; and their union (*coincidentia oppositorum*) was depicted in the form of Mercurius, an androgynous or hermaphroditic/intersex spirit. In 1565, the Italian philosopher Bernardino Telesio (1509-1588) wrote of the alchemical marriage: "We can see that the sky and the earth are not merely large parts of the world universe, but are of primary, even principal rank." In the occult sciences of the Renaissance, the theory of correspondences or doctrine of signatures became especially significant in the practice of magic. As expressed by the early (al)chemist and professor (at Marburg) of medicine Oswald Croll (*c*. 1560-1609): "[A]ll herbs, plants, trees and other things issuing from the bowels of the earth are so many magic signs." Indeed, in spite of the Church's general stance on nature, many persons of the Middle Ages and Renaissance, especially those who continued to labor in a rural setting, continued to adhere to an organic theory of nature and of life itself. As Carolyn Merchant in *The Death of Nature: Women, Ecology and the Scientific Revolution*, relates that the "daily interaction with nature was still structured...by close-knit, cooperative, organic communities ...[C]entral to the organic theory," she continues, "was the identification of nature, especially the earth, with a nurturing mother; a kindly beneficent female who provided for the needs of mankind in an ordered, planned universe. Nature remained female, now wild, bringing storms, droughts, and general chaos, now gentle, reposing in a calm, Arcadian landscape.

The Sephardic, Jewish-born, Christian convert, Dutch philosopher Benedict Spinoza (1632-1677) distinguished *natura naturans*, which he related to the creative action of an abstract god (not unlike the God of the Bible in certain respects, although less anthropomorphic), from *nature naturata*, that nature which is the product of God's creation and which is basically passive. Spinoza's pantheism (from *pan*, "all," and *theos*, "god") is chiefly concerned with the notion that God cannot be represented as two powers, that of transcendent godhead and that of nature, but rather must encompass both. In his insistence on monism, Spinoza's philosophy ultimately encouraged a view of God(dess) as Nature that commenced to return, to a certain extent, to the pagan worldview's veneration of nature and its privileging of immanence over transcendence. As Skrbina explains it, pantheism "means that the Cosmos has a divine quality, that all material objects (including humans) are part of that divinity, and that the divine is a unity. It also typically implies...that there is no transcendent realm of the Divine."

A few words about immanence. Of great significance to the earth-centered worldview, immanence refers to the presence or the indwelling of divinity in the world. Transcendence is very seldom privileged above immanence. Indeed, what might appear to be transcendent, within an earth-centered context may in fact more nearly approach what I shall call "invisible immanence." For example, where concepts and practices related to death and to beings such as fairies are concerned, otherworld and afterlife locations are often experienced as simultaneously sacred and tangible or corporeal. For the most part, within the earth-centered worldview, divinities, as those of humans and other-than-human persons/beings, as well as other realms of a multidimensional reality, are woven into the warp and woof of nature. As Abram relates, "Poseidon...is the very life and fury of the sea itself; Helios, 'lord of high noon,' is not distinct from the sun." Perhaps it is in a mythopoeic or "erotic" (in its Marcusian usage) rather than a strictly philosophical context that the term "pantheistic" may best be attributed to the pagan worldview; I am thinking here of a remark made by Fedotov in *The Russian Religious Mind*: "Beauty dwells in nature. And the beauty of nature for the Russian is the embracing, the enveloping, rather than the contemplated....[This is] pantheism of a sensual...kind. Sacred matter rather than spirit is the object of veneration."

To return to pantheism, I should point out that pantheism resonates with what I am calling here the earth-centered worldview only up to a point. Like pantheism, the earth-centered worldview, as we shall see, insists upon the sacrality of nature; it further insists upon a profound association of that sacrality with divinities. The earth-centered worldview does not, however, adhere to the monism of Spinoza's pantheism; the divinities of earth-centered spirituality are myriad, and the concomitant worldview, while recognizing 'the One,' simultaneously insists upon the existence and significance of 'the Many.' Moreover, the divinities of earth-centered pantheons are hardly what one might describe as "non-personal;" to the contrary, they are typically intensely personal. And while, resonating with pantheism, deities may correspond to or embody natural forces and entities, they are typically neither identical to nor bound by those entities or forces.

Deism and Romanticism, in the eighteenth and nineteenth centuries respectively, likewise promoted the earth-centered worldview in certain respects and defied the hegemonic stranglehold of the dominant Western worldview. With Christianization and the Scientific and Industrial Revolutions, earth-centered traditions of venerating nature were becoming ever-increasingly defiant. To participate in revived or reconstructed ancient traditions constituted, at least to a certain extent, resistance against ideological and theological assimilation.

In the earth-centered worldview and the traditions that emerge(d) from it, nature is held sacred. Stones, trees, and other entities are considered as sacred *per se* because they are embodied by sacred energy; they are often also guarded by divinities. This double source of sacrality is reflected in the understanding that "rocks and plants are alive" and ensouled and simultaneously "under relative degrees of control by their respective deities (of forest, field, storm and so on)." The veneration of nature typically depends upon specific topographical locations and is typically associated with specific entities, including non-human and divine beings inhabiting those locales. This veneration often takes the form of offerings and sacrifices. And this veneration often assists in the creation of deep, empathic bonds between humans and other-than-human beings.

Moreover, as Bernard Rio observes in *L'Arbre Philosophal* (*The Philosophical Tree*, 2001), in the earth-centered worldview, nature is not opposed to culture. The Romantics and Symbolists, who brewed a mélange of revolutionary politics, veneration of nature, and sacred hybridity, defied the Christian and Cartesian views that dominated late eighteenth- and nineteenth-century; as in the French poet Baudelaire's (1821-1867) "Correspondences," they frequently deployed the doctrine of sympathies or theory of correspondences (e.g., Venus—Friday—roses—love) to express an earth-centered view of nature:

Nature is a temple wherein living pillars
Let loose sometimes bewildering speech
Man traverses these forests of symbols
Who observe him with a familiar gaze.
Like long echoes from far away that are fused
In a tenebrous and profound unity,
Vast as the night and as brightness,
Perfumes, colors and sounds respond to one another.[4]

In sum, the indigenous European earth-centered worldview's veneration of nature stands in close relationship to the worldviews of the Yorùbá, the Ojibwe, the Shawi of the Amazon, and Japanese practitioners of Shinto, and practitioners of ancient Chinese religions/traditions. In my view, if we are to come to better comprehend the European earth-centered worldview, we need to acknowledge it as a generally indigenous European material-sacred worldview informed, over the course of millennia, by other indigenous worldviews, such as, possibly if not probably, those of certain African (including Egyptian), Asian, and Indigenous American peoples, as well as the imperial material-sacred worldviews of Greeks and Romans. Although these material-sacred worldviews and their concomitant practices differ(ed) from each other in numerous respects, they share(d) in common numerous elements including veneration of nature, resonating to a certain extent with animism and pantheism. These elements and the worldviews that have intersected, overlapped, or cross-pollinated one another have, in the face of Christianization (in other places, Islamization) and other manifestations of religious imperialism and universalism, persisted more tenaciously than we might imagine, enough so that Panspsychist philosophers, Modern Pagans, as well as those indigenous peoples who have not been the victims of deicide and religiocide, and others are able to draw nourishment from them at the dawn of the twenty-first century.

In the earth-centered worldview, as Baudelaire believed and as Rio relates, nature is a sacred text: "An elementary text, nature conserves the diffuse memories of the past," "above and beyond lengthy colonizations and ephemeral invasions." It is a "place of memory and reflection."

David Abram, in *The Spell of the Sensuous*, writes of present-day indigenous shamanistic traditions in a way that resonates uncannily with the pagan worldview, revealing the distance of both of these from the dominant worldview of the present-day West: "[I]t is not only those entities acknowledged by Western civilization [like animals and plants that are] "alive"…but also the meandering river…the torrential monsoon rains, and the stone that fits neatly into the palm of the hand. The mountain, too, has its thoughts." Even at present, for many cultures on the earth, the "enveloping and sensuous earth remains the dwelling place of both the living *and* the dead…[In] indigenous cultures, the sensuous world itself remains the dwelling place of the gods, of the numinous powers."

Earth-Centered Urbanites and Material-Sacred Centers

Many present-day Pagans, Wiccans, and kindred spirits share a common belief, or perhaps an idyllic vision, that earth-centered cultures were strangers to urbanity. While it is the case that many practitioners of earth-centered traditions were rural dwellers, since the bulk of the labor force was devoted to agriculture through the Middle Ages, it is also the case that many practitioners of earth-based traditions inhabited cities, towns, and villages. Thus, the veneration of nature was practiced by rural and urban practitioners of earth-based traditions alike. Although it is evident that urbanites were under much greater pressure than rurals to convert to Christianity, many European village-, town-, and city-dwellers continued to venerate nature during the Middle Ages and thereafter, just as city-dwelling Egyptians, Greeks, Romans, Nahuas (Mexicas/Aztecs), and others honored the forces of nature.

In the early tenth century, Archbishop Unni (d. 936) was sent to Birka ("Birch Island"), an island in Lake Mälaren, twenty miles west of present-day Stockholm, Sweden to convert its inhabitants. Birka was at the time a "heathen" urban center, indeed, a major trading center, including for the Vikings, in the Baltic Sea region, where products from Finland, Russia, Arabia, China, and elsewhere were traded, with products including finely crafted weapons, pottery, fabrics (including wool from what is now Germany as well as Chinese silk), women's attire, and jewelry. A vivid example of "heathen" tolerance of other faiths, it appears from archaeological evidence that Christians, Jews, Muslims and practitioners of earth-based traditions practiced their faiths alongside each other until the end of the tenth century. Its abandonment and the consequent rise of the town of Sigtuna as a trading center was an effect of Christianization.

Similarly, Hedeby was a town in southern Denmark, its name meaning "town on the heath." It has been described as the "largest town in the North during the Viking period." Travelers were impressed that "every house had dug a well fitted with a wooden pipe." They also noted the rather unusual diet of the inhabitants, a predominantly vegetarian one despite the raising of animals – with the addition of fish – including "barley, wheat, hazelnuts, walnuts, apples, cherries, plums, sloes, elderberries, blackberries, raspberries, [and] wild strawberries." And they noted the inhabitants' keeping of cats and dogs in their houses. Like Birka, Hedeby was a trading center; but it was also known for its own industries, including farming (inhabitants raised pigs, cows, sheep, and goats) as well as "iron-smelting, weaving, industries using bone and horn, bronze-casting, glass-making, minting of coins, and potteries," the making of "weapons and jewelry," and the construction of boats and ships from oak and ash. In the mid-tenth century, Hedeby remained a "heathen" urban center when it was visited by the Sephardic Jewish merchant Abraham ben Jacob (a.k.a. Ibrahim ibn Yaqub Al-Tartushi, d. 966 CE) from the Caliphate of Cordova, Spain. Al-Tartushi, as he was most commonly known, described Hedeby as a "large town at the very far end of the world ocean." By ben Jacob's day, pagans, then a majority, whom he, perhaps mistakenly, identified as worshippers of Sirius, and Christians, then a minority, were living and working together in Hedeby. He continued, "The inhabitants' principal food is fish, which is plentiful....[W]omen have the right to claim a divorce; they do this themselves whenever they wish. There is also an artificial makeup for the eyes; when they use it their beauty never fades, on the contrary it increases in both men and women." The town remained chiefly "heathen," at least through the mid-tenth century. During this period, practitioners of earth-based traditions and Christians lived together peacefully for over a century. Hedeby was, however, tragically burned to the ground near 1050 during a struggle between two Christian convert kings, Harald Hardrada of Norway (b. 1015—d. 1066) and Swein Estridsson of Denmark (b. *c.* 1018—d. *c.* 1074). King Harald was jubilant and a song with the words "Burnt in anger was Hedeby from end to end" was composed to commemorate its destruction. Hedeby never recovered.

Jumne lay in what is now Poland, near present-day Wollin. It appears to have reached its heyday in the late eleventh century. In this large and prosperous city, Slavs and Germanics lived together with Greeks. Jumne was especially known as a trading center. One of its most significant sites appears to have been a great lighthouse. It seems that many of its inhabitants, remaining pagan through the late eleventh century, worshipped, probably among other divinities, a sea-god comparable to Neptune, possibly Porenut.

Beyond cities and towns, certain inhabited sites in Lithuania, Sweden, and elsewhere, were thought to be sacred or were considered material-sacred centers. One such site was Roma, on Gotland Island, which lies between Sweden and the Baltic states. Roma was among the most renowned Viking settlements. Here, practitioners of earth-based traditions convened "for meetings and rituals," especially for the Gutna Althing, as well as to take advantage of the thriving market. Nearby were sacred stone sites, sacred groves, and exquisitely carved picture-stones as well as prosperous farms. Roma was Christianized in the twelfth century. Today, with its ruins and museum, it forms part of an island-wide park known as Gotland Viking Island.

More famous was Gamla, or Old, Uppsala, Sweden. More than a city per se, Gamla Uppsala, inhabited from around 300 CE, appears to have served primarily as a material-sacred center, royal residence, site of large assemblies, called Things, and trading center with great market fairs. However, agriculture and military training were also practiced there. As a material-sacred center, Gamla Uppsala included a temple, especially serving the gods Odin, Thor, and Freyr, a sacred grove, and a necropolis, and its rites included special celebrations in honor of the Mother Goddesses, the Dísir, as well as animal sacrifices. During the late eleventh century, the bulk of its population continued to practice indigenous traditions; many did so a century later, although the twelfth century also witnessed the destruction of Gamla Uppsala's great temple and the forced Christianization of Swedes.[5]

Chapter 2
Sacred Stones

...on the Moor we have Mis Tor, a height on whose consecrated rocks there is found so large and perfect a rock-basin as to be called by the peasantry Mis Tor Pan. ...[T]he heathen god still possesses his eminence...

Anna Eliza Kempe Stothard Bray, *The Borders of the Tamar and the Tavy* (1879)[6]

In Darnton towne ther is a stane,
And most strange is yt to tell,
That yt turnes nine times round aboute
When yt hears ye clock strike twell.

Anonymous lyric[7]

My maternal grandmother's father's ancestors lived for a long time in the village of Ackmenischken, as it is called in Old Prussian, or Akmeniskiai, as it is known to Lithuanians. It derived its name from the word "*akmuo*," meaning "stone," with "*akmenauti*" referring to "collecting stones" and "*akmenynas*" meaning the "place abounding in stones." "Ackmenischken" means "belonging to the stones." Its name recalls a time when the people who lived here venerated stones as sacred entities. They did so at least until the late medieval period, when Church authorities forbade such veneration.

Veneration of stones is a common element of many ancient and indigenous traditions. In *Talismans and Trojan Horses*, Christopher Faraone notes that among the Greeks, stones called *diopetês*, which had or were thought to have fallen from the heavens, including meteorites, were considered especially sacred. They believed that such stones, as well as other sacred stones, "to be inherently numinous or animated." Both Greeks and Phoenicians set up sacred stones, *baityloi*, or *lithoi empsychoi*, "animated stones," "at the gates of cities and temples." Faraone adds that according to "Phoenician belief, these stones served simultaneously as abode, image, and altar of the deity, who protected the building at whose entrance it was placed; offerings of blood and oil were regularly poured upon them." According to Homer, white stones consecrated with oil "stood before the front door of Nestor's palace in Pylos." Some Greeks believed that one should not "pass one of the smooth stones set up at the crossroads without anointing it with oil from his flask and prostrating himself before it." Stones dedicated to Hecate were sometimes offered wine. Some also believed that, together with "anointing it with oil," a stone could be sacralized by way of "draping it with wreaths and garlands." Pausanius tells of a stone at Delphi (not the omphalos) that was offered oil each day and wrapped in wool on feast-days. Sacred stones were placed at thresholds, as at gates and entry doors, and at crossroads. These included stones representing Apollo in various hypostases: Thyraios (Of the Door); Prothyraios (Before the Door); Prostaterios (Who Stands Before the Door); and Apotropaios (the Averter). Other stones represented Pan, Aphrodite, and Hephaistos/Vulcan. Still other stones were housed by Greeks in sealed jars, jugs, pitchers, and urns. Stones, as well as figurines and statues, representing deities were also placed behind doors, including those dedicated to Hermes, Hecate, and Apollo. Stone representations, including herms, of Hermes Strophaios were "set up behind the door of the house...to protect the house against thieves" and other malefic persons and forces. Ancient Hebrews also considered certain stones sacred, animate, and even capable of speech and prophesy and made kindred offerings to them or to the force they embodied; "[a]fter his dream about the ladder ascending to heaven, Jacob [set] up a stone in the desert, pour[ed] oil on it, and call[ed] it *beth-el*, "house of God."

Indigenous American Ojibwe, according to Graham Harvey, believe that "stones...are not treated merely *as if* they are persons, they are treated *as* persons. This is not human performance towards an object upon which human-likeness is projected, but an encounter with persons who intentionally act towards and communicate with other persons."

Similarly, in a conversation with Jeremy Narby, a young Canadian anthropologist and author of *Intelligence in Nature: An Inquiry into Knowledge* (2005), Nahwiri Rafael Chanchari, a spokesperson for the Shawi people of the Amazon, observed in 2001: "We Shawi think that all living beings have souls, which are their own spirits.... Take a stone, for example.... [F]or the Shawi, a stone has its own soul, as does water.... For us, everything is alive."

In the religion of the Yorùbá of West Africa and its New World manifestations, *ori*, consciousness, "encompassing both the rational and spiritual aspects of human thought," is not limited to humans; "all forces of nature also have it," including stones.

Stones play very significant roles in worship. J. Omosade Awolalu, in *Yoruba Beliefs and Sacrificial Rites* (1979, 2001), observes of rites in Nigeria, "Rocks...are believed to be the symbol and, in fact, the residences of some divinities....In consequence of this idea, many religious ceremonies are associated with large rocks and they serve as shrines." He continues, "At every shrine, there is an altar.... where sacrifice is offered...hence we have a heap of stones, or piles of iron, or a mound of consecrated earth or a large stone upon which the offering may fall." Sacred stones, as Joseph M. Murphy explains in *Santería: An African Religion in America* (1988), represent "the most fundamental symbol of the deities', the *orishás*,' presence: "ocean stones for Yemayá, river pebbles for Oshún, meteorites for the thunder king Shangó."

Indeed, numerous concepts and practices found in present-day Yorùbá-diasporic sacred practice, such as the placing of offerings and sacrifices on or near stones and the pouring of blood and its vegetable likeness, red palm oil, on stone representations of the *orishá* Eleggúa, who is comparable to the god Hermes, resonate with those of the Greeks mentioned above. Murphy notes, "As embodiments of the *orishás*, the stones [*otanes*, which one receives at initiation] must be treated as the living things that they are, and so they are lovingly bathed in cooling herbs, cleaned and oiled, and fed with the blood of animals."

Some sacred stones were thought to have fallen from the heavens. Vykintas Vaitkevicius writes: "They connect[ed] different spheres: the earth, the underworld, the heavens, the worlds of the living, the dead, and the gods." Some gatherings of sacred stones, such as Stonehenge, appear to mark special events of the ancient calendrical cycle such as the winter solstice. Drilling a "round hole into a stone was to fecundate the earth force which resides in the stone."

Stones as Living Beings and as 'Persons'

Archaeologist and historian Vykintas Vaitkevicius (1998), focusing on indigenous beliefs in Lithuania, observes that stones were "believed to possess qualities peculiar to living beings: they grew as plants and human beings did."

One of the ways stones manifested their agency or 'personhood' was by moving. The menhir of St. Martin-d'Arcé, France "rotates at the stroke of midnight," while the Bulmer Stone, a "water-worn boulder-stone of Shap (Westmorland) granite," of Darlington (a.k.a. Darnton town), England, near Northgate House the Bulmer Stone was thought by nineteenth-century inhabitants to revolve nine times whenever the clock struck twelve. Another menhir, that of Culey-le-Patry, France "moves only to the sound of the cock's crow." Still others twirl, rise up from the ground, and, at Plouhinec, Brittany, move to the "river to take a drink."

George Henderson (1911) recounts that in Scotland and Ireland, certain stones were thought to be 'good listeners,' hearing with empathy and keeping the secrets of others; Scottish Highlanders spoke of "telling it to the stones" (*ga innseadh dha na clachan*). Henderson also notes: "Stones were formerly believed to have a soul, and certain large ones were held to be in intimate connection with spirits." Indeed, in Scotland, certain stones were thought to house the spirits, or *coach anama*, "of famous men."

Some stones were believed to speak, although only certain persons could hear and understand them, such as alleged Scottish witches Katherine Carey (fl. *c.* 1617) and James Knarstoun (fl. *c.* 1633). Stones collected from different sites, such as one from the shore, one from a hill, and one from an ancient sacred site or churchyard, could assist, by speaking in a roaring voice, the practitioner in determining which sacred entity might be harming an ill person.

Kinds of Stones and Stone Structures

There are various kinds of sacred stones and stone structures. Other than the megalith, the general name for a sacred stone "of large dimensions," or a menhir, a standing stone, they include: the cairn, a "tumulus [an "artificial mound covering a burial deposit"] or mound of a megalithic tomb made up of small stones;" a dolmen, an "open burial chamber, generally megalithic, covered with a tumulus and used to hold several burials" (also used more broadly for any megalithic structure); and a henge, a "ditch, usually accompanied with an earthen mound and/or a series of standing stones."

Sacred stones were (and are) categorized according to shape, location, markings/engravings, and other features. They were often marked with symbols. In *The Goddess of the Stones: The Language of the Megaliths* (1991), George Terence Meaden draws our attention to labyrinths, lozenges, lunar crescents, spirals, triangles, and zigzags on stones at Newgrange and Knowth, Ireland, in the Orkney Islands, and elsewhere; and of Baltic countries, Gimbutas observes: "Stones found in the Baltic lands were often incised with symbols of suns and snakes, much as they were elsewhere in northern and western Europe from the Bronze Age onward."

In the *Denham Tracts* (1895), Michael Aislabie Denham recalls stones he became aware of during his childhood in nineteenth-century Scotland:

> When I was a boy, the large flat stone on which the mistresses of households knocked their linen webs when bleaching, which lay beside the well at a farm-place in Berwickshire, had on its upper surface an excavation resembling a small female foot, which was reckoned to have been impressed by a fairy footstep. Another stone with a corresponding impression by which people crossed a miry part of the road leading to St. Helen's Church, Oldcambus [in the parish of Cockburnspath, Berwick, Scotland] was regarded as a "Mermaid's Stone."[8]

Probably because of the later Christianization of Lithuania and Lithuania Minor than other regions of Europe, a greater amount of data regarding the veneration of stones has been preserved for this region. Vaitkevicius relates that various kinds of stones found in Lithuania include: cup-marked stones (*akmeno; su pėdomis*); bed-stones (*akmenys lovos*), throne or armchair stones (*akmenis kreslus*); table stones (*Dievo stalu*) and sacrifice (*aukuras*) stones, on which offerings and sacrifices were made; fairy stones (*laumio akmenys*); and menhirs (*stovintys akmenys*). Sacred stones were frequently found near sacred hearths. Certain stones are marked with rune-like inscriptions and with symbols; exemplary of the latter is the carved stone known as the "Pillars of Gediminas," found at the sacred site of Rambynas. The trident-like symbol carved on this stone was employed by Gediminas (c. 1275-1341; r. 1315-1341) as a coat of arms and, despite prohibition of its use by both late medieval Christians and twentieth-century Soviets, has survived as a symbol of Lithuanian unity. In Scotland, the shapes of stones often indicated powers they possessed; for example, "large stones, shaped like teeth, were believed to be able to relieve the pain of toothache, while those shaped like chairs were thought to help fertility problems or [to ease] childbirth."

In regard to kinds of stones, we might also make brief mention of the significant place of gemstones (precious- and semi-precious stones, jewels) in earth-based sacred traditions. In Greco-Roman embodied spirituality, for instance, the emerald belongs to Aphrodite/Venus as a goddess of nature, whereas the ruby belongs to her as a goddess of passion, and the sapphire to her as a goddess of wisdom. In Germanic tradition, the thunder-god Thor, when he dresses as the goddess Freyja to deceive a giant, has his "breasts" decorated with precious stones. Moreover, in terms of correspondences, the sapphire and carnelian belong to Thor, while the emerald, ruby, and cat's eye belong to Freyja (or Frigga), and the lodestone, amethyst, and turquoise belong to Odin/Woden. Also in Germanic tradition, dwarves are guardians of precious stones. Among Slavs, the hair of the Rozhanytsi, goddesses of destiny, "is adorned with precious stones."

Stones and Divinities

As Vaitkevicius points out, stones were often linked to divinities. Tamra Andrews, in *A Dictionary of Nature Myths* (1998), observes that in "many lands people connected the worship of rocks and stones with reverence for the earth mother. Solid and immutable, the rocks were the great goddess's bones, the foundation from which she gave birth, and the framework that protected the hollows of her womb." In this light, Gimbutas recounts of divinely embodied stones: "From a description given in 1836 we learn that in Lithuania there were stone monuments — usually about six feet high, smoothly cut, and surrounded by a ditch — which were dedicated to goddesses who spent their time at the stones spinning the fates of men." She notes that in "1605, a Jesuit reported a stone cult in western Lithuania: 'Huge stones, with flat surfaces, were called goddesses. Such stones were covered with straw and venerated as protectors of crops and animals.'"

Jean-Pierre Mohen, who received a doctorate in prehistory from the Sorbonne, provides evidence, in *Megaliths: Stones of Memory*, for Mother Goddess stones, including a carved Neolithic stone from Guernsey and an engraving on the wall of the hypogeum of Razet à Coizard, France. In southern Russia, *Kamennaia Baba*, "Stone Mothers," is the name given to megaliths thought to embody female divinities; *baba* stones were also found in Lithuania Minor and in Warmia and Mazury in what is now northeastern Poland. These examples indicate another significant element of the earth-centered worldview, namely, a matrifocal or goddess-centered element.

Among the Celtic Gauls, Alisanos was god of stones. In Lithuania, the thunder god Perkûnas sometimes embodied or assumed the form of a stone. In relating that the sites of sacred stones were "often the judicial and administrative focus of a community," In regard to a stone dedicated to Odin and to an event that occurred in the Orkney Islands of Scotland, where

Germanic traditions penetrated deeply, in 1781: "[A] young man who had broken...an agreement [regarding commitment to a loving relationship] made through a hole in Odin's Stone, near the Ring of Brogar, was severely reprimanded by the elders of the Orkney sessions for 'breaking the promise of Odin.'" Odin's Stone was destroyed in 1814 by a farmer who was fed up with couples plighting troth on his land. Another Odin's stone, utilized for the same purpose, was recorded by John Jamieson in his 1808 *Etymological Dictionary of the Scottish Language*; this stone – a black stone, 6'6" x 4' 6," "noticeably different from surrounding stones on the beach" – may still be seen on the beach at Veantro Bay on the island of Shapinsay. The presence not only of goddesses but also of male deities including Alisanos, Perkûnas, and Odin indicates another significant element of the earth-centered worldview, that of polytheism. In or near 1597, near Aberdeen, Scotland, alleged witches Beatrice Robbie and Margaret Og danced around a "great stone" to invoke "the Devil."

Vaitkevicius notes that "sometimes spirits lived under them [i.e., stones of Lithuania]." Scottish beings known as *gruagachs* and brownies assumed the shapes of stones and as such, that is, as *Clach na Gruagach*, were offered milk "in return for favorable harvests or other forms of good luck." Cultural layering or stratification is evidenced by the belief among Viking settlers on the Scottish island of Hoy, in the Orkneys, that a Neolithic burial tomb was a home to dwarves, Dvergasteinn. Some stone formations in Scotland were held in awe due to their association with chieftains, kings (at Twinlaw Cairns, Berwickshire; in the Lammermuir Hills, East Lothian), fairies (at Berwickshire; at Glenesk; and at Carmyllie, Forfarshire), and even mermaids (at Oldcambus). It was believed that these persons or beings had stepped upon or otherwise touched the stones, leaving traces of footprints and handprints. The Hurle Stane near Chillingham, in northeastern England, was thought to be the favorite haunt of the local fairies. As they danced around the stone, they were heard singing:

> Wind about and turn again,
> And thrice around the Hurle Stane;
> Round about and wind again,
> And thrice around the Hurle Stane.[9]

A legend persisting in the early nineteenth century linked an enormous stone (of about twenty tons) and two crags, "King's Crag" and "Queen's Crag," of a sandstone formation north of Sewingshields, Northumbria, England, to the mythos of King Arthur and Queen Guinevere.

Healing, Divination, and Magic

> I request my stone of conflagration.
> Be it no ghost of theft.
> Be it a blaze that will [cry out] victory
> before the valiant battle of Clare,
> my fire stone which delves pain.
> from *Lia Draíochta le Mogh Ruith* ("Mogh Ruith's Magic Stone"), an ancient Irish *rosc* (magical chant)[10]

Certain stones were thought to possess healing, divinatory, and magical powers. These stones were often passed down "through generations of the same family." Scots, as mentioned above, often considered certain stones capable of healing illness. Such were the Toothache Stone at Port Charlotte on Islay and the Clach Thuill ('Holed Stone') at Crossapol on Coll. Joyce Miller, in *Myth and Magic: Scotland's Ancient Beliefs and Sacred Places* (2000), writes: "The Clach Bhan, or Wife Stone, at Linn of Avon between Braemar and Tomintoul, [Scotland] was used by pregnant women in the belief that it would provide some help with the pain of childbirth...[U]nmarried women would also visit the stone, not initially to get assistance with childbirth, but in the belief that it would help them find a husband." "Until quite recently," Gimbutas reports, "Baltic peasant women coming home from work would stop by such stones to cure their aches and pains by washing themselves with the water." Scots often used crystals as healing tools, either by passing them over the bodies of ill persons or animals or else, as among Balts, washed the sick in water in which crystals had been dipped. White and rose quartz, which Scots envisioned as belonging to the fairies, were used in treating fever, rheumatism, and tuberculosis. Into the late nineteenth century, some Irish rurals believed that pain in the hip or limbs might be cured by rubbing three green stones, picked from a brook between midnight and dawn, "several times up and down on the naked limb," while they chanted, "Wear away, wear away,/ There you shall not stay,/ Cruel pain, away, away!"

Certain stones divined whether or not a person was telling the truth; such were the Truth Stone on the Isle of Skye and the "black slate stone called the Cremave or Swearing Stone" on an "island in the Shannon." Some stones, such as the Lia Fail, the Irish 'stone of destiny,' were thought to possess oracular powers; the Lia Fail roared when it recognized the man who should reign over Ireland. The Brahan seer of Lewis, Scotland, Kennoth Odhar (b. *c.* 1650) "had a small blue stone which he used as an aid for divination." Some stones aided persons in removing the evil eye or otherwise protected them from or countered the effects of destructive magic. Protection in battle was, needless to say, of great importance.

Other stones, especially stones with holes in them, as well as the rainwater that seeped into them, "are said to have aphrodisiac power" and also magically promote fertility. W. G. Wood-Martin describes cairns, piles of stones, found in Ireland called "hags' beds" or *leabas* that, in the late nineteenth century, continued to be visited by women, sometimes accompanied by their husbands, hoping to dispel barrenness and promote childbirth. Padraic O'Farrell notes, "Expectant women passed part of their garments through one such stone at Clocnapeacaibh in Cork." Such stone structures, also found in Scotland and Wales, sometimes carry the name of "Cailleach," such as the Cailleach na Mointeach Kerbed cairn, or the Old Woman of the Moors, found on Scotland's isle of Lewis; these stones are thought to be consecrated to the Celtic triune goddess called the Cailleach. Also in this regard, Gimbutas relates, "A huge stone in the shape of a woman's torso, known from Lithuania in the nineteenth century, was believed to possess magical qualities that would bestow fecundity on allegedly barren women."

Mohen observes: "[H]uge phallic monuments promote love, fertility, and health.... In France young women would pull up their skirts to straddle the Pierre-de-Chantecoq or the pillar of La Roche-Marie, and they would slide, legs astride, down the leaning menhir of La Tremblais at St.-Samson-sur-Rance." He continues, "To assure themselves beautiful progeny, husbands and wives would rub their naked bellies along the two sides of the menhir of Kerloas at Plouarzel, and at Nohant-Vic, barren women were advised to suck on a chip of red sandstone taken from the slab of a dolmen." In a similar manner, "slabs with holes were known to confer virility."

A related ceremonial function of stones was the conferring of royal power. Leslek Pawel Slupecki, in *Slavonic Pagan Sanctuaries* (1994), explains that in Slavic areas, stones "played an important role in the enthroning ceremonies of Slavic rulers. A prince sat on a stone, whose tough matter symbolized eternity and permanence...sanctifying the ruler by placing him in the center of his domain. The stone throne gave the ruler majesty and power."

Still other stones secured favorable winds and enabled people to fly. In Scotland, people sometimes wore amulets or talismans of quartz for such purposes as those mentioned above.

Not surprisingly, certain stones were also used in magical rites of cursing. At Cromarty, Scotland, a boulder called Clach na Mallachd was employed by practitioners by kneeling upon it and pronouncing curses. The alleged Scottish witch James Reid, tried in 1602, was thought to have sought to ruin the crops of David Libberton, a baker, by casting nine enchanted stones onto his field.

Stones and Humans

The telling of secrets and sorrows to stones is one of several indicators of the often deep, occasionally familial and/or totemic, bonds humans shared with stones. Ancient Celts, for whom veneration of stones was known as *ail adrada*, may have believed that the souls of the dead transmigrated into stones. Other stones were believed to be people who had turned to stone. In the nineteenth century, on the Scottish Isle of Lewis, "certain families...were held in secret esteem as 'belonging to the stones.'" Also in Scotland, stones enjoined humans to tell the truth and were often employed as sites of punishment when they failed to do so. Loving partners swore engagements, handfastings, and marriages in the presence of sacred stones – especially handfastings. A handfasting "was an arrangement – without any supervision by a minister or priest – between a man and a woman that they would live together as husband and wife for a year and a day. If for any reason they did not wish to stay together at the end of the year, they could separate without any penalty." In Scotland, couples journeyed to Odin's Stone in the Stones of Stenness complex, Orkney, for this purpose.

Western Balts of antiquity typically surrounded burial pits with stone circles; this practice persisted for thousands of years. Even apparently mundane objects such as stone hearths and ovens and stone walls surrounding farmsteads acquired sacred meaning for Balts due to belief in stones as embodying sacred energy.

Offerings to Stones

People who venerated stones and/or the divinities associated with them honored them with offerings, including of bread, cheese, milk, and colorful rags. In Scotland, certain stones, called *Clach na h-Iobairte*, 'Stone[s] of the Offering[s],' were particularly acknowledged as sites where offerings to stone-spirits were made. In Scotland, stones, or the spirits thought to embody them, which were thought to possess healing power were sometimes gifted with offerings. For example, when a member of her family became seriously ill, the mother or another woman of the family might bake a cake to offer to a holed stone in the vicinity of Dingwall, Scotland. As mentioned above, *gruagachs* and brownies assuming the shapes of stones were offered milk in exchange for good fortune and prosperity.

Tampering with Stones

Due to their sacredness and their aliveness, it was considered in some places, despite centuries of Christianization, disrespectful to tamper with sacred stones, other than making offerings to them; "In the Highlands," according to Henderson, "it is regarded as a source of danger to make use of pillared stones (*clachan carraghan*) in building human or other dwellings." Michael Aislabie Denham writes in his collection of British folklore (published 1846-1859):

> A large stone in the middle of a field, or laid in cumbrous bulk by a pathway side, has little to commend itself to the attention of the passer-by...to the individuals, however, [who inhabit]...its neighborhood, it [represents]...more than a mere aggregation of unconscious matter...[I]n all likelihood, [it] has become interwoven with their higher principles, the reverence with which they regard things of ancient date, and the veneration attached to the works and memories of their sires.... Perhaps it stands as one of those primitive landmarks, which it would be sacrilege to remove...[11]

Chapter 3
Flora

I, I have become a green maple; you, near me, a slender fir . . .

from a Bulgarian folksong[12]

The plant realm, as one might imagine, plays an extremely significant role in indigenous European, earth-centered, pagan traditions.

Flowers

Divinities of flowers are found in abundance – the Greek/Roman Chloris/Flora, the Celtic Rosmerta, and a myriad others. Many deities, such as the Slavic gods of springtime Yarilo and Pogoda, wear floral crowns. Other deities, like the Celtic Matres, hold baskets of flowers. Particular flowers are associated with certain deities – the rose with Aphrodite/Venus, Cybele, Dionysus/Bacchus, Hecate, the Graces, the Muses, and Freyja; poppies with Demeter/Ceres, Nyx, Hypnos, Morpheus, Thanatos; and so on.

One of the most well known European myths concerning flowers is an Irish one: the tale of Blodeuwedd. Arianrhod, the mother of Lleu Llaw Gyffes, a manifestation of the Celtic god Lugh, has forbidden him to marry a mortal woman. For this reason, Lleu's uncle, Gwydion, creates a partner for him by way of magic, from the "flowers of oak, broom, and meadowsweet," the last of which signifies "sensual pleasure." Legend has it that she falls in love with someone else, and her lover and she decide to kill Lleu. Before he dies, however, Lleu transforms into an eagle. Eventually returning to human form, he punishes Blodeuwedd by transforming her into an owl. Her name signifies either "owl" or "flower visage."

In Germanic tradition, the cowslip belongs to the goddesses Freyja, Holda, and Bertha. In 1898, Lizzie Deas recounted a tale in which children, enticed by the trellis of cowslips framing her arched doorway, enter into Bertha's enchanted garden. Only those who have revered and made offerings to Bertha throughout the year are permitted entrance. In the garden, the children are permitted to search, in vessels ornamented with cowslips, for treasures that the goddess has placed in the vessels for them. Also in Germanic tradition, the lily of the valley is sacred to Ostara (or, Eostre). Likewise, in Germanic tradition, roses are sacred to the goddess Holda and are sometimes protected by elves.

Fruits

Goddesses including the Celtic Aeracura, the Celtic/Germanic Nehalennia, and the Roman Copia hold baskets or cornucopias of fruits. In Roman tradition, the goddess of fruits and fruit trees is Pomona, whereas in Celtic tradition, the Dagda and Aengus (or, Aonghus Óg, Angus Og) possess trees that incessantly produce fruit.

Cranberries belong to the Slovenian divinity of fire, Netek; whereas figs, rich in erotic imagery, are sacred to Ishtar, Juno Caprotina, Priapus and Pan. Grapes and wine are Dionysus's treasures; while pomegranates belong to Hera/Juno, Persephone, and Cybele. Strawberries speak to the love, lust, and joy that Freyja brings. "May you live/ And flourish/ Like an apple tree."

So goes a traditional Romanian wish or spell, as recounted by Marcu Beza in *Paganism in Roumanian Folklore* (1928). The apple, tree and fruit, on which we'll focus, embraces numerous attributes, including abundance, fertility, love, destruction and death, and immortality. Apple trees are sacred to the Celtic-Roman mother goddesses, the Matronae; apples appear in the cornucopia they hold. Brigid presides over an apple orchard in the otherworld to which bees travel to obtain magical nectar. The apple is also sacred to the classical goddesses Aphrodite/Venus, Artemis/Diana, Pomona, and Vesta and to the sea-nymphs Hespere, Aegle, Erytheis, and Hestia (or Arethusa), the last of whom guard the magical apples that grow in the paradise of the west known as the Garden of the Hesperides.

In the Netherlands, apples appear in the basket of the goddess Nehalennia. The Germanic goddess Iðunn guards the magical apples "of immortality which [keep] the gods forever young." It's said that in "Freya's garden are the golden apples." In this tradition, both red and golden apples are given as tokens of love; in this regard, they are special foods of the goddess Frigg and the god Freyr. Also in Germanic tradition, apples are sacred to the goddess Holda (or, Holle); she "brings the red apple, symbol of life, back to earth from the well into which it fell at harvest."

Apples may have occasionally betokened death, as evidenced by an eleventh-century poem by a man who thinks his wife is trying to kill him with the apples of Hel, the goddess of the underworld. Could it be that this tale inspired that of the poisoned apple in "Snow White"? The writers of *Witchcraft Medicine* suggest that between myths such as the previous and the wicked queen of "Snow White"'s apple may lie the demonization by Christians of Freyja, transforming her from the goddess into the "Devil's Grandmother." Poetically speaking, the apple as sinister fruit is associated with the so-called "Sleep Apple" (*Schlaf-Apfel*), which is in fact a "mossy sort of excrescence [found] on the wild rose" and which was allegedly deployed by witches who wished their husbands to remain asleep when they gathered at sabbats. This "Sleep Apple," in being linked to the wild rose, is recalled in the fairy tale of "Sleeping Beauty," or "Briar Rose." In Slavic tradition, Perûn employs golden apples as weapons; the Baltic deity Perkûnas may have used them similarly.

As she commences reposing, the Baltic sun goddess Saulë has been compared to a red apple; and apples appear to have been offered to her. When the moon god Menulis has his way with her daughter Auðra, the dawn, Saulë laments, "The golden apple has fallen from the tree." This association of apple and sun may have led William Butler Yeats, in his poem "The Wanderings of Aengus," to pen the beautiful lines which in turn led Ray Bradbury to title a book of short stories *The Golden Apples of the Sun*; the particular myth of Saulë led present-day artist Joanna Powell Colbert to her depiction of *Saulë and the Golden Apples of the Sun*. In Lithuanian traditional culture, as Algirdas J. Greimas, following Basanavièius, relates in *Of Gods and Men*: The apple inspires the desire for love [note: apples are also given as love tokens]; the apple can change one's gender; the eating of love's apple makes one beautiful; and the apple returns health to the ailing.

Apples have served in the British Isles as magic talismans assisting humans in entering other worlds, including afterlives and the realm of fairies. In Arthurian legend, Arthur is transported to Avalon, the Vale of Apples, as he lies dying, so that he may live as an immortal there. Over the centuries, apples have come to play significant roles in seasonal celebrations including Halloween and winter wassailing. In Herefordshire, north of London, it was considered an act of sacrilege to destroy an apple orchard; into the final years of the seventeenth century, growers there as well as in Somerset continued to light midsummer fires near the orchards "to bless the apples." In Christian folklore of England, apples are considered "pagan" until July 15th, when they're miraculously christened by St. Swithin.

Fruits and deities associated with deities are as plentiful as the cornucopias that Aeracura, Nehalennia, and Copia hold, but alas, we can only consider a very few herein.

Herbs and Other Plants

As many of you will know, the term "herb" is often given to plants that might otherwise be grouped as flowers or as aromatic plants. These include, for example, aconite, arnica, autumn crocus, hemp, mugwort, and yarrow. In Germanic tradition, aconite (*Aconitum*), or monk's hood, represents the "cap of darkness" or of invisibility. Those who, especially at night, carry aconite on their persons can become invisible to others. Aconite is said to be sacred to, and used in magical works invoking, Odin, Thor, trolls, witches, and the Devil. For these reasons, aconite is sometimes called "Odin's helmet" or "troll's hat."

Because much of this information will be found in the marvelous book *Witchcraft Medicine*, I will limit my remarks here.

Arnica (*Arnica montana*), known for its "antiseptic, anti-inflammatory, and regenerative properties," belongs to Freyja. Autumn crocus (*Colchicum autumnale* L.), which is believed to be able to protect against frostbite and rejuvenate the body and is said to be eaten by witches, belongs to Holda and Frau Holle. Likewise, hemp (*Cannabis sativa*) is a gift bestowed by Freyja, Holda, and Frau Holle. Similarly, mugwort (*Artemisia vulgaris*), used in women's health matters "to bring on missed menses, hasten birth…expel a dead fetus," is sacred to Holda and Frau Holle. Likewise, yarrow, belonging to Freyja, is also deployed in women's health matters, as well as in divinatory practices, and in love magic. Yarrow is also claimed by Thor, perhaps in his capacity as the lord of marriage. There are, of course, many other herbs associated with deities.

Trees and Groves

In or near 1256, according to the *Livlandische Reimchronik*, a Christian army unit discovered a sacred forest in Lithuania Minor/East Prussia. When they found it, they "vowed not to rest until it had been cut [down]." For centuries, my ancestors lived very near the forest known in recent centuries as Ibenhorst. Under yew trees, sacred to the local inhabitants, signifying death and regeneration, elk dwelt within the forest, together with many other beings.

Veneration of trees, as of other flora, is a common element of many ancient and indigenous traditions. The Ojibwe believe that "[l]ike all trees, the birch, *wiigwaas*...is animate, and to remove its bark, *wiigwaasike*, is to act towards a person." As in their relationships with stones, they believe that relating to a tree is not about personifying a tree but rather about "an encounter with persons who intentionally act towards and communicate with other persons." Similarly, for the Shawi people of the Amazon, "[t]rees exist, as matter, as wood, as firewood. But the material existence is not all there is to it. Deep down, they are also beings.... We Shawi think that all living beings have souls, which are their own spirits." Chanchari, a present-day Shawi, relates: "A tree has a soul like a human being does. The Christian world considers that humans have souls. It is the same with a tree.... [T]aken together, trees have their mother, meaning to say mother of the forest, and mother of the species." Chancari's view is echoed by present-day spiritual teacher Sobonfu E. Somé, whose *The Spirit of Intimacy: Ancient Teachings in the Ways of Relationships* (1997) illuminates the sacred concepts and practices of the Dagara of Burkina Faso, West Africa: "[T]here is such a thing as a pool of ancestors – it doesn't have to be a person...it can be a tree out there." In the religion of the Yorùbá of West Africa and its New World manifestations, trees, like humans and other beings, possess *ori*, consciousness. Trees, especially those bearing medicinal leaves, play very significant roles in worship. For many in Benin, the iroko, in which the spirits of the dead wait to be reborn, and the leaves of which are believed to possess the power of rejuvenation, assumes the position of World-Tree; in Cuba, the ceiba has replaced the iroko as the most sacred of trees in the Regla de Ocha, the Cuban manifestation of the the Yorùbá religion.

In Shinto, evergreen *sakaki* branches, *tamagushi*, are among the holiest of offerings (*tamagushi harei*); as 'soul-connectors' (*tamashii*, soul; *kushi*, to connect), they serve to intimately connect the devotee to her or his own soul and to the *kami*, the divinities. From archaeologist Vaitkevicius' works, especially *Senosios Lietuvos Šventasvietes* and *Studies into the Balts' Sacred Places*, we learn that ancient and medieval Lithuanians regarded trees (*medžiai*) as linking the earth and the heavens. In such veneration were they held that they were typically considered untouchable. Among Western Balts, trees were also often regarded as being good or evil. For example, the hazel and rowan were typically considered beneficent, while the asp and the alder were considered evil.

Still other trees, such as the birch, were regarded as expressing ambiguity; such was the birch, which protected against lightning but which also served as a broom for *laumës* (fairies) and which was treasured by the sometimes sinister god Velnias. Likewise, trees have been venerated since antiquity among Germanic peoples. At the end of the first century CE, the Roman historian Cornelius Tacitus (*c.* 56 CE-d. after 117 CE) reported in *Germania* (98 CE), "Their holy places are woods and groves." Veneration of trees continued into the medieval period in France and other parts of Europe.

Trees as Living Beings and as 'Persons'

"Rigid pine, delicate birch, stalwart oak, each had its effect," Alfred Biese relates in *The Development of the Feeling for Nature in the Middle Ages and Modern Times* (1905), upon pagans who venerated nature. Tamra Andrews observes: "People revered trees for the energy within them, for the spirit that inhabited the tree and infused it with life. Sacred trees seemed alive with this spirit. They moved and swayed, they spouted sap like precious milk, and when the wind rustled through their branches, they appeared to speak in whispers."

Trees were envisioned as alive and akin to humans; they were even thought to bleed like human beings. In Celtic belief, Bernard Rio, in *L'Arbre Philosophal* (*The Philosophical Tree*, 2001), trees were considered as entities possessing souls, intellect and/or wisdom, and agency. In *The Folklore of the Cotswolds* (1974), Katherine Briggs relates that in seventeenth-century England, oaks were said to shriek when chopped down. The belief that trees possessed souls, etc., and that they could feel pain was also common among Germanic peoples and continued into the nineteenth century. Austrians continued to believe that trees possessed souls as well as that they could "feel injuries done to them." Also in the nineteenth century, woodcutters of the High Palatinate west of the Rhine (present-day southwestern Germany) would plead with trees to forgive them before they felled them.

Many also believed that trees possessed the gift of communication. As late as the nineteenth and early twentieth centuries, some persons, including in the High Palatinate west of the Rhine (present-day southwestern Germany) and France, believed that certain trees possessed the power to speak. A peasant of Plougasnou, France reported, for instance, that he had overheard a conversation between two beech trees.

The World-Tree

In Germanic cosmology, one of the chief representations of the cosmos focuses on the sacred ash tree Yggdrasill, "where the gods sit in council every day." Yggdrasill "rises to the sky, and its branches spread over the entire world. It is supported by three roots: one stretches to the world of the dead, another to the world of the frost giants, and the third to the world of men. At the foot of the tree are several springs [including] the spring of the goddess of fate, Urðr." The tree's sap, *heiðr*, is comparable to the *élan vital* or mana. The Irminsul was a treelike pillar meant to signify Yggdrasill.

A similar world-tree is known to Baltic traditions. This cosmic tree is typically signified by either an oak or a linden, perhaps indicating masculine and feminine hypostases, respectively. To a lesser extent, the world-tree may also manifest as a pear tree, poplar, pine, fir (or spruce), or rose bush. The world-tree is also associated with other plants, including flax, hemp, rye, peas, raspberries, wormwood, lavender, thyme, rue, sweet clover, lilies, and sunflowers. In *The Balts*, Gimbutas describes the Baltic world-tree and its artistic representations: "A peculiar cosmogonical tree of the Baltic peoples was the wooden, roofed pole topped with symbols of sky deities — suns, moons, stars — and guarded by stallions and snakes." She reports that "[r]ight up to the present century, roofed poles as well as crosses with a sun symbol around the cross-arms could be encountered in Lithuania in front of homesteads, in fields, beside sacred springs, or in the forests." These representations of the world-tree "were erected on the occasion of someone's marriage or illness, during epidemics, or for the purpose of ensuring good crops." With Christianization, "Christian bishops instructed the clergy to destroy the poles and crosses before which the peasants made offerings and observed other pagan rites." However, representations of the world-tree "managed to escape destruction because the people fixed some of the Christian symbols to them, and gradually they came under the protection of the Catholic Church."

In present-day Bulgaria (2004), the world-tree is celebrated on January 1 during the New Year's festival of Sourva, Christianized as St. Basil's Day. Decorated branches of cornel (related to dogwood) trees represent the world-tree Sourva. The *sourva* branches are ornamented with "multicolored woolen threads, popcorn, dried fruits, hot peppers, seeds, raisins, and colored papers." Children, typically boys (with women performing other roles in the festival), carry them; the boys represent "mediators between the worlds." In Romania, the same rite is known, with the tree branch called the *sorcova*.

Trees and Divinities

The Hispano-Roman writer Columella (fl. first century CE) speaks of the veneration of trees in relation to their potential to embody divinity: "Seek not a statue wrought by Daedalus or Polyclitus or by Phradmon carved or Ageladas, but the rough-hewn tree trunk of some old tree which you may venerate, as god Priapus in your garden's midst."

If, as Ernest Renan (1823-1892) claimed, in the *Histoire du peuple d'Israël* (1887-1892), that "the desert is monotheistic," then, says Bernard Rio, "if we must accede that Manichaeism be our lot," then the "forest is polytheistic." Gimbutas observes in *The Balts*, "Forests had their own goddesses and gods." In acknowledgment of the history and chronology of the cultural stratification and Christianization of Europe, let us note that in Celtic tradition, the goddess Arduinna guards the forest and its inhabitants; in Greco-Roman tradition, Artemis/Diana; in Latvian tradition, the "forest mother," "forest father," and "mother of shrubs;" in Lithuanian tradition, the goddess Medeina (whose name signifies "tree") and the god Giraitis; in Finnish tradition, Tapio and his wife.

In the Middle Ages, trees were frequently thought to embody female divinities; as such, they were addressed as "Dame," "Lady," or "Frau." In Germanic tradition, certain trees, referred to as *bo-träd* ("abode trees," or "habitation trees"), were once thought to be the homes of elves, particularly of elves called *Löfjerskor*: "If a lime or other tree, either in a forest or solitary, grew more vigorously than the other trees, it was called a habitation-tree...and was thought to be inhabited by an elf...who...dwelt in its shade, rewarded with health and prosperity the individual that took care of the tree, and punished those who injured it."

Trees and Humans

Trees play a significant role in the human life cycle and participate in deep relationships with humans. George P. Fedotov, in *The Russian Religious Mind* (1946), states that within Slavic paganism, a "human being...is identified with, rather than compared to, some animal or vegetative being....The destiny of human and animal or vegetative beings are blended in one: they blossom or die together."

Among the Celts, sacred trees may have served as the patrons of certain families, and these families may have shared totemic relationships with the trees. This familial, totemic bond is suggested by surnames such as Mac Cuill, "son of the hazel," Macc Dara, "son of the oak," Macc Cairthin, "son of the rowan," and Macc Ibair, "son of the yew," suggest.

In numerous regions of Europe, trees were traditionally planted upon the birth of children; these were envisioned as lifelong companions of the children. In Baltic tradition, specific trees were planted for children in regards to gender and other categories. For example, the fir (or spruce), linden, pine, and cherry and apple trees were planted for female children, while the ash, birch, juniper, maple, and oak were planted for males. Trees were also planted when couples married; as the trees continued to grow, so would the love between the partners. Lithuanian wedding ceremonies included fir trees decorated with flowers and topped by geometrical straw ornaments. In Germanic traditions, especially during the Middle Ages, "when a person set out on a journey, he would frequently place his welfare in the keeping of a tree, or rather in the spirit or genius of the tree." Trees were frequently the site of the securing of covenants. In Scotland, such trees were known as *covin*-trees. Among the kinds of covenants that were secured beneath these trees were troths plighted by lovers. Witches were also thought to convene beneath *covin*-trees; in the *Denham Tracts* (1895), we find: "The witches of Auldearne [Scotland] met in *covines*, and the prettiest of them was called the maiden of the *covine*."

In regard to trees planted for children, as long as such trees flourished, the individual generally remained healthy, but should the tree decline, wither, or be chopped down, the health of the individual would decline rapidly, or else she or he would die at that time. Such trees were known as *Vård-träd*, or guardian trees, similar to *naguales/tonales*, or totem animals, in Nahua (Mexica/Aztec) tradition. In Copenhagen, into the nineteenth century, elder trees often served as guardian trees. In this light, there is an adage saying that to cut a cemetery tree is to do evil to the deceased.

Indeed, trees have often been associated with death and rebirth in pagan traditions. Romanians held that certain trees lamented the dying and mourned the dead; a Romanian folksong concerning a dying hero includes:

> Beeches and maples
> Bending their heads,
> Offered solace,
> Cooling his brow,
> Gently kissing
> His hand
> Singing their rustling lament.[13]

Romanians sometimes substituted a fir tree for a human corpse in a coffin if the deceased had died in a foreign land and his or her body could not be retrieved. The tree was dressed in attire belonging to the deceased or similar to that he or she would have worn. Romanians also believed that certain trees, especially the fir and the maple, served as guideposts, bridges, and/or psychopomps leading the soul from this world to the next. In a funeral dirge, one finds:

> In the abyss of the Seas,
> Where the Fir of the Fairies [Zînelor] stands,
> The gorge of the waters lies,
> The soul paused awhile,
> And entreated me:
> O, my dear fir-tree,
> May you be my brother:
> Stretch out your treetops
> So I can catch them
> And walk on them
> As on a bridge,
> And reach the other shore
> To my world across the sea.[14]

Traditional Balts often carved images of trees on burial urns; moreover, for Balts, trees often served as repositories for the souls of the dead. Lithuanians believed that upon death, the *siela*, one of the multiple souls or else multiple aspects of the soul that each of us possesses, might take up residence in trees to wait there until rebirth. Porteous notes that in "Croatia witches were formerly buried under old trees in the forest, and it was believed that their souls passed into these trees." In nineteenth- and early twentieth-century France, some persons continued to believe that the souls of humans could migrate into trees upon death. A peasant of Plougasnou was certain, for example, that, upon their deaths, the souls of his parents had taken up residence in beech trees. Alternatively, others believed that humans might be reincarnated *as* trees. Count Angelo de Gubernatis (1840-1913), in *La Mythologie des plantes* (1878-1882), observes that in a popular Bulgarian folksong, a deceased lover sings to his beloved:

> I, I have become a green maple;
> you, near me, a slender fir;
> and the woodmen came,
> the woodmen with sharp-edged axes,
> they cut down the green maple,
> then the slender fir,
> cut them into white boards,
> make beds of us,
> they will place us near each other,

and thus, my dear,
we will be together.[15]

A Grove of Sacred Trees

As we explore the significance of certain trees within the context of the pagan worldview, let us recall the metaphors of tree rings and layers of sedimentary stratification, remembering that by the Middle Ages, much of Europe had been exposed to Old (or indigenous) European, Celtic, Germanic, and Greco-Roman (and with that, Egyptian) religions/traditions. To a lesser extent, certain parts of Europe were also exposed to Slavic, Baltic, Finno-Ugric, and other traditions and religions, including Buddhism, Islam, and Judaism. Earlier pagan influences were eventually subjected to Christianization. The rings or layers of influence were, however, more porous than one might discover with trees or stones, culminating in a kind of sacred bricolage or assemblage.

The alder, used to make shields by Celts and Germanic peoples, is, as a living being, thought to bleed. It is the sacred tree of the Celtic hero deity Bran the Blessed. In medieval and post-medieval Germanic culture, it appears as a female divinity, an "alder woman" nicknamed "Rough Else" who transforms periodically from a hag to a beautiful woman and back again, enticing men who wander in the woods. In the Austrian Alpine province of Tyrol, it was once thought to be favored by wisewomen and is said to possess the power to return the dead to life.

The ash tree speaks of the life-force, the mystery of death and rebirth, and occasionally, of cruelty. Sacred to the god Bran, the ash of Uisnedr, together with the oak of Mughna and the yew of Ross, numbered among the most sacred of trees of Celtic tradition; their destruction in the seventh century "symbolized the triumph of Christianity over paganism." Druids are alleged to have made wands from ash branches. In post-medieval Ireland, its branches were "wreathed round the horns of the cattle, and round the child's cradle to keep off evil influences." In Greco-Roman tradition, the ash is sacred to Poseidon/Neptune and to the Meliai, ash-divinities who sprang "from the blood of Uranus." Yggdrasil, the World Tree of Germanic belief, is most commonly considered an ash. In Germanic *Eddic* lore, the first couple was created from trees: a man from the ash, and a woman from the elm. The ash is sacred to Thor. Odin is thought to have hanged himself "from this magical tree to receive illumination in the shape of the runes." The runes were first marked on "tablets of ash." Also in Germanic and as well in Baltic tradition, a staff of ash is believed to protect against destructive magic. Its wood was once used in ships to protect against storms raised by the Germanic sea goddess Rân, who patrons the sailors she drowns. Alexander Porteous, in *Forest Folklore, Mythology, and Romance* (1928), relates: "A Scandinavian legend tells how some people once got an ash tree from a giant, who told them to set it on the altar of a church he wished to destroy. Instead of doing this, they placed it on a mound over a grave, which instantly burst into flames."

The Askafroa, a frequently destructive

being whose wrath can be propitiated via sacrifice, guards the ash tree in medieval and post-medieval Germanic tradition. Within a Christianized milieu, offerings of milk and beer are made to the Askafroa on Ash Wednesday. The ash is a favorite tree of wisewomen. It gradually replaced the birch as the tree most favored for the Maypole. In Slavic belief, it is inhabited by the Vila, Slavic female, fairy-like beings of the forest. Traditional Lithuanians believed that the souls of men (as opposed to those of women) sometimes transmigrated into ash trees. In March 1832, the antiquarian Anna Eliza Bray took a guided tour of Wistman's Wood. Her guide, a farmer named Hannaford, warned her to beware of adders and taught her how to charm them with an ash wand: "He...initiates me on the spot into the pagan rites of charming adders." He also told her that "an animal bitten by this venomous reptile may be cured by having a kind of collar of ash-twigs suspended from his neck." In 1870, Christian officials complained that the inhabitants of Makrickai, Lithuania, rather than attending church on holidays, convened at a sacred ash tree to offer it wool, clothing, corn, money, and eggs.

The beech is the sacred tree of the Celtic god Ogma, a great warrior, a patron of eloquence and literature, and inventor of the Ogham script, a kind of hieroglyphic alphabet based on trees. Similarly, the tree is sacred to the Germanic god Odin as patron of the runes, with those knowledgeable of runes carving them into beech branches. In this regard, the beech possesses divinatory powers. In medieval Germanic culture, witches held "dances and weddings on a great beech tree."

In traditional Irish belief, the birch is called the Mother of Learning. Some shamanistic traditions view it as the world-tree. It is also a tree of death and rebirth. It is sacred to the Celtic goddess Brigid and is associated with Blodeuwedd, a "beautiful maiden conjured out of the flowers of oak, broom, and meadowsweet." The birch is also sacred to Lugh, the Celtic god of arts and crafts. The first Ogham (rune like) signs were said to have been carved into birch. Among Romans, it is sacred to Venus. The word "birch" derives from the Old High German *bircha* "shining white;" it belongs to the Germanic goddesses Frigga, Freyja and Eostre, and to the god Thor. Ragnarok, "the final battle of the gods, will be fought round a birch tree." Lithuanians believed that the souls of certain men (as opposed to those of women) transmigrated into birch trees. Fred Hageneder, in *The Spirit of Trees*, in regard to the tree's divinatory associations, notes: "Birch also gave its name to the Germanic rune *berkana*, meaning motherhood, bosom, and protection." Birch logs are often used in Yule fires. Birch brooms are used to sweep out the "spirit of the old year." Birches also often become May branches and Maypoles. Infants' cradles are sometimes made of birch. Birch branches may serve as a token of love and as magical totems promoting love. In Irish tradition, the body of the deceased is sometimes carried to grave in a blanket of birch leaves. Hageneder relates, "Celtic chieftains of the German Hallstatt period [*c*. 900-800 BCE] were buried with a small conical birch bark hat, which is believed to represent the guardian of passage and a proud warrior's submission to the cosmic mother, entrusting himself to her in death and rebirth."

The elder bleeds like humans. It is linked to fertility, pregnancy, birth, and infants. It is also, however, associated with death. Pagan "Frisians buried their dead under elder trees." In medieval and post-medieval Germanic tradition, the elder is sacred to the Germanic goddess Holda, to a healing goddess named Hildi, and/or to another female divinity. Holda/Holle in particular uses the elderberry in healing. The tree is also called Dame Eilhorn. She is said to possess the "secret of medicinal plants." She protects those who revered her from misfortune and illness. Porteous notes, "Should any person desire to cut down an elder tree, or take a branch therefrom, he had first to ask permission from the Hyldemoer, otherwise some misfortune would befall him. The elder should never be cut without asking its permission: one should chant, "Hyldemoer, Hyldemoer, allow me to cut thy branches.

The elder is the dwelling place of the Lithuanian deity Puskaitis (Latvian, Pushkait). Bread and beer are offered to him at the base of the tree. In Baltic tradition, the elder is, by way of Puskaitis, also associated with elemental beings called *barstukai* and *kaukai*. The elder is a favorite tree of fairies; indeed, each cluster of its flowers corresponds to a fairy. One must ask the fairies before cutting an elder. When one falls asleep beneath an elder, its flowers may transport him or her to the realm of Fairy. Witches are thought to be able to transform themselves into elder trees. Enid Porter observes in *Cambridgeshire Customs and Folklore* (1969): "In Cambridgeshire [in England] the elder was associated with witchcraft.... [I]t was particularly lucky to have a[n elder] tree growing in or near a farmyard, because it kept away evil spirits and promoted fertility among the stock." Gimbutas imparts that among Balts, a "stick from...a twig of...elder...[was] regarded as effective...against the evil spirits." In nineteenth-century Copenhagen, a certain elder tree in the Nyboder quarter was thought to move from its spot at dusk and to look into the windows of houses to catch a glimpse of the children inside. Hageneder observes: "In the eighteenth and nineteenth centuries, many customs still believed in the protective powers of [the] elder, and the benevolence of this tree was appreciated by the people amongst whom it grew: the Swedes offered milk; the Prussians, bread and beer; and the Scots left cakes and milk in its shade." A traditional rhyme speaks of a maiden who goes to the "fields at break of day" on the first of May to wash herself in the dew of the hawthorn tree to ensure she'll retain her beauty as she grows older. tree.

In Celtic tradition, the hawthorn is the tree of the maiden Blodeuwedd and of the princess/sun-goddess Olwen. For Romans, the tree is sacred to the goddess Diana. Both Blodeuwedd and Diana speak to the hawthorn's association with virginity; for this reason, it was considered disastrous to marry in May. Somewhat ironically, however, it assumed a role in the May celebration of the lusty goddess Flora. Also among Romans, the tree is sacred to the god Janus, who is said to have bestowed his beloved Carna with a hawthorn. In

Germanic belief, the hawthorn was born from lightning. It is the tree of the god Thor. Like the elder, it is a favorite tree of fairies. Indeed, female fairies are sometimes referred to as 'women of the thorn,' which may have led to the Virgin Mary's manifestation as Our Lady of the Thorn. In Brittany, "Viviane enchanted Merlin to sleep under the hawthorn until his reawakening in another age," a legend which may have inspired the tale of "Sleeping Beauty." The hawthorn guards wells and springs. It is especially valued as a tree with healing powers; it protects against negative sorcery; may be used to make magical brooms; and may bring love, marriage, fertility, and prosperity. Like the birch, the hawthorn may serve as a May bough or Maypole; Gifford notes, "In traditional May Day rites, the hawthorn blossom symbolizes love and betrothal." It is envisioned as a liminal tree growing on the border of this world and the Otherworld. Because of its liminal symbolism, it is especially valued during the festival of Samhain, when the veil between the worlds of the living and the dead is rent. In this connection, Germanic tradition sometimes employs hawthorn to construct funeral pyres.

The "destruction of hawthorn trees is attended by great peril." In the early nineteenth century, a farmer who owned land in Garryglass (a.k.a. Durraghalicky) in County Cork, southern Ireland, cut down the only remaining hawthorn of what had once been a grove on his property. This tree was connected to a sacred stone, with the site on which it stood being called the "Place of the Stone." "All his cattle died and his children also. He lost his money and was evicted. The next possessor, as well as his successor, were equally unfortunate. They never prospered." A similar fate visited two brothers surnamed Bergin who lived on a farm near Ballyroan, Ireland (southwest of Dublin). During the last decade of the nineteenth century, they chopped down the hawthorns on their property. Those who knew the brothers were convinced that one brother was "fairy-stricken;" "no remedies had any effect on him." In the case of the Garryglass hawthorn, conditions finally commenced to improve when a farmer succeeding the others planted a hawthorn on the site where the old one had been. It seemed that the fairies dwelling in the vicinity of the tree finally returned: "on winter nights, lights are seen coming from this Rath (here, a barrier formed by trees)." "Even today," Jane Gifford observes in *The Wisdom of Trees*, "hawthorns...are often covered with wish rags, pieces of material tied to the tree to bring luck, love, and happiness."

In "The Song of Wandering Aengus," Irish W. B. Yeats (b. 1865-d. 1939) chants: "I went out to the hazel wood,/ Because a fire was in my head,/ And cut and peeled a hazel wand." In Irish tradition, "nine hazel trees surround the source of all wisdom, known as Connla's Well." The tree itself is thought to be wise. The hazel is thought to embody a female divinity in Germanic tradition and as such is called Dame Hazel. The tree is thought to promote fertility and to possess divinatory powers. Wands are made from hazel branches, which should be gathered on Wednesdays, as they are a tool of Odin; his is carved with runes. The hazel tree is also sacred to Thor. Hazel nuts cracked over a fire on Halloween may determine "the fate of lovers."

The juniper is, in Germanic tradition, thought to embody a female divinity and as such is called Frau Wacholder, Lady or Dame Juniper. In late nineteenth-century Germany, numerous persons continued to venerate the juniper tree or bush and to identify it with Frau Wacholder; as such, she was offered wool and bread. Lady Juniper is invoked and employed in magical practice, including in seeking to capture thieves: "A branch of the juniper bush is bent down to the ground and kept down with a stone, the name of the real or supposed thief being repeated at the same time, with injunctions to bring back the booty. Whenever the desired result comes about, the stone is removed and the branch set free." The juniper is also invoked to heal children. Gimbutas relates, "A...twig of juniper...[was] regarded as effective...against the evil spirits." In the British Isles, juniper twigs are "hung above doorways at Beltane [i.e., May Eve]; and juniper "is ritually burned at Samhain [October 31]."

"Under the linden/ in the heather/ that's where our double bed was," commences Walther von der Vogelweide's (b. *c.* 1170- d. *c.* 1230) celebrated lyric "Under the Linden." The linden is sacred to the Germanic goddess Freyja in her aspect as goddess of love and fertility and is in that tradition also a tree of elves, dwarves, and fairies. In Germanic tradition, the tree is also linked to wisewomen or witches. From medieval into nineteenth-century Germany, the Dorflinde, or village linden tree, "was cared for, often visited and well loved; the tradition was still alive in the nineteenth century as it was in medieval times. Linden trees were also revered in Slovenia. In 1629, a Catholic traveler sent a letter to the Pope, sharing with him his shock on seeing alleged Christians and Muslims gathering together near the spring equinox to honor a linden tree with candles and offerings, in the hope that this would heal them of illnesses and bring prosperity.

Among Lithuanian deities, Laima, goddess of destiny, is most often associated with the linden. Among Lithuanian practitioners of earth-based traditions, the souls of certain women (as opposed to those of men) are thought to transmigrate into the linden. Vaitkevicius notes: "In the Annals of Lithuania of the sixteenth century it is said that in the sacred place called Pajautas Grave lime [or, linden] trees were worshipped." In one of the most significant groves of linden trees, Lezu Swiato Liepie, near Trakai, a collection of sacred stones was also revered. Dismayed Jesuits observed of the Lithuanian reverence of trees in the *Annual Report* for 1606: "Some have two particular trees: one is an oak, the other a lime [i.e., linden]. They call the oak masculine and at fixed times put two eggs beneath it. They call the lime feminine and offer it butter, milk, cheese, and fat, for the well-being and protection of their children."

At the foot of Rambynas Hill, a sacred pagan site in southwestern Lithuania, near my maternal great-grandfather's ancestral home, many persons continued to venerate a linden tree sacred to the goddess Laima in the nineteenth century.

For Romanians, the world-tree, as oak, also serves as guidepost to the other world and serves as well as a site of initiation into manhood and warriorhood. In the magical Welsh text of *The Mabinogion*, an oak is recognized to be none other than the hero-deity Lleu Llaw Gyffes: "Oak that grows between the two banks;/...Shall I fail to tell him by his wounds:/ This is Llew!"

The oak "represents the sun's strength" and is symbolic of longevity. It is also said to be a compassionate listener; one may take one's sorrows to the oak. In Celtic tradition, it is the sacred tree of the Dagda, the father god of wisdom, as well as of the Gaulish thunder god Taranis (or. Taranus). The priestly class of Druids may have taken its name from the oak. The oak of Mughna, together with the ash of Uisnedr and the yew of Ross, numbered among the most sacred of trees of the Celts. At Angoulême, France, Celts divinized the oak as Deo Robori. In Greco-Roman belief, the oak belongs to Artemis/Diana, Demeter/Ceres, and Zeus/Jupiter; it is also a favorite haunt of nymphs, dryads, and hamadryads. In Germanic belief, it belongs to Thor. St. Boniface (b. *c.* 675—d. 754), the "Apostle to the Germans," destroyed numerous sacred trees and shrines of the Frisians, including the mighty oak of Donar/Thor at Geismar in Hesse; its wood was used to build a church. Finnish tradition attributes the oak to the god Ukko (Oak). Medieval tradition associates the oak with Merlin, wisewomen or witches, and Robin Hood.

A Greek chronicler of the tenth century reported that pagan Ukrainians, especially merchants from Kiev sailing down the Dnieper River, worshipped at an altar beneath a great oak tree on Khortytsia Island. In Slavic tradition, a great oak "grows on the island of Bujan, among the branches of which the sun disappears for repose every evening, to rise again therefrom refreshed in the morning." Traditional Balts ascribe the oak to the thunder god Perkûnas and believe that the souls of certain men transmigrate into oaks. For centuries, a perpetual fire burned near a sacred oak at the Old Prussia/Lithuania Minor grove of Romuva. Likewise, Balts traditionally believed that souls traveled by boat to the far west, where the "cosmic tree" existed, typically an oak tree "with silver leaves, copper branches, and iron roots; sometimes it is an enormous linden or apple-tree. It stands on [a] [grey] stone, at the end of 'the way of the Sun.' The Sun hangs her belt on the branches, sleeps in the crown of this tree and, when she rises in the morning, the tree becomes red."

Oak logs are traditionally burned in midsummer bonfires. Certain oaks are not to be tampered with other than for use in ceremonies. An oak tree growing in the seventeenth century in Norwood, England was graced with an abundance of mistletoe. Several persons cut bunches of mistletoe from its branches in 1657 in order to sell them for ten shillings each to pharmacists in London. This eventually led to the felling of the oak. Shortly thereafter, one of those who participated in the destruction of the tree broke his leg, a second became paralyzed, and a third lost sight in one eye; it was "as if the Hamadryades had resolved to take ample revenge for the injury done to their venerable oak."

Russians used to call Latvians *podubniki*, "those standing under the oak," because during a funeral procession, they stopped at every oak tree. In the Central Balkans, alleged witches have traditionally met under oak trees.

In pagan Lithuania Minor/East Prussia, near my maternal great-grandfather's ancestral home, at Heiligenbeil (present-day Mamonovo in the Kaliningradskaya Oblast), "there existed in [a] sanctuary an oak, which was supposedly always green, both in summer and winter. The leaves of the tree," Janina Kuršite recounts in in "Baltic Sanctuaries" (2005), "were considered medicinal, and people applied them to ailing parts of the bodies of humans and animals alike." The villagers of Heiligenbeil were devoted to Perkûnas, for whom a sacred fire burned. Tragically, this area is known now as having been the site of a Nazi concentration camp. In the late sixteenth century, Žemaitijans of western Lithuania, Jesuits complained, seemed to forget or tire of Christian concepts and practices and returned to remaining sacred oak groves to honor Perkûnas, the god of thunder. They made offerings of eggs to oaks in the early seventeenth century. Lithuanians were devastated when, in 1618, at Kraziai, the Jesuits chopped down a sacred oak dedicated to Perkûnas. In the vicinity of Ragnit, a particular oak, as the tree of Perkûnas, was venerated; in *Deliciae Prussicae (Curiosities of Prussia*, 1684), Matthäus Prätorius (b. 1635—d. 1707) reports: "They showed me an oak in the surroundings of Ragaine [Ragnit] [which the] people thought…to be sacred…My landlord was [an] old and rich [and] superstitious farmer…he thought that they do not…sin [who] do not harm the tree. And that was…worshipping, as he understood it."

A sacred oak of Kausai, Lithuania continued to be venerated in the nineteenth century; its honoring also demonstrates the 'bi-religiousness' of the local population: "They sacrifice a ram to the oak on Sunday mornings and then proceed to the local church for Christian services. Afterward, they would return to the oak, where they would "cook the ram and celebrate."

In 1863, insurgents taking part in a Lithuanian uprising against Russian rule returned to sacred oak groves in the vicinity of Kegriai and Saravai to pray; unfortunately, the revolt failed. Indeed, oaks in the vicinity of Azuolija and Pagirgzdutis continued to be venerated in the late nineteenth century.

As living beings, pine trees bleed when they are cut. The pine, in Greco-Roman paganism, is sacred to Demeter/Ceres, Persephone/Proserpina, Hades/Pluto, Pan/Faunus, and Cybele and her consort Attis. When Demeter searches for her lost daughter, a pine torch lights her way. In medieval and post-medieval Germanic tradition, the pine is thought to embody a female divinity and as such is called Frau Fichte. Vaitkevicius relates that in Lithuania, pines are linked to the soul's continuity after death and "grow where innocent people die or are buried." Many persons continued to venerate pine trees in Žemaitija (western Lithuania) in the nineteenth and early twentieth centuries.

In Celtic tradition, the rowan is "a symbol of the hidden mysteries of nature and the quickening of the life force. It was thought to have first grown in Ireland after a rowan berry was dropped by one of the

Tuatha Dé Danaan as they arrived from another world. It is alleged that among Druids, "the rowan had an important oracular use. Fires of the wood were used to conjure up spirits who could be forced to answer questions when rowan berries were spread on the newly flayed hides of bulls."

The rowan is sacred to the Germanic deity Thor, due in part to "the redness of its berries," red being Thor's color. Porteous relates: "[W]hen Thor was crossing the River Vimur, which had been caused to overflow its banks by a sorcerer, on his way to the land of the Frost Giants, he was aided by a rowan tree voluntarily bending to enable him to grasp it. Consequently that tree became known in Scandinavian countries as 'Thor's Helper.'" He also notes that "Norse ships used to have a piece of rowan-tree wood inserted in them to protect them from the wrath of [the sea goddess] Ran." In Finnish tradition, the rowan is sacred to the goddess Rauni, the wife of the god Ukko. The rowan is considered a fairy tree. It protects against evil. Its berries are thought to possess the power to restore youth. A tree of death and rebirth, its wood is used in funeral pyres. In Ireland, houses are decked with rowan at New Year's; and rowan branches often serve as May boughs. In the late eighteenth century, Thomas Pennant (b. 1726-d. 1798), in *A Tour of Scotland and Voyage to the Hebrides* (1772) noted that "farmers protected their cattle by tying twigs of the rowan tree...above their byres on 2 May."

The spruce or fir tree rejuvenates and repels negativity and evil. Although much of what has been said about the Druids remains speculative, the tree is sometimes said to be sacred to a Gaulish/Celtic goddess perhaps named Druantia, 'Queen of the Druids.' The spruce or fir is the sacred tree of Borute and of Dziewanna, Slavic goddesses of the fir forest and of hunting, respectively. Nineteenth-century Silesians (in present-day Poland) envisioned the spruce tree as Frau Fichte, a female divinity. As Frau Fichte, the spruce "possesses great healing powers" and is thought to provide protection for humans and animals; thus, spruce boughs were carried in a ceremonial procession to stables, where they were hung to "preserve the animals from harm." Traditional Lithuanians believe that the souls of certain women may transmigrate into fir trees as in the well-known tale of "Egle and Žaltys." Fir trees have, like birch trees, have traditionally served as Yule logs.

The walnut, a lunar tree, speaks of fertility and of "that which is hidden." The walnut tree is sacred to the goddess Karya, and indirectly, to Artemis/Diana and Dionysus/Bacchus. The latter fell in love with her. She died suddenly. Powerless to restore her to life, Dionysus transformed her into a walnut tree. Artemis told her father of the tragedy; he built a wooden temple to honor the memory of Karya, most probably from walnut, with pillars shaped like a young woman. The Greek village of Karya, well known for its walnut groves, bears her name. Her name also provides that of the genus of the tree: Caryophyllaceae. Artemis' role in the myth links the walnut to the moon; while Dionysus' role may link the walnut to women convening to dance ecstatically in the presence of a deity.

For Romans, the walnut tree and its nut were ambivalent entities. On the one hand, it signified the mysterious and sometimes sinister night, with *nox*, 'night, becoming *nux*, 'nut.' On the other hand, the walnut promoted fertility, perhaps in part because of its shape. Newlyweds were pelted with walnuts, as others have pelted them with rice. A rich harvest of walnuts signaled that many children would soon be born. The industry of wool dyeing became linked to the walnut, as its dark juice was used to color wool; its dark shade enhanced its connection to the night, while the wool it dyed enhanced its association with women. Probably because of its increasing association with women and darkness, it eventually came to be linked to Persephone/ Proserpina) in her aspect as Queen of the Underworld. Especially in Italy, and particularly in Bologna and Benevento, from Late Antiquity onward, it was believed that female priestesses, sorceresses, or witches, convened at midnight under walnut trees. They were said to do so on various occasions, as at the summer solstice/ the Eve of St. John and at an annual dance "called the Benevento wedding." Legend has it that the walnut tree of Benevento originated in ancient times. Witches were said to also venerate serpents at the site. These serpents have been alternately described as living and as figures made of gold. One description of them suggests that they may have once belonged to a temple of Isis. They insisted that they were worshipping Diana there, and not the Devil.

Catholics honor St. Barbatus (b. *c.* 610- d. 682) for having chopped down the walnut tree. A zealot, he was determined to eradicate paganism. It seems that he managed to convince many people of Benevento to convert after the town was occupied by the army of Emperor Constans (r. 337-350 CE), and the priest promised the siege would end if they converted. He chopped down the tree and may have also melted a golden serpent to make a chalice. According, however, to legend, the tree magically reappeared "whenever a witches' dance was to be held." It is highly likely that other walnut trees existed, and these may have displaced the original site; women accused of witchcraft continued to describe celebrating Diana beneath a walnut tree in Benevento almost a thousand years after the well-known tree had been cut down. Recently, a twenty-three-foot-high, thirteenth-century mural was discovered in the town of Massa Marittima which, according to George Ferzoco, director of the Centre for Tuscan studies at the University of Leicester, depicts witches, between eight and ten (a part of the mural has been destroyed), dressed in red, gold, and indigo or black, have gathered under a tree. One woman seems to be wearing a crown. Large, dark birds, ravens perhaps, circle around the tree and the women. The women appear to be picking "fruit" from the tree. Ferzoco claims that the fruits are in fact phalli. Could this mural depict the witches of Benevento or a kindred sisterhood?

The anonymous bard who penned *Eo Rossa, Eo Mugna* bemoans the fate of one of the most renowned trees of the Celtic world: "The Bole of Ross, a comely yew/ the tree without hollow or flaw,/ the stately bole, how did it fall?"

The yew signifies "the doorway between this life and the next," the intersection between this and other worlds. It guards and purifies the dead. Irish tradition imparts that its berries are germinating souls. For these reasons, material-sacred sanctuaries were frequently constructed near yew groves and yews continue to be found and planted in cemeteries. In Celtic tradition, the yew is sacred to the goddess Danu and the god Sucellos, the lord of life and death; Sucellus' hammer is made of yew. The yew of Ross numbered among the most sacred of trees of Celtic tradition. The yew is a sacred tree of Hecate in Greco-Roman tradition and of Odin in Germanic tradition.

Yew sticks are used in divination; Hageneder notes, "A rune was dedicated to [the yew] – *Ihwaz* or *Eiwaz* is the thirteenth rune, and generally believed to represent death and rebirth." Also thought to possess magical energy or force, the yew is "used to make magical staffs and wands." In Cambridgeshire, England, it was once thought to "afford shelter to witches." Gifford relates that "in Brittany it is said that the graveyard yew extends a root to the mouth of every corpse buried around it. The custom of putting sprigs of yew inside the shrouds of the dead was similarly believed to protect the immortal soul on its journey."

Although early Christians tended to permit sacred yews to remain standing, from the twelfth through the seventeenth centuries, in various parts of Europe, yews were increasingly determined to incite pagan veneration and should therefore be chopped down. Rio, in *L'Arbre Philosophal*, reminds us that "in 1636, the bishop of Rennes in Brittany, Pierre de Cornulier, ordered the destruction of the yews of his diocese," claiming that "persons of the countryside were putting them to malevolent uses." The Parliament of Brittany, however, rather surprisingly took the side of the peasants out of respect for ancient traditions. On August 26, 1636 the survival of yews in the parishes of Brittany became legally safeguarded, since "they had long been planted for very good reasons." The bishop fought this decree until his death on July 22, 1639.

Healing, Divination, and Magic

Trees were sometimes associated with ritual specialists and with healing, divination, and magic. Some say that the name of the Druid ritual specialists derives from the Indo-European *dervo*, "tree" or "oak," which appears in Slavic languages as *dyerevo* (Russian), *drzewo* (Polish), and *drvo* (Serbo-Croatian). Centuries later, in France, the broom-riding witch came to be called a *ramassière* – a *ramasseur* being someone who collects tree branches – in respect of her association with branches of trees. Indeed, the broom serves as a potent symbol of the deep connection of wisewomen and trees.

In Lithuania, prior to Christianization and into the early twentieth century, it was believed that certain trees possessed the power to heal. Jonas Balys states in this regard: "Even today trees...which have a cavity through the trunk, are worshipped and it is good for a man to crawl through and be healed of a disease." When someone in a Latvian village fell ill, the oldest man in the village was sent to talk to the Goddess of the forest and to the trees, to find out why the person had fallen ill and what offering the village might send to the trees to heal her or him. Usually a barrel of beer was among those items offered (reminiscent of wassailing). If the person did not get well quickly, the village would double its offering.

Trees were often believed to reveal secrets regarding destiny to those who possessed the wisdom to interpret their communicative methods, typically, via leaves rustling in the wind. This had occurred in Greece at Dodona, where oracles interpreted the 'voices' of oaks, and was practiced many centuries later by peasants of Saint-Jean-de-Boiseau in France.

Perhaps the most well known association of trees and magic is that found in the early medieval poem *Câd Goddeu*, the "Battle of the Trees," attributed to the legendary Welsh bard Taliesin, who possibly lived during the sixth century CE, and who was allegedly a child of the goddess Ceridwen and born on Beltane. Despite the fact that Taliesin is said to have converted to Christianity, and although the poem possesses Christian elements, I have chosen to mention it here because *Cad Goddeu* also contains numerous pagan references and themes. It focuses on a battle fought between the Britons, led by Amathaon and the magician Gwydion, sons of the goddess Don, on the one hand, and an army, possibly of the Otherworld and possibly led by a woman or goddess named Achren (whose name suggests "Otherworld" and/or "Trees"), together with Arawn, Lord of the Underworld, and the god Bran, ruler of the Island of the Mighty, on the other. The battle is fought over the possession of a deer, dog, and lapwing and possibly also over the possession of an oracular shrine. The battle is won through magic, when Gwydion transforms the troops of the Britons into trees and other flora. Alders form the "advance guard," while the birch, due to its height, is placed at rear to survey the action. Of all the trees, the hazel exhibits the greatest "warlike rage." It is the oak, however, which makes "heaven and earth quake./ He was a stout guardian against the enemy,/ his name is much revered."

Rites and Groves

In Celtic belief, Rio explains in *L'Arbre Philosophal*, forests were considered sacred, in part because they were thought to be guarded by divinities, but primarily because they were considered sacred in and of themselves. The forest was also envisioned by Celts as a place of initiation and as a gateway to other worlds. Likewise, for Lithuanians, the forest (*giria*) and the sacred grove (*miskelis*) were "considered as...a different world, or as a way leading there;" this was also true for Slavs.

Ceremonies conducted in sacred groves during the medieval period – ceremonies which were condemned by the Church – included the taking of vows, feasting or making food offerings, holding marriage rites, and performing divination. To some sacred trees, called *blót trés* ("blood-trees"), animal and, occasionally, among Germanic peoples, human sacrifices were offered. In Lithuania, certain trees, called *baublys*, were hollowed out in order to place shrines and offerings in them; in Christianized Lithuania, these transformed into shrines displaying figures of saints.

Many persons of the British Isles continued to worship in sacred groves in the eighth century, as evidenced by an "eighth-century list of superstitious and pagan rites [which] speaks of *sacris silvarum quae nimidas vocant*, 'shrines in groves which they call *nimidae*,'[or, Nemeton]." They sometimes constructed small shrines made of tree branches. On the Isle of Maree in Loch (Lake) Maree, Scotland, local inhabitants venerated a sacred grove of "oak, ash, willow, wicken, birch, fir, hazel, and enormous hollies," dedicated to the god Maree and to St. Maelrubha, for many centuries. From Robert Hunt's description of Wistman's Wood in *Popular Romances of the West of England* (1865, 1881), we may assume that this wooded area of Cornwall – one of the few that remains in what was in the past Dartmoor Forest and which now lies within Dartmoor National Park – was once a sacred grove, probably during the medieval period. In Hunt's view, its name of Wistman is related to "Wusc" or "Wisc," which he argues relate to the Germanic/Anglo-Saxon deity Odin/Woden. This deity's presence is underscored by the fact that the oaks growing here are sacred to him. In later centuries, Woden was identified with the Devil, in his hypostasis as Wistman, who visited the wood with his Wish Hounds to capture lost souls.

In the late tenth and early eleventh centuries, one of the most renowned sacred groves in Scandinavia was that of Sœlundr, "Sea-Grove," on the island of Seeland in Denmark, a grove of beech trees where sacrifices to the gods were made. The purposeful destruction of sacred trees and groves in Scandinavia and their displacement by Christian churches is evidenced by archaeological remains, as Olof Sundqvist notes in *Freyr's Offspring: Rulers and Religion in Ancient Svea Society* (2002): "[The] *Hervarar saga* may contain a reference to a sacred tree at Uppsala.... Archaeological and iconographic materials indicate the existence of sacred trees in eastern Scandinavia." He draws our attention to the "altar of the medieval church at Frösön, Jämtland, [where the] bones of...six...bears were discovered spread round a stump. The stump has been interpreted as a tree in a grove, on which the sacrificial animals were hung." Sundqvist suggests that sacred groves and other outdoor sanctuaries, indicated by terms including *vi*, *harg*, and *lund*, remained common in Sweden until the end of the thirteenth century. He writes convincingly that "[i]nvocations of groves, mounds, [and other] sacred sites" continued to be performed in Sweden "at the end of the thirteenth century." Sundqvist observes that the "verb O Gut haita 'invoke' [found in Christian texts prohibiting the practice] (cf. OSw *heta*, *haeta*, *haita*, ON *heita*, Lat *vocare*)...indicates that it was the groves and mounds themselves which were regarded as divine and thus worshipped."

Despite condemnation and prohibition by the Church, many Europeans continued to venerate trees and, as Lecouteux recounts of the Saxons, to consecrate forests and groves to their gods. Adam of Bremen (d. after 1076) relates, "It was above all leafy trees and rivers that seemed to them worthy of cultic worship."

Bartholomew Iscanus (1161?-1184), in the late- twelfth-century Anglo-Norman

Penitential, found it necessary to reiterate the prohibition of "making vows beside trees or water." Also in the twelfth century, we learn from a bull of Pope Eugenius III (pope, 1145-1153) that the priory of Saint-Laurent-au-Bois in France claimed as its property a forest called Bellen Silva that may have been a sacred grove dedicated to the Gaulish deity Belenus.

Like other practitioners of earth-based traditions, Slavs venerated trees. One of the most well known of such groves was that of the Slavic/Wendish god Prove. This grove, or *gaj* ("enclosed space"), stood on a hill in the vicinity of Starigard (or, Oldenburg-in-Holstein) in what is now Germany. It was either primarily or entirely comprised of oaks and was fenced in with a decorated gate. Devotees gathered there to make offerings on holidays, and once a week, justice was dispensed there. The grove of Prove was still in existence and functioning as a sacred and political center in the early twelfth century, over a century after the official Christianization of the area. Another groves was Boku. Boku, which means "beech tree," was fenced and gated, and animal sacrifices were made within it. Another was Swiety Bor at Schkeitbar/Rapitz, near Lützen and Leipzig. *Sweity* or *zuti* means "sacred," while *bor* or *bure* refers to a coniferous forest, or a forest in a damp area. Borute is also the name of a Polish/Slavic female divinity of the forest to whom this grove may have been dedicated. Thietmar (b. 975—d. 1018, chronicler and bishop of Merseburg 1009-1018) notes that this sacred grove was "venerated from time immemorial, [and was] never...violated" until the eleventh century.

Lithuanian and Old Prussian sacred groves (*šventa giria*) could be found in many places including at Kernaye, Trakai, and in the vicinity of Vilnius. They were often found together with sacred stones, hearths, and springs. Of this region, Adam of Bremen related in 1075: "In the Prussian land...it is forbidden [for Christians] to visit woods and springs which in their opinion would be foul[ed] by the visits of Christians." In the mid-thirteenth century, the theologian, preacher, and writer Thomas of Cantimpré (d. 1272), in *The Universal Good of Bees* (2.57.17, 1263), observed of the newly Christianized region: "Even today pagans in Prussia consider woods sacred to them and, not daring to set foot in them, never enter them except when they want to sacrifice to their gods in them."

Perhaps the most sacred grove, consisting wholly or primarily of oaks, in the area of Old Prussia and Lithuania was Romuva in Nadrovia, in present-day Kaliningradskaya Oblast. The name "Romuva," derived from the root *rom-*, signifies a place of silence or of peace. Although certain scholars have challenged the significance of Romuva and the assertion in the fourteenth-century *Chronicon terrae Prussiae* (*Chronicle of the Prussian Land*, 1326) that a very powerful ritual specialist, called a *krive* lived there, Vaitkevicius has recently (2004) argued convincingly in favor of the significance of Romuva and the actual existence of the ritual specialist. Kuršite relates, "It was in this sanctuary that the [Old] Prussians burnt a third of the spoils of war as a sacrifice to their gods."

Evidence suggests that from the eighth through the thirteenth centuries, persons of authority from most or all parts of the Baltic region convened, on invitation from the *krive*, probably annually, at Romuva to discuss important matters; near 1275, the main cultic center of the area may have relocated to Romainiai, Lithuania. Kuršite stresses that although Romuva has long been considered the mecca of the Baltic faith, "in the territories inhabited by Prussians...there were smaller, less significant *romows* in each neighborhood."

Trees and groves are often found in connection with deities, humans, animals, bodies of water, stones, and other entities, all of them together creating a holistic, sacred cosmos. For example, Slupecki relates that for Bulgarians, a "sacred place had to contain water and a tree...supplemented with a stone." He notes that this was also true for Wends and Bohemians. Similarly, as Pierre Audin observes in "Les Eaux saintes de la France de l'ouest: Des croyances issues de la préhistoire" ("Sacred Waters of western France: Beliefs issuing from prehistory," 1992), numerous sacred rivers and other bodies of water lie near sacred oaks, such as at "Coutre, or the Coudray-Macouard, in Maine-et-Loire, or Lavenay, in Sarthe, Le Pré-d'Auge or Rully in Calvados." Rio links this conception of collaboration to the theory of correspondences, by way of a passage from Pliny's *Natural History*, which associates "the mistletoe with the oak, the oak with the Druid, the Druid with the new year, the new year with the new moon, the crescent of the sixth day of the moon with the bill-hook of gold."

Nicole Roskos, in "Cathedral Forests and the Felling of Sacred Groves" (2005), observes that at the present time, "conservative religious groups, such as the Acton Institute for Religion and Liberty, refer[ring] to the [heroic] 'anti-idolatry' actions of St. Boniface," celebrate present-day capitalist ventures of deforestation. On the other hand, as Fred Hageneder concludes in *The Spirit of Trees*: "Trees are vital for the survival of all life forms on Earth. If the last extensive woodlands...are destroyed, Earth will become uninhabitable. Trees and humans stand and fall together." When my aunt Frieda, a stauch Baptist, scolded my Czech, tenant farmer Uncle Jim Machalicek for not attending church with her, he replied, "My church is under a tree. I'll pray there with my dog."[16]

Chapter 4
Animals

Science now shows that humans are fully related to other species. We are built like them and have brains like them. It also shows that other species are clever in their own ways.

Jeremy Narby, *Intelligence in Nature* [17]

Although we live in an age in which animal rights has become a significant sociopolitical, and some would add, spiritual movement, it seems to me that a majority of humans continue to live under the influence of either a particular interpretation of religious (typically Abrahamic) teachings or under that of René Descartes (1596-1650) in relation to the way they view animals. Descartes believed, like many Christians, that only humans possess souls and, moreover, that animals feel no pain; as Narby notes, Descartes "pioneered the practice of vivisection, or the dissection of living animals." This mentality reached critical mass several decades ago, when behaviorists like B. F. Skinner began speaking of animals as "stimulus-response machines;" Skinner wrote, "Pigeon, rat, monkey, which is which? It doesn't matter." Presently, a number of scientists, including Narby, are joining with the trailblazer Jane Goodall and others to try to repair some of the enormous damage wrought by centuries of misguided scientific thinking. Perhaps their work will assist in our more lucidly and respectfully comprehending and considering the beliefs and allied practices of our indigenous and pagan ancestors.

Marija Gimbutas, in *The Balts*, relates that "animals like the stag, bull, stallion, he-goat, ram, cock, swan and other birds, and such reptiles as snakes and toads were all believed to exercise a great influence on the development of...human life." One of the primary reasons why animals appear to have been venerated was because of the wisdom they were believed to possess and the emotions they were thought to express, particularly in regard to their relationships with humans. Ancient Finns called animals the "folk of the forest." Pliny the Elder (Gaius Plinius Secundus, 23-79 CE) speaks of animals in relation to language, healing, prophecy, and devotion. He notes that elephants and dogs recognize their names, while parrots and magpies imitate the human voice, and that starlings, nightingales, and ravens can comprehend human language; that stags heal themselves with dittany and wild artichoke, while weasels heal themselves with rue, and storks heal themselves with marjoram; that mice, spiders, ravens, and other animals forecast "dangers in advance;" that apes delight in playing games, while nightingales and dolphins delight in music; and that elephants, horses, dolphins, snakes, and other animals have been known to develop profoundly loving relationships with humans.

With the increasing privileging of transcendence over immanence, the bonds between humans and animals transformed somewhat over the millennia, but only with Christianization of the West would they sink to the level of the dominator and the dominated, as animals came to be seen increasingly not as kindred subjects but as objects to be possessed, without consciousness, soulless, acting solely upon instinct.

Veneration of Animals

Generally speaking, practitioners of earth-based traditions have embraced profound respect for animals; as Filotas asserts in *Pagan Survivals*: "Paganism...treated the relationship between humans and animals as potentially sacred."

In the pagan worldview, which is decidedly animistic, it is believed that animals possess special gifts; that animals are guarded by or are embodiments of or manifestations of divinities; that animals and humans form families or communities; that humans are linked to animals through totemic relationships; that humans may metamorphose into animals or hybrid, were-beings; that human souls may transmigrate into animals. The veneration of animals and human bonds with them have also manifested in the forms of ritual offerings and sacrifices made to animals and in animal sacrifice. Deep respect for animals and belief in their wisdom also persisted into the seventeenth and eighteenth centuries, including the belief that they shared with seers and fairies the gift of prophecy:

> [B]irds and beasts, whose bodies are much used to the change of the free and open air, foresee storms...[they] are more sagacious to understand by the Books of Nature things to come, than we...the deer scents out a man and [gun]powder ... at a great distance ... the raven, a carrion: their brains, being long clarified by the high and subtle air, will observe a very small change in a trice.[18]

In the pagan worldview, animals are thought to share particular relationships with goddesses, gods, similar beings, and heroines and heroes, numerous of whom continued to be revered in the Middle Ages and thereafter. Janina Kuršite, in "Changing Borderland Identity: the Curonian Spit and Curonian Problems" (2006), observes that wooden figures of turtles and toads may yet be found on Curonian tombstones; the Curonian Spit is a long, thin, curved peninsula bordering the Baltic Sea to the west, and the Curonian Lagoon to the east, not far from Lithuania proper and the Kaliningradskaya Oblast, also to the east. Those for women are carved from linden trees; those for men are carved from oak. These animals, Kuršite explains, are associated with the goddess Mara, "also called the Mother of Milk," in her role as bringer of death and rebirth. Kuršite notes that as "late as the first half of the nineteenth century...the inhabitants of Kuržeme County [in Latvia] revered the swamp turtle or toad as a zoomorphic sign of the goddess...toads were fed with milk and porridge at the...inhabitants' homes." Kuršite cites the historian Konrads Sulcs, who wrote in 1832: "They honored both snakes and toads as deities, which they fed with milk and other food served in special pots decorated with spikes and flowers." Kuršite further notes that it was believed that kindness toward and respect for toads increased milk production in cows. Farmers were to feed toads porridge on Friday evenings beneath the stove and to call them in by saying, "Come, come, you big ones and small ones."

Michel Meslin, in *La fête des kalendes de janvier dans l'empire romain: Étude d'un rituel de Nouvel An* (1970), strongly suggests that one of the chief reasons why Christians were so troubled by the persistent practice of dressing up as a stag during the January Kalends was that those who did so were basically becoming possessed or embodied by a hybrid stag-human god, probably synonymous with or akin to the Celtic/Romano-Celtic god Cernunnos, when they did so: "[t]he assimilation of the stag-god by the wearing of its skin is a magical act that inspires the individual with the vital power and energy of the god as one moves into the new year. To "make the stag" is, in other terms, is to identify totally with the god in order to take into himself the principles of fecundity and wealth."

It is, in my view, important to acknowledge, indeed, to insist, that these hybrid deities were revered as such because of animistic and sometimes shamanistic dimensions of the pagan traditions; their animal dimensions were not simply metaphoric or mythopoeic. Rather, they spoke to the profound kinship between humans and other animals, and to the power of metamorphosis.

From Bears to Wolves

As with tree lore, animal lore forms a kind of sacred bricolage or assemblage within the pagan worldview. The bear is the sacred animal of the Greek goddesses Athena and Artemis/Diana (as A. Brauroneia; her priestesses were called "she-bears"). In Celtic/Gaulish tradition, the bear is the companion of the goddess Dea Artio. Germanic tradition links Thor and Odin, in his hypostasis as Björn, to the bear. Odin's "*berserkrs*," the bear-warriors, were sometimes considered hybrid human-bear beings. Slavs associated the bear with Volos, the god of cattle, wealth, and trade; Volos is sometimes depicted as bear-headed. In the past, near the approach of winter, when bears began to hibernate, and again in spring, on awakening from hibernation, bears were honored at the Kamajezica with a ceremonial meal of turnips, oats, lentils, maize, wheat, and peas. Simultaneously corresponding to the earth and the moon, the bear is thought to resemble humans more closely than many other animals are. In caring for its young, the bear signifies the commencement of life as well as the role of the mother; in its hibernation, it speaks to the mysteries of death/rebirth, metamorphosis, and sacrifice.

The bee is devoted to the classical goddesses Demeter/Ceres, the Muses, Aphrodite/Venus, Artemis/Diana, Cybele, and the Lithuanian goddess Austėja and the god Biczbirbius. In a hybrid indigenous-Christian milieu, the bee came to be associated with the Black Madonna. The bee is "brave, chaste, industrious, clean, living harmoniously in...the hive." The sweetness of the bee's honey signifies eloquence, and its golden color brings wealth. The bee also signifies the soul and the mystery of death and rebirth; the "'path of bees' was a Germanic way of referring to the air as filled with the souls of the dead."

In Lithuania, the bee "was considered a sacred insect. Even the trees which the bee favored (e.g., the oak, ash, linden) were deemed holy. Mead, the alcoholic beverage produced from honey, was held to be a drink which the gods themselves enjoyed." Moreover, bees were "venerated so much that they were neither bought nor sold; they were given...as...a present, inheritance, or dowry." This exchange brought the giver and receiver into relationship, even if they had not been previously: they were now *bièiuliai*, "friends." This relationship of *bièiulystë* also came into being when several "apiculturalists [*drevininkai*, or *bartininkai*] kept their colonies together." On the other hand, to drive bees away, to steal honey, and to chop down trees in which bees lived constituted crimes. Beekeepers often paid taxes to rulers in honey and beeswax. In recent years, as Narby, in *Intelligence in Nature*, imparts, scientists have learned that although "bees have brains the size of pinheads, they can master abstract rules."

An ancient Irish lyric, attributed to the legendary bard Tuan mac Carill, reads: Today, I am a boar,/ I am king, strong and victorious. For both Celts and Germanics the boar is an aggressive, fearless warrior who inspires courage in battle, an "animal incarnation of the death goddess or god."

In *Shamanism and Old English Poetry*, Stephen O. Glosecki suggests that the boar was a totemic icon of the "seasoned warrior" among Germanic peoples from at least the seventh century BCE. He stresses that images of boars ornamenting Germanic, including Anglo-Saxons,' warriors' helmets were fashioned by smiths who were both master craftsmen and magicians, that the images, like boars themselves, were thought to be imbued with the life-force and with the particular energy of the boar. He writes: "Thus these boar-bodies wrought in metal...were strong guardians for ... warriors ... [T]hey were magical, suffused with sympathetic properties equally important to the smiths who made them and the warriors who fought beneath them." He further proposes that "the boar-adorned battle-mask...suggests a shamanic ritual, where animal masks are used to identify the wearer with the [totemic animal] whose power is essential to his practice," and that by cutting away boar images from a warrior's helmet, it was believed that the warrior would forfeit the boar's sacred force. Finally, due to the belief that the boar's force was embodied in boar images on helmets and weapons – together with the fact that other animal images were also deployed in this way – "war gear was ritualistically 'killed' [after battle] to get rid of...residual spirits of...slain enemies."

The pig or sow brings fertility and prosperity. Pigs, boars, and/or sows are sacred, in Celtic tradition, to the goddesses Brigid, Ceridwen (the 'Old White Sow'), and Dea Arduinna, and to the Gaulish-Roman god Mercury-Moccus. In classical tradition, they are sacred to Demeter and

Persephone, and in Germanic tradition, to Freyr and Freyja. Roast pig is the favorite food of residents of the warriors' paradise Valhalla. Baltic tradition links the pig to the earth-goddess Žemyna and sacrifices "black suckling pig[s]" to her.

"I am the bull of seven battles," reads a famous line from the *Book of Leinster*, attributed to the bard Amergin. The bull is associated with masculine vitality, prowess, and potency. It is also associated with the feminine divine, signified by its lunar horns; as such, it is known as "the bull of the mother." Bulls are also linked to sacrifice and to mysteries of death and rebirth. Bulls are sacred in Celtic tradition to the goddesses Mórrígán, to the legendary Celtic Queen Medb (who morphed into Queen Mab of the fairies), and to the Gaulish god Esus, and are represented by the godlike bull Tarvos Trigaranus, and the Brown Bull of Cuailnge. Bulls correspond to Zeus/Jupiter, Dionysus/Bacchus, Attis, and Mithra in classical tradition. In Germanic tradition, bulls are sacred to Thor and to Freyja, to whom they were sacrificed. In Lithuanian tradition, the bull embodies "virile, life-bringing power."

Cows are a "uniformly positive force" in the pagan worldview, speaking to "the maternal, nurturing powers of the earth." They are also considered lunar animals. They are sacred to the Celtic goddess Brigid, and the water goddess Boann ("She of the White Cattle"). In Germanic tradition, one finds the goddess-like cow Audumla, who, at the time of creation, "licked the first man out of salty blocks of ice; she herself was the first creature to emerge from the 'yawning abyss' [of] Ginnungagap"

Beauty, transitoriness, metamorphosis, death and rebirth, the soul (psyche): the butterfly embodies these. In ancient art, the butterfly is often stylized as an axe and is found on tombstones. According to Gimbutas, "The butterfly was [a being] in whose hands was the magic transformation from death to life...[T]he Greek, Germanic, and Slavic *mora*, *mara*, or *morava* mean both "nightmare" and "butterfly"...indeed, there is a very thin borderline between life and death, between the butterfly and the Goddess in her destructive aspect."

Resonating with Gimbutas' statement, Narby, in *Intelligence in Nature*, writes: "Butterflies are transformers as they metamorphose from worm into winged insect...shamans are transformers changing into animals...life itself is a transformer." In classical tradition, the butterfly is an epiphany of Artemis/Diana. In medieval and Renaissance Europe, the butterfly was linked to both witches and elves. Certain persons in Suffolk, England spoke with butterflies; while in western Scotland, some fed butterflies. The Irish banshee occasionally appears as a butterfly; the mother of Martin Gallagher from Tyrone reported having seen a "butterfly banshee" in the twentieth century.

A strange yet charming tale of love concerns the Celtic god of love, Aengus, and a beautiful maiden named Etaine. Aengus' friend Midir asks him to assist him in winning the hand of Etaine. The jealous sorceress Fuamnach, however, transforms Etaine into a butterfly. The butterfly alights on Aengus' cloak. He finds her familiar and finds himself loving her. He gives her a home in a sunny chamber of his; he fills the room with flowering plants and decorates it in purple for her. She is free to come and go. They sleep beside each other every night. She grows accustomed to her metamorphosis for a time, and "thrive[s] on the flowers."

In the nineteenth century in the northern Ireland parish of Ballymoyer, as a young girl chased after a butterfly, her friends remarked, "That may be the soul of your grandfather." William Shaw Mason reported in 1884 that in northern Ireland, "a butterfly hovering near a corpse was regarded as a sign of everlasting happiness."

Cats and felines, are in Celtic and British tradition a companion to, or embodied by, the Cailleach Bheur (the Blue Hag of Winter) and Black Annis/Gentle Annie (an avatar of Celtic goddess Danu). Ancient Egyptians revered the feline goddesses Bast and Sekhmet and further linked felines with Isis. In classical tradition, the cat and other felines are associated with Artemis/Diana, Hecate, and Cybele. The Germanic goddesses Freyja and Holda ride in chariots drawn by cats; and Germanic *völva* priestesses, who wore catskin gloves, may have journeyed in the form of cats to communicate with divinities. It is conceivable that this connection of cats with Germanic priestesses informed the ever-increasing depiction of the cat as the witch's familiar. It is abundantly clear, however, that medieval conflation of beliefs in women gathering to worship Diana were conflated by Christian scholars and Church officials, particularly from the twelfth century onward, with beliefs regarding the existence of Satanic or Luciferan cults (which I strongly believe may have existed, although quite apart from female, goddess-centered gatherings). In or near 1182, Walter Map described a Satanic or Luciferan cult wherein the Devil assumed the form of a gigantic black cat, whose posterior was kissed by devotees (incidentally, descriptions of this sect also linked Satanism with ceremonial same-sex intimacy). If this sect in fact existed, it appears to have been concentrated in Germany. Later Christian scholars and officials reiterated Map's description notion. If the association of witchcraft, Satanism, and cats had not already crystallized by the time of the trial of the wealthy Lady Alice Kyteler (d. *c.* 1324), the first person to be tried for witchcraft in Ireland, it certainly did so at this time. Kyteler confessed that a 'demonic' spirit, Robin Artisson, who served as her familiar, sometimes assumed the form of cat. Increasingly, artistic depictions of witches, such as that on a doorway of Lyons Cathedral, portrayed them in the company of cats.

While eggs have in many cultures signified fertility, chickens and roosters have almost as frequently signified sacrifice and rebirth (or regeneration). In this regard, in Germanic traditions, chickens were sacrificed and placed in graves with human remains. In these traditions, it was believed that a sacrificed rooster would "immediately com[e] to life again" upon entering the "Other World." In Slavic traditions, cocks were sacrificed in sacred groves. Chickens and roosters are sacred to a number of goddesses and gods, including the Egyptian Osiris, the Greek Zeus and his beloved Ganymede, the Roman Mars, and the Sámi Great Goddess Sáráhkká.

Several roosters play significant roles in Germanic traditions; these include Gullinkambi ("Golden Comb"), a golden rooster who dwells in the warrior paradise of Valhalla who awakens the dead to new life and heralds the commencement of Ragnarök; Fjalar, a red or black rooster who "heralds the cataclysmic events of [the apocalypse] Ragnarök;" Viðofnir, a golden rooster who sits in the World-Tree Yggdrasil (in its manifestation as Mimameiðr) and belongs to the beautiful maiden Menglöð, a manifestation of the goddess Freyja; and Salgófnir a rooster who awakens sleeping warriors, including deceased warriors dwelling in Valhalla.

Chickens and roosters (especially black ones), also playing a significant role in Slavic sacred traditions, are associated with the thunder god Perûn; Volos, a god of cattle, wealth, and trade as well as of the earth, the underworld, and magic; the crone-witch-goddess Baba Yaga; the sinister water being Vodyanik; Polevik, a guardian of crops; (the) Leshy, guardian of the forest; (the) Domovoi and Kikimora, guardians of the household; and (the) Ovinnik, patron of the threshing floor.

In Baltic sacred traditions, roosters (especially red and black ones) have been associated with and sacrificed to the thunder god Perkûnas; Vejopatis, a god of wind and storms; Aitvaras, a guardian of the household; and Dimstipatis, a patron of the farmstead.

The deer embodies gentility, strength, beauty, grace, agility, and metamorphosis. The stag's antlers correspond to the "sun's rays" and, due to their "periodic re-generation," to "rejuvenation, rebirth, and the passage of time." The deer is sacred to the Greco-Roman Artemis/Diana, and to the Celtic goddess Flidhais and the god Cernunnos. "[D]eer are 'cattle of the fairies' and messengers between the world of the gods and that of the mortals." In Celtic tradition, both fairies and banshees are thought to herd deer; indeed, deer are sometimes called "fairy cattle." In Germanic tradition, "four stags graze in the highest branches of the world-tree Yggdrasil, eating buds (hours), blossoms (days), and branches (seasons)." In Lithuanian tradition, the stag embodies "virile, life-bringing power." The deer possesses the ability to recognize healing plants; "its skin [has been employed as] an amulet against snakebite, and powdered antler [has been utilized] as protection for seed corn against black magic."

The dog is known in pagan traditions primarily for its loyalty and vigilance and as a guardian of portals between worlds. It is faithful companion to the Celtic/Gaulish goddess Epona, the god Nodon, and the demi-god and hero Cú Chulainn, the 'Hound of Culann;' and to the classical deities Hecate, Asclepius, and Hermes. In Germanic tradition, the trickster Loki sometimes manifests as a dog. The dog, in Baltic tradition, is an avatar of the goddesses Ragana and Þvërûna, who embody wildness, "death and regeneration."

The goat's virility and lustiness are condemned by some, yet celebrated by many others. It is sacred to Pallas Athena (who wears a Libyan garment of goatskin) and to Pan; satyrs and fauns are its kin. The goat is also sacred to the Germanic god Thor and the goddess Freyja, who sometimes appears as a she-goat. Among Balts, the male goat is the companion or steed of the thunder-god Perkûnas' and in this light is a "symbol of virile power and a weather-prophesying animal. Also in Baltic tradition, goats are sometimes born from linden trees, and are thus also sacred to the goddess Laima; moreover, this form of birth suggests transmigration. Not surprisingly, when Lithuania was finally Christianized, the goat became symbolic of the Devil.

Although hares and rabbits differ in numerous respects, in pagan traditions, they are frequently considered together. They are both considered lunar animals, known for their speed, vigilance, fertility, and lustfulness. They are the companions of numerous goddesses including Aphrodite/Venus and Hecate and the god Eros. In ancient Greece, hares were presented as gifts of love to both heterosexual and same-sex lovers. Among Anglo-Saxons, the hare belongs to the goddess Eostre. Baltic tradition links the hare to Medeina, goddess of the forest. According to Gimbutas, "[This] animal helped the goddess to protect her forests, especially by leading hunters astray... Even the Lithuanian king Mindaugas... would not hunt in the forest if he saw Medeina's hare. Clearly, the animal was sacred, a double of the goddess." Hares and rabbits appear in rites of spring as well as in harvest rites. In medieval and pot-medieval Europe, witches were thought to be capable of transforming into hares. In Irish lore, "the black hare [is] certainly a witch."

The horse is sacred to the Celtic goddesses Macha, Epona, and Rhiannon; the Greco-Roman Artemis/Diana and Ares/Mars; the Germanic goddess Dame Gaue and the god Odin/Woden; and the Slavic gods Redigast and Svantovit. Often a solar animal, the horse is honored for its vitality, speed, and nobility. Hans Biedermann observes, "Germanic sacrifices of horses, followed by the eating of the meat of the animal, led after the Christianization of Europe to the taboo that is still attached to the consumption of horsemeat in many societies." Among Balts, "[m]ost prominent among the divine animals was the horse, the escort of [the 'wise old man' god] Dievas and [the sun goddess] Saulë. In mythological songs, the horse (Lithuanian *zirgas*, Latvian *zirgs*) is so intimately related to *Saule*, the Sun, that sometimes it seems to stand as a symbol for the sun."

In England, veneration of the horse was reflected in sacred art, including in hillside sculptures, "the largest reaching 374 feet and dating from the first century BCE." Ancient, medieval, and post-medieval rites and folk dramas included male participants donning horse masks sometimes made from preserved horses' heads, as well as participants riding brooms meant to resemble horses or men dressed as horses. In these rites and dramas, incidentally, horses were often associated with persons having black skin and with transgender persons.

Horses also came to play a part in narratives of witches and witchcraft. Sometimes the deity or cult leader was alleged to have appeared in equine form. On other occasions, divinities, cult leaders, and/or participants were alleged to have ridden on horseback, or else on brooms that were meant, as in shamanistic rites of various cultures and in English folk drama, to signify horses. In my view, however, the most intriguing association of the horse with narratives of witches and witchcraft concerns alleged witches being ridden like horses by "the Devil," either himself or else pagan divinities or spirits falsely identified with Satan, and/or by other participants. For example, both Isobel Shirie, in the 1660s, and Ann Armstrong, in the 1670s, were allegedly ridden in this manner. I find this especially intriguing because in various religions/traditions, as in Vodou, possessed or embodied initiates are described as being "ridden" and as the "horses" of the gods.

The raven, immortalized by Edgar Allen Poe, is sacred to the Celtic triple battle-goddess Badb (the Raven of Battle), the Welsh underworld-goddess Rhiannon, and the divinized heroes Lug and Cú Chulainn. In classical tradition, the bird is sacred to Apollo, and in Germanic tradition, to Odin/Woden; the latter's constant companions are the ravens Huginn, "Thought," and Muninn, "Remembrance." The raven is both guide and trickster-thief. The raven is a herald of death. Although the raven has been punished for divulging secrets, the bird is nonetheless aware of all that transpires. Intriguingly, in this regard, Narby reports: "Western observers have long minimized the mental capacities of birds – hence the term *birdbrain*.... [O]ne crow, the Clark's nutcracker, can remember up to thirty thousand hiding places for the pine seeds it gathers and buries for safekeeping."

Samuel Hibbert, in *A Description of the Shetland Islands; Comprising an Account of Their Scenery, Antiquities and Superstitions* (1822), compares Marion Pardon, a wisewoman who lived in Shetland during the middle of the seventeenth century, to Odin, in part because her familiars were, like the ravens who sat on Odin's shoulders, "two corbies, that hopped on each side of her" on her frequent journeys from Brecon to Hillswick.

The snake or serpent embodies, simultaneously, vitality, happiness, prosperity, danger, the mystery of death and rebirth (particularly as reincarnation, or transmigration, signified by its shedding of skin). In *The Balts*, Gimbutas notes, "The very name for "snake" in Lithuanian, *gyvatò*, shows association with *gyvybò*, *gyvata*, "life," "viability." The "house snake [that is, a snake fed by humans]...can represent the blessings of departed ancestors." For Gimbutas, the snake is an avatar of a primordial goddess; she is depicted in the form of Old European figurines or statuettes and reliefs dating from Crete, Bulgaria, and elsewhere from the sixth millennium BCE onward.

Roman maidens honored the snake as a companion, like the goat, of the goddess Juno. Within her sacred grove at Lanuvium dwelt a prophetic serpent to whom young women would offer barley and cakes, in exchange for certain prognostications, including whether or not their families could expect an abundant harvest. In Celtic tradition, the snake becomes the companion of the horned god Cernunnos, and in classical tradition, that of Asclepius and Hermes, signified by the serpentine staff called the caduceus.

In Germanic tradition, the snake is typically ambiguous, with the beloved god Odin being nicknamed Ofnir and Svâfnir, linking him totemically to snakes, while Jörmungandr, a huge snake who coils in repose around the earth, will awaken to assist in the destruction of present world. Snakes are also sacred to the Slavic deities Perûn and Volos; the Prussian deity Patrimpas; the Latvian goddess Brehkina and the female snake-divinities, the Peena Mahtes ("Milk-Mothers"); and to the Lithuanian Perkûnas. In the Spreewald, a region of marshland, meadows, and forests in Brandenburg, Germany, rurals who persisted in performing pagan practices until fairly recently often kept two snakes, a male and female, in their houses and cared for them with great respect.

Slavic peoples often employed snakes in magical practice. The bishop Merkelis Giedraitis in 1587 wrote that in the greater part of the Samogitia diocese [Žemaitija, in western Lithuania], people "worship[ped] grass snakes" and continued to offer the snakes milk. Slavs and Balts number among groups who have honored and fed grass snakes milk and encouraged them to dwell in their houses, believing that they are divinities and that they will bring prosperity to the family. Maria Kravchenko, in *The World of the Russian Fairy Tale*, notes: "Belorussians and Ukrainians had great respect for the house snake Domovoi Tsmok (sometimes called Damavik), which lived behind the stove, and were careful to put milk out for it each night." In Finnish paganism, the snake is the "*tietäjä*'s [roughly, the shaman's] helper, which [can] be summoned to his presence by whistling." *Tietäjäs* typically kept snakes in cellars, feeding them and communicating with them. Once, a renowned *tietäjä* named Kusti Ihalainen asked his snake to demonstrate to his guests how many persons were in the room, "at which point the snake nodded its head as many times as there happened to be visitors." When a sacred snake died, it was customary for the *tietäjä* to sew its body into a belt.

The wolf – dangerous, predatory, shrewd, cunning, leading warriors to victory — is sacred to Apollo Lycius and to Mars. A female wolf is honored for having nursed Romulus and Remus, the legendary founders of Rome. In Germanic tradition, the wolf is sometimes a companion to Odin/Woden; on the other hand, "the mighty wolf Fenris [or, Fenrir] must be tied up but then in the final battle breaks its bonds, swallows the sun, then is killed in combat by Odin." Thus, the "time of wolves" refers to the end of the world as we know it. Also in Germanic tradition, warriors were generally called "friends of wolves," with a certain class of warriors being known as *ulfserkrs*. In Sweden, priestesses or sorceresses known as *Vargamor* ("Wolf-crones") were thought to have wolves as familiars. This association of wolves with priestesses and sorceresses may have been linked to the portrayal of wolves as the " 'hounds' of the Norns." The death-bringing goddess Skaði, who "eats the bodies of the dead," is also identified with the wolf. Perhaps due to this association with death, the gallows, in Hamðismal, is nicknamed the *vargtré vindkold*, the "wind-cold wolf-tree." Certain Slavs, practitioners of earth-based traditions and later Christianized Slavs practicing religious hybridity, particularly Poles, Bulgarians, and Dalmatians, honored wolves during the winter with Vilci Prazdnici, "Wolf Holidays," which might last from November to February. During these periods, wolves were nicknamed "carolers," and carolers dressed in wolf skins.

Cruelty to Animals vs. Animal Sacrifice

Unfortunately, there is evidence that some pagans practiced forms of animal cruelty. It is believed, for example, that the "cruel amusement" of torturing bears via bearbaiting, the setting of fierce dogs onto a chained bear, "was introduced into Europe by the Romans." This atrocious "amusement" became increasingly popular over the centuries and was not halted by Christianization; among its chief supporters was James I. Another abhorrent "amusement" of this caliber is the practice of cock-throwing on Shrove Tuesday, as practiced in Oxfordshire, England. Such practices often occurred during Carnival. For example, during Carnival at Hildesheim, apparently as a seasonal sacrifice, cats were fastened to baskets in the tops of fir trees and apparently left to die there should they not manage to escape. It may surprise some readers that bull-baiting was a popular sport in England until 1835, when it was banned by Parliament; other acts of animal cruelty were also banned at that time. Other abuses of animals were clearly a product of Christianization; for example, a hideous Irish Christian custom, perverting an ancient holiday, encouraged the stoning of hares on May 1st because they were thought to be shape-shifting witches.

Although I find it a bit problematic to characterize the following as animal cruelty outright, I am inclined to categorize certain uses of animals in medicine amounts as such, as, for example, the treatment from which the expression "a frog in the throat" is alleged to originate. For an infant ill with thrush, a frog was held tightly in a cloth in the infant's mouth until it died; this was believed to cure the infant. This treatment persisted into the nineteenth century in the British Isles. Another such treatment, thought to cure epilepsy, involved the sacrifice of a black cock, by way of burying it alive beneath the floor where the sufferer had experienced his or her first epileptic episode. Such treatments do not, however, personally disturb me as much as realizing that at present, "[m]illions of animals – dogs, cats, rats, mice, guinea pigs, and rabbits – are used for testing...nonessential cosmetic products such as deodorants, shampoos, soaps, and eye makeup" – the primary responsibility for which lies neither with ancient nor present-day pagans.

Unlike many persons living today, particularly those involved in organizations such as PETA (People for the Ethical Treatment of Animals), for whom animal sacrifice is regarded as cruelty to animals, among past practitioners of European traditions, as with practitioners of Yòrubá-diasporic traditions, the practice of animal sacrifice was not thought to lessen or invalidate respect for animals; it was not considered animal cruelty but instead as an aspect of veneration. As in numerous indigenous traditions, animals were believed, on certain occasions, to offer themselves as sacrifices to the gods or ancestors so that another or others, both humans and animals, might be healed. Such animals were supposed to be treated with utmost care prior to the sacrificial rite; at times, however, this was not always the case, as when chickens were walled up within an English house while still alive. The preceding is also true for a number of present-day indigenous and African-diasporic sacred traditions.

One of the primary ritual practices performed by Roman agricultural workers of late Classical antiquity, discussed by both Varro and Cato, is animal sacrifice. Goats were offered to Bacchus [i.e., Dionysus, Liber], while pigs were offered to Ceres, Janus, Jupiter, and Juno. Certain animals were never to be sacrificed to particular deities; for example, cattle were never offered to Ceres, because they were considered her attendants, members of her entourage. Together with animals, these sacrifices included an offering of cakes and wine and the burning of incense. They frequently occurred prior to "harvesting spelt, wheat, barley, beans, and rape seed" and before the clearing of a grove of sacred trees. Such sacrifices were thought to promote protection of one's household and prosperity in terms of one's crops. When an area of land required purification, a triple sacrifice, called the *suovetaurilia*, was made: a pig to Janus; a ram to Jupiter; and a bull to Mars. To avert or drive away plagues, Greeks sacrificed black sheep to Hades and Persephone, sweetening the sacrifice with pure water, perfume, and incense, or else a cow to Gaia or a reddish male goat to Apollo.

Archaeological evidence indicates that Celts may have sacrificed bulls, dogs, and other animals to goddesses and gods, with dogs being offered primarily to mother goddesses. In Germanic tradition, boars were offered to Freyr, bulls to Freyja, and bulls and goats to Thor. After a portion of the meat was given to the deity, devotees consumed the remainder at a great feast (this is what typically occurs, incidentally, in West African-diasporic traditions). In the mid-tenth century, a Spanish Jewish traveler from Cordova wrote of inhabitants of the market town of Hedeby, Denmark: "They hold a feast where all meet to honour their god and to eat and drink. Each man who slaughters an animal for sacrifice – ox, ram, goat or pig – fastens it to a pole outside the door of his house, to show that he ha[s] made his sacrifice in honor of the god."

In the nineteenth and early twentieth centuries, in Sussex, horses and calves were sacrificed on the branches of trees to increase fertility among the remainder of their kind; some believed this type of sacrifice to be rooted in the ancient reverence of Odin.

Sacrificial blood, *blaut*, was considered very sacred and potent. A bowl of blood was kept in Thor's shrine, and blood was sprinkled on shrine's walls.

Some believed that the gods possessed the power to restore life to sacrificed animals. The *Prose Edda* relates a tale that resonates with many found in shamanistic traditions in which "Thor, lodging with a farmer, 'sacrificed his goats for dinner and cooked them in his cauldron and after the meal he collected the bones and skins, and restored them to life by raising his hammer over them.'" In 1982, a deposit was discovered in the river Hull at Skerne, near Driffield, England that speaks to Viking sacrifice of animals during the medieval period. A gathering of about twenty animals – cattle, dogs, horses, and sheep – appears to have been sacrificed to the river or to a deity or similar being associated with it.

In England, Scandinavia, Russia, and elsewhere, it appears that animals – including cats, chickens, deer, dogs, goats, horses, and sheep – were sometimes sacrificed when a house or building was being constructed, apparently to protect it from fire, destructive magic, and other harm, from the Anglo-Saxon period onward. A noteworthy comparison: in Chinese tradition, "[c]hicken blood, believed to repel demons, was…sprinkled on the building site to restrain…dark forces."

In Slavic tradition, as we have previously noted, cocks were sacrificed in sacred groves. Gimbutas recounts that among indigenous Balts, "The usual animal offerings were boars and pigs, he-goats, sheep, calves, cocks and hens, as testified by the excavations and the historical records." Sacrifices to the goddess Laima of hens (for girls), roosters (for boys), and sheep took place at the time of childbearing. Lithuanians in particular sacrificed a sow to the earth when founding a town. In a *daina* (Lithuanian folksong) of unknown date, the sacrifice of a goat is performed to bring agricultural fertility and prosperity:

In order that the crop be bountiful,
One need bring a little black goat
As a sacrifice
To the altar on the hill,
Where it must be strangled
For the glory of the gods.[19]

In July, 1525, Christian Protestants condemned and commenced persecuting inhabitants of Samland/Sambia, in the vicinity of the region in Lithuania Minor/East Prussia/Kalinigradskaya Oblast, who continued to "pay homage to the Steinbock." "Steinbock" translates as "Capricorn;" the implication is that inhabitants of this region were continuing to honor a deity or deities, most probably the lord of thunder, Perkûnas, with sacrifices of goats, as the ancient Sudovians had done before them. Protestant authorities sought the aid of anyone who might know someone who continued to practice this tradition and warned that those who were caught doing so would be punished. This persistent veneration and sacrifice of the goat was also described by Hieronymus Meletius in *Warhafftige Beschreibung der Sudawen uff Samland sambt ihren Bock heyligen und Ceremonien* (*True Description of the Sodovians in Samland along with their Goat Sacrality and Ceremonies*, probably 1561/2). In this tradition, the goat sacrifice ceremony included confessions by those persons who'd committed transgressions as well as determinations regarding punishments.

Animal sacrifice also occurred during seasonal rites. In late sixteenth-century France, alleged witches sacrificed black cocks or hens during a rite held on or near February 17th.

On the occasion of the spring equinox, Poles traditionally sacrificed a rooster, thought to embody "beauty, masculinity, vital forces, and fertility," to "the deities of fertility and harvest;" commencing in the eighteenth century, live roosters were often replaced by artistic representations of roosters.

In Ploy Field, in the village of Holne in the county of Devon in southwest England, animal sacrifice persisted in the nineteenth century in the form of the annual Ram Feast, celebrated on May 1 (Beltane). It appears that this sacrifice was linked to homage paid to sacred stones and/or to the divinities inhabiting or associated with them. Young people gathered around a menhir of about six or seven feet in height to sacrifice a young ram at noon, after which dancing around the menhir, drinking cider, and feasting occurred. In Savoy, a fox or cat was sacrificed, and in Languedoc, a "cat, a snake, or a mole" at midsummer. Bulls were sacrificed each August 25th on the island of Innis Maree, Scotland until 1678; they were offered to the mysterious divinity Mourie to encourage fertility of livestock. In France, Germany, and elsewhere, goats, cats, and cocks were decorated and sacrificed at harvest-time.

As late as the seventeenth century, Latvians sacrificed "in December, about Christmas time, at cross-roads a goat to the wolves, 'with strange idolatrous rites', to induce the wolves to spare the herds and flocks during the ensuing year." Scots and others of the present day continue to serve boar's head at Yule, a dish that may return us to the sacrifice of a boar to Freyr. In certain pagan and pagan-based traditions, cakes shaped like bears, cows, deer, goats, and pigs, for example, those traditionally baked in Poland on the occasion of the winter solstice, replaced animal sacrifice.

Many animal sacrifices in the seventeenth and later centuries were undertaken to prevent or cure disease. In England, cocks were sacrificed in an effort to cure consumption (tuberculosis). In Ireland, two pigeons or two chickens were sacrificed to cure a person suffering from bronchitis. A Scotsman named Thomas Grieve sacrificed an unspecified animal in 1623 in the hope that this act would cure his extremely ill family. In 1650, at Lochbroom, Ross, Cromarty, Scotland, Margaret Dow sacrificed a lamb at the threshold of her house "as a preventative against the death of the rest of her beasts." In 1686, peasants of Autun, France, sacrificed a heifer to Our Lady (Autun having been a seat of Cybele's worship) to obtain protection against the plague. A black hen was sacrificed in Gerona, Spain in the nineteenth century to "cure nausea and sickness [in pregnancy] which was attributed to the evil eye." In nineteenth-century Ross-shire, Scotland a black cock was sacrificed in an attempt to heal a child of epilepsy; the "animal was...buried alive, after which an incantation was muttered over it by a 'wise woman.'" When he was a youth, Sir James Simpson (1811-1870), the discoverer of chloroform, aided his father in sacrificing a cow in an attempt to cure a herd of the disease of murrain. During this period, cows and bulls were sacrificed for the same reason near Haltwhistle in Northumberland, England, in Cornwall, in the county of Moray in northeastern

Scotland, and in Wales.

Animal sacrifice was to a certain extent appropriated by the Church (which, of course, also drew upon Biblical tradition in regards to this practice). For example, during the medieval period in England, the sacrifice of deer to Diana was transferred to St. Paul. When the "Primitive Methodist chapel was built in Littleport, Cambridgeshire, in 1897, a horse's head was placed in the foundation trench and a glass of beer was poured over it."

Occasionally, it would seem that animal sacrifice and animal cruelty became indistinguishable, not in view of our own ethics, but in view of those of the time in which they occurred. For example, it is not difficult to imagine that many living in the late sixteenth century might have looked upon the tossing of a cat, like a ball, into the sea in the hope that this offering would be accepted by the Devil, who would then assist witches in stirring a tempest that might result in the death of King James VI/I (1566-1625; r. Scotland 1567-1603; England and Ireland 1603-1625), as an act of both sacrifice and cruelty.

Animals and Humans: Bodies and Souls

In the very earliest time
when both people and animals lived on earth,
a person could become an animal if he wanted to
and an animal could become a human being.
Sometimes they were people
and sometimes animals

....

All spoke the same language.

from an interview with Nalunqiac, an Inuit woman, by ethnologist Knud Rasmussen, early twentieth century [20]

In both Germany and England, particularly in Cornwall, "traditions tell of snakes that live together with a child, whom they watch in the cradle, eat and drink with it. If the snake is killed, the child declines and dies shortly after. In general, snakes bring luck to the house in which they take up their abode, and milk is placed for them as for the domestic sprites." In certain parts of England, "every farmhouse has two snakes, for the master and mistress; they appear upon the death of either, and the one bonded with that one dies."

In Lithuania, the "death of a farmer had to be immediately announced to his horses and cattle, and when a beekeeper died, the bees had to be told; otherwise, the animals and bees would die out...In prehistoric times, it was believed that the animals went to the other world to live there with their master. Human and bee communication, and the profound, familial bond humans and bees share within the pagan worldview, is evidenced by documentation pertaining to beekeepers of Herefordshire and Cambridgeshire, England. In *The Folk-Lore of Herefordshire* (1912), Ella Mary Leather observes that although the custom of telling "cart horses of the death of their master" had been practiced for many years, it had apparently died out by the early twentieth century. On the other hand,

Bees are regarded with respect, and the general custom of telling them of a death in the family of their owner is not yet [circa 1912] extinct.... In Weobly, it was thought they would die if not told. ... I have heard of one case of which the bees in twelve hives died after a death, a loss attributed to neglect of the custom of announcing it to them.... There is at all times a fear of offending bees; they must not be bought or sold...bees are lovers of peace, and will not stay with a quarrelsome family.[21]

Leather cites an event which occurred in Herefordshire, at Pembridge, in 1838, and which was written up in the *Hereford Times* (March 20, 1838). A medical doctor attending a funeral for a young man was greatly troubled by actions performed by the local clergyman and the entourage. At some point prior to the burial, the clergyman halted the procession and stopped at a crossroads to announce the death of the young man to the local bees. "[T]hey foolishly affirm," the doctor carped, "that if they do not, the bees will all be sure to die." Leather mentions a similar event that occurred in 1873, at a "large apiary at the Moor, near Hay." When the beekeeper died, "no one told the bees. It was noticed shortly afterwards they all disappeared."

Where animals themselves were concerned, because they were often viewed as other-than-human persons, they were respected as such upon death. In *Slavic Mythical Beliefs* (1982), Frank Kmietowicz relates: "When an ox became old, they let it go free in the pasture, and when it died, they buried it with the same respect as they buried their [human] dead, with crying and lamenting."

As late as the 1960s, Enid Porter reports in *Cambridgeshire Customs and Folklore* (1969), it was "a common practice for Cambridgeshire beekeepers to make their bees a part of their household by imparting to them the news of such important family events as births, engagements, weddings, and especially deaths. If this is not done, the bees will either fail to thrive or will forsake the hives." In Cambridgeshire, human communication with bees did not always take the form of verbal communication. For example, in 1951, an eighty-year-old man recalled that when, in 1893, his grandmother died at Barrington, his "grandfather tied pieces of black material to all the bee-hives."

Sometimes animals were also thought to confer a kind of immortality, or at least a lengthy state of suspended animation, upon humans, as suggested by the tale of the desire of the Witch of Berkeley, who allegedly lived in eleventh-century England, to have her children to sew a stag's skin around her body upon her death.

Early peoples appear to have envisioned themselves as protected by totemic animals; Slavs, for example, saw "animals as the forefathers of the tribes." Tribesmen who considered the wolf their forefathers" took the name Vuk, "wolf." Such totemic relationships are also suggested by the Scottish Highland tribal name of the Caereni, or "sheep-folk," and the Highland place-name of Caithness, relating to the "cat-folk." Similarly, the Ossorians of Ireland were thought to be "descendants of the wolf."

A legend told of when St. Patrick was Christianizing Ireland goes: "[T]here was one race more hostile to him than the other people that were in the land. …And when he preached Christianity to them as to other men, and came to meet them when they were holding their assembly, then they took counsel, to howl at him like wolves." St. Patrick then prayed that God would punish them for howling at him: "And great punishment and fit…has since befallen their descendants; for it is said that all men who come from that race are always wolves at a certain time…[S]ome become so every seventh year."

Scots believed that the clans of Iver/Maciver and Donnachaidh, or, Robertson shared a special relationship with serpents and that no serpent would harm a member of those clans. Certain Scots of the nineteenth century, when celebrating St. Bridget's Day, said of the serpent, whom they sometimes referred to as "the Queen": "I will not hurt the daughter of Iver, neither will Iver's daughter hurt me." Likewise, the Scottish clan of MacLeod was thought to have the horse as a tutelary animal; the clan of Matheson/MacMhathain/Macmaghan, the bear; and that of MacCulloch, the boar.

Occasionally, relationships between animals and humans are associated with theriomorphic metamorphosis. Transformation into animals often takes the form of wearing animal masks and skins or hides. For example, in pagan Poland, persons wearing masks of horses, turons (aurochs, a wild bovine animal that inhabited Polish forests but that became extinct in the seventeenth century), and other animals sang at the winter solstice,

Where our Horse goes

Rich rye grows
Where our turon puts his feet
There stands a rye heap.[22]

This fertility rite, once linked to the Slavic deity Radegast, has continued into the present.

Theriomorphic metamorphosis may also take the form of hybrid were-creatures. For example, in the late sixteenth century, the English travel writer Fynes Moryson (1566-1630) reported that "in Upper Ossory and Ormond [in Ireland] are yearly turned into wolves." We have already noted that some members of the Scottish clan of MacCodrum and of the Irish clans of Connolly and Lee and were thought to metamorphose into selkies. Notably, belief in the existence of selkies continued (at least) into the late nineteenth century; it was claimed in 1895, for example, that Baubi Urquhart of the Shetland Islands was "the great-great-granddaughter of a seal-woman."

Occasionally, the bond between humans and animals indicates that humans possess animal souls while living and/or embraces the concept reincarnation, metempsychosis, or transmigration. In traditional Germanic belief, humans are believed to possess several souls, or, alternatively, a multidimensional soul. Soul and souls are frequently discussed as being synonymous with guardian entities. One or more of these souls or aspects of soul may assume the form of an animal, often a bird, a goddess, or a goddess companioned by or riding on an animal; according to some sources, this is the *hamingja*; according to others, the *fylgia*. These souls or aspects of soul may manifest when humans sleep as forms like those called astral bodies by spiritualists, or upon death. Although descriptions of *fylgia* tend to be incomplete and less than lucid, it would appear that each person has a masculine and feminine *fylgia*, the *mannsfylgia* and the *fylg-jukona*, respectively, which resonate with Jung's conception of the animus and anima. It also appears that each family possessed its own guardian, the *oettarfylgia*.

In the Orkney Islands of northern Scotland, it was believed in the past that "everyone had a *varden* or companion spirit, in the shape of an animal, which accompanied him everywhere, and which moaned dismally if he was about to die."

In Slavic tradition, the human soul might assume the form of a bee, a fly, a moth, a butterfly, a bird, or a mouse. Maria Kravchenko, in *The World of the Russian Fairy Tale* (1987), states: "Since it was believed to leave the body upon death and was associated with the air and flying, it became natural to imagine the soul as a bird, butterfly, or some other winged creature. In Yaroslavsk province the butterfly is still called *dushinka*, 'little soul'." She notes that in Bulgaria, it was traditionally believed that the "soul in the form of a butterfly or a bird sits on the nearest tree to the grave until the funeral is over, and then flies off on its distant journey with its guide."

When migratory birds returned in spring, Slavs rejoiced in the return of ancestral spirits in bird form and fed them "corn, flax and hemp seeds." Similarly, Lithuanian sacred tradition holds that there are several souls or several aspects of the soul. One of these is the *siela*, of which we have spoken above in relation to trees. The *siela* is "related to the Roman *anima* or the Greek *pneuma*, meaning a living power which [does] not depart from the earth." It often assumes the form of an animal, typically a bird ("women into a cuckoo or a duck, men into a falcon, a pigeon, a raven, or a cock") or a "butterfly, a bee, a mouse, a toad, [a] snake," a wolf, a bear, a dog, a horse, or a cat. Humans transmigrating into bees and bears is a belief especially found among Romany "gypsies" in southeastern Poland, near Pryslop.

It should be noted that reincarnation in the form of transmigration has engendered extreme prejudice in spiritual authorities and others who typically insist that humans represent a higher form of life than all other life forms and that animals possess no souls. Justin Martyr (*c*. 100-*c*. 165 CE), a Church Father, a believer in reincarnation, argued that only souls deemed unworthy in the eyes of God are reborn as animals. Hermetic writings argue that a human soul cannot enter the body of an animal. Prejudice against human-animal transmigration on evolutionary grounds continues in the present, incidentally, such as in statements made by Joseph Head and/or Sylvia Cranston in *Reincarnation: The Phoenix Fire Mystery* (1977, 1998), where this form of rebirth is denigrated as a "complete reversal of the natural evolutionary processes."

Belief in transmigration was shared by many Celts. Peter Berresford Ellis (1992) relates, "Souls migrated from the Land of the Living to the Land of the Dead and vice versa. They also migrated through various births." In *The Celts: Uncovering the Mythic and Historic Origins of Western Culture* (1976,

1993), Jean Markale writes of human-animal transmigration: "[A]nimals are...regarded as the reincarnations or the original embodiments of heroes." animals that shared this connection with humans included the boar, cow, crow, eagle, raven, salmon, and wolf.

Medieval Germanic tradition included the belief that upon death, the soul may pass into another entity, or assume the body of another entity; just as it may pass into or be reborn as a flower, especially a lily or rose, so it may pass into or assume the body of a soul as a dove, duck, raven, or swan. Among Balts, the cuckoo "is the main incarnation of the dead mother." Similarly, the astral body may assume the form of a snake when we dream.

Some Scots, during the nineteenth and early twentieth centuries, believed that upon death, the human soul might transmigrate into the body of a cuckoo, magpie, raven, swan, or deer; during the same period, certain persons of Brittany likewise believed that the human soul might embody a raven. A Scottish carpenter repairing a cottage, resting to eat lunch, watched as a deer passed him and walked into the house. The deer then proceeded to walk up the staircase, and when the carpenter tried to force it to leave, the deer wouldn't budge. The carpenter became convinced that the deer was "the spirit of a former occupant, now deceased, that had come back in deer guise." Also during this period, a gamekeeper at Cornwall refused "to fire at a fox that haunted a certain house" in the area. The gamekeeper "was not deterred by any fox-hunting scruples, but by the conviction that the animal was really 'poor Mr. Frank,' whose spirit returned to an earthly form."

Also during that period, some elderly people of Wales asserted that "white moths were the souls of the dead who in this form were allowed to take farewell of the earth." The soul has assumed the form of a butterfly since ancient Greece. In certain parts of Europe during the medieval period, it was thought that butterflies embodied the souls of witches and elves. Belief in the human soul assuming the form of a butterfly persisted in nineteenth-century Brittany, Scotland, Ireland and on the Isle of Man; Highlanders spoke of this state of being as *dearbadan Dé*, *tarmachan Dé*, being the Highland names." In 1810, a girl in Armagh, Northern Ireland was scolded for "chasing a butterfly, because it might be the soul of her grandfather;" and in 1869, an elderly woman living in Maryfort, Ireland "scandalized her neighbors by asserting that butterflies were the dwelling [place] of the human soul, and that her own soul would go into a 'blessed (tortoiseshell) butterfly' [upon her death]." Such beliefs persisted in early twentieth-century Russia. Felix J. Oinas, in *Essays on Russian Folklore and Mythology* (1985), relates that birds were considered mediators between the realms of the living and the dead and it was believed that upon death, the human soul could assume the body of a bird (particularly the grey pigeon) or butterfly. For these reasons, feeding pigeons gained a sacred aspect. When villagers visited graves they took offerings of rye, wheat, and oats with them, believing that the dead might appear to them as birds; and many persons permitted pigeons to dwell in their homes as "pets" or family members. Not surprisingly, to kill a pigeon was seen as a great crime. When the writer Leo Tolstoy (1828-1910) died, peasants who loved him "honored his memory by strewing grain for birds on his grave every night."

In the spring of 1964, as my maternal grandmother and I sat together in south Texas watching butterflies flutter among the roses, she pointed to one of them and said, "When I'm gone, I'll come back to you like that."[23]

Chapter 5
Elements and Celestial Bodies

'Hail to thee, Lady Sun!
Art all the world's delight.'
When ye see the sun glad,
The fair day to her ye ascribe,
To her ye give the honor…
a thirteenth-century anonymous

German poem to Frau Sonne [24]

Firmicus Maternus, a pagan astrologer who became a zealous Christian convert, commenced condemning earth-centered concepts and practices around the third decade of the fourth century. He especially attacked the veneration of elements by ancient peoples: "Egyptians, water; Phrygians, earth; Syrians and Carthagians, air; and Persians, fire."

Within Yorùbá and Yorùbá-diasporic belief, the elements, including "winds," air, and "mountains," earth, possess *ori*, consciousness; "[e]very element and force of nature is spiritual and self-aware." Although the elements of ancient Chinese sacred practice differ somewhat from those of African, European, and other religions/traditions, they are likewise venerated. Earth brings forth; water is the great nurturer; wood activates, catalyzes; fire transforms; metal brings culmination.

Jordan Paper, in "Chinese Religion, 'Daoism,' and Deep Ecology" (2001), describes a Chinese tradition that is linked to Daoism and that resonates with the earth-centered worldview: Rujia. He explains that many persons practice both Daoism and Rujia. Rujia, in accord with animism, acknowledges that life feeds on life. Rujia emphasizes the creation of "ritual ceremonies (*jiao*) that celebra[te] cosmic renewal and…that reinfor[ce] the connections between humans and the spirit realm, including Earth, Waters, and Sky." Rooted in an agriculture-based economy, Rujia rites have been performed for over 2,400 years. In earlier epochs, "the imperial couple sacrificed to Sky and Earth; regional governors, as well as the emperor, sacrificed at altars to Soil and Grain; and farming families…sacrifice[d] at small shrines in the farm fields to Grandmother and Grandfather Earth," the last, a practice that Paper reports continues to be practiced today. Veneration of elements and celestial bodies is a common element of many indigenous and ancient religions/traditions, including those of the Egyptians, Mesopotamians, Greeks, Romans, and many African and Indigenous American peoples.

Elements and Elementals

Both the English librarian (of Christ's Church College, Oxford), scholar, and Anglican clergyman Robert Burton (1577-1640) and the Greek scholar Leo Allatios (*c.* 1586-1669) acknowledged seventeenth-century belief in elementals.

Allatios referred to elementals, as well as house-spirits, as *stoicheia*. Although he was reared in the Orthodox Church and converted to Catholicism, he openly acknowledged both his own and his mother's belief in earth-based, non-Christian *stoicheia*. "The *Stochion* was said to haunt our house in the form of a snake." These elementals were born in "fire, air, [earth,] and water, [demonstrating] that there is nothing in this universe which lacks a soul, nor does it lack the natural life of the higher animals." *Stoicheia* could be cruel or kind to humans depending on how they were treated. If treated well, they would foretell the destinies of members of the household and would tell them news of persons living, and events occurring, far away. *Stoicheia* sometimes manifested as harmless lizards and snakes. Practitioners of magic could summon the energy of elementals into amulets, figurines, and the like.

One should bear in mind that in *The Anatomy of Melancholy* (1621), Burton frequently conflated elementals with pagan deities and with "demons" as described by Christians. Of course, Burton was himself drawing upon earlier beliefs and texts such as Paracelsus' (1493-1541) *Liber de nymphis, syphis, pygmais et salamandris* (1566). Burton's gargantuan text is significant in that within it he has collected a great deal of material from antiquity through the sixteenth century regarding various conceptions of spirits. He notes that while, in his view, the Sadducees, Galen the physician, Aristotle, Peripatetic philosophers, Epicurus, and atheists did not believe in spirits, Socrates, Plato, Plotinus, Porphyry, Iamblichus, Proclus, Hermes Trismegistus, and Pythagoras did, and Talmudists and Christians do. He asserts that spirits "know the virtues of herbs, plants, stones, minerals, etc." Possessing the power of metamorphosis, they can manifest as various objects as well as colors, sounds, smells, and tastes. "They can produce miraculous alterations in the air, and most wonderful effects...and [they can] alter human...projects." He also indicates how divinities may have been transformed by Christian scholars and practitioners of ceremonial magic into demons. He does so by describing numerous classes of demons, some of which are clearly linked to divinities. For example, he relates that the "first rank" of "bad spirits" are "those false gods of the Gentiles." Those Christians who uphold this system assert, unsurprisingly, that these gods are governed by the demon Beelzebub. The second and third ranks of "bad spirits" are also comprised of deities, and it is not clear how they differ in status from the first rank; these ranks include as members Apollo and Thoth. The rank to which the latter belongs is governed by the demon Belial. This classification suggests how if an individual or group continued to pay homage to such deities in the sixteenth or seventeenth century, their reverence might have been reduced to, or collapsed into, veneration of the demonic by Christians, who equated the ancient and indigenous European with the demonic. Burton's classification of elementals is also intriguing. In France and elsewhere in Europe, many continued to believe in and interact with other elementals, including the gnomes or elves of the earth, the ondines of the water, the sylphs of the air, and the salamanders of fire. Around two and three-quarters centuries following Burton's *Anatomy*, Michael Aislabie Denham claimed that in the mid-nineteenth century, many inhabitants of the British Isles alone acknowledged the existence of over one hundred elemental beings and kindred spirits, including very well-known beings like fairies, elves, leprechauns, and Robin Goodfellow, as well as many lesser known, probably more localized, beings like Dick-a-Tuesday, Jack-in-the-Wad, and Jinny-burnt-tail. Some scholars have rejected the notion that belief in such beings demonstrates a persistence of earth-centered paganism, *as if Robin Goodfellow sprang fully-grown from the pages of the New Testament*. Typical of such a nonsensical notion is a claim made by Boris Rauschenbach in "The Development of Kievan Rus' in the Wake of Christianization" (1988). Because Christians were afraid of *demons* who had *once been* pagan household beings but who had *now been classified as demons* by the Church, rather than being afraid of household beings *per se*, this proves, he claims, that "continuing belief in household beings is in no way evidence of the survival of paganism as is sometimes claimed." In this respect, Christian evangelists who rant and rave about pagan elements in music and such seem more observant and honest and, indeed, less Christocentrist than a number of scholars I have read in recent years. Moreover, in regards to the 'evolution' of paganism, it is evident that earth-centered traditions continued to develop in many Christianized milieus. Exemplary of such development or innovation, a Russian law of 1469 stipulated that punishment of robbers should include the cutting off of one of their ears. Not long after, certain beings of the forest were depicted as possessing a single ear. Over three centuries later, after a number of soldiers deserted the Russian army in 1834 and went into hiding in a thick wood, forest beings came to be depicted as wearing military uniforms.

Earth

From earth life arises, and to earth life returns. For this reason, earth has often been perceived as a Mother Goddess (we will take up this topic again when we consider reverence of the Earth Goddess). Veneration of the earth includes that of the earth itself, of soil, stones and trees, and of hills and mountains and other features of the landscape. For the Greek philosopher Empedocles, earth, together with water, air, and fire, works to create "love" or "strife" in the cosmos. George P. Fedotov, in *The Russian Religious Mind* (1946), stresses that the "sky or the heavens is rarely mentioned by a Russian Slav with particular warmth, awe, or romantic longing. It is on the earth that he has concentrated all his religious devotion to natural powers." Likewise, in *The Rise of Russia*, Robert

Wallace notes that during forced Christianization, spiritually recalcitrant peasants were considered "black-earth" people.

In Germanic tradition, practitioners of earth-based traditions swore to abide by contracts by way of mingling grass and earth together in their hands; and to die was to "kiss the earth," to "sink into the earth," and to "fall back into the womb of Terra Mater." Jonas Balys (b. 1909), writing of Lithuanians and Lithuanian-Americans living in the early- to mid-twentieth century, observes that the "earth is worshipped by old people even today and regarded as mother and provider of food for all living beings."

Germanic deities were often thought to dwell on mountains, or were associated with mountains, as evidenced by such names as Wuotansberg (Odin's/Woden's Mountain) and Donnersberg (Thunder's, i.e., Thor's Mountain). In Lithuania, hills and mountains (*kalnai*) connect the earth and the heavens. They are frequently the abodes of divinities, having names like Saulė kalniai (Sun Goddess' mountains), Auðrinës kalnai (Dawn Goddess' mountains), Kauko kalnai (Homely Sprites' mountains), Laumiu kalnai (Fairies' mountains), and Raganu kalnai (Witches' mountains). Certain hills and mountains are also associated with the rites of younger and older women, Mergakalniai and Bobkalniai, respectively. In *The Balts* (1963), Gimbutas notes that among the most sacred hills of Lithuania Minor was Rambynas Hill, "on the north bank of the lower Nemunas near Tilsit, mentioned in records ever since the fourteenth century," in the vicinity of my maternal great-grandfather's ancestral home. Its name, derived from *ram-*, signifies a place of silence; this root is often found in names of sacred sites. Kuršite points out in "Baltic Sanctuaries" (2005) that the related *ramit* signifies "to grieve" or "to mourn the dead." Gimbutas explains that in ancient and medieval times, "A stone with a flat surface formerly crowned this hill and votive offerings were placed on it by newly married couples seeking fertility at home and good crops in the field. The water found up on *Rambynas* was eagerly sought after for drinking and washing." In *Landscape and Memory* (1995), Simon Schama, describing hills, sometimes natural, sometimes artificial, used as tumuli, or barrows, to bury heroic dead, observes: "Lithuania was the last pagan nation to be converted to Christianity as late as the fourteenth century. And the ancient native tradition has endured by memorializing the nation's martyrs and heroes in the form of a *kopiec* – a grassy mound."

Witches were thought to congregate on certain rock formations, hills, and mountains: the Brocken in the Harz Mountains, Germany; the Hörselberg, also in Germany; the rock Blakulla in Sweden; the Barco of Ferrara and the Paterno of Bologna in Italy; the Puy de Dôme near Clermont in the Auvergne, France; in Spain on the plain of Cirniegola; Mount Szatria in Lithuania; and elsewhere. Of these, the Brocken came to be known, especially in the mid-eighteenth century, as the site of a very mysterious occurrence: the "Spirit of the Brocken" referred to a phenomenon involving the gigantic mirroring of the human observer in regard to both image and words spoken.

Janina Kuršite relates that "[t]hroughout Latvia certain hills were considered sanctuaries, known as the *zilie kalni* (blue hills). Records have survived that show nine such blue hills...the most important of these is...located not far from the city of Valmeira." This hill had a sacred spring, thought to possess great healing power, and a sacred grove. Latvians congregated here and presumably on other blue hills to celebrate the summer solstice and probably other occasions as well. During the seventeenth century, several women, including a mother and daughter, were burned to death after confessing to having participated in secret gatherings on the blue hill near Valmeira.

One of the most renowned sacred mountains of Europe is the lofty, forested Sleza Mountain, found in Lower Silesia, present-day southwestern Poland. The area has been a sacred site since the Neolithic. Stone sculptures depicting the sun, a bear, a boar, a mushroom, and a woman (probably a goddess) with a fish, dating from between 1300 and 500 BCE, have been found here, and it appears that trees and springs have been venerated here since very early times. Slavic, Polish, and Celtic tribes appear to have intermingled here by 400 BCE. The area around Sleza was a major material-sacred center until the Christianization of the area in the tenth and eleventh centuries. Thietmar wrote of Sleza in the early eleventh century: "This mountain was worshipped by all the townsmen for the reason of its enormity and its destiny as accursed pagan rituals were carried out over there." In the nineteenth century, spiritually hybrid celebrations, particularly on the summer solstice, continued to be held on Sleza until they were officially prohibited by Church authorities.

Earth elementals, whom Burton associates with "lares, genii, fauns, satyrs, wood-nymphs, foliots [i.e., *follets*], [other] fairies, Robin Goodfellows, [and] *trolli* [i.e., trolls]" as well as with the deities "Dagon...Bel...Astarte...[and] Isis and Osiris," include those who "dance on heaths and greens...[and] leave that green circle, which we commonly find in plain fields, which others hold to proceed from a meteor falling, or some accidental rankness of the ground."

Among the most widely known and venerated of European earth elementals were the 'wild women of the woods.' Also called 'forest nymphs,' 'wood-wives,' 'wish-wives,' 'moss women,' and 'bush grandmothers,' they are known to Germans, Swedes, Czechs, Poles, and others by many names, including: *bereginy*, *buschgrossmutter*, *dirne-weibl*, *divje devojke*, *divozenky*, *dziwozony*, *femmes sauvages*, *finz-weibl*, *holz-frauen*, *holzleute*, *holzweibel*, *lundfolk*, *lundjungfrur*, *moosfräulein*, *moosleute*, *napeas*, *silvestres*, *skogsrå*, *waldleute*, *wilde leute*, and *wildiu wîp*. Wild Women emerged during the Middle Ages, suggesting, perhaps, an innovation of paganism; they were frequently spotted during the eighteenth century, and their veneration persisted into the nineteenth century. They were depicted as alternately smaller than and equal in height to humans. Long-haired, they were also alternately depicted as beautiful or as shaggy and covered with moss. Sometimes, as in

Sweden, they appeared as very beautiful women except for having claws instead of hands and fingers. They often wore broad-brimmed hats. Sometimes they went naked, and stored their clothes within oak trees. Occasionally, like the Celtic Matronae, Red Riding Hood, or the Evil Queen of "Snow White," they appeared as women carrying baskets of apples. Disillusioned with the world of humans, they withdrew into forests, dwelling in huts and caves. Like certain wisewomen or 'witches,' are considered knowledgeable in the art of herbal medicine. What they love most: to sing and dance wildly, and the smell of baking bread. Wild Women can be dangerous: they can stir up destructive winds, and sometimes herald death. They feel it their duty to abduct children from abusive parents and to protect wives from, and take vengeance on, abusive husbands. To those who venerate them, however, and offer them flax, freshly baked bread, fresh fish, and licorice, they assist in baking, spinning, weaving, fishing, hunting, and healing, and reward their devoted with gifts, protection, and prosperity. When mortals assist them willingly, Wild Women often offer them gold in return for their kindness. Wild Women were celebrated primarily on Midsummer's Eve and at the winter solstice. Claude Lecouteux, in *Au-delà du merveilleux: des croyances du Moyen Age (Beyond the Marvelous: Beliefs of the Middle Ages*, 1998), suggests that Wild Women may have eventually been largely displaced by fairies. However, they nevertheless persisted as Wild Women within Christianized Europe, occasionally envisioned as beneficent elementals taking refuge from the Devil in Christian sanctuaries. The Wild Women bear striking resemblance to the Slavic Mavka. Mavka is the transformed spirit of a girl or woman who has died an unnatural death. She is typically depicted as a beautiful maiden who wears flowers in her hair, wears a transparent shift, dwells in a cave decorated with exquisite rugs, and dances to the accompaniment of a flute played by a faun-like figure. She delights in erotic play. Until very recently, celebrations were held in her honor in springtime. Mavka appears in Mykhailo Kotsiubynsky's *Tini zabutykh predkiv*, *Shadows of Forgotten Ancestors*, on which Sergei Paradjanov's acclaimed film is based.

Among Greeks, the ancient werewolf-like *kallikantzaros*, also known in Romania, is an ambivalent elemental who spends part of each year above the ground and part below it. The *kallikantzaros* probably originated as a member of a class of centaurs, joining the equine-mortal hybrid being and other types of centaurs. He was probably a creature that inspired awe, but he does not seem to have commenced as the monster or carnivalesque creature that he has become in Christianized Greece. Rather, he was, like the satyr, a member of the court of Dionysus who may have been honored alongside the god at the January Kalends. *Kallikantzaroi* typically dwell in caves and mainly eat toads and snakes. Christians, repulsed by these beings, sometimes referred to them as *paganá*, that is to say, "pagan beings." In Christianized Greece, they are said to spend most of the year trying to destroy the World-Tree so that the world will fall into chaos. At some point, many people came to believe that *kallikantzaroi* were born human and only later, and for only certain periods of time, transformed into werewolf-like creatures. According to tradition, males born at Christmastime are particularly susceptible to becoming *kallikantzaroi*. As Allatios points out, *kallikantzaroi* continued to be acknowledged in the seventeenth century. In the late nineteenth century, it was customary to offer the *kallikantzaroi* "sweetmeats, waffles, [and] sausages" in wintertime. In exchange for these treats, the *kallikantzaroi* wouldn't play tricks. In the early twentieth century, the Romanian folklorist Marcu Beza (1882-1949), a lecturer at King's College at London University, recounted that some of his drivers believed that *kallikantzaroi* lived in a cave in a mountain in the region of Clisura Dunarii and that it was often possible to hear them when they held their nightly revels. Today, many continue to believe in the existence of *kallikantzaroi*; although, in heavily Christianized Greece, they are depicted as ugly, carnivalesque, mean-spirited prankster-monsters. Nevertheless, some Greeks continue to make offerings to them at Christmastime, scattering pancakes on the roofs of houses.

Another being known to Romanians is Muma Padura, a female being who assists children who are lost in the woods. Slavic peoples are familiar with many other earth beings, including: a Wendish being who likewise assists travelers lost in the forest, but whose original name has been lost and replaced by the Christian term Bludniki, 'fornicator;' Morozko, a Russian patron of the forest and frost, an azure-coated gift-giver who was first demonized as Jack Frost and then Americanized into Santa as the Soviet Union was displaced by the present-day Russian capitalist totalitarian state; and Snegurochka, the kind and beautiful Snow Maiden, who may have contributed, ironically, to the misogynistic portraits of Andersen's "Snow Queen" and C. S. Lewis's White Witch.

One of the most well known of Slavic earth beings is the Leshy, derived from the Russian *lesu*, "wood," "forest." Each forest is thought to be protected by a Leshy. The Leshy is a shapeshifter who can manifest as a shepherd, a hairy man with green eyes, a horned giant, and a tree; he casts no shadow. He dwells in the depths of forests, sometimes living in a birch tree, at other times in a cave or an abandoned hut. He loves to whistle and sing. If people journeying into the forest are respectful of him, he will guide them safely through it and may even offer them an animal if they are hunting. Those who do not respect him, he leads astray. The Leshy is said to perish every October and to be reborn in spring. Unlike many other such beings, he is often married with children. Although some persons continue to believe in the Leshy at present, much of his role has been appropriated by St. George. When one wishes to invoke the Leshy, one places birch branches in a circle with the cut ends facing its center. One also offers salted bread or sacrifices a cow. Then the supplicant turns his or her face toward the east, then bends his/her head, and commences to invoke the Leshy: "Uncle Lieschi, ascend thou, not as a grey wolf, not as an ardent fire, but as resembling myself." Then, if he wishes to do so, the

Leshy manifests.

Finno-Ugric Karelians of northwestern Russia have traditionally venerated Meccän Isäntä, the Master of the Forest. Hunters often invoke him in autumn to assist in their hunting, by calling him in chant or song, scraping the silver from three coins as an offering to him, and by bowing to the forest three times. Sometimes, especially if they are lost, travelers will find their way to his hut. If he is not at home, they may stay there, but only if they formally, by way of invocation, ask his permission. Otherwise, he will return home in the middle of the night and, infuriated, will make so much noise that they will not be able to sleep.

Practitioners of indigenous Finnish traditions also venerated – and often feared – certain *genii loci* known as *hiisi*. *Hiisi* were usually linked to sacred forests or sacred stone sites; they were also linked to the elk, bear, and other animals. In Christianized Finland, they were reduced to a singular demonic being, or else were simply equated with the Devil. *Hiisi* continued to be propitiated in the late seventeenth century, as evidenced by a report documenting a rite undertaken by a man named Turuinen in 1672. Turuinen offered beer to the *hiisi* during the harvest festival of Kekri, which in Christianized Finland was conflated with Michaelmas.

Water

Water, the Greek philosopher Thales concluded, is the "cosmic *arche*, the fundamental principle underlying all material things." Many persons living in medieval Europe continued to venerate bodies of water. Water was often thought to possess the power to protect persons from, and heal them of, serious diseases as well as to purify the body (baptism preceded Christianization among Germanic and other peoples) and, occasionally, "to change the bather's sex." Water could cause great harm, and must therefore be propitiated. Veneration of water continued into the medieval period in France and other parts of Europe, as evidenced by St. Eligius' (also, Eloi, Loy, *c.* 588-660) seventh-century condemnation of this practice as pagan.

In 1835, Samuel Reynolds Hole, in *Thaumaturgia, or Elucidations of the Marvellous*, reported

> …even now, in many parts of Devonshire and Cornwall, the vulgar may be said to worship brooks and wells, to which they resort at certain periods, performing various ceremonies in honor of those consecrated waters; and the Highlanders, to this day, talk with the genius of the sea; never bathe in a fountain, lest the elegant spirit that resides in it should be offended and remove; and mention not the water of rivers withot prefixing it to the name of *excellent*; and in one of the western islands the inhabitants retained the custom, to the close of the last [i.e. the eighteenth] century, of making an annual sacrifice to the genius of the ocean.[25]

> …we may justly wonder at the inhabitants of Devonshire and Cornwall thus worshipping the gods of numerous rivers…[26]

Western Balts utilized water in numerous

rites, as, for example, during wedding ceremonies, when a deep ditch is dug to signify the threshold and the couple, the guests, the marriage bed, the household, and the domestic animals of the homestead were all asperged with water in order to purify them. Western Balts also held that rivers served as roads to the afterlife; this was especially true of the Prieglius River, the name of which indicated an abyss or the world of the dead.

In *Senosios Lietuvos Šventvietes*, Vaitkevicius observes of lakes: "The world of the lakes is very lively; in the legends they move from place to place...[T]hey moan an wail." Vaitkevicius relates that in medieval Lithuania, there were over one hundred sacred lakes (*ežerai*), fifty sacred rivers (*upes*), and 150 sacred springs (*šaltiniai* or *versmës*), each one having a patron divinity. Many sacred lakes were thought to contain submerged houses and sacred structures.

In Celtic, including Gaulish, tradition, Brigid presides over many wells; Sequana is goddess of the Seine; the Romano-Celtic Apollo Grannos is patron of curative springs with his consort Sirona; and the goddess Sulis, "the greatest British curative deity," presides over the "gushing hot springs under the great temple at Bath." Celtic Taranis brings storms at sea. In 1838, Anna Eliza Bray observed in *Traditions, Legends, Superstitions, and Sketches of Devonshire*:

The atmosphere of Dartmoor deserves particular notice; it is at all times humid.... [When the rain] pour[s] down in torrents...attended by thunder and lightning...one would think that the peasantry still...worshipped thunder as [the] god Tiranis; for they call a storm...conjuring time...mingling their pagan superstitions with some ideas founded on Christianity ...[27]

In Germanic tradition, Mimir is the primordial ocean or spring that flows from the sacred tree Yggdrasil; Njorð calms the seas; and Freyr brings rain that fertilizes the earth. When storms arise, one knows that the god Aegir, Odin, Thor (also, Donar), or the goddess Rân is at work. Tamra Andrews observes that Ymir is the frost giant born of the "mingling of ice and fire." The incessant struggle of frost giants with fire giants eventually leads to the destruction of this world.

The Germanic Skaði is a "beautiful giantess, the snowshoe goddess, wearing a white hunting dress, fur leggings, and snowshoes or skis and carrying a hunting spear that glittered with the frost of winter." She is a goddess of death whose name means "to harm" or "to kill." Driffa is goddess of snowstorms. The goddess Holda, who rose to prominence in the medieval period, is said to be shaking out the feathers of her bed when the snow flies. These may be ancestresses of the Snow Queen of fairy lore.

Slavic tradition speaks of the *rusalki* and *vodynoi*, elementals of the water, and Perûn, god of storms; Baltic tradition, of the goddess Laima and the fairy-like *laumës*, who preside over many bodies of water, and of Perkûnas, god of the tempest. Lithuanian wetlands were associated with certain deities, including Perkûnas, Ragana, and Velnias, and elementals including *kaukës* and *laumë*s; Finnish tradition makes Ukko god of storms. Healing spirits of the British

Isles whose names are no longer remembered were once honored at sacred wells, such as that of Tobar Bial na Buaidh, the 'Well of the Tree and Virtuous Water,' near Benderloch in Argyll, Scotland; this well "had a tree beside it where offerings were left to placate the guardian spirit of the water."

Despite Christianization, many Europeans have venerated certain wells from ancient times into the present. At sacred wells, people hoped to secure health for themselves and animals, fertility, beauty, protection, prosperity, and favorable winds. Well veneration was, like many other practices, subjected to hybridizing, layering or mixing Celtic, Roman, and Germanic elements.

Although with Christianization, the ancient names of many wells were replaced by Christian ones, some wells retained indigenous, non-Christian names into the twentieth century. At Thorsas, Norway, for example, Thor's Well retained its original name, with the exception of the title of saint prefixed to the god's name. In England, in 1995, one also found a Thor's Well (Holme on Spaldingmoor, East Yorkshire), together with wells dedicated to the goddess Brigid (who transformed into St. Bridget), Mab (the Fairy Queen), Nicker (a water divinity), Puck, and fairies. Fairy wells of Scotland included those of Minchmoor, near Peebles, and the Fairies' Well, near Doonies in Moray. Cheese was left as "an offering to the fairies." At other wells, bent pins were the most popular offerings. Other wells continued to acknowledge the nearness of sacred trees, such as those named after ash, elder, elm, hazel, holly, maple, oak, and willow trees. Wells were often visited on the occasion of indigenous holidays, including Beltane (May Eve) and Samhain (Halloween), as was Braemou ('Physick') Well in Moray, Scotland. Physicians acknowledged the healing power of the water of Braemou during the seventeenth century. At the English well at Tullybelton, Perthshire, a "totally unchristianized" rite continued to be held in 1811 on Beltane (May 1) morning, when "local people drank from [the] well, circumambulated it three times, and then did the same at a nearby 'Druidic' temple." As James Rattue – whose attitude toward the earth-centered worldview is, notably, exceedingly hostile – observes in *The Living Stream: Holy Wells in Historical Context* (1995), the renowned hot springs at Bath, dedicated to the Celtic water goddess Arnemetia and later to the Roman Minerva, "were never formally Christianized."

Among the most well known ancient springs and wells which continues to be visited by pilgrims is that near Loch Shiant, the "sacred lake," on the Isle of Skye. It is thought that in ancient times, an "oak copse which was deemed so sacred that no person would venture to cut the smallest branch of it" bordered the lake, spring, and well. Divination, especially pegomancy (including observing bubbles in water and movements in water when stones are dropped in it), was undertaken here. Eventually, the well came to be called the Fairies' Well. The well's water was believed to possess healing powers. Into the nineteenth century, ill persons, hoping to recover, would bring offerings of bread, flowers, pins, and colored threads and rags to the well. They would turn three times deosil before the well before drinking its water and making an offering.

Indigenous Lithuanians provide an example of the earth-centered worldview's attribution of healing and magical powers to water. Gimbutas, in *The Balts*, says of its healing power: "No one dared soil their life-giving water, which had purifying, healing...properties.... The...animals were sprinkled with it to keep them healthy." "Washing with clear spring water would heal eye and skin diseases;" and of its magical potency: "The fields were sprayed with holy water to ensure good crops."

Because water was venerated and was frequently associated with divinities, and also because it could cause great harm, offerings and sacrifices were made to lakes, rivers, and other bodies of water. The eighth-century *Indiculus superstitionem et paganiarum* (*Index of Superstitions and Paganism*) listed sacrifices to water as a pagan practice continuing into the medieval period. Burchard of Worms, in his *Corrector* of the early eleventh century, asked persons suspected of participating in non-Christian practices if they had visited a spring to light a candle there or to offer bread or another offering in hope of being healed of illness. Offerings and sacrifices to bodies of water in the British Isles from the Middle Ages through at least the Renaissance included coins and weapons (including miniature weapons).

Among the West Slavs, the spring of Glomac was held especially sacred. It lay two miles from the Elbe River and at its center was a large morass. In the late tenth and early eleventh centuries, natives thankful for good crops and peaceful times made offerings of "wheat, oats and acorns" on its morass. Thietmar (975-1018, bishop of Merseburg 1009-1018) claimed that the locals revered "that spring more than any church."

Gimbutas, in *The Balts*, observes of bodies of water in Lithuania: "If one gave them holy water, flowers, and trees would blossom bountifully." Vaitkevicius recounts that Lithuanian lakes required offerings and sacrifices annually, if not more frequently. At least thirty-two lakes required sacrifices, typically pigs or horses, to be made to them by devotees. Some rivers required the sacrifice of sheep, oxen, and possibly even humans. Sailors often sacrificed pieces of copper, bread, and beads to the divinities controlling the Nemunas River (also, Neman, Nieman, Memel) the beads were "for the fairies [of the river], to adorn themselves." To sacred springs, the faithful offered coins and eggs; this practice lasted into the eighteenth century. Surrounding wetlands belonging to divinities – Perkûnas, Ragana, and Velnias, and spirits including *kaukës* and *laumë*s – were offered dairy products, jewelry, and weaponry.

In early twentieth-century Romania, in the region of Clisura Dunarii, many persons continued to leave offerings of hair, kerchiefs, basil, cakes, and coins at a certain "Fairies' Spring" for the nymphs who inhabited it, in the hope that in return they would be healed of illness and bestowed with prosperity.

Wells, as mentioned above, were often visited on the occasion of ancient holidays, including, in the British Isles, on Beltane

(May Eve) and Samhain (Halloween). Of Balts, Gimbutas notes: "At the beginning of summer, during the sun festival (the present St. John's night), people would go swimming in the holy waters so that they would be healthy and beautiful and so that young people would soon marry."

Despite Christian bans, many Norwegians and Swedes continued to venerate bodies of water and wells in the eleventh and twelfth centuries. In the early fourteenth century, the chronicler Peter von Dusburg documented sacred bodies of water in Prussia where no one dared fish. In 1479/ 1480, P. Callimachus reported that Lithuanians continued to venerate lakes; and in 1525, Nicolas Hussovianus (c. 1470-c. 1533) wrote: "Lithuanians drop fruits into the river, worship gods of rivers and believe that the benevolence of destiny and the fertility of their herds depend on the will of these gods." A distraught Martynas Mazvydas (1510-1563) reported in the preface to his *Catechism* of 1547 that many Lithuanians and East Prussians continued to "worship...rivers...as gods;" at that time, some persons also continued to sacrifice a white pig to the river god Upinis so that "the water would be clean and bright."

In Brittany, on New Year's Day, 1610, women made offerings of bread and butter to the elementals of village fountains. In Lithuania in the seventeenth century, when women who "were faithful to old customs and [who] offended the norms of Christianity" were being persecuted as witches, certain rivers sacred to indigenous deities appear to have acquired the reputation of being haunts of witches and fairies; these were called *raganines*, "Witches' Depths." Watery elementals, whom Burton (1621) associates – rather peculiarly – with "[certain] fairies ... Habundia ... Diana, [and] Ceres," are said to assist mortals in hydromancy, divination via water. Negatively, as Petrus Valderama (fl. c. 1610), relates, they can cause great floods.

In regard to Classical watery beings, Nereids, originating in antiquity, continued to be acknowledged into the late twentieth and early twenty-first centuries. In recent centuries, Nereids have often been called by euphemistic names resonating with those given to fairies, including "the Ladies," "Our Maidens," "the Good Queens," the "Lucky Ones," and the "Kind-Hearted Ones." Nereids are typically described as very beautiful except for having one or two animal legs, as in "one donkey's foot," which brings to mind demonic descriptions of the Biblical Queen of Sheba. Alternatively, they are described as having very long legs, which in Greece carries erotic significance. In this light, Nereids are said to sometimes transform ambulatory-challenged young women into Nereids. Charles Stewart notes, "they are often described as brides, dressed in white, wearing crowns, and celebrating weddings in the wilds." They are said to "appear at, and seem to reside in, outlying places such as caves and water sources." Mountain caves where they reside are called *neraïdovoúni*, while springs where they reside are called *neraïdovrysi*. They love to play musical instruments and dance at night in riverbeds. Sometimes they entice humans into joining them in their dance. They are said to be led by a queen known as the "Beauty of the Mountains." Persons wishing to receive her assistance made offerings of honey and other sweets to her on August 1st.

While journeying in Crete in 1833, Robert Pashley learned of continuing belief in Nereids. Dwelling both near the sea and in the mountains, Nereids, Pashley observed in *Travels in Crete* (1837), "show themselves to very few persons," "always pass their nights in dancing," and occasionally, in the manner of fairies, "change one of their young Nereids for the child of a woman." Some spotted Nereids laying out their clothes on rocks to dry.

Nereids often appear when a child is born. As they love mortal children greatly, some have thought it wise to protect mother and child against them in the event that they, as mentioned above, decide to switch the human infant with a changeling. Nereids possess a paradoxical relationship to healing. They are often both the source of an illness and the only ones who can heal it (a rather common phenomenon in indigenous traditions): "A spell from northern Greece…for a nereid-possessed person (probably suffering from a fever) makes it clear that it is the nereids themselves who must come and 'mark' the glass of water that is left out overnight in order for the afflicted person to recover."

In regard to healing, if "one 'sweetens' the nereids by spreading honey on the floor around a sick person, then they will help to heal" that person. In the late nineteenth century, women continued to visit a "spring in a grotto" in Kozáni (Kozane), Macedonia, Greece, the water of which was said "to issue from the Nereids' breasts." This water could "cure all human ills." James Rennell Rodd relates: "Those who would drink of it must enter the cave with a torch or lamp in one hand and pitcher in the other, which they must fill with the water, and, leaving some scrap of their clothing behind them, must turn round without being scared by the noises they may hear within, and quit the cave without looking back."

Nereids can also impart the gift of healing. In the nineteenth century, for instance, one lyre player from Rhodes was said to have been the gift of healing sore throats by a Nereid. Also in the not-too-distant past, certain wisewomen were trained to heal illnesses inflicted by Nereids who had been ignored, insulted, or injured. They appear to have invoked the Nereids by burning incense, which included gunpowder, to them. When the Nereids came, they would discuss with them what needed to be done, such as offerings made, so that the ill person's health might return. On one such occasion, in the twentieth century, a man was hunting when a Nereid, attracted to him, approached him, and the man, feeling something brushing against him but not seeing anything, brushed her away. In return, he was struck with swelling of the face and a stretching to one side of his mouth. He was healed only after a wisewoman conversed with the Nereids.

Over the centuries, many accounts have been related of mortal men who have fallen in love with Nereids and whom the Nereids have gifted with treasures. During the nineteenth and early twentieth centuries, it was said that "[s]ometimes…young men...marr[ied] nereids and...settle[d] down and [had] children that are called 'nereid-engendered.' These offspring are thought to be exceptionally beautiful and talented." During this period, "certain families [were] pointed out as [being] of Nereid descent. Such a family," Rodd relates, "is said to exist in the little village of Menidhi, near Athens."

According to Rodd, for a late nineteenth-century Greek woman "to be compared to a Nereid is the greatest of compliments; to be said to have a Nereid's eyes or a Nereid's hair is the praise that is bestowed on beauty; to be said to sing, to weave, or to sweep like a Nereid, is the praise that the housewife desires." A century later, in some parts of Greece, "it is still said of a woman skilled at cookery that she cooks like a nereid."

In late twentieth-century Greece, many persons continued to believe in the existence of Nereids. Unfortunately, Nereids have been increasingly demonized by the Greek Orthodox Church and other less influential Christian groups. Moreover, the Nereid has increasingly become a symbol for everything that a "modest, humble, self-effacing" Greek woman "actively concerned with prayer" should *not* be. Nereids, to the contrary, "are not dominated by any power" and are a "model for free sexuality." Not only this, but some present-day Greek women are taught to fear and despise Nereids because the latter may try to take away their husbands.

In a rather peculiar instance of sacred hybridity, Nereids have come to be associated with the Virgin Mary and with Jesus Christ. Chapels dedicated to the Panagía, the Virgin Mary, are often built in the vicinity of Nereid locales. Many Greeks believe that one should not swim on August 6th, the feast of the Metamorphosis of the Savior, because Nereids are "thick in the water" on that day and may drown people as, distraught, they search for their brother Sotíris, the Savior, who died on this day.

In the last decades of the twentieth century, however, Orthodox priests expressed their disgust with "blond-haired tourists who swim naked and sleep on the beaches" by comparing them to Nereids. Thanks to Hans Christian Andersen and Disney, we are perhaps most familiar with mermaids. In *The Balts*, Gimbutas describes them as "beautiful women with long breasts, very long blond hair and a fishtail. They were mute. When people happened to see them, they would stare back silently, spread their wet hair and hide their tails."

In 1619, during the reign of Christian IV 1577-1648; r. 1588-1648), a company of Danish officials, led by Oluf Rosenspar and Christian Holck, was returning by ship from a conference in Norway when they observed and captured a merman. The merman, extremely agitated, kept tossing and turning in the net. Finally, one of the company remarked, "It must be a wonderful God that has created such humanlike creatures to dwell in the water." To which the merman replied, "Yes! If you knew that as I do, you might say so! If you do not instantly restore me to the water, neither you nor your ship shall ever reach land."

The company then returned the merman to the water. In 1687, the *Aberdeen Almanac* of Scotland, in its prognostications for 1688, predicted that on May 1, 13, and 29, as well as "in divers other times in the ensuing summer," as well as on October 7 and 14, those traveling on water might well see "a pretty company of mermaids, creatures of admirable beauty, and likewise hear their charming sweet melodious voices." In or near 1701, two fishermen

> drew up with a hook a mermaid, having face, arms, breast, shoulders, &c., of a woman, and long hair hanging down the neck; but the nether part from below the waist hidden in the water. One of the fishermen, in his surprise, drew a knife and thrust it into her heart; where upon she cried, as they judged, 'Alas!' and the hook giving way, she fell backwards, and was seen no more.[28]

In *A Description of the Shetland Islands* (1822), Samuel Hibbert describes mermaids and mermen as

> resembling, in form, the human race...possessed of surpassing beauty, of limited supernatural powers, and liable to the incident of death. They dwell in a wide territory of the globe far below the region of the fishes, over which the sea, like the cloudy canopy of our sky, loftily rolls...Unfortunately, however, each merman or merwoman, possess[es] but one skin, enabling the individual to ascend the seas [; thus] if, on visiting the abode of man, the garb should be lost [or stolen], the hapless being must unavoidably become an inhabitant of our earth.[29]

Hibbert continues:

> I could obtain little satisfaction from the Shetlanders relative to the nature of the country beneath the sea; but a native of the Isle of Man once visited it by means of a diving-bell, that drew after it a rope double the distance of the moon from the earth. After passing the region of fishes, he descended into a serene atmosphere, and at length arrived at the bottom of the submarine world, which was paved with coral and unknown shining pebbles, where were large streets and squares on every side, pyramids of crystal, and buildings of mother of pearl. ...[T]he mermen and...mermaids...were greatly alarmed at the sight of the diving-bell and its occupant.[30]

Certain Irish families, including the Hennessys and the Flahertys, are believed to have merwoman ancestors.

Other hybrid water beings resembling merwomen and mermen include swan maidens and selkies. Belief in, and tales of, swan maidens proliferated in the Middle Ages. Swan maidens often come into being as a result of sinister magic performed by older on younger women. They are capable of shapeshifting, and when they assume human form, men often fall in love with them. Sometimes men, in an effort to hold onto the swan maidens, hide their swan 'shifts' from them. At other times, love alone causes the swan maiden to be restored to human form permanently. Swan maidens are thought to be expert at divination.

Selkies, hybrid seal-human beings, are hybrid creatures who are torn between worlds and who deeply love marine life. Certain Irish and Scottish clans, including the Lees, Connollys, and MacCodrums share a profound, totemistic kinship with seals and selkies and are sometimes thought to metamorphose into selkies, human-seal beings (as depicted in the masterful film *The Secret of Roan Inish*); should one of the members of these clans slay a seal, he or she will be cursed. Belief in selkies was a "matte[r] of undoubted credence" into the late nineteenth century. In 1894, the Reverend Archibald Macdonald wrote: "It was said that a woman of the same surname [i.e., MacCodrum], and probably lineage, as the bard [i.e., John MacCodrum], used to be seized with violent pains at the time of the annual seal hunt, out of sympathy, it was supposed, with her suffering relatives."

A very ambivalent being, the Slavic Vodny Muz (or, Vodianik, Vodyanik, Vodyzh, Votash, Wodny Muz) often manifests when a drowned man's soul gains a new body, Vodny Muz alternately lures men to watery deaths, protects mariners, and provides fishermen with plenty of fish. He is also a patron of millers. He is portrayed as a plump, bald-headed, elderly man with longish green hair. He sometimes has black skin. He wears a cap of reeds and a belt of rushes. When he appears at the marketplace, he tests the fairness or greed of humans by buying grain; if he is overcharged, he will initiate famine. Those who honor him with sacrifices of black sows, cows, sheep, and horses smeared with honey are greatly rewarded.

Unquestionably, the *dracae*, or Water-drakes, are among the most mysterious and often sinister of water beings. Their name is linked to both "dragon" and "Dracula" and appears to be of ancient Indo-European origin.

In the later Middle Ages, *dracae* were said to abduct human women to assist them in delivering and nursing their infants. Although they lived in the depths of rivers (including the Rhône) and lakes, they assumed human form and garments when they traveled to the surface, often encountering humans at, and abducting women from, the marketplace. As a subset of the belief that human infants who died without undergoing baptism remained "pagan," many believed that deceased, unbaptized infants transformed into *dracae*. Gervase of Tilbury (b. *c.* 1160—d. *c.* 1211) encountered a woman who had once been washing clothes in a river when she was abducted by a Drakos. For several years, she was made to serve under the water as nanny to his son. One day, the Drakos gave her an eel pastry to eat. From that time forward, she could see clearly all that lay under the water and could distinguish *dracae* from other beings. After a number of years, she was permitted to return to her family. One day, at the marketplace at Beauclaire, France, she spotted the *drakos* who'd abducted her. When she inquired about the health of his wife and child, he asked her which eye she could see him with. He then thrust his finger into the eye, and blinding her in that eye, vanished.

In Greek tradition, the *drákos* was "traditionally an ogre who lived in a cave and blocked the water supply of a nearby settlement until given the tribute of one young girl." In Norway, belief in *dracae* persisted into the nineteenth century, when they were described as shapeshifting, dangerous, death-bringing sea-beings. In late twentieth-century Greece, "*drákos* is a name given to stranglers and rapists such as the one who killed several young women in

Athens during a period in 1983/84."

Peg Powler is thought to be the patron of the River Tees, especially in the vicinity of Pierse Bridge, in northern England. Unfortunately, I have not as yet been able to discover anything about her origins; however, her memory, and perhaps her veneration, persisted into the nineteenth century. She is a death-bringing divinity or related being, depicted as a siren with long, flowing, green hair. She seeks to be nearer to mortals by drowning them. Parents of the nineteenth century warned their children not to wander too close to the riverbank, should she be tempted to take them. She has a second hypostasis or a sibling named Nanny Powler, who is patron of the Skerne, a tributary of the Tees. She is reminiscent of the Germanic sea goddess Rân, who patrons the sailors she drowns. Peg may be related to Jenny Greenteeth, a "malevolent spirit" of water in northern England "who drags down those who come too near." She may also be related to an ancient goddess of the River Dart, in Devon, England, in the vicinity of Dartmoor, who allegedly demanded the sacrifice of a human life each year. Reminiscent of Peg, Jenny, and the goddess of the Dart is Nelly Longarms, a.k.a. Helena Longimana, who grabs children who walk too near the water's edge and takes them to live with her in her watery lair.

Another pagan or perhaps pagano-Christian being linked to the element of water, Old Nick, a name popularized by English sailors, was paradoxically linked to both the Devil and, as "St. Nick," to Father Christmas.

This being, also called Nix, speaks to a hybridizing process that interwove Classical and Germanic figures into a potentate of the seas. This weaving appears to have included Neptune and Odin; "*nic*," an old Germanic term for "washing," forms a part of Odin's hypostasis as Hnickar (or, Hold Nickar, Old Nikkar) as a powerful patron of the waters. Belief in Old Nick continued in the nineteenth century; the "British sailor, who fears nothing else, confesses his terror of this terrible being, and believes him the author of almost all the various calamities to which the precarious life of a seaman is so continually exposed." Old Nick could, however, also be joyful and helpful if he was given respect.

In the Scottish Highlands, he traditionally appears as a grey water-horse emerging from a lake. He may have also been associated with the Scottish female divinity Nicneven. Old Nick was associated with beings called "nickers." Nickers love to sing; they foretell the future and bring rain, fertility, and prosperity.By way of *Jungbrunnen*, springs of rejuvenation, cause elderly people to become young again. Pools and wells sacred to the ruling patron Nick and his entourage of nickers persisted into the nineteenth century; unlike many other pools and wells, their names were not Christianized. English wells sacred to Nick and the nickers include Nicker's Well (Church Holme, Cheshire), Nicker Pool (Wimboldsley, Cheshire), and Nykarspole (Lincoln, Lincolnshire). In the nineteenth century, people of western Germany continued to "throw bread and fruit every year into the Diemel [River] as an offering" to Nix. In Brittany, nickers were sometimes called "Mary Morgans."

Rusalki (sing., *rusalka*) are among the best known of water spirits, combining traits of the Classical nereids and sirens, and mermaids. Wends know them as *vodni panny*. They typically appear as beautiful maidens, either naked or dressed in white, red, or green shifts. They sometimes possess green hair, and their heads are garlanded, often with sedge. *Rusalki* originate in the souls of drowned female infants or in those of women who have committed suicide. They dwell in magnificent crystal palaces at the bottoms of rivers or else within celestial rivers. They spend their days and nights bathing, combing their hair, singing, playing music, and dancing. In springtime, they love to swing from trees overhanging lakes and riverbanks; in summer, they leave the lakes and rivers to frolic in the woods among birches and willows. They can prove very dangerous, luring both men and women to their deaths with their haunting music. To protect themselves from succumbing to the *rusalki*, humans carry wormwood or loveage on their persons. Those who acknowledge their presence and venerate them offer them strips of fabric as well as red-dyed eggs, pancakes (*byliny*), bread, butter, and cheese. In return, they assist women with their spinning and farmers with the raising of rye, the growth of which is promoted by their dancing. They are celebrated in springtime and in summer, in Christianized Slavic regions near Easter and the Eve of St. John the Baptist, at which time young women thought to embody them are dressed in red shifts and led around villages. *Rusalki* are linked to Zorya, an archetypical priestess and divinity who heals with water and lives on the paradisal island of Bouyan.

They find male counterparts in the *strömkarl* of Sweden and the *fossegrim* of Norway. These are elementals who offer instruction in music, particularly how to master stringed instruments, in return for the sacrifice of a black lamb or white male goat. In Christianized Scandinavia, they were said to ask that the musician pray for their salvation. In the mid- to late twentieth century, Karelians of the Kestenga region reported seeing female "water mistresses" who resembled *rusalki*; they perceived them as sitting on stones near the water and combing their long, black hair.

Air

Euros of the east, Notos of the south, Zephyrus of the west, and Boreas of the north: these are the wind gods of Classical antiquity. Their personae stretch from the (usually, although not always) mild and loving Zephyrus to the harsh and bitter Boreas. Together, they stir the universe; they signify its "creative breath." Aeolus is keeper of the winds. For the Greek philosopher Anaximenes, air is the fundamental principle animating the universe. Claude Lecouteux, in "Le radeau des vents: Pour une mythologie des nuages au Moyen Age" ("The Floating of Clouds/The Cloud-Float: For a mythology of clouds in the Middle Ages," 1995), argues that the element of air is not held in as much esteem as the other elements in the Medieval world; that "they didn't make much of a distinction" between air, wind, the whirlwind, mist, fog, rain, hail, etc.; and that, when paganism is expressed, it is much more difficult to find divinities of air than those of other elements. On the other hand,

Richard Perkins, in *Thor the Wind-Raiser and the Eyrarland Image* (2001), argues that wind, at least, was extremely important to the Medieval world, as much of its economy depended upon sailing: "The wind...was one of the most powerful forces known to man...a favorable wind was a highly desirable asset which could confer enormous advantages...At the same time, the wind was a capricious, incomprehensible, enigmatic phenomenon, its true causes virtually unknown and mysterious."

In Perkins' view, Germanic, Slavic, and other European peoples attributed the power of controlling the wind to deities and tended to hold in awe those deities, persons, and others whom they thought possessed the power to control the wind. Among Germanic peoples, Thor, Odin/Woden, and Holda were primary guardians of the air and the wind, as was a goddess or female troll, Kajsa. In deified form, the heavens were sometimes envisioned as a divine being called Vindofnir, the "weaver of the winds." The wind is linked not only to deities but also to giants and elves. Slavs called the four winds the "sons of one mother [the implication is of a mother goddess]" and "Stribog's grandsons." Slavic tradition envisions the whirlwind as a destructive female being, Polednice, while witch lore links the whirlwind to the Biblical Herodias (who is actually Salome, the dancing daughter of Herodias and Herod). Balts envisioned the winds as being of different ages; the east wind is a beardless youth, while the west wind is a wise old man with a long beard. The winds are themselves controlled by the Mother of the Winds.

Medieval and Renaissance practitioners of healing, divination, and magic include persons who "sell" winds to others, becoming latter-day, somewhat commercially-oriented incarnations of Aeolus. Usually embodied by knotted threads, these winds may be favorable, as desired by sailors, or unfavorable, as desired by those who wish to harm another (King James VI/I believed that the witches of North Berwick had attempted to kill him by means of such a wind).

As for clouds, mist, and fog, in Greco-Roman tradition, they are utilized by deities to conceal and protect, as when Aphrodite saves Paris by hiding him in the 'breast' of a cloud. Gwyn ap Nudd, a warrior, hunter, and king of the Otherworld, is in Celtic, specifically Welsh, tradition "ruler of the mountain mist. Germanic tradition views clouds as evocative of other realms, realms which may also appear vague or invisible to the untrained eye. The term *nifl* evokes the mystery of clouded, obscured realms, as suggested by Niflheim, a land of shadows and clouds. As Lecouteux has argued, however, Niflheim is also depicted as not only this but also an otherworld region of darkness steeped in fog and mist, inhabited by giants. *Nifl* also evokes the Nibelungen of the *Nibelungenlied*, a thirteenth-century epic. The Nibelungen are first those who possess a treasure forged by dwarves; but they are later identified with the Burgundians, who dwell under its curse. Lecouteux suggests that in their original manifestation, the Nibelungen, who, in Icelandic, are called the Niflungar, may be, beyond any earthly identity they may possess, cloud beings from another world.

Germanic tradition also sometimes places the Valkyries in a landscape of clouds, mist, or fog. A mist or fog also surrounds the Celtic Isles of the Blessed, or Avalon. Clouds, mist, and fog, like wind, play a role in magical practice. The goddess Thorgerðr Hördaröll, as recorded in the *Saga of the Jóms Vikings* (*c.* 1200), assists Hakon in winning a battle against the Jóms Vikings by causing a great, destructive storm cloud to appear amidst the Viking troops. An ancient magical practice that involved clouds was blowing a horn or trumpet to keep menacing clouds away. Although this custom was anathematized in the eighth century, as indicated by the *Indiculus superstitionem et paganiarum*, it managed to persist into the nineteenth century in the Alps.

According to Burton, aerial beings, whom he calls sylphs, produce whirlwinds, tempests, and floods. Also in the seventeenth century, the inquisitor Petrus Valderama echoed Burton, adding that aerial beings bring hail, snow, and frost.

Burton writes, "According to the Western cabalists, the sylphs flew through the air with the speed of lightning, riding a 'peculiar cloud.'" They assist "witches and sorcerers" in Lapland, Lithuania, and Scandinavia in acquiring winds to "sell...to mariners."

Fire

Associated with vitality and purifying power of the sun, as well as with its destructive power, fire "consumes, warms, and illuminates, but can also bring pain and death." Food cooked over flame provides nourishment for the flesh, as lamps and candles nurture sacred illumination. Fire transforms flesh into spirit. For the Greek philosopher Heraclitus, the fundamental animating, ensouled "life-energy" of the universe is fire. Fire is sacred to the Celtic goddess Brigid, who is said to have been born "at dawn in a pillar of fire." The Druids allegedly lit fires against their enemies. Prometheus steals fire from heaven. The goddess Demeter, wishing to make the child Demophoon immortal, places him in the hearth fire. Hestia/Vesta, goddess of home and community, guards the hearth fire and the eternal flame; the Vestal Virgins guard her sacred fire. Shepherds encountered the fire of purification at Roman festival of the Parilia in honor of the goddess of flocks, Pales.

In Germanic tradition, fire signifies the hearth and nurturance; vital force, often destructive, needed for battle; trickery and cunning; passion; and purification and transformation. As Hilda Ellis Davidson observes in *Roles of the Northern Goddess* (1998), "women have always ruled the hearth." Baking bread is among the most sacred of activities, with bread being the basic ceremonial food. Germanic goddesses of the hearth include Nehalennia (who also oversees navigation) and Hlodyn, the mother of Thor. The vital force of fire is embodied by Thor. Davidson relates in *Gods and Myths of Northern Europe* (1975): "Thor's temple ...'was the place for the fire which was never allowed to go out. This they called the sacred fire.'...Thor's power over the lightning, the fire from heaven, must not be forgotten, and this aspect of the god was...emphasized by the imitation of thunder within the temple itself."

The Germanic god Loki, like fire, plays pranks, is not to be trusted, can be destructive. Fire's ardor burns in Freyja's fiery necklace, the Brisingamen. Fire purifies and transforms flesh into spirit: even after the Church banned cremation, fires were lit near graves, and incense burned.

The Slavic god Svarog, sometimes called Ogon (from the Sanskrit *agni*, "fire;" one finds here a rather uncanny homophonous association with the Yorùbá god of iron, Ogún), the Slavic Perûn and his Lithuanian counterpart Perkûnas, share guardianship of fire with Gabija, Lithuanian goddess of the hearth. Slavs greeted the hearth fire with the prayer "Hail the light! Hail, holy fire!" and insisted that the faithful treat it as a deity, with great respect. In indigenous-Christian hybridity, fire was equated with Jesus; when lighting it, Slavs prayed "Hail, Jesus Christ!" Gimbutas, in *The Balts*, observes: "Fire was a goddess, who required offerings. She was fed and carefully guarded and covered over at night by the mother of the family. The Latvians call this flame "mother of the fire," *uguns mate*; in Lithuanian it is *Gabija* (from the verb *gaubti*, 'to cover'); in Prussian *panike*, 'the little fire.'" Of the Lithuanians, Old Prussians, and Latvians, Gimbutas relates: "[They] were great venerators of fire. Fire was sacred and eternal. Tribes had official sanctuaries on high hills and on riverbanks where fire was kept, guarded by priests, and in each house was the sacred hearth in which fire was never extinguished."

In thirteenth-century Lithuania, Vaitkevicius notes, when earth-centered traditions were being synthesized and centralized, *šventaragiai*, sites of sacred fires, including places of cremation, became increasingly important as religious as well as political vortices.

Although bonfires and need-fires commenced in antiquity, they flourished from the medieval period onward, despite the Church's banning them. The term "bonfire" connotes a festive fire as well as, perhaps, one fashioned by a community. It may also signify the burning of bones in a ceremonial fire; in Ireland, for example, bones were burnt on certain holidays. Because need-fires (from Old German *nodfyr*) involved rubbing two sticks together to create friction and then fire, the need-fire took on associations with lustiness and fertility; in this regard, they were also called *reibfeuer*. Oak was most commonly used for need-fires. Such fires were lit in England, Germany, Scotland, Bulgaria, and elsewhere into the eighteenth and nineteenth centuries. Their efficacy depended upon "all other fires being extinguished" and upon celebrants purifying themselves prior to commencing the rite. On the Isle of Lewis, Scotland, there "was an ancient custom...to make a fiery circle about the houses, corn, cattle, etc., belonging to each particular family: a man carried fire in his right hand, and went round [in a] Dessil [i.e., deosil, clockwise] direction." In Bulgaria, two "naked men produce[d] the fire by rubbing dry branches together in the forest, and with the flame they [lit] two fires, one on each side of a crossroad haunted by wolves." Need-fires and bonfires were lit especially on the occasion of ancient holidays. Yule fires commemorating the return of light were popular in France; in

Germany, spring equinox/Easter fires were lit on mountaintops to celebrate the triumph of spring over winter; persons leapt over fires, drew cattle through them to heal and protect them, and rolled fiery wheels down slopes in France, Germany, England, Scotland, Russia, Old Prussia, Lithuania, and elsewhere on Beltane/May Eve and Midsummer Eve/the night of St. John the Baptist.

Veneration of fire continued in eighteenth-century Lithuania. Norbertas Velius, in *The World Outlook of the Ancient Balts* (1983, 1989), relates that in the logbook of the pastoral activities of Vilnius Academic College for 1718-1719, one finds: "Even now offerings are made to fire in a superstitious way." Lithuanians traditionally offered the fire bits of food, salt, and a bowl of fresh water. Jonas Balys recorded a late nineteenth- or early-twentieth century Lithuanian prayer: "Every evening the housewife puts the glimmering coals and ashes together in the fireplace and prays: "Dear fire, little Gabija, do not burn, if not intentionally fired; you are nicely covered, then sleep, please, and do not walk in this house." The Reverend Peter Sirvaitis, in *Religious Folkways in Lithuania and their Conservation among the Lithuanian Immigrants in the U. S.* (1952), asserting that approximately of 30% of Lithuanian-Americans living in the mid-twentieth century were "for the most part atheists" – by which he appears to mean persons who practice an indigenous-Christian hybridity – observes: "Fire is still venerated by the Lithuanian people. Some Lithuanians of the second generation know of this respect for fire, by signing it with the sign of the cross in the morning, or on leaving the house, and not allowing any spitting into it, and so forth."

Burton (1621) speaks of fiery elementals as salamanders. They often inhabit volcanoes such as Vesuvius and assist mortals in pyromancy. In the eighteenth century, some continued to believe in the existence of flying dragons, or "fiery drakes," which Edward Gibbon (1737-1794), known primarily for his *Decline and Fall of the Roman Empire* (1776-1788), thought had entered English tradition by way of encounters with "Arabian magic" during the Crusades. In nineteenth-century France and elsewhere in Europe, many continued to believe in and interact with salamander elementals. These fire elementals included the Slavic *perelesnyk* (also, *litavets*), a being akin to incubus that can take form of a flying, fire-breathing dragon.

In nineteenth-century Wales, some continued to see mysterious, fiery spirits called *tan-we(d)*. These took the form of laser-like beams that, when manifesting and darting through an area, lit up everything in the vicinity with a brilliant glow. They were sometimes thought to either prophesy or bring on death.

Before leaving the elements per se, I would like to point out that in some sacred traditions, sets of elements – earth, water, air, fire – taken together often bore a relationship to the theory of correspondences. For example, in a tradition of medieval Germany, earth corresponded to the goddess Perchta; water to the goddess Holda; air to the god Wuotan (Odin); and fire to the god Donar (Thor).

Celestial Bodies

"The animate and dynamic forces of the heavenly bodies — the sun, moon and stars...and the rainbow...were all believed" in the indigenous Baltic worldview, as Gimbutas explains, "to exercise a great influence on the development of plants and of animal and human life. The divine significance of the life- and light-bringing powers inspired the personification of the sun, moon, morning and evening stars.

Swearing by "heaven or by the earth or by the sun or by the moon" was also prohibited from the eleventh century onward.

In the early eleventh century, Burchard of Worms (d. 1025) found it necessary to interrogate ostensibly Christian individuals as to whether or not they were continuing to venerate celestial bodies: "Hast thou observed the traditions of the pagans...that is,...worship[ping] the elements, the moon or the sun or the course of the stars, the new moon or the eclipse of the moon?" Had they asked the heavenly bodies to bring them good fortune? "If thou hast, thou shalt do penance for two years." It is noteworthy that this question was still being asked of persons suspected of holding cosmos-centered beliefs in the sixteenth century. Also in the eleventh century, the English King Cnut (or, Canute, d. 1035, r. 1016-1035) found it necessary to forbid earth-centered veneration of, and the making of offerings to, the sun and the moon. Norbertas Velius, in *The World Outlook of the Ancient Balts* (1983, 1989), recounts that veneration of celestial bodies continued in eighteenth-century Lithuania; in the logbook of the pastoral activities of Vilnius Academic College for 1718-1719, one finds evidence of persons worshipping the heavenly bodies and pleading with the deities of those bodies to heal them. They continued to invoke Saulë the Sun, Menulis the Moon, and other celestial bodies.

Sun

The sun "warms the earth, bringing about the growth of plants, guarding the crops from harm, and moderating the thunder-god's enthusiasm." Apollo of the Greeks and Romans, Lugh of the Celts, Dazhbog of the Slavs: these are gods of the sun. As a male, the Slavic sun is a prince who lives in the far east, in a "golden palace," in a "land of eternal summer and abundance." His children are variously depicted as the two aspects of Venus and the signs of the zodiac. But the sun is also, and just as frequently, envisioned as a goddess: she is the Basque Eguski Amandrea, Grandmother Sun; the Slavic Kolyada, goddess of the "newborn sun" emerging at the winter solstice; Saulë, the Baltic sun goddess; and Baiwe of the Sámi. Slavs prayed to the sun each morning and evening. In Christianized areas, these prayers merged with Christian ones, resulting in hybridized prayers like "Hail, welcome, divine light, which shines upon the whole world, upon me, a sinner!" However, travelers to Christianized Slavic areas asserted that Slavs frequently "renounced the Christian faith, preferring to worship the sun and other celestial bodies." Like other Europeans, Slavs followed a *deosil*, or solar-directional, pattern during "magic rituals."

In Baltic tradition, the sun is often divided into a mother-daughter pair, Saulë and Saulës meita, respectively. Fire is sometimes also envisioned as the sun's daughter. The sun also shares a complementary relationship with the female earth, often as two mothers. On the other hand, the sun's relationship with the male moon is oppositional, with the former corresponding to "red, female, hot, blood, fire, summer," and the latter corresponding to "white, male, cold, semen, water, [and] winter." The sun's rays are horses or their riders. Red "gooseberries are said to be the sun's tears. The sun is used to determine numerous rites and its path the direction of dancers and other ritual participants. Indeed, on festival days, the sun, unable to restrain its joy, dances. "If the sun be tardy in rising, then it has gone to keep the orphans warm," sings the performer of a *daina*, a folksong. There are thought to be two suns, one in the land of the living, the other in that of the ancestors; the dying person is said to "sleep between two suns." In Rev. Sirvaitis' *Religious Folkways*, we find that among Lithuanian-Americans living in the mid-twentieth century, some continued to venerate the sun and moon; in Shenendoah, Pennsylvania, it was considered "improper to point to the sun or the moon with one's finger."

Moon

> When Diana lighteth
> Late her crystal lamp,
> Her pale glory kindleth
> At her brother's fire:
> ....
> Moonlight falleth,
> And recalleth
> ....
> ... love's delight . . .
> from *Dum Dianae vitrea*,
> attributed to the Archpoet (fl. 1159-1167)[31]

The moon speaks of cycles, reflecting those of plants, animals, and humans; in its waxing we consider our growth; in its waning, our decline; in its return, our rebirth. It speaks of intuition and of sacred descent and the attainment of wisdom.

The moon, like the sun, has been alternately envisioned as female or male. The moon corresponds to the classical goddess Artemis/Diana, the Basque goddess Mari, and the Baltic goddess Ragana. The moon has been Christianized as Mary Magdalene. But the moon also corresponds to male deities: the Slavic Myesyats and the Baltic Menulis. As a male, the moon often forms a couple with the sun goddess. The "man in the moon" is an old man carrying a burden on his back, holding a lantern, and accompanied by a dog.

Of veneration of the moon, Bernadette Filotas, in *Pagan Survivals, Superstitions and Popular Cultures in Early Medieval Pastoral Literature* (2005), writes, "[T]he moon, with its evident connection to growth and decay and the feminine cycle, played a[n] ...important role in agrarian popular religion." Many beliefs, later called "superstitions," flowed from veneration of the moon. At the new moon, one should sow crops that grow above ground, collect healing herbs, wean cattle, count one's money, move into a new house, and marry. During the full or waning moon, one should perform "operations involving severance or dissolution, cutting down or leveling:"

one should cut wood, hunt game, and annul marriages. One should also sow crops that grow beneath the ground. In the eighth century, veneration of the moon was condemned in the *Indiculus superstitionem et paganiarum (Index of Superstitions and Paganism)*: persons continuing to practice pagan-based traditions shouted "Triumph, Moon!" on the occasion of lunar eclipses and continued to believe in the power of certain "women [to] command the moon."

Germanic Thuringians are thought to have held rites on the occasion of the new moon and perhaps on occasions marking its other phases as well. Slavs offered various prayers to the moon, particularly to the new moon. Some, tossing a coin toward the moon, prayed, "Here you are. Have some money. Give me health!" Others prayed, "I greet you, dear new moon, because you cure toothaches and headaches!" Still others prayed, "Rejuvenate me like you rejuvenate yourself!" Young women seeking partners prayed, "O, you splendid moon in the sky! You look at the earth and see everything, even my future husband. Make it so that I can see him in my dreams!" Like many other Europeans, Slavs planted by the moon and picked herbs and worked magic according to the phases of the moon. Frank Kmietowicz recounts in *Slavic Mythical Beliefs* (1982): "A girl in Poland was to go naked on the first Thursday night after the new moon and look for the herb called Nasiezrzal (*Ophioglessum vulgarum*) [which was] good for love magic." Indeed, so linked were the moon and loving unions that Slavic wedding ceremonies were often performed during the new or full moon, and special cakes called *korowaj*, decorated with horned moons, were baked for weddings. On the other hand, the dark of the moon was associated with sinister personae and events: "Southern Slavs maintained that boys born in this phase would [become] werewolves, [while] girls [would become destructive] witches." Slavic tradition also held that when the moon appeared dark, it was shining in the land of the dead.

In fifteenth- and sixteenth-century Western Europe, particularly in Germany, the Moon and those patroned by the Moon, the "Children of Luna," came to be associated with the ancient wisewoman Circe. Her male assistant was depicted as a magician, resonating with the later Tarot image of the Magus (thus also perhaps corresponding to Hermes/Mercury). This chain of associations linked the Moon to witchcraft, magic, fluidity, and itinerancy.

John Aubrey (1626-1697), following John Blau of Amsterdam, known for his *Atlas* of Scotland (1654), reports that Scottish highlanders of the mid-seventeenth century continued to pay homage to the moon, especially "worshipping...the new moon." This is particularly true of women, who "make a curtsey to the new moon." Aubrey adds, "I have known one in England who does it, and our English women in the country do retain (some of them) a touch of this Gentilism still;" some of these pray to the moon to divine future husbands: "All hail to the Moon, all hail to thee!/ I prithee, good Moon, declare to me,/ This night who my husband must be." This practice closely resembles that of Slavic women.

In the late eighteenth century, according to Samuel Johnson, the belief in the moon's power to guide in the planting of crops and the rearing of farm animals held strong in the western islands of Scotland. In 1773, the essayist, critic, poet, and lexicographer Samuel Johnson (1709-1784) and his young friend James Boswell (1740-1795), a diarist and Johnson's biographer, journeyed to the Hebrides, the western islands of Scotland; their works on this journey are considered classics of English literature and continue to be studied in the twenty-first century. Johnson was a peculiar mix of keen interest in the "superstitions" of indigenous peoples and profound skepticism. He reported, somewhat prematurely, that many indigenous concepts and practices had been "almost extirpated" by way of the "diligence of the ministers." Despite this, Johnson acknowledged that "[t]he moon has great influence in vulgar philosophy," he wrote disparagingly.

In his *Etymological Dictionary of the Scottish Language* (1808), John Jamieson (1759-1838), a Scottish lexicographer and son of a minister, quotes a minister of the early nineteenth century who is complaining of the persistent-become-resistant practice of divination and its link to veneration of the moon in Scotland: "It is strange that in a land so long favoured with clear gospel light some should still be so much under the grossest superstition that they not only venture on divination but in their unhallowed eagerness to dive into the secrets of futurity, even dare directly to give homage to the 'Queen of Heaven.'"

Western Balts prayed to the moon to heal various illnesses, including warts and weakness in arms and legs. They made "offerings of bread, wool, linen, and money" to the moon to encourage its assistance. Sirvaitis observed of Lithuanians and Lithuanian-Americans living in the mid-twentieth century: "Some Lithuanians still say a prayer when they see a full moon. The farmers still believe in the effects of the different phases of the moon on plants and corn." My maternal grandmother, grandfather, and step-grandfather, like many American immigrant farmers, planted by the moon, marking the moon signs under the eaves of the roof of their house on Bandera Road in San Antonio, Texas.

Marcu Beza wrote in *Paganism in Roumanian Folklore* (1928), "In my childhood, I myself prayed to the moon... No doubt faded remnants of such pagan usages linger also in other parts of the world." Beza recounts:

> I still remember how my grandmother used to approach me in a soft whisper: "Come, dear, the new moon!" Then she would put a loaf of bread or a specifically prepared cake on my head, and a silver coin in my pocket, and at the same time give me two brass vessels filled with water to hold. All these objects naturally stood for symbols of prosperity, and the water of the vessels was known as *apa muta* or *apa nençeputa*, speechless, virgin water. Making me turn three times and look straight at the moon, my grandmother would slowly utter, with deep religious solemnity, the verses, which I murmured after her:..."Moon, new moon, let goodness be like the dew; as much sand in the river, so the purse of the father; as the cinders in the house, so many guests at our table; thou like me,

and I like thee!"[32]

According to Beza, early twentieth-century Romanians continued to plant according to the phases of the moon. They also continued to believe that the moon possesses the ability to heal, to protect, to bring prosperity, and to remove negative spells. In regard to these, Beza first praises the moon – "A new moon has put on a crown of precious gems. / Luminous moon, / who art in heaven and seest everything on the earth" – and then tells the moon of his troubles: he finds "no rest" in his home; his enemies have "risen up;" and so on. Then he pleads with the moon to "takest [away] the spell" that has been placed on him and his family.

Stars and Constellations

In Celtic tradition, the constellation of Cassiopeia is called Llys Dôn and is the throne of the goddess Dôn (Welsh) or Danu, mother of the Tuatha Dé Danaan; the Corona Borealis, also known as the Northern Crown, called Caer Arianrhod, is the castle of Arianrhod, daughter of Dôn; and the Milky Way, Caer Gwydion, is the castle of Gwydion, son of the goddess Dôn and brother of Arianrhod. An early account of Dôn and her children – Arianrhod, Gwydion, and others – suggests that the Tuatha Dé Danaan may have descended to earth from the stars. Charles Squire, in *Celtic Myth and Legend: Poetry and Romance* (1912), further suggests that "they landed in a dense cloud upon the coast of Ireland on the mystic first of May [Bealtaine] without having been opposed, or even noticed."

The Milky Way, in Germanic tradition, is a "path of ghosts," the road that deceased warriors take to the paradise of Valhalla. Likewise, Slavs envisioned the Milky Way as the "Way of the Souls." It was also called the "Way of Birds," as human souls often took the form of birds. Lithuanians likewise described the Milky Way as the road of the dead. This association of the Milky Way with divinities and the dead appears to be a very ancient one and is found in many cultures, including numerous Indigenous American ones such as the Ojibwa, Mi'kmac, Iroquois, Cheyenne, Skiri Pawnee, and Maidu. Indeed, it is conceivable, as evidence of primordial trails out of Africa demonstrated by the National Geographic Genographic Project suggest, that this sacred association may return us to the very origins of human spirituality; according to some of our most ancient ancestors, "the Zulu and Ndebele people of southern Africa, the stars are the eyes of dead ancestors, keeping watch on the living from above." In the Middle Ages, some living in the Netherlands referred to the Milky Way as the "street of Vrouelde," or Vrouelden-straat, referring to the goddess Vrouelde/Pharaildis.

The Aurora Borealis, similarly, reveals the movements of the Valkyries. Among Estonians, it depicts a great celestial battle. In Germanic tradition, Eridanus is the Rhine, "where the mist folk Nibelungen hid the treasures they had robbed from earth;" Orion signifies the distaff of the goddess Frigga; while Ursa Major (the Big Dipper) is the starry counterpart of Odin or Thor, as well as the wagon of Odin (Wuotanes wagan) or Irmin (Irmines wagen), the latter variously described as a god of the heavens, war, and wisdom. Interestingly, Ursa Major was Christianized as Himmel Wagen, or "Heaven's Wagon," and Odin and Irmin were displaced by Hans Dumken, a poor dwarfish man who was kind to a stranger who turned out to be Christ. Slavs envisioned the Pleiades as a group of crone-like divinities, calling the constellation Baby, i.e., the "grandmothers."

Some Slavs and Lithuanians identified the goddess of dawn with Venus as the Morning Star. For Slavs, she was Zorya; for Lithuanians she was Auðrinë. Until recently, in Poland and Russia, peasants "took off their hats, and crossing themselves...prayed, 'Hail O Morning Star, brightest Maiden!'" When Slavs, especially Poles and Ukrainians, could not spot Venus, they claimed that the planet had been stolen by a witch and hidden in a vessel or else carried off by *boginkas*, often sinister fairy-like beings. Latvians considered Venus "god's son[s]."

According to Slavic tradition, exposing herbs, cauldrons filled with water, and rings to be used in healing, divination, or magic to the stars on starry nights promoted their efficacy. When soldiers died in battle, said the Slavs, or else (in partially Christianized areas) unbaptized infants died, stars fell. Similarly, among Lithuanians, Verpeya, the "spinneress, begins to spin the thread of the newborn on the sky, and each thread ends in a star; when a man [or woman] is dying, his [or her] thread snaps, and the star turns pale and drops [becoming a shooting star]."

Increasingly linking the veneration of celestial bodies to astrology, Christian writings from the sixth through at least the eleventh century condemned the "pagan traditions [of] observ[ing] or honor[ing] ...the moon or the course of the stars or the empty falsehood of signs for building a house, planting corn or trees, or contracting a marriage."

Rainbow

The rainbow assists, with rain, in bringing fertility to the earth. In Celtic tradition, it is the throne of the goddess Ceridwen; in Greco-Roman tradition, it is the bridge of Iris; in Slavic tradition it is the joyful female divinity Raduga (or, Paraduha, Radauka, Raduha; also, Veselka) or else the bow of the thunder god Perûn; and in Baltic tradition, it is the sash of the goddess Laima and "the girdle of the fairy (*laumës juosta*)." Some Slavs also believed that passing beneath a rainbow or drinking water from a well near a rainbow could result in a transformation of one's sex. In Germanic belief, the rainbow is the bridge Bifrost that leads from Midgard, the human realm, to Asgard, the realm of the gods; the "gods rode over it daily to their tribunal held under the Yggdrasil Tree, and the Valkyries crossed it [as they did the Milky Way] to choose the heroes from among those slain in battle for Valhalla. The heroes marched back over it in triumph to the great wassail held to welcome them."

Finns envisioned the bow of the god of thunder, or, alternatively, a "divine maiden sit[ting] on the rainbow and weav[ing] golden raiment."

* * *

In my view, with all due respect to those who argue that ancient and pre-twentieth century paganism/s do not give evidence of being a nature-based religion or sacred system, I would argue that the foregoing evidence makes it abundantly clear that the ancient, indigenous, premodern sacred traditions of Europe, like those of many other cultures possessing resonant beliefs and practices, were most assuredly nature-revering, earth- or cosmos-centered traditions, and that they remained so for a very, very long time.[33]

Chapter 6
The Wheel of the Year

It is, I believe, universally allowed that no custom has a higher claim to heathen antiquity than the erection of a May-pole, garlanded with flowers, as the signal-post of mirth and rejoicing for the day.

Anna Eliza Kempe Stothard Bray, *The Borders of the Tamar and the Tavy* (1879)[34]

Most of us are all familiar with the pagan days of the week, which in some places have been Christianized or secularized. An eighteenth-century poet (whose name is unfortunately not listed) wrote of these:

The Sun still rules the
Week's initial Day,
The Moon o'er Monday
yet retains the sway;
But Tuesday, which to Mars was whilom given,
Is Tuesco's subject in the Northern Heaven;
And Woden [Odin] hath the charge of Wednesday,
Which did belong of old to Mercury;
And Jove himself surrenders his own day
To Thor, a barbarous god of Saxon clay:
Friday, who under Venus once did wield
Love's balmie spells, must now to Frea
[i.e., Freyja, or, Frigga,
in some versions] yield;
While Saturn still holds fast his day...[35]

One might almost be tempted to agree with John Sharp (1643-1714), Archbishop of York, when he decries in Sermon VIII, "[W]ere it not for that happy institution of the Lord's day...we should...in a little time...scarce be distinguished from heathens." We shall, however, concentrate here on pagan elements of the seasonal rather than the weekly cycle. In *On Agriculture*, the Late Antique Roman writer Columella stresses the significant relationship between the seasons, agriculture, and the sacred; for example, he states that in near the Lupercalia, one should plant Cappadochian lettuce, which belongs to Pan; on the Kalends of Mars, Tartessian lettuce; on the Kalends of Venus, Paphian lettuce; and so on.

The following poem, appearing in a seventeenth-century anthology (unfortunately, neither the name of the poet nor the date of composition is given), is in accord with the table of months given in Diderot and Le Rond d'Alembert's *Encyclopédie, ou, Dictionnaire raisonné des sciences, des arts et des métiers* (1781) and is somewhat reminiscent of the passage from

Columella:

> By Juno January's ruled and driven,
> Wet February is to Neptune given;
> March to Minerva, may whose wisdome screen us
> From April's procreant goddess, lovely Venus:
> Apollo hath the charge of flowrie May,
> while Mercury on June
> exerts the sway;
> July is Jove's, the thundering King of Heaven;
> And August is to yellow Ceres given:
> September is ascribed to Old Tubulcain,
> Which mythists make to be the same as Vulcan :
> Instead of March fierce Mars hath got October,
> Who with new wine replete is never sober:
> Chaste Dian treads the covers in November,
> And makes the mangled Hares her shafts remember,
> Whom burning Vesta roasts in dull December.[36]

"Among the pre-Christian peoples of Western Europe and elsewhere," Bernadette Filotas observes, "the most important festivals of the year were associated with the lunar and solar calendars" and stressed the "birth, growth, death and rebirth of nature." Following Károly Kerényi, she refers to this cyclic, or what others describe as a spiraling, view of time as a "sacred festive...[conception of] time." In this regard, in *The Festival of the Dead* (1863), Robert Grant Haliburton offers an intriguing hypothesis, namely that the Celtic calendar, with its primary divisions of the year signaled by November and May, may have been based on observation of the Pleiades, only to be later changed to an equinox-solstice-based calendar; he states:

> In place of the seasons of the Pleiades commencing in November and May, a year of two seasons regulated by winter and summer was substituted by the northern nations of Europe. ... Halloween was transferred to Christmas Eve, or Yule ... while May day was shifted to the summer solstice, and began at St. John's Eve.[37]

He continues: "Both [May Eve & St. J's] still share in many singular features. We have the May queen reappearing on St. John's eve, and the May pole again set up."

In *Folk Song in England* (1967), A. L. Lloyd stresses the relationship of seasonal celebrations to the "economic reality of the farming year." In Lloyd's view, the cycle of the ceremonial farming year can be divided into two or three parts; if the first, or first and second, is/ are comprised of "a set of rites accompanying the preparation (October to February) and augmentation (March to June) of the crops," the final part is devoted to "rites accompanying the harvest (end of summer, beginning of autumn)."

George Caspar Homans, in *English Villagers of the Thirteenth Century* (1942), makes a point concerning seasonal rites that, in my view, cannot be overstressed, namely, that "husbandmen formed at least nine-tenths [G. C. Coulton claims a somewhat smaller proportion, 80%] of the population" of medieval England (and beyond England, I think we may safely attribute the same rough figure to the rest of Europe) and that the "traditional year governed the behavior of most men [and women] and was represented as common to all."

One need only look at the traditional Lithuanian calendar to get a sense of how much the year was tied to the cycles of nature and to agriculture: January, Sausis, the month of snow; February, Vasaris, winter's end approaches; March, Kovas, struggle between winter and spring; April, Balandis, doves return; May, Gegužis, the cuckoo sings; June, Birželis, the month of the birch; July, Liepa, month of the linden; August, Rûgpjûtis, month of rye; Rugsëjis, another month of rye; Spalis, October, month of flax; November, Lapkritis, falling leaves; December, Gruodis, frozen soil. In regard to Lithuania, agricultural practices were frequently ritualized. For example, "[d]uring rye harvesting, people wore clean or white clothes...[W]omen gave their men shirts 'as white as the sun.'"

Filotas stresses that Church authorities opposed celebration of seasonal festivals: "Both the cyclical concept of time and the very character of the rituals were deeply offensive to the Church" because they promoted reverence of nature and an earth-centered conception of time linked to the natural cycle. Biblical time, in opposition to pagan time, is, generally speaking, "linear, beginning with the Creation...and marching irrevocably toward the Last Judgment." The significance of this shift in the conception of time cannot be over emphasized. The notion of linear time has not only led in the West and elsewhere to a devaluation of cyclical time and to the affirmative valuation, naturalization, and normalization of progress and linear evolution but has also, among certain religious and other groups, promoted apocalyptic ideologies and actions rooted in those ideologies.

Church authorities may have also reacted against some of the more highly ritualized farming traditions, such as, for example, the Russian tradition that the "mother-in-law reaps in front of all the other; beside her on the right hand is her eldest daughter." The Church may have looked upon such rites as challenging patriarchal authority.

However, as Homans recognizes, the Church understood that "when the people of western Europe were converted to Christianity, the cycle of heathen festivals was already well geared to the traditional farming year" and thus determined that when necessary, in order to ease Christianization, it might be necessary to appropriate the dates of pagan festivals for its own celebrations: "A feast which had once been kept in honor of some heathen god was now [frequently] said to be kept in honor of a Christian saint...while the practices of the feast remained very much what they had always been." Filotas acknowledges that "[a]lthough the new Christian rituals and feasts were accepted" – I would add, often forcibly – "the traditional ones were not wholly abandoned, but often continued to be celebrated simultaneously."

Of seasonal rites during the Renaissance, Robert Muchembled observes in *Popular Culture and Elite Culture in France, 1400-*

1750: "At first sight, the calendar of the peasant year seems totally Christian. ... However, the truth of the matter is elsewhere, since many of the holidays were not uniquely, sometimes not even essentially, Christian." Muchembled further states: "Fertility was naturally the primary preoccupation of the human being whose entire life depended on good harvests and the increase of his herds. Therefore all of the festivities...were accompanied by rites to assure the fertility of fields, animals, and women."

Although it is generally agreed upon that peasants and other rural inhabitants of medieval and Renaissance Europe continued longer than many urbanites to celebrate seasonal and kindred rites of ancient origin, in this way often becoming characterized as "pagans" or "heathens," it is important to recognize, as Fernand Braudel puts it in *The Structures of Everyday Life* (1981), that "town and countryside never separate like oil and water." Indeed, in medieval and Renaissance Europe, "the countryside had to support the town if the town was not to live in a constant state of anxiety with regard to its subsistence. ... Moreover, even the large towns continued to engage in rural activities up to the eighteenth century. ... As for the innumerable small towns, they could barely be distinguished from country life."

A great amount of interaction occurred between townspersons and country dwellers. "The inhabitants of the towns," for instance, "often spent only part of their lives there: at harvest-time, artisans and others left their houses and trades behind them and went to work in the fields." This suggests that townspersons, especially those, including artisans, working in the fields, may have joined country dwellers in celebrating harvest and possibly other seasonal rites. By the same token, country dwellers traveled to cities and towns seasonally and at other times to sell produce at markets. For example, vintners transported "thousands of barrels" of wine to cities and towns "every autumn; cities like Florence were "transformed into...enormous market[s] for new wine." While visiting cities and towns, country dwellers may have taken advantage of such experiences as attending the theater; while certainly many country dwellers were not poor, those who were less well-off than others may have taken advantage of discounted prices such as those offered to "groundlings" at the Globe. Country dwellers may have also shared traditional wisdom and descriptions of seasonal and other rites with townspersons. In this way, townspersons, especially artisans, working in the fields and country dwellers selling produce in towns and cities may have ultimately contributed to an interpenetration of arts and rural, including earth-based or –inspired, traditions; triumphal processions, in which nobles and commoners, urbanites and country dwellers, etc., participated demonstrate evidence of this interpenetration.

I find it significant that in the early sixteenth century, persons employed by King James IV of Scotland (1473-1513; r. 1488-1513) were paid from Candlemas to Beltane, Beltane to Lammas, Lammas to All Hallow, and All Hallow to Christmas. Somewhat ironically, Celtic and Roman holidays appear to have been celebrated by some practitioners alleged to be witches, whom James fiercely persecuted. In the witch trials one finds numerous references to rites and celebrations at Imbolc/Candlemas, Midsummer, and Samhain/Halloween.

Although I might have commenced this discussion of seasonal rites with January 1, the New Year's of the later Roman and our own calendar, or else October 31, the traditional New Year's of Celts and nowadays of Wiccans, I have decided to begin here with festivals bidding adieu to winter and welcoming spring, based in part on the fact that numerous traditional folk calendars of Europe, some rooted in the pre-153 BCE Roman calendar, commence(d) around the beginning of March.

Farewell to Winter and Welcoming of Spring

In the mid-sixteenth century, Thomas Kirchmaier (a. k. a. Naogeorgus) wrote of Carnival, noting its homage to Bacchus: "Now when at length the pleasant time of Shrovetide comes in place,/ And cruel fasting-days at hand approach with solemn grace:/ Then old and young are both as mad, as guests of Bacchus' feast."

Carnival, often at February's end, with its Mardi Gras, owes something to the Germanic festival of Sporkelmonat, as it owes something to the January Kalends, the Roman Feast of Fools, and the Liberalia in honor of Bacchus (held in March). Among Germanic peoples, and continuing among some present-day Germans, the festival of Sporkelmonat (Latinized as *Spurcalibus*) may have begun as a rite of animal sacrifice, specifically of pigs, to the Vanir deities Freyja and Freyr, becoming increasingly carnivalesque over the course of time. In recent years, I've begun collecting marzipan pigs at Christmastime, which may reflect both the boar sacrifice at Yule as well as, perhaps, that of Sporkelmonat. Church authorities have reacted to Carnival, and more specifically, to the festival of Sporkelmonat, in contradictory ways. Although, generally speaking, the Church accepted the celebration as a sort of necessary ceremony of release of repression, it was condemned on numerous occasions, particularly during the mid- to late-eighth century, including by Charlemagne, who "commanded bishops sedulously to investigate pagan customs, such as divinations, phylacteria, incantations, and 'all the *spurcitias* of the heathens'."

During the Carnival of the Renaissance, men and women, children and adults, rich and poor joined in feasting, dance, song, and playing cards and other games. Some ran "naked about the street," while others dressed in the attire of the opposite gender ("the men in maids' array,/ And wanton wenches dressed like men"), and still others "like wild beasts [did] run abroad in skins." Nobles and their families, not to be outdone by commoners, nodded to the crowds from sumptuously decorated wagons. It seems that the ancient tradition of animal sacrifice also persisted; as Muchembled relates, "The animal sacrifices of Carnival and Lenten games were perhaps votive offerings or means of warding off maleficent forces before the awaited return of generations." On Shrove Tuesday, or Mardi Gras, the day before Ash Wednesday and the onset of Lent, Aubrey reports that in seventeenth-century England, "as soon as the clock strikes nine, all the boys in the school [i.e., Eton] cry, 'Io Bacchus! Io Bacchus! Io Bacchus!' as loud as they can yell, and stamp, and knock with their sticks and then...run out of the school."

In Lithuania and Lithuania Minor, Carnival, called Uþgavënës, was originally celebrated at the time of the spring equinox, but with Christianization, it was moved to the end of February. This festival honors the ancestors (resonating with Celtic Samhain/Halloween, at this time the dead walked among the living), pits Winter against Spring (Death against Life, Thin against Fat, etc.), and celebrates fertility and prosperity with a host of earth-based carnivalesque figures, ceremonial cross-dressing or mixed gender attire, and in ancient and early times, ceremonial eroticism.

With the last day of February and its turning into March, we return, in Umbria, Italy, in the fifteenth through early eighteenth centuries, to February's ancient Roman rites of the Lupercalia and Ceres' search for Proserpina. The historian Polydore Vergil (*c.* 1470-1555), followed by the theologian Jean-Baptiste Thiers (1626-1703), who condemned a ceremony involving children running through fields with lit torches to promote fertility, believing that the rite had originated in, or else been patterned after, one devoted to the goddess Ceres.

The month of March was primarily devoted to festivals honoring goddesses, women, and mothers and to celebrations marking winter's end and the commencement of spring. In ancient Rome, the Matronalia, held on March 1, honored women in general and mothers in particular. Because the Matronalia honored women, it was also known as Foemineis Calendis. The primary goddesses honored on this day were Juno Lucina and Diana, reflecting in part a continuation of the celebration of the return of light after the darkness of winter, as well as Minerva. Male deities appear to have also been honored on this day, including Mars, Jupiter, and Faunus and Picus, the latter couple being rustic divinities of the forest. In their translation of Ovid's *Fasti*, A. J. Boyle and R. D. Woodard write of this festival: "On the Matronalia, a day of great revelry, presents were given to the married women of Rome...Roman matrons themselves visited the temple of Juno Lucina and...prepared a meal for their slaves. The event appears to be something of a feminine version of the Saturnalia."

The *Canons* of the Council of Trullo, held in Constantinople in 691/692 CE, indicate that the Matronalia was still being celebrated in the late seventh century, not only at Rome but also more generally in the Mediterranean and Asia Minor. At this time, Church authorities moved to ban the very popular holiday: "We have determined that...the festival celebrated on the first of March [is] to be removed completely from the life of the faithful." Several days after the Matronalia, typically on March 5, the festival of Isis, called Navigium Isidis, the "Promenade of the Ship of Isis," was held at a number of European sites during the Middle Ages, perhaps especially at Aix-la-

Chapelle (Aachen, Germany), where it was celebrated as late as 1133.

Other festivals celebrated the culmination of winter and the commencement of spring. Classical antiquity acknowledged this transformation of seasons in the form of tales and (sometimes accompanying) rites concerning the cycle of life-death (often via sacrifice)-rebirth (or regeneration), as in the experience of Persephone, who transforms from innocent maiden into Queen of the Underworld. The ancient self-sacrifice of Attis, the consort of the goddess Cybele, and his subsequent transformation into a bunch of violets,, together with similar narratives of the death and rebirth of young gods (into flowers), was remembered in springtime. The annual commemoration of Attis' death may have played a role in early Roman commemor-ations of the death and resurrection of Jesus Christ.

In the main, European festivals of March alternately emphasized a battle of the seasons, with spring triumphing over winter, or the metamorphosis of a goddess of winter into a goddess of spring; honoring ancestors (similar to the present-day Mexican Dia de los Muertos); and fertility, returning us to the celebration of women, mothers, and goddesses.

"In pagan times," W. E. S. Ralston relates, "the gods were supposed to walk the earth at Springtide." On March 9 or thereabouts, Russians and Ukrainians celebrated Stricha, the return of the larks (*zhaivoronky*). Agricultural workers made clay and cloth figures of larks, which they smeared with honey, as if to feed them and thus bring them to life, and crowned with tinsel. They carried the clay and cloth larks on branches in procession. Moreover, women baked pastries shaped like larks and other birds. These pastries, like King Cakes, were filled with coins, buttons, and other small objects that became divinatory clues for those who found them. Some of the pastries were thrown up into the air by children. As farmworkers and others processed in parade, they sang songs to Lada, the goddess of spring. Together, these rites were meant to usher in springtime and ultimately to bring fertility to crops, animals, and people and the prosperity that would follow. In Lithuania, the return of the, the larks, was likewise celebrated at this time.

In traditional Russia, and indeed in Christianized Russia, transformation of winter into spring is sometimes called Provody. In early (and in some places, more recent) manifestations of the holiday, the goddess Maslenitsa (or, Masliana) magically transformed from the patron of winter into that of spring, reminiscent of Persephone/Proserpina's transformation. As the goddess of winter, Maslenitsa is sometimes portrayed by a straw figure that is ritually burned at the end of her festival to symbolize the end of winter. As such, she is associated with Snegurochka, the Snow Maiden. (It's noteworthy that both Hans Christian Andersen and C. S. Lewis transformed the Snow Maiden into an evil queen.) As Maslenitsa, emphasis is placed on her name, which derives from *maslo-*, butter "bringer of good things to eat" due to her being perceived as a gourmand, she is nicknamed Polizukha, "the licker," Blinoeda, "pancake-eater," Shirokoro-zhaya, "the broad-cheeked," and even Obzhora, "the glutton." Her special food is pancakes, *bliny*. Pancakes, as a circular food, were meant to signify both the sun and the cycle of life – birth, death, and rebirth. Maslenitsa may have also been envisioned as pregnant. As the centuries passed, Maslenitsa's image transformed; she eventually became, in some places, a young woman with "black eyebrows ...carefully groomed" wearing a "blue fur coat." Her part was sometimes taken by a girl or young woman crowned with a wreath of wildflowers and holding a green branch. A song to Maslenitsa goes: "Broad-cheeked Maslenitsa,/ We sing your praises./...And eat our fill of pancakes."

Pancakes were typically made by the oldest woman in the family, were supposed to include water from snow, and, when baked, they were to be placed on a windowsill in moonlight before being eaten. The woman who had baked them would chant, "Moon, moon, little gold horns, peep through the window and blow on the batter!" At this time, the dead were also offered pancakes. Participants in the festival would offer pancakes to ancestors by placing them on windowsills, or would offer them to homeless persons, who stood in for ancestors.

The dead were also offered colored eggs, placed on their graves, to signify rebirth. Likewise, at Velykos, Lithuanians offered red-dyed, and later on, diverse colors of and richly decorated, eggs, marguciai *i*, to their ancestors. In Poland, as in Russia and the Ukraine, eggs (in Polish, *pysanky*), like larks, serve to beckon or invoke springtime. It is significant that in many parts of Europe, the dead were honored on at least two primary occasions, one at the time of the spring equinox and the other in late autumn. Boris Rybakov writes of the springtime commemoration of the dead: "People visited the cemeteries on those days bringing their grandparents boiled sweetened wheat, eggs, and honey, believing that the ancestors would help the wheat grow....The custom of offerings on parental days was retained until the nineteenth century." This celebration also included the ploughing, sowing and decorating of fields, as well as decorating farmhouses, with greenery.

In Poland, the triumph of spring over winter appears to have been similarly celebrated in the form of a contest between Marzanna, the crone goddess of the harvest and winter, and Dziewanna, the maiden goddess of springtime as well as of forests and hunting (and thus corresponding to Diana), probably on the occasion of the spring equinox. In Lithuania and among early Lithuanian immigrants to America, incidentally, Morë, like Marzanna, represented winter and its end; carried around in a cart, she held a flail in one hand and a broom in the other. It is conceivable that a figure of Marzanna was submerged in a body of water to represent the cessation of the old year. If this was indeed the case, then on March 7, 965, near the end of the Early Middle Ages, the ancient significance of the submersion was severely twisted by Church authorities; it was attached to a Christianizing ceremony of chopping up figures of pagan deities and then drowning them in bodies of water to signify conversion to Christianity. The procession, burning, and drowning of Marzanna, represented by a large doll made of grass and tree branches, dressed in female attire, came to be called Topienie Marzanny. The major contest was thus transformed from one between two goddesses to one between a pagan goddess who came to represent "all evil" and the Church. Marzanna's role as the representative of evil was generally amplified in Christianized Poland. However, in some places, the Church succeeded in erasing her from the rite entirely and replacing her with Judas. The role of Dziewanna, as the representative of spring and the blossoming of the new year, was downgraded or erased, sometimes replaced by the Gaik Zielony (or, Nowe Latko), a pine or spruce decorated with "ribbons, flowers and paper suns." (Was the Maypole perhaps originally a figure representing a goddess?) In some locations, however, Dziewanna appears to have been remembered into the nineteenth and twentieth centuries. In 1855, Frédéric-Constant de Rougemont reported that "the Poles, the Silesians, and the Bohemians, to this very day, continue to throw into a river or pool, the image of a woman who bears the name of their ancient goddess the Earth, and which has the two names of Ziéwonie or Life, and Morena or Death." Dziewanna's continuing presence is also documented by a 1948 photograph.

Near the end of the month, and into the month of April, many Europeans celebrated the spring equinox and the season and continued to do so after Christianization, although often in disguised, increasingly carnivalesque, forms. Moreover, as with eggs offered at graves morphing into Easter eggs, serious rites frequently transformed into children's games.

Celebrations at this time embraced themes expressed earlier in March but emphasized Goddess reverence and fertility. In Cambridgeshire, Hertfordshire, and Worcestershire, England, into (at least) the late nineteenth century, it was customary to bake, give as gifts, and eat hot cross buns. Although Christians appropriated this custom for Easter, in particular, for Good Friday, the roots of the tradition, according to Peter Hampson Ditchfield in *Old English Customs Extant at the Present Time: An Account of Local Observances* (1896), lay in Dianic worship brought by the Romans:

> This custom is as old as the Romans, who were accustomed to present to their gods consecrated bread. Two loaves were discovered at Herculaneum marked by a cross. The Romans divided their sacred cakes with lines intersecting each other at right angles, and called the quarters quadra. ...
>
> Much has been written concerning the origin of hot cross buns. The Romans made their sacred cakes in honour of Diana, whose festival was observed soon after the vernal equinox. The original home of the custom, where it is chiefly observed, is Cambridgeshire and Hertfordshire. There the old Roman roads the Ickneld Street and the Armynge Street crossed. There stood in Roman times the altar of Diana of the Crossways, to whom the Romans offered their sacred cakes. There, too, the custom of eating hot cross buns is chiefly observed... This is a curious survival of the Roman times.[38]

Others have argued that hot-cross buns

originate in the reverence of Eostre; legend has it that when Christians could not stop women from baking the buns at this time of year for this purpose, they insisted that the women place crosses on them. Still others maintain that over the centuries, the custom of buns being offered to Eostre became enhanced by the Biblical narrative of women offering "cakes to the Queen of Heaven." In some places, these cakes took the form of crescents and were called "Easter moons," reflecting a connection of the festival with a lunar goddess. It is probably the case that in England and elsewhere, Celtic, Roman, Germanic, Biblical, and perhaps also other traditions were interwoven into a spiritually hybrid festival. Baked and eaten on the spring equinox, hot cross buns were believed, when "hung in the kitchen," to avert ill fortune, and "when grated [to be] an excellent remedy for various illnesses."

In Russia, the Goddess of the earth, as Žemlya or in her hypostasis as the "bright" goddess Svyetlaya, gives birth at this time. Boris Rybakov has described this festival as a "boisterous and orgiastic celebration of the spring equinox, a welcoming of the sun and exhortation of nature." Not surprisingly, earth-centered traditions were incorporated into Christianity in Russia and the Ukraine as they were elsewhere, to the great dismay of some Christians. For example, in tenth-century Italy, Atto of Vercelli (885-960/ 961) condemned the non-Christian elements of the Easter celebration as originating in the reverence of Venus and Liberus (i.e., Dionysus/ Bacchus). In certain places including in Silesia (now parts of Germany, Poland, and the Czech Republic), a Dionysus-like deity, a "very soft and feminine male," represented by bronze figures on staffs in rituals, appears to have been celebrated at this time.

Various scholars have suggested that Germanic peoples honored Freyja, Holda, Herke, and Eostre at this time (these may ultimately have been hypostases of the same goddess). "In sixteenth-century England," Robert Muchembled relates in *Popular Culture and Elite Culture in France, 1400-1750*, "the feast of Easter was accompanied by fertility festivals, secret ceremonies connected to the cult of mother goddesses." It is possible that these ceremonies are suggested by the Heffel Fair at Heathfield on April 14, when an "Old Woman," perhaps a reference to an elder goddess, releases a cuckoo, a bird associated with marriage, via the coupling of Juno and Jupiter, and with destiny.

In the late nineteenth century, according to an article that appeared in the *New York Times* on April 10, 1898, the "heavy hand of the police, urged on by the hidden hand of the churchmen, put a stop to" Prussian celebrations in honor of Ostara that included "bonfires and races, with burning brands and mummeries."

In France, a hybrid pagano-Christian spirituality combined the veneration of fairies with that of the Virgin Mary (whom, according to some, fairies despise).

In later centuries, particularly in nineteenth-century Germany, celebrations of the spring equinox and Easter embraced the figure of the Green Man, a "young peasant dressed in boughs brought from the forest." It also seems that in Bavaria on this occasion, a celebration of Thor involving a type of fireworks eventually metamorphosed into the Judasfeuer, the "Judas Fire," transforming one of the great Germanic gods into the betrayer of Christ.

Other than moveable springtime feasts, one other significant April holiday appears to have persisted for many centuries: the Parilia. This festival was celebrated in Rome with offerings and sacrifices to the goddess Pales, patron of herds, flocks, goatherds, and shepherds. According to John Aubrey, "Sheep-shearings, on the Downs in Wiltshire, and Hampshire," rooted in the April 21 festival in honor of Pales, guardian of herds persisted into the seventeenth and eighteenth centuries, being "kept with good cheer, and strong beer...The Fiddler and the Tabourer [i.e., drummer or tambourine player] [attend] this feast." According to William Grant Stewart in *The Popular Superstitions and Festive Amusements of the Highlanders of Scotland* (1823), this festival was also celebrated in Scotland, where it appears to have converged with the feast of May Eve, or Beltane. At this time,

no victim [i.e., animal] was killed, and nothing was offered but the fruits of the earth. The shepherds purified their flocks with the smoke of sulphur, juniper, boxwood, rosemary, etc. Then they made a large fire, round which they danced, and offered to the goddess [Pales] milk, cheese, eggs, etc., and holding their faces to the east, [they] utter[ed] ejaculations peculiar to the occasion.[39]

Stewart claimed that "until of late," that is, possibly into the late eighteenth century, this celebration of the Goddess and of flocks "remained pretty entire in some parts of the Highlands." On April 23, pagan Romans traditionally celebrated the Robigalia, the purpose of which was to make offerings to the goddess Robigo and her spouse Robigus so that they would bless the fields and protect the crops from "late spring frosts" and from mildew. Around the eighth century CE, this festival was Christianized, first dedicated to the emperor Constantine the Great and eventually becoming the Rogation days; its purpose, however, remained the same for centuries.

The Fertility Cycle

Robert Muchembled, in *Popular Culture and Elite Culture in France, 1400-1750*, notes, "May was the popular festive occasion that had best resisted Christianization." The Eve of May and May 1 celebrations possess numerous origins including Greco-Roman, Celtic, and Germanic, as evidenced, respectively, by celebrations of Maia as the mother of Hermes/Mercury and as the eldest of the Pleiades and the Floralia; Beltane; and Walpurgisnacht.

In terms of the Roman celebration of Maia, she was not only considered the mother of the Pleiades but also, by many, as the mother of the earth. In this way, Cybele became linked to Maia, gaining the nickname or alternate name of "Maja." The Roman festival not only honored Maia as a Mother-Goddess, including as the mother of Mercury, but also the heliacal rising of the Pleiades, with the Seven Sisters, like the Hyades, being linked to the zodiacal sign of Taurus. Some scholars have suggested that the names "Maia" and "Maja" may be related to the Sanskrit "Maya," as well as to the terms *magnus*, "great," *magus*, "practitioner of magic," and *majus*, a "May branch."

In regard to the Floralia, it is important to note that medieval and later scholars, Church authorities, and writers were aware that, and pointed out to penitents, congregations, and others that, the rites of May returned to pagan homage to the goddess Flora, patron of lovers and courtesans. In this light, it is conceivable, indeed quite probable, that many of those who celebrated the rites of May in the Middle Ages, the Renaissance, and thereafter were also made aware that the rites they were enacting owed had sprung from paying tribute to a pagan goddess.

Among Celtic peoples, the festival appears to have been held in honor of the solar god Belenus. There is, however, educated controversy on this point. In 1823, for example, William Grant Stewart took exception to this view; according to Stewart, "Beltane" does *not* signify "Ba'al's Fire" but rather the Greek goddess Pales' "fire," that is, "Paletein." This view hearkens back, of course, to the Parilia we have described above. Whichever the case, in its ancient Celtic manifestation, Beltane was associated with the arrival in Ireland of the Tuatha Dé Danaan "in a cloud that settled on the mountains of Connacht."

St. Eligius's condemnation of the rites of May in the seventh century suggests that a continental Germanic celebration was popular in ancient times. "Walpurgisnacht is thought to have its origins in a heathen Spring festival," Jennifer M. Russ explains in *German Festivals and Customs*, "in which Woden [Odin] and Freya [Freyja] begat Spring (Lenz)…The 'drink of love' (*Trank der Minne*) formed the center of these celebrations, and was thought to have the power to rejuvenate. The ever-popular green 'May Punch' (*Maibowle*), containing woodruff, is possibly a development of the 'drink of love'." Others have proposed that the festival paid homage to Freyr and/or Thor.

The May rites included ceremonial animal disguise and ceremonial cross-dressing or mixed gender attire; the drinking of May wine, a heady brew of wine and herbs, possibly meant to be a love potion; the construction of beds for lovemaking deploying flowers and herbs sacred to Freyja; and amatory magic employing menstrual blood.

The Maypole, Russ suggests, may have originated, at least in part, in a birch tree that was decorated for Freyja. During the High and Later Middle Ages, numerous Maypoles and sites of their raising, such as those of London, became more permanent items and well known as ritual objects; such were the Maypoles of Cornhill (known in Chaucer's day) and Aldgate Wards, the latter housed at the Church of St. Andrew the Apostle, which came to be called "St. Andrew Undershaft" because of its housing of a Maypole shaft taller than the Church's steeple.

Maypoles were typically "covered all over with flowers and hearbes, bounde rounde aboute with stringes, from the top to the bottom, and some tyme painted with variable colours." Similarly, the May branch, bush, or tree (in French, the *mai*; in German, the *Maibaum*; in Italian, the *maio* or the *palo per le danze di calendimaggio*) was chosen by young men for young women with whom they wished to spending May Eve. Indeed, the May branch, bush, or tree served as a token of love. The branch, bush, or tree was also believed to protect livestock against negative sorcery.

The assimilation of the Maypole, bush, and tree and the rites of May to a Christianized culture was not, needless to say, joyfully accepted by many Church authorities. In the early thirteenth century, for instance, Robert Grosseteste (*c.* 1175-1253), Bishop of Lincolnshire, forbade his diocese to celebrate the rites of May due to their pagan elements.

During the Later Middle Ages and the Renaissance, the month of May was alternately claimed to be governed by Apollo or Venus; the rites of the eve and first of May, also known as the Floralia and Beltane, were especially associated with the latter, as well as with the goddess Flora and, to a lesser extent, with other pagan deities and similar beings. It is important to bear in mind, I would note, as we consider Renaissance rites and deific and folkloric figures associated with them, that the Romans not only left traces behind them in Italy but also carried their traditions and deities with them as they colonized Britain and other parts of Europe.

In fourteenth-century France, the rites of May, not surprisingly, became linked to the subculture of the troubadours and to courtly love, the pagan-inspired dimension of which we've already noted; at the Jeux Floraux, a kind of poetic Olympics held in southern France, troubadours competed to win the Golden Violet. In Florence, during the Later Middle Ages and early Renaissance, the rites of May were celebrated majestically. Called the Calendimaggio (Feast of the Kalends of May), they opened a ritual cycle that culminated in the Feast of St. John the Baptist in June. Jean Delumeau, in *Catholicism Between Luther and Voltaire: A New View of the Counter-Reformation* (1977), states, "These May-day antics were fairly widespread in Europe, and seem to have been, in Italy at least, a survival of the ancient Floralia." Similarly, Mirella Levi D'Ancona, in *Botticelli's "Primavera,"* asserts that the Calendimaggio signified a conscious renewal or "revival of the Roman festivity of the Floralia" held in honor of the goddess Flora. Florence, in part because of a pun, came to be looked upon at some point as being under the patronage of Flora; and in Renaissance Florence, Flora came to be regarded as a special patron of the Medici family. D'Ancona relates, "[T]his was a feast of love and flowers, where all sorts of licentiousness was permitted. Groups of young men would go around Florence carrying flags and throwing oranges at their sweethearts, who would answer back by throwing down flowers from balconies, terraces, and windows." In a meticulous study of Botticelli's painting that speaks to its wider cultural context, she notes that oranges were associated in Renaissance Florence, as they had been in Greco-Roman antiquity, with love and marriage, the goddess Flora, the Three Graces (given by them as a gift to celebrate the nuptials of Zeus/Jupiter and Hera/Juno), and the Hesperides (as Latin *pomum* may not only refer to apples but also generically to fruit, the 'apples' of the Hesperides may in fact have been oranges); in the Renaissance, oranges also came to symbolize the Medici.

A great carnival was held, with triumphal processions as well as chant, music, and dance competitions and jousting matches (*armeggeria*). C. Clifford Flanigan observes that triumphal processions were "not, of course, the invention of...Christian communities," but rather "were taken over from late antique religious...practices." On this occasion, Denis Raisin-Dadre relates, "Florentines, wearing masks, would parade through the streets singing the old 'May songs.'" If we wish to have a virtual experience of the *Calendimaggio*, he continues, "[W]e must...imagine all the colour and atmosphere of the carnival, with its floats, tableaux, the powerful sound of the 'high instruments'" – i.e. shawms and trumpets –"the grotesque masks, the standards painted by the great masters living in the city, and the general jubilation and high spirits of the event."

Both female and male participants dressed exquisitely, their garments often lined with pearls; indeed, to dress well was as important as, if not more important than, to perform well. The women's primarily singing and dancing and the men's jousting evoked the coming together of Venus and Mars – and the ultimate triumph of Venus, and love – on this occasion.

Dances linked to the rites of May were lively and sensuous; among the most popular was the morris. Although the morris's name and perhaps certain of its movements refer to Moorish civilization and to the combat of Christians and Muslims during the Crusades, its origins are ancient. Typically danced to "pagan god(s)" by males wearing bells or dressed as women or animals, the morris celebrated "the return of vegetation" and was thought to possess and attract "magic power" and to "bring luck" to participants. The morris, like other rites of May, was linked to Venus; French, German, and other engravings and artworks of the fourteenth and fifteenth centuries depict the Goddess as presiding over the dance.

During the reign of Henry VI (1421-1471, r. 1422-1461, 1470-1471), the aldermen and sheriffs of Stebunheath Parish in London hosted a banquet celebrating May 1, inviting commoners as well as others. The poet John Lydgate (*c*. 1370-1450), a Benedictine Catholic priest best known for his devotional and moralistic poems, penned a poem for the occasion, which commenced,

Mighty Flora! Goddess of fresh flowers, –
Which clothed hath the soil in lusty green,
Made buds spring, with her sweet showers
By the influence of the sunshine;
To do pleasance of intent full clean,
Unto the States which now sit here,
Hath Venus down sent her own daughter dear.[40]

This poem is particularly significant in our context because it names the goddesses Flora and Venus as presiding over the rites of May and was recited to sheriffs and commoners in the fifteenth century; if they had not been aware before then that the rites were rooted in earth-centered spirituality/enspirited materiality and patroned by goddesses, they were aware of it now.

The coming together of various economic

and social classes was typical of the pagan-rooted holidays of the English calendar, as was also true for other European countries, but was perhaps especially common where the rites of May and midsummer were concerned. Stow observes in his *Survey of London* (1598) that "in the month of May, the citizens of London of all estates...[took part in] mayings." The evangelical author and pamphleteer Philip Stubbes (c. 1555- c. 1592/ 1610) probably exaggerated, however, when he railed, misogynistically, against the rites in *The Anatomie of Abuses* (1583), in which he insisted that at least one third of the women who participated in them were willingly deflowered during the night. The rites of May were, however, most assuredly the Valentine's of pagan-inspired Europeans. As Muchembled relates, "in the custom of "maying" (*esmayer*)...[a] *mai* – small trees or mixed bunches of branches – was planted in front of or fixed onto the house of each marriageable girl." Young men, by doing so, announced their desire to spend May eve in the forest with the young woman of their dreams. As mentioned above, the May branch, bush, tree, or pole was linked to love, magic, and, as a natural combination, to amatory magic. Many would "go to the woods, and groves, some to the hills and mountains...where they [would] spend all the night in pleasant pastimes" which included lovemaking. Muchembled insists, "The rites of the month of May were first and foremost agrarian and sexual;" and "The May games celebrated the growth of the fruits of the earth and the fruits of love." When the celebrants returned to their villages or cities from the woods, they brought a great tree trunk with them, as well as "birch boughs, and branches of trees, to deck their assemblies withal." Sometimes the Maypole was carried in a decorated wagon drawn by equally decorated oxen:

> [E]very Ox [has] a sweet Nosegay of flowers tied on the tip of his horns, and these Oxen draw home this Maypole...which is covered all over with Flowers and Herbs, bound round about with strings from the top to the bottom, and sometimes painted with variable colors, with two or three hundred men, women and children following it, with great devotion, and thus being reared up, with handkerchiefs and flags streaming on the top...[...] And then [they] banquet and feast [and] leap and dance about it, as the heathen people did, at the dedication of their Idols.[41]

These assemblies were filled with singing, morris dancing, "warlike shows, with good archers," and evening bonfires in the streets. Many poets celebrated the rites of May, including Spenser in his *Shepherd's Calendar*:

I saw a shole of shepherds outgo
With singing, and shouting, and jolly cheer;
Before them yode a lusty Tabrere,
That to the many a horn-pipe play'd,
Where to they dance each one with his maid.
To see these folks make such jouissance,
Made my heart after the pipe to dance.
Then to the greenwood they speeden them all,
To fetchen home May with their

musical:
And home they bring him in a royal throne
Crowned as king; and his queen attone
Was Lady Flora, on whom did attend
A fair flock of fairies, and a fresh bend
Of lovely nymphs—O that I were there
To helpn the ladies their May-bush to bear![42]

Another of the principal rites of May during the Later Middle Ages and early Renaissance in Italy and elsewhere was the "May Bath" (in Germany, the *Maibad*).although public bathing was practiced at other times of the year, it acquired special significance on this occasion. May bathing alternately took place in rivers and other bodies of water, in saunas or spas, or in outdoor tubs or large fountains, as evidenced by calendar illustrations and other works of art. In certain places, ceremonial bathing, rather than, or in addition to, taking place on the eve or first of May, took place on Midsummer Eve or on the Eve of St. John the Baptist. Germans, incidentally, appear to have been more at ease than Italians and other Europeans with mixed-gender bathing. Not surprisingly, the May Bath was thought to be overseen by Venus.

Artistic and other evidence from Germany, Italy, and elsewhere suggests that the May Bath included bathing, drinking, feasting, dancing, and lovemaking – activities governed by Venus – and had as ceremonial aims the enhancement of general health and fertility.

The May Bath was also associated with prostitution, and it is conceivable that courtesans and prostitutes numbered among its participants.

Writing on May 18, 1416 of the baths of the spa at Baden, the Italian humanist Poggio Bracciolini suggested that when "Venus departed Cyprus," she must have journeyed to Baden, "where they follow her customs and continue [to emulate] her licentious conduct." He contrasted the ambiance at Baden, a pagan, Venusian paradise of joy, eros, freedom from inhibitions, and an Eden-like innocence with the predominant, Christian-hegemonic culture of his day, which, in his view, cultivated backbiting, greed, guilt, jealousy, mistrust, pessimism, and shame. Trottein, in *Les Enfants de Vénus*, remarks: "Briefly put, one could almost employ the term 'Club Med' [to describe the baths], as the image that the twentieth century created of an earthly paradise...Water, nudity, banquets, bacchanals, music, and dance all contributed to an ideal of sensual pleasure."

So delighted was Bracciolini with the baths' "gaiety and extravagant amusement," and particularly with the bathhouse musicians, who struck him as the very embodiment of "winged Venus," that he barely had "time for lectures or philosophy, in the midst of all the troops, flutes, citharas, and songs."

Musicians playing trumpets, chalumeaus, cornets, harps, lutes, board zithers, organs, and other instruments associated with Venus assumed significant roles in bathing rites, not only by accompanying dancers but also by announcing that the water was warm enough for bathing to commence, by singing songs explaining the rules of bathhouses, and by entertaining participants with joyful songs (in Germany, the *Singbad*).

In Scotland, the celebration of Beltane was becoming increasingly associated with gatherings of witches, leading many Protestants there to seek its prohibition. In 1597, at the trial of alleged witch Margaret Aiken, the "great witch of Balwery," the court learned of a great "convention" of witches held on a hill in Atholl in the Scottish Highlands at Beltane, with an alleged 2,300 witches in attendance. In 1657, Jonet Anderson was alleged to have met with other witches at Newton-dein on Beltane, "where was the devil dressed in green clothes, with a black hat on his head."

The Puritans – that gloomy group that left for America in search of a religious freedom they did not wish the English or anyone else who disagreed with them to have – banned the Maypole in England commencing in 1644; this last seventeen years. The renowned diarist Samuel Pepys (1633-1703), joyful upon the restoration of the May in 1661, wrote of his wife and friends going with him to Woolwich to celebrate May by spending the night in the countryside and "gather[ing] May-dew" the next morning. The *British Apollo* reported in 1708 that it was now commonly held that the Maypole rite had commenced with "the ancient Britons, before converted to Christianity," who sought to thereby worship the Roman "goddess Flora." The Anglo-Irish satirist Jonathan Swift (1667-1745), author of *Gulliver's Travels* (1726) and "A Modest Proposal" (1729), celebrates May and comments on the Puritans' fanatical ban, in "A Maypole:"

Depriv'd of Root, and Branch, and Rind,
Yet Flow'rs I bear of ev'ry Kind;
:
My Head, with Giddiness, goes round;
And yet I firmly stand my Ground:
All over naked I am seen,
And painted like an Indian Queen.[43]

Swift describes the ring dance around the Maypole as a rite undertaken by many amorous peasants. While the Anglican priest does not condemn the pole or rite, "Yet hypocrite Fanaticks cry,/ I'm but an Idol rais'd on high." Speaking of the period when Puritans forbade the Maypole and reminiscent of the destruction of the Maypole at Merry Mount, the personified pole reports that after a number of years, she and her rites have been restored:

And once a Weaver in our Town,
A damn'd Cromwellian, knock'd me down.
I lay a Prisoner twenty Years;
And then the Jovial Cavaliers
To their old Posts restor'd all Three,
I mean the Church, the King, and Me.[44]

Swift, a devout Anglican, purposely closes his poem with a trinity, comprised of the Church, the King, and the Maypole; it would seem that he supports the continuing of this earth-centered tradition and views the coexistence of it with Anglicanism as unproblematic.

Stukeley, in *Itinerarium Curiosum* (1724), notes that a hill especially consecrated to the Maypole may be found near Horn Castle, in Lincolnshire, England. He believes that during Roman times, a herm stood here. He reports that in his day, young male students "keep up the festival of the Floralia." As symbolic of the gods who patron this "religious festival," they carry "a white willow wand, the bark peel'd off, ty'd round with cowslips, a thyrsus of the Bacchanals." In the evening, they dance around their bonfire.

In *Antiquitates Vulgares* (1725), Henry Bourne wrote of the May celebration:

> On the calends or first of May, commonly called May day, the juvenile part of both sexes were wont to rise a little after midnight and walk to some neighboring wood, accompanied with music and blowing of horns, where they break down branches from the trees and adorn themselves with nosegays and crowns of flowers...[T]he after part of the day is chiefly spent in dancing round...[the] May-pole; and being placed in a convenient part of the village, [the Maypole] stands there, as it were, consecrated to the Goddess of Flowers, without the least violation being offered to it in the whole circle of the year.[45]

In the late eighteenth century, Beltane continued to be celebrated in England as well as in the Scottish Highlands. Regarding Scotland, special bannock cakes were baked, with a coating of "custard of cream, eggs and butter...decorated with nine bosses [decorative nobs]" and offered to non-Christian, unnamed entities and to birds and beasts of prey – "Here's to thee, Fox, spare my lambs!" – so that they would not harm "flocks and herds." These rites were often held in the ruins of stone circles or in the vicinity of sacred stones. In England,

> ...not only the common people, but those of every rank in the vicinity of the place, joined in the tumultuous dissipations of the day...[The crowd] gave a free indulgence to...riotous and disorderly practice, dancing through the streets in wanton attitudes...[...] Even the priests, joining with the people, [went] in procession to some adjoining wood on the May morning.[46]

London's *Morning Post* reported on May 2, 1791: "Yesterday being the first of May...a number of persons went into the fields and bathed their faces with the dew on the grass, under the idea that it would render them beautiful."

In seventeenth- and eighteenth-century Ireland, Scotland, and elsewhere, May Eve or Beltane continued to be celebrated with bonfires. At this time, it continued to be thought that Beltane honored the ancient sun god Belenus; Donald McQueen noted in the *Gentleman's Magazine*, February 1795: "The Irish have ever been worshippers of fire and of Ba'al [i.e., Belenus], the god of light], and are so to this day. This is owing to the Roman Catholics, who have artfully yielded to the superstitions of the natives, in order to gain and keep up an establishment, grafting Christianity upon pagan rites."

Many people participated in kindling bonfires in spite of their being prohibited by ecclesiastical ordinances. It was reported that on May Eve, "fire is at this day kindled in the milking yard, the men, women, and children" leap over it. In the mid-1790s, the beverage syllabub became extremely popular with May revelers; a concoction of cream, sugar, and white wine or cider, it was served with cakes. In an intriguing rite of eighteenth-century Scotland, special foods including oatcakes, cakes in the form of breasts with nipples, custards, whiskey, and beer were offered to what appears to have been a manifestation of the Earth-Goddess. One participant who received an oatcake blackened with charcoal was said to be symbolically sacrificed to the earth. As offerings were made, celebrants recited, "This I give to thee, preserve thou my horses. This I give to thee, preserve thou my sheep."

During the French Revolution, the rites of May took on a revolutionary aspect. The fête now stressed the joy in being liberated from oppression; Maypoles were often referred to as "liberty trees" (*arbres de la liberté*); and the signature red beret-like cap of the Goddess of Liberty began to appear as a crowning object of Maypoles somewhat like the traditional star on the Christmas tree. Moreover, while tools of agricultural laborers had previously served as ornaments on Maypoles to call beloved ancestors to the rites, these tools as ornaments now accentuated the revolutionary leanings of these laborers. Somewhat similarly, in August 1765, an elm tree in Boston had been ornamented with images of English oppressors, whom Revolutionaries had proceeded to mock, suggesting another kind of liberty tree. To a certain extent, the famed seventeenth-century Maypole of Merry Mount, Massachusetts also signifies defiance of oppressive authority. The French Revolutionary Abbé Henri Grégoire (1750-1831), in *Essai historique et patriotique sur les arbres de la liberté* (1794), stresses the connection of trees, revolutionary fervor, and pagan traditions. He reminds his audience of trees and other plants dedicated to divinities: the oak to Ceres; the vine to Bacchus; the poplar to Hercules. Grégoire credits American Revolutionaries with promoting the radical dimension of the Maypole celebration: "[O]n the banks of the Delaware...maypoles became the citizens' rallying signal in every community."

With the arrival of the nineteenth century, the battle of Summer, typically played by a "Green Man" wearing branches and leaves, and Qinter, typically played by a man dressed in women's attire, with the latter's defeat, continued to be celebrated in many regions of Europe. In the British Isles, Beltane fires continued to be lit so that cattle could be driven through them to promote fertility. In Ireland, many continued to believe that fairies held revels on May Eve at the Grey Rock south of Mallow in County Cork, led by Cleena (or, Cliodhna) the Fairy Queen. In 1802, John Audley wrote in *A Companion to the Almanack*: "Some derive May from Maia, the mother of Mercury, to whom they offered sacrifices on the first day of [the month];" and in 1812, John Brady wrote in *Clavis Calendaria* that the popular folk figures of his day, "The May Lady, Maulkin, Jack in the Green, and...all...are merely variations in the mode of representing the goddess Flora." A few years later, Washington Irving (1783-1859) wrote, "I shall never forget the delight I felt on first seeing a Maypole. It was on the banks of the [River] Dee [near the city of] Chester."

In the rites, chimney sweeps and milkmaids played fiddles and danced. In

Cambridge, children and others carried around a figure called the May Lady or the Maulkin, begging money for her, "Pray remember the poor Lady May." At some point, she was placed on a table and offered wine. Offerings in Cambridge in 1802 to the "May Lady," which also included meats, give evidence that this was a revered figure and not simply a doll. Male youths participating in this festival also carried "Maygods," the "god" being a "white willow wand, the bark peeled off, and tied round with cowslips." In Perthshire, locals continued to perform a "totally un-christianized" rite at the well at Tullybelton, including circling around the well three times. Ceremonial cross-dressing or mixed gender attire continued to be popular in the rites of May. Some London chimney sweeps dressed in feminine attire assumed a key role in the May festivities. In Hertfordshire male couples comprised of the the cross-dressing "Mad Moll and her husband" took part in the rites; an observer remarked, "The men-women looked and footed [i.e., danced] so much like real women, that I stood in great doubt as to which sex they belonged to." In 1844, a London cross-dresser or transgender woman named Marmselle Molliowski, "attired in a remarkably short gauze petticoat, beneath which were displayed a pair of legs that had been brought to a most extraordinary state of muscular development," performed a festive dance. In London, as young women sold flower garlands for the rites of May, they sang a popular song,

Rise up, maidens! Fy for shame!
For I've been four long miles from home:
I've been gathering my garlands gay:
Rise up, fair maids, and take in your May.[47]

And at the culmination of the rites, participants sang:
We have been rambling all this night,
And almost all this day;
And now returned back again,
We have brought you a branch of May.
:
The life of man is but a span,
It flourishes like a flower;
We are here today and gone tomorrow
And we are dead in an hour . . .[48]

In nineteenth-century Germany, many continued to believe that Holda and her witch devotees danced on the Brocken in the Harz Mountains. In the early twentieth century, some Germans founded a Walpurgis Society and held annual celebrations for a number of years; as Jennifer M. Russ reports in *German Festivals and Customs*, "770 people attended the event in 1903. In 1911 a splendid festival was held, involving ...dancing [and] a dinner consisting of such dishes as 'cave bear ham in red magic sauce'...After the meal there were fireworks at midnight and the communal singing of the famous song 'May has come' (*Der Mai ist gekommen*)." In County Kerry, Ireland, May bonfires continued into at least the 1920s.

Other goddesses and similar female beings were celebrated later in May, including: the continental Germanic goddess Hertha (/Nerthus), the "goddess of peace and festivity" (on or near May 17);" the Russian *rusalki* (on May 23); and the Lithuanian goddess of flax, Petronele (May 31).

Ancient Romans honored their beloved dead by placing roses on their graves during the Rosalia (or, Rosaria, Rousalia). The early Christians kept the tradition but focused on honoring martyrs. Eventually, the fête evolved into the feast of Pentecost. In parts of Italy, where the holiday was called the Pasqua Rosa, "roses were thrown from the roofs of churches on the worshippers below." In Campania, Christians continued in the nineteenth century to honor the dead by decorating their graves with flowers. The late May celebration of the *rusalki* – the name of whom has been linked to the Rosalia – is noteworthy in regard to its paying homage to deep friendship among young women; Y. M. Sokolov, in *Russian Folklore* (1938), describes the rite as follows: "In the grove the girls kissed each other...gave one another the oath of friendship and adoption," and sang: "Let's adopt each other as sister, let's adopt each other;/ Let us love each other, sisters, let us love each other."

Midsummer nights, from June 21-24, are those "when the earth reveal[s] its secrets and ma[kes] ferns bloom to mark places where its treasures [are] buried." Midsummer rites typically include ceremonial bathing, feasting, singing, dancing, eroticism, and healing, divination, and magic.

Gina Iannella, in "Les Fêtes de la Saint-Jean à Naples," accurately points to at least one of the main pagan origins of this fête when she notes that "ancient Romans...purified themselves in the water of the Tiber River" at this time. This ritual, Sandra Billington, in *Midsummer: A Cultural Sub-Text from Chrétien de Troyes to Jean Michel*, explains, was called the *Tiberina Descencio*, occurred on June 24, in Rome and elsewhere in the Roman Empire, and was performed in connection with the goddess Fortuna. Others have suggested that European midsummer rites might have Celtic origins. Indeed, like most festivals, celebrations of the summer solstice undoubtedly possess multiple origins.

It's been suggested that in medieval Europe, midsummer may have honored the goddess Diana in certain places and that in this connection she came to be linked to the legendary Lady of the Lake, Viviane (or, Niniane), loved by Merlin.

A chain of correspondences links the Roman goddess Fortuna and midsummer song-dances called *caroles* to sacred stones. Wace (*c*. 1100- d. after 1174), the Anglo-Norman author of the *Roman de Brut* (1155), speaks of *caroles* as megalithic stone circles constructed by giants dwelling in Ireland. From Geoffrey of Monmouth (c. 1100-1154), in the *Historia Regum Britanniae* (*History of the Kings of Britain*, *c*. 1135), and Giraldus Cambrensis (Gerald of Wales, *c*. 1146-1223), we learn that these stones were thought to have been carried to Ireland, to "the plains of Kildare, near Naas," from Africa by the giants, who combined great physical strength with "artificial contrivances." The "Giants' Circle (or Ring, or Dance, the *Querolle aus Jaienz*)" was later transported by the wizard Merlin from Ireland to England's to Salisbury Plain during the (fifth century CE?) reign of an early British ruler, Aurelius Ambrosius. The stone circle, which came to be known as

Stonehenge, was meant to commemorate the massacre of three hundred noblemen by Hengest and the memory of Uther Pendragon. This massacre occurred during "the last week of June," as Philippe Walter points out in *La Mémoire du Temps*, "that's to say, precisely at the time of the summer solstice." Walter suggests that "ritual dances," such as in memory of the fallen heroes and at seasonal junctures, may have been performed "around the cultic stones on the occasions of the summer and winter solstices," and that this association of stone circles and round song-dances may have given rise to the use of *carole* to describe both. Walter observes that very old songs speak of "always go[ing] on the Eve of St. John/ To dance at the Roque Balan." The "Roque Balan," which appears to refer to Stonehenge, probably does not refer to the tragic knights Balan and Balin but rather to the Celtic solar deity Belenus, whose main feast, Beltane, was, as Peter Berresford Ellis notes, "claimed for Christianity and merged with the [midsummer] feast day of St. John the Baptist." Walter suggests that the ritual dances at Stonehenge and elsewhere at seasonal junctures, especially in association with the goal of honoring fallen heroes, may have not only been performed in honor of the god Belenus but also in honor of the ancestral dead. He further suggests that dances at such sites may have been meant to evoke Otherworlds including the land of the dead and Tír na nÓg, the Land of Youth. Associations with the dead and Otherworlds suggest that such dances may have been performed at such sites not only on the solstices and at Beltane but also at Samhain.

Water, as mentioned above, and fire comprise the two primary elements that play significant roles in the rites of midsummer. In ancient Rome, it involved purification of the body in the Tiber, while in medieval Germany and continuing into the nineteenth century, "the women of Cologne were wont at sunset on the eve of St. John to wash their arms and feet in the Rhine, thinking that thus they washed off all the potential ills of the year to come. This custom still survives in the Walloon country."

In Russia, the very name of the midsummer festival is Kupalo, from *kupati*, "to bathe." The Russian holiday, like the Roman and the German, focuses on "the traditional custom of ceremonial ablution, [with] bathing [being viewed] as a manifestation of 'lustrational' (purificatory) magic." Thus, it is hardly surprising that as Christianization advanced, the midsummer festival was conflated with commemoration of St. John the Baptist. In Naples, in the fifteenth and sixteenth centuries, on the Eve of St. John the Baptist, as documented (for the early sixteenth) by Benedetto Di Falco in *Descrittione dei luoghi antichi di Napoli* (*c*. 1549), participants gathered at the Church of San Giovanni à Mare (St. John at the Sea) and then processed to the sea, where they partook of ceremonial bathing synonymous with that undertaken in May. Ceremonial, nude, mixed class and gender bathing was thought to purify both body and soul. As in the May rites, singing, dancing (possibly nude circle dances at the seashore) and lovemaking occurred. Unfortunately, after being banned repeatedly, ceremonial bathing at midsummer all but vanished in Naples by 1734.

As for fire, bonfires were ritually lit at midsummer in England, Scotland, France, Italy, Russia, Estonia, and in many other places in Europe during the Middle Ages, the Renaissance, and into the nineteenth century. According to Muchembled, "[t]he bonfires…chased off demons and purified agricultural space for crops and women's wombs alike." Monaghan adds, "animals were herded around these fires, so the sacrificial smoke could bless them for the year." One of the rites included a nocturnal dance around the fire, with certain dancers jumping over the fire to test their strength and courage.

In Swabia, in Bavaria, the midsummer fire, rather than being called *Johannisfeuer*, "St. John's Fire," kept its pagan name, *Himmelsfeuer*, "Celestial Fire," through the nineteenth century. In seventeenth-century England, the bonfires came to be linked to the dances of witches and fairies, with Midsummer Eve coming to be called Witches' night. The rites also included fiery wheels being rolled down hills and mountains. In sixteenth-century France, these wheels were known as *les roues de fortune*, the wheels of the goddess Fortuna. In Russia and the Ukraine, the god Kupalo was likewise represented by a fiery wheel which was "rolled down a hill as a symbol of the declining life-giving powers of the sun after the solstice." This fête, Muchembled adds, "was probably aimed at galvanizing all available energy for the coming harvest." In regard to celestial bodies it was, of course, the sun that was most honored at the summer solstice. In both Latvia and Lithuania, the sun is traditionally thought to dance at midsummer; in the latter country, she – the sun-goddess Saulë – is envisioned as wearing silver shoes and a garland of "red fern blossoms."

Plants also played a key role in midsummer rites; as Muchembled relates, "Thus the night was also favorable to gathering magical plants." In the tenth century, Atto of Vercelli (d. 961) wrote of a pagano-Christian rite held on the Eve of St. John the Baptist during which celebrants 'baptized' sacred trees and grass, referring to these flora as godparents, "co-parents," or comrades, indicating a veneration of plants and a belief in a bond of kinship between plants and humans. In the late fourteenth century, Parisians "made up wreaths of herbs to break spells cast on the possessed. Many illnesses, epilepsy, for example, were thought to be curable at this particular time." During the High Middle Ages, in the British Isles and elsewhere, it was traditional to collect collecting fern-seed, which was sacred to the Fairy Queen, for its magical properties on Midsummer Eve. Shakespeare wrote of collecting fern-seed in *The First Part of Henry IV*: "We have the receipt of fern-seed; we walk invisible." In early twentieth-century Russia, many persons continued to gather special herbs on Midsummer Eve.

In the traditional culture of Brittany, we find a rite combining ceremonial fire and plants, as described by Constance Gordon Cumming in the nineteenth century:

> Thus, on Midsummer's-eve, all the lads and lasses in Brittany assemble at divers

groups of old weather-beaten stones. The lads wear green corn, the girls a bunch of flax, with blue blossoms. They lay their corn and flax on the great grey stones, and dance round them till sunset. Then, according as they find their flowers fresh or withered, they read the fate of their love; and return home, each lad leading his lass by one finger. As the darkness closes in, bonfires are lighted on every hill-top, lighting up all the laud with their red glow, and the young people dance wildly round them, hurrying from one bonfire to the next; for all manner of luck in love and life attends those who have danced round nine fires before midnight.[49]

Animals, especially snakes, played an important part in midsummer celebrations; as Robert Grant Haliburton noted in the mid-nineteenth century: "In Cornwall it is the opinion of the vulgar that 'it is usual for snakes to meet in companies' on Midsummer Eve; when, by joining their heads together, by their hissing they form bubbles which harden into the magic 'snake stone,' the sacred amulet of northern nations."

Where divinities are concerned, Sandra Billington, in *Midsummer: A Cultural Sub-Text from Chrétien de Troyes to Jean Michel*, explains that the summer solstice was called the *Tiberina Descencio* in Rome and elsewhere in the Roman Empire and was performed in honor of the goddess Fortuna.

Fortuna, the Roman manifestation of the Greek goddess Tyche, is a goddess of luck, chance, and wealth. In medieval art, she is occasionally depicted as possessing numerous sets of arms and hands; in one illustration, three sets, in another, six. In the *Decahedron* (1322), Giovanni Boccaccio (1313-1375) speaks of her as having "one hundred hands and as many arms, to give, and promote men to acquire, worldly goods, and to pull to the depths and elevate to the heights the men of this world." Noteworthy is Jurgis Baltrušaitis's observation, in *Le Moyen Age fantastique: Antiquités et exotismes dans l'art gothique* (1981), that this multi-armed depiction of the Goddess may reflect Asian spiritual influence, which would signify a novel contribution to pagan iconography. He notes that such European figures "conserve the look and even the rhythm of the dances of Buddhist and Brahmanic [Hindu] deities;" and he points to the Venetian traveler Marco Polo's (1254?-1324?) description of images of Buddhist deities of Japan, who possess numerous faces and hands; some "have four [hands], others have twenty, and still others have as many as a hundred. Those who have the most hands are considered the most powerful." Marco Polo's portrait resonates with that of the Christian theologian Thomas of Cantimpré (1201/1204-1263/1272/1280), who, in his *Opus de natura rerum* (1290-1315), refers to multi-armed Hindu deities who distribute karmic gifts.

In terms of guiding human affairs, Fortuna is also associated with divination, two of her best-known oracles being at Praeneste and Antium. In part, her rites on 24 June spoke to her governance of change and mutability.

One of her attributes is a rudder, which symbolizes her guidance of human affairs as well as her association with water. Her

Greek name further links her to water, as Tyche numbers among the Oceanides, the nymphs of the ocean. She is also a patron of women seeking relationships and of married women who desired to remain attractive to their husbands. Ovid, in the *Fasti*, speaks of Fortuna's association with water and more specifically, with bathing. Even more specifically, the ceremonial bathing associated with Fortuna is linked to beauty, courtesans bathing in men's baths, attracting a mate, and the goddess Venus. Ovid chants of the fête of 24 June: "Go, celebrate with joy the goddess Fors [i.e. Fortuna].../...Garland yourselves, boats, and carry parties of the young./ And let wine be drunk aplenty mid-stream."

Billington explains that early Christians, once their faith triumphed, became extremely hostile toward reverence of the goddess Fortuna. They looked upon her connection with chance, change, and mutability as undermining the new religion, as threatening its still uncertain stability. Indeed, argues Billington, Fortuna became a "greater danger than any other" deity or belief of "pagan religion, and the tracts of Lactantius [(250-c. 317 CE)] and Augustine [(354-430 CE)] aimed to extirpate her." In particular, in "Augustine's *Retractiones*, composed at the end of his life, he denied that he had referred to 'any goddess, but rather to the fortuitous outcome of events.'" Her extirpation was carried out in numerous ways: her "shrines and images were destroyed, worship banned, [and] sacrificed punished by death." The poet Palladius (fourth century CE), bewailing the turning of one of her temples into a tavern, remarked that Fortuna, having once been a maker and breaker of fortunes, was now reduced to a "barmaid." However, as Billington observes, in medieval Europe, despite Christian hostility toward the Goddess, summer solstice celebrations continued to be associated with Fortuna. Boniface was allegedly so infuriated by the persistence of a cult of Fortuna in eighth-century Germany that destroyed her image and attempted to destroy a shrine or temple to her; he was, however, at least for a time, "prevented by the fury of the heathen[s]" from accomplishing the latter.

Fiery wheels, mentioned above, signified Fortuna's solar Wheel of Fortune, and perhaps also the seasonal cycle or "wheel of the year." Fortune's Wheels also "hung in some medieval French churches. It is also possible that rose windows in churches were designed as solar wheels" signifying Fortuna. Fortuna's Wheel was also mirrored by the round *caroles*, or song-dances, mentioned above in association with sacred stones.

Although eventually Christianized as St. John and then hybridized or somewhat re-paganized as the folkloric "Ivan Kupalo," it appears that into the seventeenth century, a pagan deity or deities were honored at midsummer at some Russian sites. It is possible that the festival originally paid homage to a single Goddess of earth and/or agriculture, at least one of whose hypostases was called Kupala, "the Bather." Or, alternatively, it is possible that several deities were honored. It is evident that over time, several deities, who eventually came to be conflated, were honored. These may have included a female Kupala and a male Kupalo as well as the goddess Morena,

Kostrob (oddly, a god primarily of winter), and the god Yarilo. Eventually, goddess or deities morphed into a deity of love, eroticism, fertility, sacrifice, and the harvest, named Kupala/o, who was Catholicized as St. John and was described, in the seventeenth-century *Gustyn Chronicle*, as corresponding to Demeter/Ceres. In Logroño, Spain, the Feast of St. John the Baptist is also thought to have originated in a festival to Demeter/Ceres. In Estonia, the Earth-Goddess Ma-Emma was honored: "Fires were lit in celebration of her fruitfulness; animals were herded around these fires, so the sacrificial smoke could bless them for the year."

It is noteworthy that by the late sixteenth century, midsummer rites were (once more or still? –it's not clear) being attributed to an ancient goddess or goddesses. I find no reason to insist that this attribution was not occasionally shared with, or perhaps even offered by, persons, including rurals and urbanites alike (as, for example, the late fourteenth-century Parisians mentioned above), who continued to celebrate these rites – as the spirit of my high school drama teacher June Smith – who, incidentally, was teacher to actors Randy and Dennis Quaid and New Age spokesperson Marianne Williamson– reminds me, *"Remember the groundlings!"*

In *De Miraculis Occultis Naturae* (published *c.* 1600), Levinus Lemnius (1505-1568) suggested that the midsummer rites might have originated in part from fires lit in ancient Rome at this time of the year for the goddess Cybele. In the mid-seventeenth century, Aubrey reported of rites in England, "they make fires in the fields in the ways…to bless the apples…this custom is derived from the Gentiles, who did it in remembrance of Ceres…and the people might think, that by this honor done to the goddess of husbandry, that their corn…might prosper the better."

In 1775, the Scottish minister Lachlan Shaw rather surprisingly reported that "in the middle of June, farmers go round their corn with burning torches, in memory of the Cerealia," the rites of Demeter/Ceres. In many Christianized milieus, the festival became increasingly carnivalized; exemplary of this carnivalization is the assumption of the Goddess' role by a comic cross-dressing figure in the eighteenth century. "Junius" wore a long wig, a crown of flowers, and a petticoat stitched with coins and carried a box filled with coins, throwing them at the crowd during played a charivari parade.

As was typical of such feasts, special attire was worn; in Russia, a "crowd of both sexes" wove head "garlands for themselves from edible herbs, or roots, and gird[ed] themselves with grasses." Special foods were prepared and consumed: in Russia and the Ukraine, for example, an "integral part of the festivities was a supper of eggs, *varenyky*, and liquor;" in Germany, fried elderberry blossoms and Black Forest Cherry cake were served in later times.

Chant, music, and dance, particularly around the fire, as mentioned above, were also key elements in the rites. Again in Russia, as Elizabeth Warner and Evgenii Kustovskii explain in *Russian Traditional Folksong* "wild, abandoned dancing" from evening until dawn around the bonfire was accompanied by "the music of tambourines, pipes and stringed instruments" and "clapping in time to the music and stamping of feet." Participants sang *vesnyanki*, chants to welcome the summer, to "invok[e] the Bather," and to catalyze eroticism and fertility; as Warner and Kustovskii relate, "The magico-functional nature of *vesnyanki* is attested by the fact that the peasants did not even regard them as songs."

Like so many other seasonal rites, three of the chief pursuits undertaken at the midsummer rites were healing, divination, and magic. As M. Mushynka relates of the Ukrainian festival of Kupalo, "herbs could protect one from the evil forces of nature and even cure illnesses in humans and animals. ...The sick would roll naked in the dewy meadows in the belief that this action would help them get well, and farmers would run their cattle through...meadows in the belief that this...would prevent disease."

In Christianized, eighteenth-century Estonia, many persons practiced healing at a pagano-Christian manifestation of the holiday. They gathered at nine o'clock in the evening in the countryside to build a fire near a sacred stone. The ritual was led by three women, "one of whom [was] the most venerable and something like their priest," who sat around the fire. For Estonians, this midsummer festival appears to have focused on healing. A special wax was prepared by two priestesses, while the chief priestess conducted offerings and sacrifices. Then ill persons would approach the priestesses, receive ale, which they would offer to the fire and stone three times, and then receive waxed bandages, which they placed, or which would be placed, on their bodies at or near the source of suffering. All would join in a prayer which may have included invocations of pagan deities and which included the prayer, "O help us, St. John!" The waxed bandages were then removed from the afflicted, handed to the chief priestess, and burned in the fire. Participants believed that healing would ensue. The following year, those who were healed brought thank-offerings to the ritual, typically a candle or a human figure made of wax.

Philippe Walter emphasizes the importance of divination and magic in French medieval midsummer celebrations. Divinations incorporated fern-seed (which also grants invisibility), "the breaking of hen-eggs," and other items in order to "see what their fortune will be."

Aubrey recounts an event he witnessed one Midsummer Eve in seventeenth-century England:

> I...was walking in the pasture behind Montague House. It was twelve o'clock [midnight]. I saw about two or three and twenty young women, most of them well habited, on their knees very busy, as if they had been weeding. I could not presently learn what the matter was; at last a young man told me that they were looking for a coal under the root of a plantain, to put under their heads that night, and they should dream who would be their husbands: it was to be found that day, and hour.[50]

In Lithuania, Poland, and the Ukraine during the late nineteenth and early twentieth centuries, "Girls float[ed] wreaths on rivers to find out their prospects for marriage. The farther their wreaths float[ed] the sooner they [would] get married."

In regard to magical practice, what occurred in Russia and the Ukraine was typical of much of Europe: "On the morning of that day girls washed themselves with the dew that had fallen on Kupalo eve, which they collected in a bowl left outside overnight, and ran barefoot through the bedewed fields in the belief that doing so would accelerate their opportunity to get married."

In this light, ritual lovemaking also occurred; in Mushynka's words, "It was also the only time of the year when free love received popular sanction."

Likewise, some Romanians continued – and to this day, continue – to celebrate the Noppi de Sânziene. The term "Sânziene" refers to fairies or nymphs, to the goddess Ileana Sânziana (an avatar of Diana), and to Ileana as the Fairy Queen. This festival focuses, like other summer rites, on finding mates and on promoting a good harvest.

Young women search for yellow *sânziene* flowers (*Galium verum*, Lady's Bedstraw), here linked to Ileana Sânziana (as in Germanic tradition they are associated with Frigga and/or Freyja), from which they make braided garlands (*cusitzãs*) to wear on their heads as crowns. They also search for other plants like St. John's wort which are alleged to possess special potency at this time and which they use in amatory divination, one form of which consists of placing the flowers under one's pillow in order to dream of one's future spouse. They take ritual baths in streams or lakes to become more beautiful, more fertile, and healthier. They wash their hair in a rinse made from sea grass. A *gãleata* vessel is created to represent the young women's imminent transition from virgins to brides and ultimately to signify the marital bond of a couple.

Families place wreaths of *sânziene* flowers on their roofs. If the wind doesn't manage to blow them off during the night, then they can expect good fortune. Songs are sung to the Sun, a local hypostasis of Apollo, and to the Moon, Ileana Sânziana; and dances include dancers whirling burning torches around their heads. A feast emphasizing fruits is shared. The *sânziene* are said to punish those who do not take part in the festival.

The Harvest Cycle, and Honoring the Dead and Sacred Beings

Some festivals celebrating summer continued to be held in July in premodern Europe; as Filotas points out in *Pagan Survivals*, the *Homilia de sacrilegiis* of the eighth century CE suggests that the Neptunalia was celebrated by the Franks at this time. In paying homage to the element of water, the Christian "forfeited his faith and baptism." In the main, however, late July signaled the commencement of festivals of the harvest cycle. In Kievan Rus,' on or near July 20, sacrifices were made to the god Perûn so that he would not ruin the harvest with thunderstorms. In more recent times, Russians celebrated the first fruits of the harvest with a communal feast; dressed in white and scarlet, they processed through villages paying homage to the earth goddess in the form of a sheaf dressed as an older woman. French Revolutionaries deemed July the month of the "Feast of the

Gods of Rome."

August, September, and October brought many more harvest rites, with rituals including offerings and sacrifices, bonfires, feasting, divination, and dancing. Divinities and other beings to whom homage was paid at harvest time included Lugh, Tailtiu, Odin, Ciza, Perûn, Svantovit, Žemyna, Þemininkas, Perkûnas, Vaižgantas, Petronele, Fru Gaue, and the fairies. When and where sacred hybridity occurred, the Virgin Mary and Mary Magdalene were also honored as patrons of the harvest.

In her masterful 1962 study, *The Festival of Lughnasa: A Study of the Survival of the Celtic Festival of the Beginning of the Harvest*, Máire MacNeill – whom I admire intensely for her astute remark, "The country people, who preserved so much of old custom and myth, are witnesses whose evidence must be considered" – demonstrates that into the mid-twentieth century, many people in Ireland, England, Scotland, Wales, the Isle of Man, France, and elsewhere continued to celebrate Lughnasa) in ways that subtly acknowledged earth-centered origins and persistent influence. This festival celebrated the beginning of the harvest. Its elements included the first cutting of corn or first harvesting of another crop; the picking of bilberries (which MacNeill explains is the element that has persisted the longest); the making of a special bread or cake (often with bilberries), as well as, occasionally, preparation of a special meal including cabbage, bacon, and onions; offerings (nowadays primarily of butter); the sacrifice of a bull and its magical reconstitution (in older times, uncannily resonant with a rite alleged to occur in meetings of Italian witches); dancing; athletic contests; courtship, lovemaking, and an unusual custom of temporary marriage (said to have been held until 1770); and the crowning of representatives of a goddess and/or god. The god honored was Lugh, god of the sun, male beauty, arts and crafts, war, and weather (especially thunder and rain), compared by the Romans to Mercury. It's said that Lugh established the festival of Lughnasa in honor of his foster-mother, the goddess Tailtiu. She was well-known for having cleared a great forest when it was deemed necessary to do so in order to create fertile farmland, a labor that took her life. She also appears to have been an Earth-Goddess, who doubled as Lugh's mother and his spouse in different hypostases. As the latter, she and Lugh celebrated their marriage at Lughnasa; as the former, she mourned her son as autumnal sacrifice.

In the past, one of the most important Lughnasa celebrations was held at Tailte, in more recent times, Telltown. T. F. G. Dexter, in *The Pagan Origin of Fairs* (1930), relates: "The Fair of Tailte (now Telltown)…was held "around the grave" of Tailtiu, Lug's foster-mother, who died on 1st August. Tailte, said to have been named after Tailtiu, was especially celebrated for its athletic games, which are reputed to have originated in those played by Lug at his foster-mother's funeral." He notes, "Lug was the great Irish sun-god, and from Lug, the 1st August was named Lugnasad, generally translated 'the *nasad* or games of Lug.'" Although official records stated that the fair was last held there in 1169, local residents claimed to have celebrated it as late as 1806. There is no hard evidence that celebration of it lapsed over the centuries. Indeed, marriages recalling the "marriages of the gods" there were allegedly performed there until 1770.

In the late sixteenth century, Lithuanians of Žemaitija continued to honor the Earth Goddess Žemyna and her brother, spouse, or consort Žemòpatis, in the autumn; at this time, the deities were, in celebration of the harvest, offered bread and beer as well as sacrificed animals (with most of the meat being consumed by participants. Similar rites continued in England at the end of the sixteenth century. Paul Hentzner describes an English harvest rite he observed in the precincts of Windsor in 1598:

> As we were returning to our inn, we happened to meet some country people celebrating their Harvest Home; their last load of corn they crown with flowers, having besides an image richly dressed, by which perhaps they would signify Ceres, this they keep moving about, while men and women, men and maid servants, riding through the streets in the cart, shout as loud as they can till they arrive at the barn.[51]

As with the rites of May, harvest rites, as François Laroque points out in *Shakespeare's Festive World*, made possible encounters these liaisons between persons of different economic and social classes and walks of life, occasions when, for instance, scholars might encounter farmers. He notes that the "meal that followed the harvesting was...a communal one." This is confirmed by Thomas Tusser in *A Hundreth Good Points of Husbandrie* (1557), "where he encourages farmers to display good humor at harvest time and make all welcome at their table." The presence of different classes of agricultural workers at these rites cannot be overstressed, nor can that of the occasional scholarly traveler like Hentzner, as their presence indicates that encounters occurred between commoners performing traditional rites and more learned persons who recognized these rites as rooted in earth-centered traditions. I find it extremely doubtful that the latter would have practiced the non-intervention ethics of present-day anthropologists or the crew of *Star Trek*; rather, I believe that communication most likely occurred between the commoners and others observing or attending the rites, particularly if we bear in mind that physical intimacy between those of differing classes occurred. This would suggest that at least from the sixteenth century, some persons performing traditional rites may have acknowledged their undertaking of these rites as continuing or reviving ancient rites held in honor of Ceres, who, we should recall, was worshipped in Roman England, and perhaps other pagan divinities.

I think we must vigorously question the general tendency to assume that little or no interaction occurred between performers of traditional rites and learned persons, including antiquarians (roughly, proto-folklorists and proto-anthropologists), as evidence such as that just given – not to mention the process, at least at the outset undertaken by the Church, to appropriate earth-centered traditions in order to promote Christianity, until it came to the attention of Church authorities that many commoners and others were employing this process to carry out ancient rites – suggests otherwise. In this light, I think we must also question a tendency in present-day writing on the roots of NeoPaganism to suggest that it draws primarily upon "folklore," as if "folklore" in this context seems to signify drawing primarily upon scholarly interpretations of traditional (often described as extinct) rites rather than drawing upon a lively interactive process of communication between vernacular and learned communities extending across epochs and cultures.

Nineteen years after Hentzner's observation of Harvest Home, a traveler in England observed "the country people bringing home in a cart from the harvest field a figure made of corn, round which men and women were promiscuously singing, preceded by a piper and a drum." A bit later in the seventeenth century, John Aubrey reported of this festival:

> Cerealia: Home Harvests [the first being Lammas]...are observed [more or less] in most counties of England...When they bring home the last load of corn: it is done with great joy and merriment...This custom (no doubt) is handed down to us from the Romans, who after this manner, celebrated their Cerealia [*Sacra Cereris*] [i.e., from Ceres/Demeter] instituted by Triptolemus.[52]

Aubrey quotes Ovid's *Fasti*: "The men of old...sewed spelt, reaped spelt,/ And gave cut spelt as Ceres' first fruits;" "Appease the harvest mothers, Ceres and Tellus,/ With their spelt." Aubrey also notes that autumnal festivals often embraced horned and antlered beings, rooted in part, as is the masque, in the ancient Kalends, persisted in England and elsewhere in Europe in the seventeenth and eighteenth century, with some continuing to be held in the early twenty-first century. Bearing in mind that Aubrey was either not very concerned with, or knowledgeable of, Celtic or Germanic/Scandinavian origins, his belief that the goddess Diana continued to be honored in a subtle, indirect way in these rites, which include ritualistic display of deer antlers housed in churches, is noteworthy.

He was assuredly correct in acknowledging the honoring of Diana at this time of year. Although by the fifteenth century, the Church had fairly successfully appropriated the goddess's August 13-15 festival and had displaced her with the Virgin Mary (in Spain, for instance, with the Virgen del Pino), the feast devoted to the Assumption, Franco Mormando suggests that at least some women may have continued to celebrate Diana in August.

Had Aubrey been more interested in, or aware of, Celtic origins, he would undoubtedly have also recognized the veiled reverence of the horned god Cernunnos. Evidence regarding horns, noted below, points as well to a Scandinavian origin. Aubrey, asserting that the pagan traditions were appropriated by the Church and transferred to St. Luke [in itself, probably signifying a transference from St. Paul to St. Luke] and, apparently less commonly, to St. Margaret, writes of the Horn Fair in England:

Luke [is] the patron, or tutelary saint, of the horned beasts, and those that have to do with them. Wherefore, the keepers and foresters of the New Forest [proceed to a chapel to St. Luke at Stoke Verdon, in the parish of Broad Chalke, Wiltshire] every year [on October 18] at St. Lukestide to make their offerings...that they might be fortunate in their game, their deer, and their cattle.[53]

At some point, the Horn Fair came to include persons wearing horns and antlers and the sale of cakes baked in the shape of different horns. The most popular festival of horns is the Abbots Bromley Horn Dance (mentioned in the section on winter rites), held in early September since around 1893. At this time, according to A. L. Lloyd in *Folk Song in England* (1967), "the local parson put a check on the phallophoric displays" and "obscene horseplay," considerably taming the festival.

Harvest rites also continued to be celebrated in Lithuania and Lithuania Minor in the seventeenth century. Matthäus Prätorius (*Deliciae Prussicae*, 1684) describes an autumnal ritual taking place near Metirkvieèiai near a sacred oak and a sacred stone. A pole was set up, a goatskin was draped over it, and to it was tied a bouquet of herbs and corn. An indigenous priest chanted a praise-hymn and thanked the god, probably Perkûnas, for all he had provided. Then, reminiscent of the May celebration, participants would encircle and dance around the pole. The priest would then hand them tokens of herbs, following which he would remove the goatskin from the pole and, sitting on it, would tell them of the elder faith and its traditions. After he blessed them, they enjoyed a feast.

An intriguing ceremony, one resonating with rites undertaken in Scottish as well as African and African-diasporic and other indigenous traditions, was called "feeding the sickle" and was practiced among the Finns. At the end of harvest, farmers and their workers would take bread, cheese, and other foods to the field and place them before the last "stalks of oats left uncut." Hailing and thanking the grain stalks, the maser of the farm and the laborers would share the foods they had brought. They then gathered the sickles they had used and placed them around the stalks. Acknowledging the remaining stalks as the "sickles' share," toasting the sickles, and "feeding" the sickles as they had fed the stalks of grain. "You have labored the whole summer, may the food you have now eaten bring you strength," the master would say to the sickles. Then the sickles were wrapped in oat-straw and taken to the barn, where they would remain till the following summer.

Returning to Great Britain, in the eighteenth century, William Hutchinson (1732-1814), best known for his *History of the County of Cumberland* (1794), observed:

I have seen in some places an image appareled in great finery, crowned with flowers, a sheaf of corn placed under her arm, and a sickle in her hand, carried out of the village in the morning of the conclusive reaping day, with music and much clamour of the reapers, into the field, where it stands fixed on a pole all day, and when the reaping is done, is brought home in like manner. This they call the Harvest Queen, and it represents the Roman Ceres.[54]

Like Polydore Vergil and Paul Hentzner before them, Aubrey and Hutchinson recognized these rites as linking back to celebrations in honor of Ceres/Demeter. Similarly, Dr. E. D. Clarke (1769-1822) reported that in the first years of the nineteenth century, farm festivities in the vicinity of Cambridge included a "clown dressed in women's clothes, having his face painted, his head decorated with ears of corn, bearing about him other symbols of Ceres, carried in a wagon, with great pomp." When Clarke asked the farmworkers what they were celebrating, they replied that they were honoring the Harvest Queen; the festival was called the Hawkie. In Scotland, a figure of the Harvest Queen or goddess, as the Cailleach, or "Maiden," was toasted with whiskey by all the farm laborers, who repeated, "Here's to the one that has helped us with the harvest."

Anna Eliza Kempe Stothard Bray (1790-1883), in *Traditions, Legends, Superstitions, and Sketches of Devonshire* (1838), makes an intriguing remark regarding harvest rites in a letter of June 9, 1832: "That we still have some vestiges of that [festival] sacred to Godo, the British Ceres...whose rites were observed at the time of harvest, cannot, I think, be doubted." Godo is a now little-known goddess with historical, legendary, and sacred associations. Godo, or Godgifu ("gift of God," 1004-1055), was the daughter of King Ethelred II. Another woman named Godgifu (d. 1067) is better known to us as Lady Godiva. An historical figure, married to Lord Leofric (d. 1057), she is undoubtedly the most celebrated citizen of Coventry due to a legend concerning her that may have been at least partly true. On behalf of Coventry's citizens, she argued that the taxes he levied on them were far too high. He told her he would lower the taxes on one condition: that she ride naked through the streets of Coventry. She did so, covering her breasts and private parts with her long hair. Leofric was forced to reduce the taxes. Another legend links the name Godo with Lady Godda, the Fairy Queen, who was believed to have been responsible for the disappearance of "Wild Edric," a Saxon noble who fought against the Normans. In sacred terms, Godo is an alternate name of the Germanic goddess Freyja. Godo may also be related to Gode, a female counterpart to Odin/Woden who has been linked to Holda and Ciza. It would appear that the figure of Godo/Godgifu/Godiva/Goda/Gode was eventually woven into a goddess or goddess-like figure possessing these various attributes. The local Godo to which Bray refers may have been such a persona, as well as being envisioned as a goddess of fertility and crops, especially of barley, a river goddess, and a guardian of birds. I strongly believe that learned persons may well have shared such insights with persons performing these rites, and that we need to realize that this may have been a much livelier, more interactive process than we have been led to believe. Where Anna Bray is concerned, this is most assuredly the case, as she documents such interaction in her letters. For example, in describing harvest rites, she relates:

One evening [in or near 1831], about the end of harvest, I was riding out on my pony, attended by a servant who was born and bred a Devonian. We were passing near a field on the borders of Dartmoor, where the reapers were assembled....When I asked my servant what all that noise was about, he seemed surprised at the question, and said 'It [is] only the people making their games as they always [do], to the spirit of the harvest.'[55]

Bray, continuing to describe the harvest rite, tells of her servant and herself observing as the male farm laborers tied sheaves together and decorated it with flowers to create an image of the Goddess or female patron of the harvest, perhaps Godo. As the male laborers were performing this rite, women and children were carrying boughs and flowers, singing and dancing. The male participants took the figure to a "field on the side of a steep hill," with one man holding the figure in the center of a circle, and the others raising up their scythes to it and chanting, "Arnack, arnack, arnack, wehaven, wehaven, wehaven." Although this chant at first appears to be nonsense, on closer examination, we find that "nack" is a local term for a "kirn-baby," the female figure made of sheaves. From other related chants, we can fairly safely translate this one as "Our goddess/spirit of the harvest (x 3), we have completed our harvesting (x 3)." As this chant was repeated, a cask was passed around from which each participant drank. Bray then makes an intriguing statement concerning various groups of reapers in the surrounding area shouting the chant in order for it to be heard by others and for it to resound throughout the countryside as a collective, colossal invocation: "When the weather is fine, different parties of reapers, each stationed on some height, may be heard for miles around, shouting." The rite culminated with one of the men "offering...the finest ears of corn" to the Lady of the Harvest/Goddess; Bray writes: "The man so elevating the offering is...no other than the successor of the [pagan] priest, whose duty it was to offer up the first and best fruits of the harvest to the goddess...I cannot but conclude that we have [here a] rite derived from pagan antiquity." In late nineteenth-century England, farmers and rurals continued to celebrate Harvest Home and to sing:

Harvest-home! harvest-home!
We've ploughed, we've sowed,
We've reaped, we've mowed,
We've brought home every load.
Hip, hip, hip, harvest-home![56]

Halloween (or, Hallowe'en, All Hallows) draws primarily upon the Celtic festival of Samhain (or, Samhainn, Sambhuinn, Samhein, La Samon, Samuin, Shamhna). In 1889, Sophie Willock Bryant, in *Celtic Ireland*, wrote: "It is dangerous to be out on November Eve, because it is the one night in the year when the dead come out of their graves to dance with the fairies on the hills, and as it is their night, they do not like to be disturbed." On this night, the dead were invited to come out of the tombs and a feast was prepared for them. Beyond Celtic origins, the festival may have also drawn upon Roman, Germanic, and other roots. In the seventeenth century, Aubrey surmised that the festival might draw upon the Roman Feralia, which had been held in February, and that Christianization had caused the feast to be switched to late autumn, as the Eve of All Souls. The fact that in the Middle Ages, the goddess Holda was "propitiated with a food offering [of or including meat] on the night before All-Soul's Day, Hallowe'en" suggests that the festival may have also drawn upon Germanic roots. François Laroque relates in *Shakespeare's Festive World* that this was the "time when the souls of the dead returned to haunt the living. Throughout the countryside and villages of Elizabethan England, games were organized on Hallowe'en." He notes the sacred hybridity of the celebration: "On this occasion, pagan beliefs and popular games intermingled with the atmosphere of the religious festival of All Saints' Day, which the Church had judiciously allocated to the very same date as the pagan *Todtenfest* (Festival of the Dead)." Muchembled reports similar rites in Renaissance France; these came to be known as the Fêtes des Morts. In Slavic regions, as in Poland and Belarus, feasts for the ancestors, or *dziady* ("grandfathers"), were held. Lithuanians, likewise, celebrated Vëlinës (also, Ilges) in honor of the dead.

Although the festival primarily honored the dead, Holda was not alone among divinities also honored at this time. Others appear to have included Diana, Pomona, Veliona (Lithuanian goddess of the dead and possibly also of rivers and the afterlife), Perkûnas, Vaižgantas (Lithuanian god of flax), Herodias, Nicneven, Mourie, Shony, and Puck. Lowry Charles Wimberly, in *Folklore in the English and Scottish Ballads* (1928), adds: "Tam Lin's fairy friends ride on Hallowe'en. ...[T]hey are said to ride 'throw all the world wide'..." [Moreover,] escape from fairyland was only possible when the old and new year met [i.e., at Samhain]." In Ireland, bonfires and hearth fires were sometimes lit as offerings to the fairies on this night.

Of all the earth-centered practices that persisted and that also reflect innovation in regard to Halloween, divination is foremost. In *Shakespeare's Festive World*, François Laroque notes: "Throughout the countryside and villages of Elizabethan England, games were organized on Hallowe'en...to exploit the powers of divination proverbially associated with this night." Muchembled reports similar divinatory rites in Renaissance France. The focus on divination continued into the seventeenth and eighteenth centuries. For the most part, ordinary persons rather than seers carried out these divinations using apples, nuts – by cracking them via casting them into a fire – and other items. In *The Vicar of Wakefield* (1766), the Anglo-Irish novelist, essayist, poet, and dramatist Oliver Goldsmith (1730?-1774) writes of rustics "religiously crack[ing] nuts on All-hallow Eve." Indeed, the holiday was also called "Nutcrack Night." In the nineteenth century, some divinations commenced with saying "the *pater noster* backwards." This was referred to as reciting it "*widderschynnes*" (or, "widdershins"), counterclockwise. Most divinatory consultations focused on love and marriage. Three of the most common were scrying (among Irish, while eating an apple); "wash[ing] a garment in a running brook, then hang[ing] it on a thorn bush, and wait[ing] to see the apparition of the lover, who will come to turn it;" and a third known as "the building of the house": "Twelve [bundles representing] couples are taken, each being made of two holly twigs tied together with a hempen thread; these are all named and stuck round in a circle in the clay. A live coal is then placed in the centre, and whichever couple catches fire first will assuredly be married. Then the future husband is invoked…to appear and quench the flame."

Magic was also practiced on Samhain/Halloween, often focusing on death and the dead. In Scotland, one such rite involved taking articles of clothing and a three-legged stool to a trivium (three roads meeting) and taking one's seat on the stool as midnight neared. When the clock struck twelve, one could hear the names of those who would die the following year in one's village. If, however, one offered a garment to the spirit(s) gathering at the trivium, the life of a person destined to die might be spared, one garment for one life.

Speaking of death and the dead, necromancy was among the most serious, and for some, among the most sinister, practices undertaken at this time: "Also on November Eve, by certain incantations, the dead can be made to appear and answer questions; but for this purpose blood must be sprinkled on the dead body when it rises; for it is said that the spirits love blood."

Alleged witches were said to gather for great celebrations at Samhain/Halloween. For example, in 1595, the Scottish male witch Thomas Leyis, whose father may have also been a witch, was said to have led a host of witches in celebrating the holiday at the "Mercatt and Fische Croce of Aberdeen."

This location refers to two market crosses, signaling the sites open-air markets. The first probably refers to the "Meillmercatt" or Meat-Market Cross, where meats were sold, while the second refers to the "Fische" or Fish Cross, where "fisher folk displayed their wares." However, these sites not only served as marketplaces but also as hubs for royal processions, proclamations, and punishments. Where the punishments concerned, exemplary is the case of a man and woman "convicted of adultery" in 1583, who "were sentenced to be bound and exposed at the market cross for three hours, thereafter to be burned with a hot iron on the cheeks and banished from the town." When great celebrations occurred, wine flowed from the Meillmercatt fountain. That is to say, these were decidedly public, urban sites. Thus, when Thomas Leyis and the crowd that followed him to these sites to celebrate Samhain at midnight in 1595, they must have realized that, on the one hand, these were perfect sites to celebrate and, on the other, that in choosing these sites, they risked exposing themselves to charges of witchcraft. It would seem conceivable, therefore, that among the sentiments they expressed that night as they played music, danced, and allegedly transformed into animals, may have been a certain sense of defiance.

Of course, we cannot leave the subject of Halloween without mentioning games and pranks. In the nineteenth century, Scots and others joined in apple bobbing, which was linked to apple divination:

> ...the mystic apple comes into play – the apple that so often appears in Celtic fairy lore. These swim in water, and each person in turn must catch one in his mouth. The apple when caught must be carefully peeled, and the long strip of peel passed thrice, sunwise, round the head, and thrown over the shoulder, when it will fall in the form of the true love's initial-letter.[57]

By the late nineteenth century – and probably much earlier – it had become customary to pull such silly pranks as taking gates off their hinges and such mean-spirited ones as trampling gardens. Indeed, Irish persons spoke too soon when they told D. H. Moutray Read near 1915 that they were pleased to see that the custom of playing pranks was dying out.

November and early December return us to the theme of the harvest, with the final harvest festivals of the year being held at this time. Ancient Romans held the Vinalia, in honor of Bacchus and celebrating the vintage. Ancient Celts sacrificed pigs at this time; Irish Christians appropriated the sacrifice, crediting St. Patrick with its institution.

For Germanic peoples, this was the Blotmonath, the "month of blood" during which animals were ritually slaughtered. Actions taken by the Christian zealot King Olaf Tryggvason in 996 CE indicate that Norwegians made sacrifices to Thor and Odin at this time; Tryggvason insisted – on pain of death – that they make them instead to St. Martin. In nineteenth-century Germany, however, little cakes baked in the shapes of horns and horseshoes at this time may have preserved a form of the sacrifice to Odin. In Lithuania, St. Martin's feast usurped the feast of the god of flax, Vaižgantas.

Martinmas, celebrated in many parts of Europe during the Middle Ages and after On November 11th, is named after St. Martin of Tours (*c.* 316-397 CE), a Hungarian military officer who became a monk, bishop and viciously anti-pagan missionary. St. Martin's biography connects only minimally to the feast in his honor: he was buried on that date, and he was once compassionate to a beggar (the feast is relatively democratic in promoting mixing of persons of different economic classes. Otherwise, the feast is almost wholly dependent upon its pagan precursors. As with other such holidays, one can see bricolage at work here. Martin and his feast constitute a very interesting choice to replace Odin, Thor, and other deities who had been honored and practices that had been performed at this time, particularly because of his fanaticism in converting the rural pagans of Gaul (here, present-day France). Until Martin's missionizing, "Christianity had been largely confined to the urban centres of population... : to Martin are attributed the destruction of heathen temples and sacred trees." Clearly, it was not some manifestation of respectful hybridity that guided Church authorities to claim this holiday for Martin. As Martin Walsh observes in *Medieval Folklore*, "It is ironic that the fourth-century ascetic and destroyer of pagan cult sites should become the patron of such a secular [i.e., pagan-inspired] festivity."

Laroque notes that on "the continent, particularly in France, this was the great festival of the new vintage of wine, celebrated a few short weeks after the grape-harvest; and meanwhile, in England, the beer was flowing freely." In the Renaissance, the festival included, as receipts of payment for products as services from the early sixteenth century demonstrate, sharing bread, wine, and ale; decorations of rose garlands; and performances by professional singers. "Martinmas beef" provided by slaughtered cattle was also shared by participants in some places. Some participants in Western Europe undoubtedly recalled that the holiday had Celtic, Roman, and Germanic roots, including honoring of Bacchus/Dionysus. However, during the Renaissance, Robin Hood, who was more typically associated with the rites of May, also came to be linked to Martinmas. Laroque believes that this association is rooted in the depiction of Robin Hood as patron of banquets, as well as in the fact that Martinmas included the recounting of tales of spirits and legendary heroes. It is possible that Robin Hood's association with Martinmas also originated in an expansion of the festival's association with the forest and its inhabitants and to masquerading, as demonstrated in the mid-fifteenth century by the wearing by certain Martinmas celebrants of wolf skins.

In early December, Lithuanians celebrated Samborios, the "Grain Feast." At this time, farmers and their families took nine handfuls each of three grains, typically rye, barley, and a third, and baked bread with them, after which they offered the bread and beer, together with sacrifices of a cock and hen, to the earth-goddess Žemyna. Upon the conversion of Lithuania, primarily in the late fourteenth century, this rite was appropriated by Christians. However, by the eighteenth century, the process of spiritual hybridization had led to the following prayer:

O fruit-bearing Earth,
let our rye and barley and all our grain bear fruit.
O God, and thou, O Earth,
we offer thee this cock and hen;
receive them as freely offered gifts.[58]

Joy in the Midst of Winter

In the mid-seventeenth century, the Puritan cleric Thomas Warmstry (1610-1665), ruminating on Christmas and New Year's celebrations, pondered

[w]hether this Feast had not its rise and growth from Christians' conformity to the mad Feasts of Saturnalia, kept in December to Saturne the Father of the Gods, in which there was a sheafe offered to Ceres, Goddesse of Corn; a hymne to her praise ...and whether those Christians, by name, to cloake it, did not afterwards call it Yule, and Christmas, as though it were for Christ's honour; and whether it be not yet by some, more antient than truly or knowingly religious, called Yule; and the mad Playes, wherewith it is celebrated like those Saturnalia Yule Games? and whether, from the offering of that sheafe to Ceres, from that song in her praise, from those gifts the heathens gave their friends in

the Calends of January, ominis gratia, did not arise or spring our Blazes, Christmas Kariles, and New Yeare's Gifts?"[59]

Medieval and later celebrations of the winter solstice and Christmas, as well as those celebrating New Year's, most assuredly drew upon Roman, Germanic, and other roots. Romans celebrated several winter holidays that contributed to later feasts: these included a feast for ancestors, called a "table of souls;" a feast in honor of the goddess Fortuna; the Saturnalia, in honor of Saturn as god of the Golden Age; the Brumalia in honor of Bacchus, of which we've spoken above; and the *Natalis Invicti*, the Nativity of the Invincible Sun, in honor of the gods Sol Invictus and Mithra(s).

Many winter celebrations were, not surprisingly, Christianized. This is true not only where Christmas is concerned; for example, a winter sacrifice of a doe to the goddess Diana was transferred to St. Paul in the Middle Ages, just as the cathedral named for him in London was built upon the ruins of her temple. Some Greco-Roman goddesses continued to be celebrated during winter into the Middle Ages, however; Hera, for instance, was thought, by persons of the fourteenth century, to fly over the countryside "between Christmas and Twelfth-day, dispensing earthly goods in abundance." Saturnalia and Yule persisted into the Renaissance and thereafter; seventeenth-century antiquar-ians and Puritans alike classed the traditions of Lord of Misrule, Yule log, caroling, and decorating houses with green plants, as pagan "remains." These, one need hardly point out, are *not* Christian festivals.

It has been suggested that Celts honored the Mother Goddesses, the Matronae, at the winter solstice. The goddesses Danu and Aine also appear to have been honored at this time; although it is not clear how long the custom of celebrating them in winter continued, it appears to have persisted into the Christianized period. This is true also for the Cailleach Bheur, the Blue Hag of Winter.

Although Aubrey rarely observes the Celtic role in the construction of pagan and hybrid rites, he asserts that the hanging of mistletoe – elsewhere called the "heathenish plant" – in entrance halls is most probably a relic of Celtic veneration of the oak. Although it is important to acknowledge that much data regarding the Druids is presently viewed as controversial or simply wrong, I would nevertheless point out that Stukeley, in *Medallic History of Marcus Aurelius Valerius Carausius* (1759), likewise describes the hanging of mistletoe in York Cathedral on Christmas Eve as a "remain of Druidism;" his description of a rite employing mistletoe mixes pagan and Christian traditions with emerging democratic sentiment:

This was the most respectable festival of our Druids, called Yule-tide, when mistletoe, which they called all-heal, was carried in their altars ....The custom is still preserved in the north, and was lately at York: on the eve of Christmas Day they carry mistletoe to the high altar of the cathedral, and proclaim a public and universal liberty, pardon, and freedom to all sorts of inferior and even wicked people at the gates of the city, towards the four quarters of heaven.[60]

In the late eighteenth century, Dr. Richard Chandler, known for his *Travels in Greece* (1776), reiterates this information, explaining that "where Druidism prevailed, the houses were decked with evergreens in December, that the sylvan spirits might repair to them, and remain unnipped with frost and cold winds, until a milder season had renewed the foliage of their darling abodes."

Others claim that customs linked to mistletoe originate in Germanic lore. For example, in 1896, Peter Hampson Ditchfield explained that the custom of kissing under hanging mistletoe emerged from the tale of Loki slaying Balder with an arrow dipped in the juice of mistletoe berries: "The legend is that Baldur was slain by a mistletoe dart a£ the instigation of Loki; and in reparation for this injury the plant is dedicated to his mother Frigg, so long as it does not touch the earth, which is Loki's kingdom. Hence the mistletoe is hung from ceilings of our houses…"

It is of course possible that medieval, Renaissance, and later customs related to mistletoe reflect a Celtic-Germanic sacred hybridity, and that kissing under the mistletoe, which became extremely popular during the Renaissance, reflects pagan – and most certainly not Christian – innovation.

Germanic celebrations honored ancestors, deities, and other entities such as elves. The mother goddesses or maternal beings, the Dísir, associated with the dead, prophecy, and wisdom, were offered sacrifices called *dísablót* in the great hall at Gamla Uppsala and presumably also elsewhere. This feast formed part of the great Disthing held in their honor, which also included a politico-religious assembly and a great market to which traders came from far and wide to sell their wares. During the eighth century CE, on or near December 24th, Anglo-Saxons likewise revered the Dísir at a great feast called Modranicht, "Mothers' Night." E. K. Chambers, in *The Medieval Stage* (1903), notes: "[T]he winter festival included a commemoration of ancestors…[The dead] were naturally regarded as under the keeping of the…earth-mother."

Freyr was also honored at this time of year. In his aspect as the "Sun-Boar," he signified the return of light. It was perhaps for this reason that he was honored with the sacrifice of a boar at this time by Anglo-Saxons and others.

It should be noted, however, that some say that the boar sacrifice and later customs relating to it originated in a sacrifice to the goddess Frigg.

This custom persisted into the later Middle Ages, the Renaissance, and beyond. As James E. Spears notes, "The boar's head with apple in mouth was carried into the banqueting hall on a gold or silver dish to the sounds of trumpets and the songs of minstrels." The "Boar's Head Carol," composed sometime prior to 1500, celebrates this custom (noticeably, this carol does not focus on the birth of Christ). In Sweden, Denmark, Germany, England, and Scotland, the boar sacrifice eventually morphed into breads, cakes, cookies, and marzipan in the shape of boars and pigs.

According to some sources, Freyja was also honored at this time, with the sacrifice of a pig, in the hope that she would bring peace and prosperity in the year to come. This is suggested by, among other things, the traditional sacrifice of a sow on "Sow-Day," December 17, in the parish of Sandwick in the Orkney Islands.

Odin/Woden also appears to have been honored at this time, particularly in his hypostasis as Jólnir, leader of the Wild Hunt; it is possible that the term "Yule" originates in this name. Odin's association with the winter solstice is supported by the phrase *Hugins jól*, "Raven's Feast," referring to Hugin, one of the god's totem ravens, as well as by the phrase *skölkynis jól*, "Wolf's Feast," the wolf being sacred to the god.

A type of *Iulagalt* bread or cake shaped into a wheel may have been offered to, and eaten in honor of, Odin at this time.

In association with the Wild Hunt, a horse, perhaps representing his horse Sleipnir, may have been sacrificed to Odin/Woden during this season; in Scotland, his association with horses may be evidenced by a tradition, persisting into the nineteenth century, of offering horses a special meal on Yule morning. In Germany, this occasion came to be called *Rauchnächte*, "Hairy Nights," referring to Odin and the Wild Hunt. Map notes that the Wild Hunt was observed in 1154 in England at this time. In nineteenth-century England, the custom of "hoodening," that is, of mumming while dressed as a horse or bull, persisted, with some suggesting that it recalled ancient rites performed in honor of Woden/Odin. In nineteenth-century Germany, the Wild Hunt could best be observed by standing at a crossroad at midnight on Christmas Eve.

Thor also appears to have been celebrated at this time. During the Middle Ages and thereafter, devotees of Thor dressed as the *Julbok*, "the goat or stag of Yule," perhaps a metamorphosis of an earlier sacrifice. The Yule buck symbolizes the goats that pull Thor's cart. Nowadays, the Yule buck appears as a Scandinavian Christmas decoration made of braided straw. In seventeenth-century England, on the Thursday prior to Christmas, suggesting an association with Thor, girls and boys visited the homes of others, wishing them joyful holidays and hoping to receive small gifts of fruit or money. Not surprisingly, Puritans condemned this custom as pagan – which it was.

Indeed, according to Paul Henri Mallet (1730-1807), "The Danes seem to have paid the highest honours to Odin. The inhabitants of Norway and Iceland appear to have been under the immediate protection of Thor; and the Swedes had chosen Freya for their tutelary deity, or…Frey, her brother."

Other Germanic deities who may have been honored at this time are Njorð and Skaði. Moreover, the *álfablót*, in honor of the elves, was held at this time. Other Yule customs included the sprinkling of the blood of sacrificed animals on the temple walls and on worshippers; the eating of wolf hearts by wolf-warriors to make them fiercer; and the practice of *seiðr* magic and divination, which was especially popular during this season. The sun, as a sacred entity, was also honored by Germanics at this time, as evidenced by the special bread called *Sunnugoltr*.

One Yule custom which persisted into the nineteenth century was the making of special, long-lasting candles in celebration of the festival, meant to burn for at least a day if not several; as John Jamieson noted in 1808, it was for this reason that "large candles are by the vulgar called "Yule candles." Yule candles are not supposed to be extinguished, which might result in an extinguishing of good fortune, but should be left to extinguish themselves. Jamieson relates a "Sleeping Beauty"-like tale in which a "*spakona, spae-wife*, or sybil" who feels she has been neglected at the celebration of a child's birth, cries out, "Truly, I add this to these predictions, that the child shall live no longer than these candles, which are lighted beside him, burn out."

In Romanian tradition, Ileana Sânziana, goddess of the moon, is honored during the winter festivities.

Like other winter celebrations, Russian, Ukrainian, and other Slavic ones pay homage to ancestors, signified by sheaves of wheat called "grandparents," with special plates of food being offered to souls of the dead. Animals were also honored at this time; cattle and other domesticated animals were fed special dishes, including "bread, garlic, and rose hips." One animal, often a lamb, was invited in the house to share the feast with the humans and the ancestors. Some Slavs, including Poles, also honored wolves during winter festivities, with the "Vilci Prazdnici, 'Wolf Holidays,' [lasting] from November to February. During these periods, wolves were nicknamed 'carolers,' and carolers dressed in wolf skins."

The primary deity honored on this occasion was the goddess Kolyada. She signifies the "newborn sun" emerging at the winter solstice. Like many other goddesses of winter, she "strolls about the countryside...bearing good luck" and gifts "to those who welcome her." She is depicted as a "kindly benefactor" who chops wood, heats the bathhouse, makes porridge, and feeds children, "sheltering them with her own garment." It is noteworthy that her name appears to be Greek in origin, its etymology linked to the Greek term for "kalends" (*kalendai*) and/or an offering of fruits made to the ancestors (*kollyba*). Although in recent centuries the name of the winter solstice festival has been changed to Christmas, in "some areas the pagan name of the feast—*Kolyada*—has been preserved."

In some places, the goddess Lada and the god Perûn were also fêted at this time. The season of winter itself was also honored on this occasion. When the ceremonial supper was about to be served, the head of the household took a portion outside and invited the "frost" to share in the feast.

Preparations for the ceremonial supper followed a set pattern: "[S]traw was strewn under and on top of the table,...then covered with a tablecloth. Garlic was placed at the four corners of the table while iron objects—an ax and a plowshare...and a yoke, a horse collar...were placed under the table. [On the table, a] pot of [the cereal dish] *kutia*...was topped with a loaf of bread (*knysh*) and a lighted candle. As Pëtr Bogatyrëv explains, the table served as a kind of altar and as a magical spell.

The Kolyada feast was comprised of twelve (nine if twelve was not possible) vegetarian, non-dairy dishes, sometimes including "potato dumplings (*pyrohy* or *varenyky*), cabbage rolls (*holubtsi*), *dzobavka* or *kutia* (cooked wheat or barley, honey, and poppy seeds), potatoes mashed with garlic, stewed fruit...*pyrohy* [pirogies] stuffed with poppy seeds," and other items." As M. Hnatiukivsky notes, "Even the poorest of families tried to maintain the eating ritual."

During the evening ritual, divination and magical rites were performed. For example, the head of the household threw a spoonful of *kutia* "to the ceiling: an adhesion of many grains signified a rich harvest and augured a good swarming of bees." Spells were "aimed at ensuring a good harvest and a life of plenty."

As with other winter festivals, caroling (*koliaduvannia*) is a significant feature of the Kolyada (or, Koliada). Carolers (*kolyadovshchiki*) traditionally sing for households, praising family members and asking that the families be granted a good "harvest, wealth, fertility, and marriage" in the year to come. "Where the she-goat walks," they sing, "There the wheat springs up." For doing so, they are given treats of biscuits, sausages, pancakes, small pastries shaped like animals and birds. In *Russian Traditional Folksong* (1990), Elizabeth Warner and Evgenii Kustovskii stress that both "the givers and receivers of the well-wishing were conscious of the magic function of the songs." If carolers are turned away, they sometimes curse the householders in song, as in the line "For the New Year we wish you an aspen coffin." The association of the *kolyadovshchiki* carolers with paganism is so marked that in the nineteenth century, specifically Christian groups of carolers, *khristoslavtsy*, were formed to try to displace the former. P. Odarchenko notes that the Kolyada "'holy supper' ritual and caroling are still observed, in a modified fashion, by Ukrainians in the diaspora...[and in] post-Soviet Ukraine, particularly in western oblasts."

Lithuanian winter rites share much in common with Russian and Ukrainian ones. Lithuanians celebrate two festivals at this time: Kûèios, followed by Kalëdos. Jonas Trinkunas, following Greimas, stresses that neither Kûèios nor Kalëdos has "anything in common with Christianity, which usurped or destroyed ...traditional Lithuanian celebrations." Of the two festivals Kalëdos, like many solstice holidays, celebrates the rebirth of the sun.

As Trinkunas relates, "People carry images of the sun through the fields and the towns, wishing everybody prosperity." Kûèios honors ancestors, animals, and certain trees. Ancestors (*vëles*) are invoked with candles, toasted with beer, and fed, often at a special table dressed with myrtle, fir branches, and candles. Apple trees are wassailed and offered special foods. It is believed that if the stars shine very brightly during Kûèios then the coming year's apple harvest will be bountiful. Bees are conversed with and offered food, as are farm animals.

A number of divinities are honored at this time with food, drink, and other offerings, including Žemyna, the Earth-Goddess; Žemepatis, god of the household; Dieves, the "grandfather god;" Saulë, the Sun-Goddess (documented as being revered into the eighteenth century); and Veles, the bear-headed god of the forest as well as of cattle, wealth, commerce, and trade.

As in Russia and Ukraine, a special feast is held. Prior to the feast, the family bathes in the sauna. Tables are decorated with hay and other items. Special foods are prepared, including: *kûèia*, very similar to the Russian *kutia*, comprised of "many traditional grains which symbolize regeneration: cooked wheat, barley, peas, beans, rye, poppy seeds, hemp seeds, etc., mixed with nuts and honey water;" as well as "thirteen dishes for each of thirteen moons including…borscht, mushroom dumplings, cabbage, herring or other seafood, poppy seed cookies, cranberry pudding, poppy seed milk, potatoes, apples, nuts, bread, salad of winter and dried vegetables." Velius relates that the father or grandfather "gets dressed in ritual garb like a heathen priest. He puts on a long white shirt with three heddles like that worn by every man in ancient times and girdles himself with a black sash…He dons a black cap made especially for the occasion." After supper, divination is performed for year to come, one kind being based on objects placed under the tablecloth, including a ring for marriage and a key for a house. As among Slavs, caroling forms a part of the Kalëdos celebration. Revelers dress as animals, including goats, bulls, and bears and drag a log around with them, *kaleda* or *blukis*, that's reminiscent of the Yule log.

Thomas A. Janvier's *The Christmas Kalends of Provence and Some Other Provençal Festivals* (1902) includes a late-nineteenth century monolgue concerning pagan influence on Christmastime celebrations. Commencing with a discussion about the Feast of St. Barbara and its relationship to the grain cycle, the Vidame Monsieur Vièlmur aggravates his staunchly Christian housekeeper, Misè Fougueiron, considerably when he remarks,

> The custom must be of pagan origin…But whatever…goddess may have been their patroness then, she [i.e., St. Barbara] is their patroness now…

> …It is not easy to make our Provençaux realize how closely we are linked to older peoples and to older times. The very name for Christmas in Provençal, Calèndo, tells how this Christian festival lives on from the Roman festival of the Winter Solstice, the January Kalends …Our farmers believe, for instance, that these days which are now passing – the twelve days, called *coumtié*, immediately preceding Christmas – are foretellers of the weather for the new twelve months to come…That the twelve prophetic days are those which immediately precede the solstice puts their endowment far back into antiquity. Our farmers, too, have the saying, 'When Christmas falls on a Friday you may sow in ashes' – meaning that the harvest of the ensuing year will be so bountiful that seed sown anywhere will grow; and in this saying there is a strong trace of Venus worship, for Friday – Divèndre in Provençal – is the day sacred to the goddess of fertility and bears her name. Our *Pater de Calèndo* – our curious Christmas prayer for abundance during the coming year – clearly is a pagan supplication that in part has been diverted into Christian ways; and in like manner comes to us from paganism the whole of our Yule-

log ceremonial.[61]

A number of goddesses and female beings who either originated in or whose cults experienced a dramatic surge in popularity during the Middle Ages and thereafter were honored from the winter solstice until the first days of January. Typically patrons of women, they are associated with spinning and demand that women rest from this task at this time. Some lead or join the Wild Hunt and care for the souls of the dead, particularly those of deceased infants and children. They are offered gifts of food such as fish, eggs, apples, nuts, milk, honey, porridge, dumplings, and pancakes and crepes. In exchange, traversing the earth in wagons, they give their devotees gifts including gold, fertility and prosperity. Often depicted as crones, they are embodied in rituals by women or men dressed in feminine attire. Most have persisted into the present but have been subjected to demonization and carnivalization in recent centuries; some, however, like La Befana, continue to be seen as beneficent gift-givers; most have been displaced by Father Christmas or Santa Claus. These divinities include La Befana, Chlungeri, Grýla, Frau Herke, Holda, Perchta, Rupfa, Saelde, and Tante Arie.

Constance Gordon Cumming, writing of how Yule was celebrated during her childhood in mid-nineteenth century Scotland, observes:

> On Yule morning, offerings of oatmeal and of various grains were made to Hulda [i.e., Holda], the Divine Mother, to induce her to send abundant crops; and the people feasted together. Hence the bowls of furmety or sowans, alias sour gruel, which in our childhood we always shared in the early Christmas morning. Hence too the custom of all the lads and lasses going from farm to farm, each carrying their own bowl and spoon, to share the brew of each gude-wife.

Probably it was also in her honour that those curious " Yule doughs " originated, still common in the north of England, where many a time we have assisted at the manufacture and baking of wonderful dolls, adorned with currants. Dolls masculine and dolls feminine, to be duly distributed as sweethearts to every lad and lass in the house—and many such have we received from village friends.[62]

During the Middle Ages and Renaissance, Robin Hood also became associated, by way of hunting and the sacrifice of a stag, to the rites of winter. Banquets were held for, or offerings given to, elves, fauns, satyrs, *pilosi*, elves, kobolds, wood-wives, Wild Women, Scrat, and the Fates/fairies. Iscanus's twelfth-century *Penitential* prohibited the practice of "laying tables with three knives for the service of the Fates [or Fairies] that they may predestinate good things to those who are born there." In some places, including Angus, Scotland, pagan innovation is evidenced by the translation of Yule into a divine-like being who was, in the eighteenth and nineteenth centuries, "let in" by hospitable and prosperity-seeking families and served a plate of bread and cheese.

Divinations performed at this time "especially concerned the crops and the weather for the ensuing year."

The winter rite of wassailing, which allegedly commenced as a Briton custom, but which in Germanic, Slavic, and Baltic areas may possess other origins as well, also continued to be practiced; in the seventeenth century, Aubrey reported: "[I]n Somersetshire when they Wassail...the ploughmen have their twelve-cake, and they go into the ox-house to the oxen, with the wassail-bowl and drink to the ox...and afterwards they go with their wassail-bowl into the orchard and go about the trees to bless them." In Surrey, England, during the nineteenth century, wassailers sang a spell to the trees:

> Here stands a good apple-tree
> Stand fast at the root
> Bear well at the top
> Every little twig
> Bear an apple big...[63]

New Year's, which was moved between 153 and 46 BCE from March to January, was an extremely popular festival in Late Antique Rome. The festival of Janus, during which he was invoked first among the gods, celebrated beginnings and openings and sought to invoke peace. Other deities honored on this occasion included Vesta (new fires were lit to her), the Lares and their mother Mania, Jupiter, Venus, Diana, Mars, Mercury, Saturn, Bacchus, Hercules, and Isis and Serapis. The gods were invoked by way of a masque, of which Michel Meslin, in *La fête des kalendes de janvier dans l'empire romain: Étude d'un rituel de Nouvel An*, writes, "The masque here is not a caricature [but rather concerns] the...desire to affirm...a power and an energy." Offerings and sacrifices included special cakes and lambs. Romans greeted each other by wishing each other a "happy year." It was a time of divination, forecasting the year to come, as well as of gift giving, popular presents *(strenae)* including figs, honey, earthenware lamps bearing symbols of prosperity such as the cornucopia, and money – a tradition appropriated by Christians, in opposition to many Church leaders, for Christmas. Communal meals were shared, with dishes symbolizing abundance and prosperity, and singing and dancing continued in taverns until dawn. Slaves didn't have to work and were given a double ration of wine.

John Brady wrote in *Clavis Calendaria* in 1812, "The first day of January having been observed by the heathens as a day of extreme rejoicing, and for an offering up profane and superstitious sacrifices to their idol Janus, the primitive Christians held it as a fast, to avoid even the semblance of joining in their abominable customs."

Church officials were especially distressed by the emphasis on feasting, preparing feasts for the fairies, singing of bawdy songs, dancing, divination focusing on the year to come, the embodiment of deities (they appear to been especially troubled by the portrayal by males of goddesses), the wearing of sumptuous attire, dressing as and embodying animals (especially stags and calves), and alleged non-reproductive eroticism.

Many medieval Europeans living in Christianized milieus appear to have shifted from honoring the gods at this time to offering a banquet to the fairies. Divination as well as magic continued to be performed, particularly by women, at New Year's, in Germany and elsewhere. In the eleventh century, Burchard (d. 1025)'s *Corrector* described women as "spin[ning], sew[ing]," and "wind[ing] magic skeins," possibly "in a magic circle." In England, during the thirteenth and fourteenth centuries, celebrants continued to dress as "bulls, stags, and goats" and to give gifts according "to the ancient guise of heathen people."

New Year's continued to be celebrated in England and elsewhere in Europe during the seventeenth and eighteenth centuries. John Aubrey (1626-1697) claimed that New Year's was rooted in Roman traditions of wishing one a "Happy New Year;" in Ovid's *Fasti*, one finds, "You must now speak good words on this good day" – and of giving gifts of dates, figs, honey, and money at this time. In the 1770s, in Northumberland, England and in Scotland, especially in the Hebrides, many continued to celebrate New Year's in a traditional manner. This included the "burning of the clavie," a bonfire made of casks, and the sacrifice of an ox. A young man was chosen to wear or sleep on the hide of the sacrificed animal. This rite, and the wearing of the hide in particular, had been condemned by the Church for about 1,400 years, and in England since at least the eighth century, a thousand years. In some places, the young man served as a kind of scapegoat; in most, however, he slept wrapped in the hide in order to experience visions. Some believed these ceremonies originated in the ancient Roman festival of the Brumalia (the "winter rites"), in cults of Amphiaraus or Asclepius, or in another ritual practice. Dalyell observes, "as clothing in the skin of the victim, formed part of the sanctified rites, it may be presumed that the *taghairm* [signifying a "summoning" or an "invocation"] whereby the Scottish seer, wrapping himself in a hide, sought nocturnal responses, [is] some relic of an ancient religious ritual." It is most likely from the ancient custom of dressing as, and incarnating the personae and powers of, animals, together with such rites as that just described, that he most celebrated British festival of horned animals, the Abbots Bromley Horn Dance, arose. Originally, it appears to have been on or near Twelfth Day (it is presently held in early September). It has been performed in its present form since 1226 CE or before. This dance ritual's celebrants include a Fool, a Hobby Horse, Maid Marian (traditionally played by a man), a Bowman, and six men wearing reindeer antlers that were, it would appear from testing, imported from Scandinavia in the eleventh century.

Another New Year's rite practiced in Scotland, especially in Strathaven, included the elements of water and fire and focused on protection and perhaps also purification and prosperity:

> …some of the mystical practices used on New Year's Day have reference to the worship of rivers, which Gildas accuses our countrymen of adhering to. …[T]hese rites are evidently…derived from a period anterior to the introduction of Christianity. For the protection of the family during the ensuing year a person is dispatched to draw water from a ford in the river, where both dead and living had crossed; and having filled the pitcher, to return to the house, having all the time carefully preserved silence. Neither

must the pitcher have been allowed to touch the ground, or the virtue of the water would be withdrawn. Fire was then lighted, and the inmates were sprinkled with this mystical water. They were also fumigated with the incense of burnt juniper branches. All the horses, cattle, and sheep had also the benefit of sprinkling and fumigation, which was intended to prevent any malign influence that might have otherwise assailed them through the year…[64]

In Russia and the Ukraine (where, in medieval times, New Year's occurred on March 1), special foods were prepared for the ancestors, and, perhaps in some places, for gods, particularly *kutia*; special breads and cakes were baked; new hearth-fires were lit; divination, especially concerning love and marriage and the weather, was performed by women; cattle and other domesticated animals were brought indoors, with some persons believing that they could communicate with each other, as they had in the most ancient of times; celebrants bathed in a mixture of coins and river water to invoke good health and prosperity in the year to come; and, although it is difficult to tell when this custom commenced, carolers, led by a cross-dressing person or possibly, transgender woman, sang at homes and elsewhere.

In regard to animals being brought within the household, I'm reminded of a Wendish festival that's celebrated on January 25: *Ptaci kwas*, the Birds' Wedding. "On this day," Gerald Stone relates in *The Smallest Slavonic Nation: The Sorbs of Lusatia*, "the children put dishes or plates outside the door or by an open window…[for] the birds, who are said to be celebrating a wedding…Gifts…of apples, nuts, pastries, and sweets are provided…[T]he spirits of the dead [are believed to] live on in the birds and may be placated by an offering of food."

Returning to Ukrainian New Year's, in our context, a part of this Eastern European festival that holds special significance is the ceremonial procession of Malanka. Although, in Christianized times, this rite and the figure of Malanka have been excessively carnivalized and secularized, some celebrants continue to acknowledge and pay homage to its ancient origins. Malanka is none other than the Ukrainian Persephone. Her mother, the goddess Lada, takes the part of Demeter. It appears that the people of what is now the Ukraine may have learned of Demeter and Persephone from Greeks who lived in colonies on the Black Sea Coast around 2,500 years ago. Like Persephone, Malanka, whose name means "loving" and who is also known as "Spring" or "May," is abducted by the Lord of the Underworld. She is, however, permitted to return to earth each spring bringing beautiful flowers and green grass with her. The processing of Malanka, who is alternately represented by a doll or masked person, often a cross-dressing person or possibly, transgender woman,, recalls her tale and serves to invoke her, beckoning her back to bring winter to an end. Although the Soviets banned this festival as such in the 1930s – although replacing it with what might be considered an equally pagan carnival featuring the Snow Maiden and Grandfather Frost – it has been openly practiced once more since 1991.

As most will know, Twelfth Night, the subject of plays by Shakespeare, Ben Jonson, and others, is famous for its card games, its "King Cake" or "Baby Cake," a multicolored cake – now in the U.S. primarily associated with New Orleans' Mardi Gras – in which a bean or coin, and more recently, the figure of a baby, is found, betokening good fortune, and for its reversal of roles, with men trading roles with women, masters with slaves, and so on. I would point out, however, that throughout its history, many of its celebrants have remained aware that its Lord of Misrule is none other than the Roman god Saturn; the Saturn, that is, of the Golden Age. This may have been the most potent, and perhaps most threatening, aspect of the Twelfth Night celebration: its vision of an age when people lived in peace, prosperity, and equality. It is difficult today to envision what it must have meant to slaves in a time when slavery was a very real institution to set aside a day when masters served slaves; how cruel it must have seemed the day after, yet what a vision of democratic, egalitarian hope it may have inspired in slaves, indentured servants, and others. This aspect of Twelfth Night was not lost on Isaac D'Israeli (1766-1848), who condemned the festival for its vision of what he considered to be the "false notion of the equality of men." Thus it is that a persistent, hybrid pagano-Christian-secular festival may have played a not insignificant role in inspiring and catalyzing egalitarian and democratic movements. I would also like to remind the reader that at least into the Middle Ages, it preserved a certain magic, in being one of those occasions when banquets were prepared for fairies. Moreover – and this may be an example of pagano-Christian hybridity – on this night, during the Renaissance (and perhaps earlier), houses were purified with processions of candles and incense, and crosses were inscribed on the rafters to protect the house from evil beings.

In recent centuries, one traditional Twelfth Night song became extremely popular among children and others:

Lavender blue, diddle, diddle,
Rosemary green,
You shall be King, diddle, diddle,
And I shall be Queen.[65]

Lady Maria Calcott, in *Three Months Passed in the Mountains East of Rome* (1820), offers an insight into the role of La Befana in Twelfth Night celebrations in nineteenth-century Italy:

We are not quite sure whether to class the Beffana [i.e., La Befana] of Twelfth Night *with the witches or fairies* [italics mine; intriguing question of classification]. ... [T]here are cakes and sweetmeats and fruit, and in short, all good things...The Piazza della Rotonda is particularly distinguished by the gay appearance of the fruit and cakestands, ornamented with flowers and lighted with paper lanterns. Persons dressed up to resemble the pictures of Mother Bunch or Mother Goose, and called Beffana, are led about the streets... But these visible Beffanas are nothing in importance to the invisible [ones]. When the children go to bed, each hangs up a stocking near the pillow. If the child has been good, the stocking is filled with sweetmeats and cakes before morning...[66]

An extremely unusual variation on the Twelfth Night cake took place in the not-too-distant past in the Rossnowlagh area of Donegal, Ireland:"[A] ritual almost like a séance was observed. A round cake, a flat container of dried mud [or] animal dung was placed in the kitchen. A rush candle or a piece of bog-oak representing each member of the family was placed in the 'cake' and lit." Then, in the darkness lit only by the candles or pieces of wood, they would burn out. In the order that they did so, this was thought to be the order in which the "members of the family would die.

New Year's and Twelfth Night were linked in medieval and later Europe to the Feast of Fools, roughly equivalent to the Feast of the Ass, typically held on January 7.

This may be one of the reasons that the following ceremony, practiced in early nineteenth-century England, seems to combine the aforementioned rites with ancient customs including agricultural rites (bonfires, wassailing) and the honoring of animals together with carnivalesque behavior:

> In Herefordshire, on the Eve of the Epiphany, the Farmers collect together, and go into the wheat fields, and there light [thirteen]... fires... The attendants, headed by the master of the family, ...[pass the ale around]... A circle is formed round the large[st] fire, when a general shout and hallooing takes place, which you hear answered from all the adjacent villages and fields. Sometimes fifty or sixty of these fires may be all seen at once. This being finished, the company return home, where the [women prepare]... a good supper [including a] large cake ...with a hole in the middle. After supper, the company all attend the bailiff (or head of the oxen) to the Wainhouse, where the following particulars are observed: — The master, at the head of his friends, fills the cup, generally of strong ale, and stands opposite the first, or finest of the oxen. He then pledges him in a curious toast: the company follow his example with all the other oxen, addressing each by his name. This being finished, the large cake is produced, and, with much ceremony, put on the horn of the first ox, through the hole above mentioned. The ox is then tickled, to make him toss his head: if he throw the cake behind, then it is the mistress's perquisite; if before, in what is termed the boosy, the bailiff himself claims the prize. The company then return to the house, the doors of which they find locked; nor will they be opened, till some joyous songs are sung. On their gaining admittance, a scene of mirth and jollity ensues, and which lasts the greatest part of the night.[67]

The Feast of Fools reflect/s a pagano-Christian-secular hybridity. The feast's origins lie in the Roman Feast of Fools, which was celebrated on February 17th and which is commemorated by Ovid. His description of the Stultorum Feriae is intriguing, suggesting that the festival not only celebrated silliness but also, more somberly, recognized foolishness as a kind of ignorance that resulted in senseless wars, disrespect of the Goddess of the earth, and ultimately in lack of abundant crops. Due to the recognition of Ceres' taking offense at being offered uncooked grain, and the consequent desire to cease being "foolish" and to placate her, both she and Fornax, goddess of the oven, were honored during this feast with toasted grains.

Although numerous scholars of the seventeenth and eighteenth centuries, including Charles Du Fresne, Sieur Du Cange (1610-1688), Guy-Alexis Lobineau (1666-1727), and Karl Friedrich Flögel (1729-1788) were convinced of the pagan origin of the feast, the Feast of Fools and/or the Ass has become most widely known for its/their parody of the Christian mass. Peasants and sometimes priests dressed in rags or women's clothes or even naked would frolic into churches, while bearded nuns sang hymns to asses, and others perfumed the churches with incense of burning shoes. In the mid-fifteenth century, despite the efforts of the Church, Ludovicus, the archbishop of Sens, in Bourgogne, France was still complaining about individuals who during the Feast of Fools wore "masks with hideous features," in other words, those of animals, and "dressed like women." Of course, this element of the Feast of Fools/the Ass does lead us back to pagan origins. They danced inside the church, running, leaping, and singing "indecent songs." Not only this, but the crowd included "naked men with even their private parts uncovered" who indulged in "infamous shows" too "shameful to remember."

In *Medii aevi Kalendarium* (1841), R. T. Hampson not only sheds light on a possible connection between ancient Greek feasts to Dionysus in late January and early February and the Feast of Fools/Ass but also suggests that Church authorities of the Middle Ages and thereafter may have been all too familiar with the Feast's pagan origins: "[T]he cover of an ancient missal of the Feast of Fools preserved in the library of Sens," he relates,

> is ornamented with mythological figures, representing the triumph of Bacchus, the sun, and the rising of Diana, the moon from the sea. The Bacchanalian scenes depicted agree very well with the feast which the cover represents, and in which a hundred times is repeated the very exclamation used in the Bacchanalia: *Evohe! Evohe!* The office was composed by Pierre de Corbeille, archbishop of Sen(s), who died in June, 1222...In various versions of the Feast of the Ass, participants roared *"Evovae!"*[68]

In certain places, particularly in rural England, Plough Monday followed Twelfth Night. This celebration ritualized the first ploughing of the new year. It appears to have drawn upon both the ancient Roman January Kalends celebration, as suggested by ceremonial cross-dressing or mixed gender attire and dressing as animals, as well as, perhaps, Germanic feasts in honor of the god Freyr and the goddess Freyja, possibly in her Danish hypostasis as Gefion (ultimately becoming the carnivalesque figure of Old Bessy). The case for honoring Freyr on Plough Monday is suggested by the fact that a portion of the boar sacrificed to him and baked at Yule was dried and kept until ploughing commenced. At this time, a portion of it was mixed with dried corn for the plough-horses, while another portion was distributed among the ploughmen; it is probable that yet another portion was offered to the soil, indicating Freyr's association with fertility and prosperity. It is not clear, however, how long these ancient associations remained known to the agricultural workers who practiced them.

In northeast Scotland, the advent of ploughing (not necessarily on Plough Monday) was ritualized by way of "food [i.e., bread and cheese, and drink, i.e., whiskey, being] offered to the [field, the crows of the field, the ploughman, and to the] plough itself."

Most of the important themes of February celebrations centered on light and its role as an agent of purification, together with its role in providing a lamp in the darkness for body and soul, and its role in catalyzing health and fertility (with a later emphasis on romantic love), particularly in the form of fire, reflected in the gradual return of the sun's light following the darkness of winter. For some, in this regard, February signaled reaching a midway point between the winter solstice and the spring equinox.

Among the Celts, the feast of early February was called Imbolc (or, Oimelc), signifying ewe's milk and by extension the storing of winter foods during the winter months. Held in honor of the goddess Brigid (later hybridized with St. Brigit), Imbolc celebrated health, fertility, and purification. This feast played a significant part in the construction of the Christian feast of the Purification of the Virgin Mary, called Candlemas, over the course of the fifth through seventh centuries. Among the Romans, following the Greeks, the light of February torches reminded devotees of the torch carried by Demeter as she searched for Persephone in the darkness of winter. Although in Rome this homage to Ceres was held on February 21st, with offerings of "wine [-soaked bread] and loose violets/ [Left] lying on a shard in mid-street," it nevertheless, like the feast of Brigid, played a significant part in the construction of the Christian feast of Candlemas, as acknowledged by Pope Innocent XII (pope, 1691-1700) in the late seventeenth century: "Why do we in this feast carry candles? Because the Gentiles dedicated the month of February to…Proserpina, and her mother Ceres [who] sought her in the night with lighted candles…Because the holy fathers could not extirpate this custom, they ordained that Christians should carry about candles in honor of the Blessed Virgin." In the late nineteenth century, Mourant Brock, in *Rome: Pagan and Papal*, remarked: "The Feast of Purification, or Candlemas, was…substituted for the Heathen festival…[that] commemorated the wanderings of Ceres…[T]he torches and wax tapers, formerly carried about in honour of Ceres, were now connected with the Holy Virgin…Thus Ceres went out, and Mary came in…"

Beyond Demeter's/Ceres' search, another of Rome's February rites, the Lupercalia, a feast dedicated to Pan/

Faunus and centering on purification, health, fertility, and the averting of evil beings, may have played a role in the creation of Candlemas, as John Brady suggested in *Clavis Calendaria* in 1812: "When the Christian bishops instituted this festival [of Candlemas], there can be little doubt but that they substituted it in place of the pagan Lupercalia." He continues: "[T]hey adorned their churches with numerous lights, and paraded about with flambeaux and candles, in close imitation of the pagan custom of brenning, in honor of Februa, or Juno, who, in heathen mythology, was deemed to preside over the purification of women.

In Great Britain, the Candlemas feast may also owe something to the ancient Germanic festival of Sporkelmonat, in that this festival is thought to have been held "in honor of the advancing sun." Most probably due to its significant associations with women, the feast of Candlemas eventually came to be known in England as the Wives' Feast. In the not-too-distant past in Ireland, the holiday was especially celebrated by women, including girls carrying "dolls" of Brigid, typically made of handles from butter churns, and performing ceremonial dances. Sometimes "all the women had to bow before" the image of the goddess-saint "as it was paraded about the village." In *Southey's Commonplace Book*, one finds: "On St. Bridget's eve every farmer's wife in Ireland makes a cake, called *bairin breac* [a bread/cake with cinnamon and yellow raisins, also served at Samhain/Hallowe'en], the neighbours are invited, the madder of ale and the pipe go round, and the evening concludes with mirth and festivity."

From at least the Late Middle Ages onward, Candlemas also became associated with creativity and craftsmanship, with "representatives of all the crafts and trades wearing the symbols of their craft on their breast[s]." It appears that the Wends held somewhat similar rites in February, as Thietmar, the bishop of Merseburg, noted near 1018: "The Liutizi [Wends]...the month of February, which the heathen venerate with rites of purification and obligatory offerings. [...]...this folk, called the Abodrites and Wagrii [subgroups of the Wends who occupied the eastern part of Holstein, northern Germany]."

Returning very briefly to the Lupercalia, a rite resembling that rite's averting of evil spirits appears to have been practiced into the nineteenth century in Germany, in memory of Thor, when rurals would bang wooden and other structures and objects with hammers to frighten demonic beings away.

When it comes to Valentine's, one thing is quite clear: other than its name, the holiday owes little or nothing to a Christian saint. Having said that, however, our current celebration of lovers and loved ones bears but slight resemblance to the ancient rites on which some have claimed it has sprung – although one can see how it might have evolved from such. Like Candlemas, it's said to be based on the Lupercalia; although, in the case of Valentine's, a specific rite of the Lupercalia, which involved naked males running through the streets and whipping consenting women with goatskins to induce fertility, was that aspect of the festival that may have given rise to Valentine's. On

Feb. 15, 494, many Romans, now ostensibly Christians, rebelled against Pope Gelasius I (d. 496) by celebrating the festival of the Lupercalia on the Palatine. Those who did so were branded "renegades" and were excommunicated. Over time, this rite became increasingly less wild; from a box, boys and men chose the names of girls and women to give gifts to and perhaps to couple with. As Christianization advanced, the rite remained but became increasingly secular, with many forgetting its origins in fertility rites and homage to Pan. In the ninth century, in or near 827, some Church authorities seeking to "abolish the heathen...custom of boys drawing the names of girls, in honor of their goddess Februata, or Juno, on the fifteenth of February, several zealous pastors substituted the names of saints in billets given on that day." The saint one chose was supposed to patron that individual throughout the coming year. While the custom of having a patron saint gained broad popularity, the attempt to do away with the erotic-becoming-romantic dimension of the holiday proved a disastrous failure. The popularity of Valentine's Day as a predominantly secular celebration of lovers – with occasional bows to Venus and Cupid – rose dramatically during the Renaissance. In some places, however, earth-centered elements persisted; in 1742, for instance, Pope Benedict XIV (1675-1758, r. 1740-1758) banned celebration of the Lupercalia in Italy. He later, incidentally, banned numerous "dances [and] games, and the masques of the 'Bacchanalia.'"[69]

Chapter 7
Beliefs and Rites of the Life Cycle

Procreation, Pregnancy, Childbirth

In Germanic tradition, women wishing to become mothers and couples hoping for children invoked the aid of several deities to give birth to children, to ease the pain of childbirth, and to grant fortunate destinies to offspring. Chief among these were the goddesses Freyja and Frigga and the gods Freyr and Odin. Elves and dwarves could also, if treated well, ease the pangs of childbirth. In Baltic and Slavic cultures, the goddesses Žemyna and Laima were invoked. Similarly, in Christianized medieval and post-medieval France, in the Arles district, women "invoked the fairy [or goddess] Esterelle to become pregnant."

In Germanic tradition, the world-tree holds healing power, and the souls of children are thought to dwell within it or within its fruits. A related belief holds that trees are "homes for the unborn," especially fruit trees." "In many places in Germany it is said that girls' souls are gotten from plum or cherry trees and boys' souls can be gathered from pear trees." Souls also wait in "crevasses in cliffs [and in] ponds [and] caves" for women desiring to be mothers to call them.

Certain times of the year were considered more propitious than others for impregnation. In *Witchcraft Medicine* (2003), Claudia Müller-Ebeling, Christian Rätsch, and Wolf-Dieter Storl relate: "The joyous month of May...was considered to be a particularly favorable time for impregnation...Only after the conversion to Christianity...was a May wedding warned against." Women and men desiring children "drank a wine scented with sweet woodruff, which stimulated desire and eased inhibitions....The May festival was also an occasion to 'quicken' the young women with birch and hazel branches." Similarly, certain foods were thought to promote fertility and childbearing. Among Poles, for example, women were encouraged to eat the meat of animals considered "famous for their fertility, such as rabbits and roosters."

The midwife, considered a wisewoman, played a significant role in the process of childbearing. Indeed, so significant was her role that the midwife was sometimes bestowed with the title of Earth-Mother. Müller-Ebeling et. al. relate that when "women had difficulty conceiving, they went to the wisewoman. She knew of herbs to help increase fertility. For example, footbaths made with infusions of mugwort [also called artemisia, sacred to Artemis/Diana] warmed and energized the abdomen." At a special ceremony, the "wise woman placed a bundle of mugwort in the pregnant woman's left hand, because the guardian of mothers, Frau Holle or Artemis, is present in this aromatic woman's herb."

Divination was sometimes undertaken to learn of the sex of the child to be born. In *The Folklore of Orkney and Shetland* (2000), Ernest W. Marwick explains that in Scotland, this form of divination was typically performed by a woman who practiced scapulamancy. In a simplified version of the art, the woman dropped a sheep bone into her lap several times. Depending upon which side the *spo ben*, or "prophecy bone," came to rest would tell her whether a girl or a boy was to be born.

In earth-centered as well as in Christianized Europe, interference in the birth process by evil spirits was greatly feared (this brings to mind *Rosemary's Baby* and *The Omen*). Marwick relates that in the Northern Isles of Scotland, "this tendency was all the stronger because of the supposed necessity of keeping the secret from malevolent beings who could harm mother and child." Scottish methods of averting evil included placing a knife in the pregnant woman's bed and later in the cradle (in Christianized Scotland, a Bible was added to but did not displace the knife) and in keeping a black cock at the window, as he, unlike a white cock, was believed to be able to sense the presence of harmful entities and would crow when he did so. Meanwhile, pregnant women of Slavic regions would sometimes dress in masculine attire in an attempt to deceive such beings; garlic and onions would be placed around them at the time of labor; and upon the birth of a child, the eldest woman of the family might run out of the bathhouse or house shouting that a wolf had been born, also in an attempt to deceive evil beings, or else the father might fire shots into the air to drive them away.

As the time of labor and giving birth neared, in Latvia, Lithuania, and in certain other parts of Europe, the bathhouse was ritually prepared. In Latvia, the goddess or similar being Pirts Mate ("bathhouse mother") was invoked at this time. Lotte Motz explains in *The Faces of the Goddess* (1997) that in the bathhouse, "women experienced the pain, fears, and joy of giving birth. Even if the delivery did not occur within the bathhouse, the new mother would be brought there afterward for the feast, named *pirtizas* (*pirtis* – bathhouse)."

As the mother-to-be was entering labor, she was ceremoniously led to the bathhouse. On her way there, she was met by a woman embodying the Goddess, in Baltic tradition, the goddess Laima, who was – together with the Virgin Mary and St. Anne – invoked on this occasion into the seventeenth century. Offerings were made to the presiding goddess, goddesses, or similar female beings at this time, including such items as a ring, a garter of colored wool, gloves, and stockings, as well as the sacrifice of an animal, typically of a hen, by the offspring's grandmother. Once the mother-to-be was placed in the bathhouse, the midwife began to utter invocations and prayers. The presiding female divinities were called in; in Germanic tradition, this included Mara, a goddess of cows and milk reminiscent of the Egyptian Hathor. Upon the birth of the child, "[a]mong the Germanic peoples...the midwife laid the newborn on the straw-covered earth. Thus she consecrated it to the Earth Mother, to Frau Holle...She circled the child three times and inspected it." In Germanic tradition, midwives were also seen as serving the goddess Ciza; as blessing newborns in her name (Christians would translate "Ciza" as the "Devil"); and as also holding the power to shapeshift, particularly into cats or cows. For these reasons, they were sometimes accused of practicing witchcraft. At this time also, the goddesses of destiny, in Germanic tradition, the Norns, arrived to predict the newborn's fate. These may have been represented by the midwife, and/or, in Germanic tradition, the practitioner of *seiðr* divination and magic. In Germanic tradition, the midwife, because she was considered an "embodiment of the goddess of fate and the ancestors...[often performed the role of the Norns,] prophes[ying] the child's destiny and welcom[ing] it with a blessing."

In Slavic tradition, these goddesses, perhaps represented by women wearing "beautiful, highly decorated dresses," were known variously as the Rozanicas, Orisnicas (which sounds uncannily like the Yorùbá term for deity, *orishá*), or Sudickas. Similarly, in medieval and Christianized Greece and Sicily, fairies appeared to predict the child's fate. As in the fairy tale "Sleeping Beauty" and in line with earth-centered notions of balance, two of three Fates or fairies (or a similar combination) blessed the child, while the third or last placed before it its obstacles or tribulations.

At or near this time, the newborn was bathed for the first time, also typically by the midwife. The vessel in which the child was bathed was ritually significant; for Poles, it was a bowl used in bread making, believed to promote healthy growth of the child. Just before the bath, certain items thought to promote health and good fortune were placed into the bowl or basin. Slavs, for instance, placed corn, silver, and herbs including mugwort, thyme, and lovage into the vessel. Shortly thereafter, as in Germanic tradition, the newborn was swept with a broom which had been made by the expectant mother. This broom, made of birch, oak, rowan, and linden twigs and bound with red thread, was meant to sweep away any negative forces and to promote health and growth. Interestingly, both Hispanic traditional healers, *curanderas*, and priestesses of Vodou employ sweeping in similar ways. In Germanic tradition, also shortly after birth, newborns also underwent a hallowing ceremony in which they were blessed by the god Thor via a representation of his hammer Mjöllnir.

Once the child was born, deities, similar beings, and others who had assisted in its birth were thanked. Often such thanks involved gifts, sometimes including gifts from the birthing process. In the Baltics, for instance, Laima and Pirts Mate were thanked with gifts. In Slavic regions, the Rozanicas, Orisnicas, and Sudickas were offered bread, cheese, honey, salt, wine, herbs, soap, and money. Germanic peoples "buried the 'shirt' (placenta) of the newborn and the umbilical cord beneath a tree, or they hung it on branches as an offering to Woden's ravens. For this purpose the trees and shrubs sacred to Freyja, such as linden, wild rose, birch, and fruit trees, were used." In later times, "It was...the custom to thank the fairy of the farm or village tree for the blessed birth of the child by offering it the umbilical cord or the first bathwater."

In Lithuania, the goddess Žemyna was

thanked with spirits poured on the earth. The father of the child was responsible for cooking a great feast in honor of the Goddess as well as for the mother, midwife, and others present at the birthing ceremony. Six weeks later, Žemyna was honored again with a special beer. For her role in the process, "the midwife received eggs, flour, flax, and other utilitarian and symbolic offerings. Money was also given to her."

Many superstitions accompanied the birth of a child, including the belief that a child born with a caul or at midnight possesses psychic ability; that a child born with a caul would be safe from drowning; that a sickly child might be a changeling left by the fairies or might have been sickened via the evil eye; and that, to secure good health, babies should be weaned in springtime; as well as rituals of saving the hair from the first haircut to protect its use by sinister practitioners of magic and of grinding the umbilical cord to a powder and feeding it to the child. Many of these carried over into Christianized periods. Also with Christianization, goddesses came increasingly to be displaced by the Virgin Mary and female saints, while male gods like Odin and Thor vanished from birth rites altogether.

One of the more significant rites involving infants was baptism. The ceremonial sprinkling of sanctified water over infants was a common practice among Greeks and Romans, Celts, and Germanic peoples. Godparents or foster-parents frequently played a significant role in this rite, which included chanting or singing over the child and giving a name to her or him. As we know, baptism attained a prominent place in the rituals of Christianity. In Christianized Europe, anxiety regarding the urgency of baptism became widespread, as a popular belief took hold that infants were born pagan and remained so until baptized. Although some recalcitrant pagans believed that, should an infant die before baptism, its soul would travel to the goddess Perchta, who would care for it, many other Europeans believed that should a child die before baptism, it would become a will-o'-the-wisp, a *rusalka*, or a fire-drake (or, *drakoula*). Thus, it would seem that while pagan babies are *born*, Christian babies are *made*.

Love and Marriage

Except in rare circumstances, marriage, in the premodern West, was not chiefly about love. Russian scholars Y. M. Sokolov and Pëtr Bogatyrëv have stressed that marriage was primarily conceived as an economic relationship established between two families. In *Medieval Folklore*, Carl Lindahl, John McNamara, and John Lindow stress the importance of negotiations regarding the bridal dowry in medieval Europe. As Bogatyrëv puts it in *Vampires in the Carpathians*, "The celebration of a wedding is the beginning of the life of a new economic unit." He points out that in early twentieth-century Russia, as in other cultures and as in previous centuries, "the question of money" is a significant one, and it "is natural that a whole series of rites should be dedicated to the new family's material well-being." Erotic attraction and/or love, when either or both occurred within marriage, served as a kind of bonus within the institution.

Not surprisingly, where such an important institution was concerned, the assistance of deities was often sought. In Germanic tradition, for example, those wishing to marry sought the help of Freyja, Frigga, and Freyr. Couples were also blessed by Odin as well as Thor, via a representation of his hammer. In Baltic contexts, the goddess Laima was invoked as patron of marriage. Once negotiations were settled between the families, Žemyna was ritually thanked. In Slavic regions, Kikimora and the *rusalki* were thanked.

Divination and magic also formed an aspect of the marriage rites. In Germanic tradition, the practitioner or priestess of *seiðr* was consulted regarding future marriages and their fortunate or unfortunate destiny. In the British Isles, young women wishing to marry performed divination on the occasion of seasonal festivals, especially at Candlemas, Midsummer, and Halloween. In Scotland and elsewhere, love potions and kindred items were sometimes concocted by wisewomen in order to promote loving unions. Marwick relates that a "fish of the ray family, was considered to be a powerful aphrodisiac. But many anxious lovers placed their faith in nettles, which, if gathered at Hallowe'en and placed between the blankets of the loved one, never failed to secure his (or her) affection."

Engaged couples often ritualized their bond, sometimes, as we have seen, at sacred sites, such as Scottish handfasting rites at sacred stones. Once couples were considered betrothed, they were, in some regions, permitted to engage in lovemaking, although not intercourse per se, on certain festive occasions; in Orkney and Shetland, Scotland, for example, they were permitted to do so, alongside other betrothed couples, at Lughnasa on a barn floor covered with sheaves. This kind of lovemaking sans intercourse was, incidentally, referred to as *ta haad buhelli*.

In many parts of Europe, perhaps especially in Slavic regions, marriage was seen as both a happy and very sad event. For young women, it signaled a separation from their childhood homes, an ending of virginity, and the loss of a kind of freedom associated with youth. This separation and transition was often marked by cutting a young woman's braids and by marriage laments, such as this Russian one: "My heart begins to pine for the grave./ Never in my life shall I forget my maiden freedom. When my partner David recorded songs still sung in central Texas by older Czech women in the early 1990s, such laments were among them – and when the women sang them, they permitted no men except us to hear them.

Weddings were typically held at certain times of the year and were associated to a certain extent with seasonal rites. In Russia, for example, weddings were often held in winter, close to fêtes honoring the ancestors. Among Germanic peoples, weddings were often held on Tuesdays, Thursdays, or Fridays, days of Tiw, Thor, and Frigga (or Freyja), respectively.

Marriage rites included various symbols. Brides of certain Germanic cultures may have worn gold foil talismans depicting deities and couples embracing. In Ireland, images of the sun and the zodiac were exchanged by loving couples, possibly referencing reverence of the Celtic god

Belenus. The wedding ring may have spread via Roman influence; the Romans had borrowed the custom from the Egyptians and Greeks. In the seventeenth-century England, the Puritans attempted, generally unsuccessfully, to ban wedding rings, considering them to be pagan symbols. In Poland, male bridegrooms-to-be wore special hats and scarves adorned with rosemary, thyme, artificial flowers, and red ribbons.

Speaking of red, in both Greco-Roman antiquity and in premodern Albania, Bulgaria, the Ukraine, and elsewhere, the bride often wore a red veil; and in both Classical antiquity and in premodern Finland, the marriage bed was covered with red fabric.

In Poland and Lithuania, rue served as a talisman of virginity and marriage. Prior to the wedding ceremony, young women wore headdresses of black headbands garlanded with sprigs of rue, silver and gold foil, and ribbons (often nine), sometimes in the shape of a crown. The bride-to-be presented her future husband with a wreath of rue. Rue also used to decorate the wedding *ko³acz* (bread or cake). During the wedding procession, rue sometimes served as a decoration on wedding carts in which the bride and groom were transported. When a woman presided over the wedding ceremony, she held a staff decorated with rue. Branches of periwinkle served similarly. In other Polish traditions, the wedding "rod" was made from a pear and/or pine branch and was decorated with apples, "gold and silver ribbons, artificial flowers, peacocks' and cocks' feathers," and other items. Among Lithuanians, a *sodas*, or "orchard," a tree resembling a Christmas tree, typically a "fir tree decorated with colored paper and flowers," served to signify the growth of joy, love, prosperity, and stability within marriage. When marriage vows were exchanged, Polish couples sometimes wore wreaths of rosemary. These were kept and later placed into their child's first bath.

Special praise-songs continued to be sung in early twentieth-century Poland to the goddess Lada and the god Lelum, the Polish Eros, regarding wedding garlands, scarves, and gifts:

> In Crakow town
> Our garland green was growing—
> Lelum Lado!
> In Sandomir
> Our kerchiefs they were sewing,
> Lelum Lado!
> ………………………………..
> Oh, with wondrous gifts we're laden –
> A rue garland for a maiden.
> Hand over the wreath, without delaying,
> Lelum Lado![70]

Also during wedding processions in early twentieth-century Poland, bridesmaids and best men continued, in praise-songs, to "invoke the blessings of the god Lelum (the god of love) [also called Polelum] and the goddess Lado [or, Lada]": "With thy powers bless guests of ours/ Lelum Lado."

The wedding banquet was, other than the rite of the nuptial bed, most definitely one of the most significant of the marriage rites. One of the most widespread customs was having the couple drink from the same cup. Very consciously, foods having symbolic significance, signifying erotic attraction, love, and fertility, as well as foods considered to be aphrodisiacs, were served. These included eggs, butter, wine (in regions influenced by Rome, including in England, signifying the patronage of marriage by Bacchus), rabbits, roosters, testicles of goat and bear, and honey. In Lithuania Minor as well as in the Ukraine, into the early twentieth century, honey was offered to the couple by the master or mistress of the feast, who said to them as it was offered, "May your love be as sweet as honey!" On the other hand, certain foods were avoided, such as the meat of castrated animals, as such foods might promote infertility.

The wedding cake, often in fact a masterfully ornamented, sweet loaf of bread, was in many places the most significant of the foods at the feast. In Germanic, Slavic, and Baltic regions, the cake or bread was decorated with symbols of fertility, such as chickens and roosters, as well as with nuts and apple slices. In Germany and Lithuania, a *raguolis*, or "tree-cake" decorated with flowers and greens, was sometimes served. In Russia, the bridegroom was also given a special cake "which ha[d] lain in the bosom of the bride." H. E. Kennedy notes that in early twentieth-century Poland, women continued to invoke the goddess Lada, perhaps only vaguely aware that they did so, as they baked wedding cakes; they sang,

> Oh Lado, Lado, Lado,
> Little birds swiftly winging
> Twigs from the bush are bringing,
> The cake to deck with singing.[71]

The wedding banquet often became extremely rowdy. In various parts of Europe, charivari concerts of chaotic noise were performed to rid the site and the ensuing marriage of any malefic beings. In this context, it should be noted that other practices meant to protect the couple from, and to ward off, evil beings included ritual bathing as well as closing all doors, windows, and the chimney flue, brandishing torches, and breaking objects during the ceremony.

Certain special dances were performed which symbolized the coming together of bride and groom. Bawdy songs were sung, songs promoting lovemaking. In the Ukraine, the master of ceremonies – in the Christianized Ukraine, occasionally the priest – said to the groom, bride, and other celebrants: "Go and play, all you horned oxen, cows with pretty udders, sheep with thick wool, boys with handsome penises, girls with pretty vaginas, in every corner a baby." Other priests, not surprisingly, horrified by such wild behavior, bewailed "phallic rite[s] observed at wedding-banquets, sexual promiscuity during the feast."

In Germanic tradition, it would seem that the gods, embodied or represented by costumed performers, may have sometimes made an appearance at the wedding banquet. Noting that Germanic deities were "in the habit of wandering about in disguise on such festal occasions" and that one of Odin's names was "Gestr ('guest' or 'stranger')," Marwick suggests that in Christianized Scotland, in Shetland, the ancient deities were recalled in the form of the *guizers*, "[y]oung men...fantastically got up in straw dresses with a profusion of ribbons, and with covered (or masked) faces." The leader of the guizers, the *skudler*, "danced around the room, making protective gestures with his besom over bridegroom and bride."

As the couple left the feast, foods such as rice, wheat, oats, hops, nuts, peas, beans, and little cakes were thrown at them to avert evil and promote love and fertility. In Sicily, barley signified male offspring, while wheat signified female offspring. Among persons in Lithuania Minor/East Prussia, as the couple was sprinkled with barley, wheat, corn, peas, and/or beans, a prayer was said: "May our gods give you a sufficiency of everything as long as you remain in the faith in which your forefathers died and you manage your house with industry and due care."

In England, following a Roman custom honoring Demeter/Ceres, a youth with a torch led the couple to the nuptial chamber. Rites of crossing the threshold were of course important in many places. In Lithuania Minor/East Prussia, a deep ditch was dug to represent the threshold. The feet of the couple and any others entering the chamber with them were ritually washed prior to entry. Alternatively, as in England, they were asperged with water and incensed. Objects including eggs, pots, and glass were broken either when crossing the threshold or during another part of the wedding; the breaking of these was meant to frighten evil beings as well as to signify transition from an old state of being to a new one. After crossing the threshold, the couple might circle the bedroom or its hearth in order to sanctify the space and protect themselves from unwelcome beings.

The nuptial chamber was decorated and filled with special foods and beverages similar to those at the feast. In France, couples were given spiced wine to promote eroticism and fertility. In Russia, as elsewhere, straw, flowers, and/or herbs were strewn on the floor, and a cask of beer was placed in the room. Cakes and other gifts of thanks were offered to the presiding deities and similar beings. Cas O' Connor draws our attention to a "special jeweled, embroidered belt from her husband, meant to represent that given by Vulcan to Venus on their own wedding night. The gift was hoped to evoke in the bride the qualities of the goddess." As mentioned above, the color red often predominated, as in the fabric covering the marriage bed. Alternatively, a red beet might be placed on a white sheet to signify the shifting from virginity to fertility.

In numerous places, for instance, in southern Sweden, into the nineteenth century, the bride and groom were ritually undressed in the nuptial chamber in front of at least some of the guests, after which they climbed into bed to commence making love. On occasion, songs were sung by guests outside the chamber as the couple consummated their marriage.

Near 1835, a traveler in Ireland happened to witness a "rustic marriage festival...one evening in the wilds of Kerry" County. It was probably during the early days of May, since a Maypole made from a hawthorn tree, decorated "all over with bits of colored stuff," probably rags or ribbons, with "lighted rush candles ...placed...amongst the branches," comprised the primary symbol of the celebration. The sacred hawthorn stood, incidentally, beside a stream. In Lady (Jane Francisca Elgee) Wilde's (Oscar's mother, 1826-1896) quoting, paraphrasing, or retelling of this event, the Maypole signified the "new life of brightness preparing for the bridal pair." The traveler noticed a procession of young men performing a charivari 'concert' with flutes, bones, and a tin can. They were followed by a youth taking the role of Hymenaeus or a local patron of marriage who carried a torch. He was in turn followed by the bride and groom, who walked beneath a black canopy meant to signify the "mystery of love." They were followed by two attendants bearing a "sieve filled with meal," a symbol of good fortune, fertility, and children. The procession culminated in a "wild chorus of dancers and singers" dressed as "fauns and satyrs, nymphs and bacchan[tes]." The procession halted at a bonfire and, after dancing around it three times, all present clapped, shouted, and waved branches as the bride and groom exchanged vows and kissed. This was followed by a great feast. Gifts were placed on an altar. The bride's father paid her dowry and the groom presented her with a "beautiful new dress." Singing, dancing, and feasting continued until dawn.

Courtly Love, or Fin'Amor:

A Pagan Erotic Spirituality/Enspirited Materiality

Courtly love refers to a type of erotico-sacred relationship and code that arose, chiefly between knights and troubadours, on the one hand, and noblewomen on the other, during the Middle Ages. Although it does not appear to have played a significant role in the lives of rurals or the lower classes, it would appear that earth-based beliefs they held and practices they performed contributed to its construction.

During the late 1960s, the era of so-called "free love," the notion of "courtly love" came under attack. This is particularly noticeable in a collection of papers delivered at SUNY in 1967. In a nutshell, the various conference participants (unsurprisingly, all white males) insisted that "courtly love" was a late Romantic fantasy invented by Gaston Paris (1839-1903) and that it was not only entirely useless in describing medieval relationships but that it also served to romanticize such relationships. Like many Foucauldians of a later generation, the SUNY presenters relied on the fact that Paris had coined the term "courtly love" to argue that this proved that such a phenomenon had never existed before. Perhaps they were unaware that the medieval term for "courtly love" was *fin'amor*. W. T. H. Jackson insisted, "'Courtly love' is an absolutely useless phrase." At best, said one academic, it was a game played by Christians needing release from the seriousness of their religion. Although I appreciate these skeptical views, in looking backward, their proponents seem as trapped in the academic-agnostic-existentialist ideology of the late 1960s (how well I remember it!) as Paris must have seemed to them to be trapped within Romanticism, or their more free-spirited colleagues and non-academics must have seemed to them to be trapped within the "Love Generation." Intriguingly, beneath all the maverick skepticism there seems to lie a decidedly Christocentric – except perhaps in the case of Theodore Silverstein – patriarchal, hegemonic interpretation of texts allegedly concerning courtly love. Silverstein especially condemned interpretations of courtly love that he felt had been inspired by a fascination with esotericism and/or mythology; such scholars as Jessie Weston (1850-1928) and Robert Graves (1895-1985) suffered from "bewitchment." This is reminiscent of Henri Marrou's (pseudonym, H. Davenson) 1961 characterization of scholars who promoted a pagan interpretation of courtly love as "esoteric maniacs." Rather surprisingly, Marrou and W. T. H. Jackson of the SUNY conference saved their harshest criticism for C. S. Lewis; indeed, said Jackson, "I have spent a lot of my life – as we all have – giving my low opinion of Lewis's *Allegory of Love*."

Although a number of academics have followed in Marrou, Jackson, and Company's footsteps, C. S. Lewis' vision of courtly love endures. This might be due to the fact that many of us remain hopeless Romantics, or there might just be a kernel of truth in Lewis' view. Lewis rejects a Christocentric interpretation of the development of courtly love. He argues, to the contrary, that courtly love arose as a mirror-like reaction to Christianity. Although he thinks that it would be an exaggeration to "describe it as the revenge of paganism," that is pretty much what he proceeds to do. Deploying the German term *Frauendienst*, "the service of ladies," he describes courtly love as "the love religion." He claims that during the medieval period, courtly love developed into a "rival religion" that never became "reconciled to the real religion," i.e., to Christianity. Indeed, he insists, one might even describe courtly love as the "open enemy" of Christianity, "as when Aucassin roundly declares that he would rather follow all the sweet ladies and goodly knights to hell than go without them to heaven." Despite its apparent hostility toward Christianity, or at least Christian dogma, the tradition of courtly love was nevertheless taken up by many Christians, including Moniot d'Arras (fl. 1213-1239), a monk of the Abbey of Arras and French composer of the *trouvère* tradition, well known for his chanson "Ce fu(t) en Mai" ("It Happened in May"), which describes an unrequited lover who sees the woman he loves and a knight dancing a "round dance," embracing, and kissing in a rose garden: "The game/ of love they played to their hearts'/ content [among] the flowers." They notice him, wish him well, and pray that he will find another woman to love. Resonant with Lewis' view, Roger Boase argues in *The Origin and Meaning of Courtly Love: A Critical Study of European Scholarship* (1977) that courtly love "evolved out of the folk traditions and ritual dance songs of Europe, particularly those associated with the rites of spring, or it was an actual survival of the pagan cult of Cybele or Maia, the Great Mother of the Gods." Similarly, Andrea Hopkins, who studied at Oxford and wrote her thesis on penitence in medieval romance, writes in *The Book of Courtly Love: The Passionate Code of the Troubadours* (1994): "[L]ove was …celebrated in quasi-religious terms, with the beloved woman being venerated as an object of worship…They invented a religious cult of love, with its own deities – Venus and Cupid – and its own temples, rites, prayers, priests and commandments."

Courtly love, or *fin'amor*, emerged from an amalgamation of numerous sources including Hispano-Arabic love theory and Christian heresies, especially that of the Cathars. C. S. Lewis suggests that a significant component in the development of courtly love may have been passionate friendships or homoerotic liaisons between men. "The deepest of worldly emotions in this period," he states, "is the love of man for man, the mutual love of warriors...and the affection between vassal and lord....[T]hese male affections...were themselves lover-like."

Troubadour lyrics focusing on courtly love describe the birth of spring in an earth-centered manner; as Boase observes, "This picture of the rebirth of nature is appropriate to a lyrical tradition which originated in hymns to the Goddess of Nature." Where Goddess reverence is concerned, Jean Markale, in *Courtly Love: The Path of Sexual Initiation*, observes: "[T]his is [an] erotic mysticism that has scarcely any Christian roots. The woman takes on the look of a savior goddess....Woman now...becomes the most perfect image of the divine incarnated in all forms, the initiator of human activity. The *domna*, courtly love's "lady of high rank, " was, and has been, compared to numerous goddesses including the Roman Venus and Cybele and the Celtic Danu (or, Anu, Dana, Dôn), as well as to the Virgin Mary (except in her lack of eros) and to Guinevere of the Arthurian cycle, who, in Markale's view, "incontestably represents the ancient universal mother-goddess whom people have not ceased to worship since the dawn of time." Gwendolyn Trottein, in *Les Enfants de Vénus: Art et Astrologie à la Renaissance*: "[The] iconography of courtly love insisted on veneration of the goddess Venus, who was capable of intervening in favor of lovers; Venus was depicted as enthroned in the heavens above her followers, who...implored her assistance."

Although Trottein acknowledges the controversy regarding 'Christian' and 'pagan' interpretations of courtly love and even voices her own contradictory views in this matter, she ultimately concludes that "the cult of Venus existed," at the very least, in a mythopoeic way, and that existence of her cult is born out by medieval works of literature and visual art, as, for example, the painting *Venus Venerated by Six Legendary Lovers*. Likewise, the male lover becomes the "priest of a new religion – a religion that dares not give itself a name but which develops in parallel with...the Church. The profane reunites with the sacred. Like the "worshipper of Cybele," he "declare[s] himself a 'servant' of a goddess." As Markale sees it, the lover is comparable to Lancelot, Guinevere's lover in the Arthurian cycle, who himself is the "courtly image of the pagan Irish hero Cú Chulainn," who in turn is related to the "great god and multiple craftsman Lug[h]."

The code of love exemplified by *fin'amor* has nothing to do with marriage except in the sense that it is often adulterous. Boase writes: "It was the convention in May Day songs and chansons de *mal-mariée* to scoff at the odious bonds of matrimony...The goddess, whose festival was at the vernal equinox...did not recognize marriage, but required free love from all her votaries. Courtly love was extra-conjugal." Markale adds: "[T]he idea of marriage is totally excluded from such a couple....[T]here must be either actual or symbolic adultery. After all, the perfect model of this couple is Lancelot and Guinevere, or Tristan and Iseult [/Isolde]."

The teaching of courtly love or *fin'amor* was that enlightenment results from a heady brew of mystery, yearning, passion, secrecy, suffering, and gynocentricity. When eroticism manifested within *fin'amor*, it would appear that it may have embraced nudity and non-coital, non-orgasmic (at least on the part of the man) lovemaking, with boundary lines being drawn by the woman and accepted by the man.

A Few Words about Same-Sex Intimacy and Transgenderism

To begin with, controversy continues in regard to whether or not we can speak of "gay" or "transgender" "people" in pre-modern epochs and cultures. Social constructivists, who have been winning the battle, so to speak, for the past twenty-five years, maintain that prior to the nineteenth century, we can only speak with any surety about acts of same-sex intimacy and "performances" of transgender behavior. A minority of academics, joined by many in the mainstream, argue that homosexuality and transgender identity are and have been relatively stable in numerous epochs and cultures other than our own; indeed, these identities may be linked to genetic markers and biology. In the context of our present exploration, it is, I believe, important to acknowledge that certain earth-centered cultures were well acquainted with same-sex intimacy and transgender behavior or identity (I will leave it up to you as to whether or not, to put it reductively, you side with "nurture" or "nature") and that in some of these cultures, these behaviors or identities were ritualized and comprised, for some, a significant rite within the cycle of rites including birth, maturation, union, ageing, death, and regeneration.

Commencing in the sixth century CE, European Christian penitentials and kindred religious documents addressed same-sex intimacy and, to a considerably lesser extent, transgenderism. It is sometimes difficult to categorize these practices or identities as foregrounding same-sex eroticism or transgenderism; for example, in the *Penitential of Theodore*, one finds: "Sodomites shall do penance for seven years, and the effeminate man as an adulteress." In this penitential, one also finds: "If a woman practices vice with a woman, she shall do penance for three years." These were practices or identities that must be banned because they were pagan in origin and as sins the practice of which must be punished.

Most readers will already be familiar with the practice of various manifestations of same-sex intimacy and transgenderism among Greeks and Romans, including the suppression of the Bacchic Mysteries in 186 BCE due to their inclusion of a same-sex erotic component in the initiation process, and will know that Christian-ization, unsurprisingly, brought condemnation and suppression of these.

During the sixth century CE, Christian penitentials and related documents condemning such practices or identities were addressed to Celtic peoples; these included two Welsh documents, one produced by the "Synod of the Grove of Victory" the other called *A Book of David*. In the seventh century, Irish penitentials including *The Penitential of Cummean*, the *Penitential of Columban*, and *The Penitential of Theodore* likewise condemned these practices or identities. Moreover, the *Penitential of Theodore* also addressed these as they occurred in Northumbria among persons of Germanic or mixed Celtic and Germanic heritages. Eighth- and ninth-century penitentials like that known as the *Penitential tentatively ascribed by Albers to Bede*, the *Burgundian Penitential*, and the so-called *Roman Penitential* addressed, like that attributed to Theodore, both Celts and Germanics as well as persons possessing both of these ethnicities. Eleventh- and twelfth-century penitentials like the *Corrector* of Burchard of Worms and the Icelandic *Penitential of Thorlac* primarily addressed Germanic peoples. This suggests that Christian authorities deemed it necessary to condemn same-sex intimacy and transgenderism among persons of Celtic and Germanic heritage for over half a millennium – and we haven't even mentioned the burning of "sodomites" in the centuries that followed.

That transgenderism and same-sex eroticism were considered non-Christian or pagan practices is abundantly obvious from their appearance in the penitentials and related texts. They were considered as such because, at least where Celts and Germanic peoples were concerned, they comprised, for some persons, a significant component of the rites of the life cycle.

In *Politics*, Aristotle (384-322 BCE) writes that the Celts, as well as other groups he does not name, "openly approve of homosexual attachments." Diodorus Sicilus (fl. 1st cent. BCE) states of the Gauls, a Celtic people dwelling primarily in what is now France: "Although their wives are comely, they have very little to do with them, but rage with lust, in outlandish fashion, for the embraces of males. It is their practice to sleep upon the ground on the skins of wild beasts and to tumble with a catamite on each side...[W]hen anyone of them is thus approached and refuses the favour offered him, this they consider an act of dishonour." Likewise, Athenaeus (*c.* 170- *c.* 230 CE) writes: "And among barbarians, the Celts also, though they have very beautiful women, enjoy boys more; so that some of them often have two lovers to sleep with on their beds of animal skins."

As for Germanic peoples, Sextus Empiricus (*c.* 160- 210 CE) writes in *Outlines of Pyrrhonism*: "For example, amongst us sodomy [*arrenomixias*, "male-mixing"] is regarded as shameful or rather illegal, but by the Germani they say, it is not looked on as shameful but as a customary thing." Ammianus Marcellinus (*c.* 325- after 391 CE) writes that, in the late fourth century CE, among the Taifali, "Boys couple with men in a union of unnatural lust, and waste the flower of their youth in the polluted embraces of their lovers. But if a young man catches a boar single-handed or kills a huge bear, he is exempt thereafter from the contamination of this lewd intercourse."

Procopius (late fifth century CE- in or after 562 CE) also suggests that the Germanic tribe of Heruli practiced initiatory homosexuality.

Jan Bremmer argues that, despite suppression of evidence, statements by Livy, Athenaeus, Procopius, Ammianus Marcellinus, and others indicate that ritualized, initiatory same-sex eroticism was probably widely practiced by Greeks, Celts, Germanic peoples, and other Indo-Europeans – all of whom were, of course, pagans, prior to Christianization. Thus, it is little wonder that Church authorities were determined to suppress homo-eroticism. It appears, however, that Christianization was not completely successful in eradicating either same-sex eroticism or trans-genderism, as John Boswell suggests in *Christianity, Social Tolerance, and Homosexuality* and *Same-Sex Unions in Premodern Europe*. Rather, these practices or identities were, on the one hand, condemned and banned, being punishable by death; and, on the other, were appropriated by Christianity and reshaped into often sublimated "particular friendships," same-sex ritualized unions, and transgender saints.

Death, the Soul, Afterlife, Rebirth

Europeans frequently conceived of Death as a goddess or similar female being. As such, Death's manifestations include the Germanic Hel, the Slavic Morena and Baba Yaga, and the Baltic Giltine, and Ragana. She also manifests as the Irish *banshee*, the Polish Jagusia (also, Baœka, or Zoœka), and the Hispanic/Latino la Llorona and Santissima Muerte. She announces herself by knocking on a door or window or else is announced by the cries of dogs, owls, and magpies.

Various sorts of rituals were undertaken when it became clear that someone was dying. One such ritual, practiced in Scotland, involved "old wives" cutting the nails of the dying person, particularly of someone with consumption, and putting the pairings into a small bag and then waving the bag around the person's head three times so that his or her soul would not be stolen by "the fairies."

The traditional Ukrainian funeral provides a good example of a European pagan and, later, a pagano-Christian funeral. First, all work other than preparing the dead for burial ceased. The body of the deceased was washed and placed near a window, with the person's feet pointing toward the door. When the body had been ceremoniously dressed and prepared for internment, it was carried in the coffin to the gravesite. The coffin was lined with down, and as it was being lowered into the grave, the presiding ritual specialist or priest chanted, "May the earth be like feathers for you." The funeral cortège said their farewells to the deceased, and the coffin was knocked upon three times to remind the deceased that she or he had now changed status and would (primarily) dwell among the dead.

The living responded to death with sadness, joy, or both: sadness, in that someone would no longer be present in the same way they had been in life; joy, in that the person would find his or her way to paradise or else would soon be reborn. Thus, both lamentations and entertainments occurred during funeral rites.

In Saxony, ancient hymns called *dadsisas* were sung at the graves of the dead into at least the ninth century. In Russia, keening (called *vopit,*' *plakat'sya*, and *prichitat*'), which occurred through at least the twelfth century, despite Christian condemnation, included invocation of "the forces of nature, the wind, the River Dnieper and the sun, seeking their sympathy and help" in protecting the body and spirit of the deceased; on certain occasions, the wind was begged to restore the deceased to life. In Lithuania Minor, the living rejoiced upon the death of a family member or comrade, focusing on the deceased's journey to paradise or into new life. Those who believed in reincarnation considered brave warriors to be rewarded with the most desirable destinies in their next lives. Others, whose vision focused on paradise, witnessed the spirits of warriors "flying through the sky on horseback, adorned in shining armour, with iron spear in hand, and great company proceeding into the other world," a vision reminiscent of the Germanic Wild Hunt.

Ancient, earth-centered cultures often embraced several forms of dealing with bodies of the deceased. These forms, including burial and cremation, indicated views regarding the afterlife. For example, in Kievan Rus,' burial rites were "linked to the idea of reincarnation: the bodies of the dead were put in an embryonic position as if in preparation for rebirth." In some cultures, how the body of the deceased was dealt with depended upon his or her station in life: in Lithuania Minor, rulers were typically cremated; nobles were buried; and commoners might be buried or cremated.

Burials where the skull has been detached from the body and is then either buried with the rest of the body or separately represent a very ancient form of burial in the British Isles and elsewhere. This practice appears to have arisen from a Celtic belief that the soul was located in the head and that it lived on through transmigration. As Dorothy Watts explains in *Religion in Late Roman Britain* (1992), "the head is more powerful/ apotropaic/ talismanic when detached. If the head is removed, then the spirit is released and is free to move into another body or person." A subset of such burials includes that wherein the mandible has been separated from the remainder of the skull. This practice appears to have been associated with the ability of powerful women, particularly queens and wisewomen, to utter effective spells even after death. From evidence gathered at Rushton, Northamptonshire, England, decapitated and skull burials appear to have continued into the ninth and possibly into the late twelfth century in defiance of Christian prohibitions. Watts observes: "The cemetery was undoubtedly in existence by the time England was ostensibly Christianized, yet the burials were clearly pagan (that is, south-north orientation and with disturbed and decapitated burials)...The longevity of the rite once again reinforces the strength of the commitment of the native Britons to their old religious practices."

Cremation was practiced by numerous European cultures, including Germanics, Balts, and Slavs. Bodies were sometimes cremated or buried in or near sacred groves.

Because the practice of cremation was so common among pagan Europeans, it was banned as such by Charlemagne in the eighth century.

In medieval Žemaitija (or, Samogitia), bodies were cremated in sacred groves, "along with each dead person's horses, saddles, and finest garments." The sacrifice of horses, as Gimbutas explains, was not considered animal cruelty but rather signified the "last traces of the great love that existed between man and animal....[I]t was believed that the animals went to the other world to live there with their master."

When Lithuanian warriors were cremated, about one third of their possessions were burned with them. Likewise, when Lithuanian rulers were cremated, an "immense pile of grave goods" accompanied them. Among the last Lithuanian rulers to be cremated in a sacred grove was the Grand Duke Algirdas, who was "solemnly burned in 1377 in the Kokiveithus grove not far away from the Masiagala castle and settlement." Gimbutas observes: "The custom of cremation persisted long after the introduction of Christianity and was abolished only as the result of a fierce struggle against the practice by the Christian missionaries. Lithuanian kings and dukes were cremated with great pomp until the end of the fourteenth century." Similarly, Ukrainians were buried with their favorite things and objects signifying social status. Many persons of the British Isles, especially rurals, into the late nineteenth century, placed pieces of quartz and diversely colored stones – especially white, black, red, and green – in graves, apparently for magical purposes.

David Wilson, in *Anglo-Saxon Paganism* (1992) documents the discovery by archaeologists examining Anglo-Saxon cemeteries of deliberately broken items including combs, brooches, and other personal effects. This practice is described as "killing" the objects. It is possible that the underlying belief motivating this practice concerned the object being 'translated' into one which might become useful to the dead, one whose daily existence had been 'broken,' somewhat resembling the practice of burning incense so that it might reach the realm of the gods, or else the "transporter" of *Star Trek*, which transforms matter into energy and back again. Moreover, archaeologists have also discovered cremation urns that have been deliberately damaged, including being pierced; the holes made in them have been described as "ghost holes." These holes have "been explained as being a means by which the spirit of the dead was released from its container." Anna-Leena Siikala reports that the ritual breaking of objects was also practiced by indigenous and pagano-Christian Finns; she writes: "The breaking of objects...brought out the contrast between the worlds of the dead and the living. Things broken in the human world were whole in the other world."

This practice bears an uncanny resemblance to ones of the Yorùbá of Nigeria and the Mimbres of New Mexico, who also break objects linked to the deceased. In *Dwellings: A Spiritual History of the Living World* (1995), the Chickasaw writer Linda Hogan relates, "The Mimbres 'killed' their pots by breaking a hole in the center of each one. It is thought that the hole served to release the spirit of the pot from the clay, allowing it to travel with them over land and to join them in their burial grounds. It is called a 'kill hole.'" A mysterious custom in regard to the relationship of the living and the dead involved toasting corn "in the place where a dead man lay, for the health of living men."

Europeans held divergent views of afterlife existence. Often, within the same tradition, several views were held simultaneously. The notion that a body was being returned to the earth from whence it had come was widely accepted. For some, both body and soul remained in the earth, while for others, this was a temporary resting-place for the soul before recommencing its journey. Whichever of these alternatives was voiced, however, Mother Earth was honored for her role in giving birth to this life and in taking it back into her womb. In Lithuania Minor, offerings of mead or beer were poured on the earth at this time, with this prayer being said to the Earth Mother Žemyna: "Be joyful, Žemynėle, receive this soul and guard it well."

In some cases, alternate views of afterlives resulted from a belief that humans as well as other-than-human beings possessed multiple souls and that each experienced its own afterlife. Germanic peoples, like ancient Egyptians and Greeks, believed in multiple souls, or, alternatively, in a multidimensional soul.

One of the souls or parts of the soul in Germanic tradition is the *hugr*, which is similar to the ethereal body or 'double;' while another is the *hamingja* (in Orkney, a *varden*), a sort of animal soul, like the Nahua (Mexica/Aztec) *tonal*.

Another common belief, one we have previously encountered, was that in reincarnation or metempsychosis. In Slavic tradition, between lives, souls sojourn in the orchard paradise of Irej (or, Rai, Raj, Ray; also, Bouyan, or Buyan), which lies in this universe, just beyond the sun. Lithuanians believed in a soul or aspect of a multidimensional soul called the *siela*. This is the soul or aspect of the soul that is reborn in "trees, flowers, animals, birds. It would leave the body as a breath, a vapor, and immediately find a lodging in plants, animals or birds. Sometimes it would issue directly from the mouth in the shape of a butterfly, a bee, a mouse, a toad, a snake...[or] a lily."

The belief that the deceased lived on in the tomb was commonplace. In Germanic, Slavic, and Baltic traditions, ghosts of deceased ancestors often communicated with the living and visited their old homes on certain nights. Where Ukrainian tradition is concerned, P. Odarchenko explains in "Ancestor Worship:" "According to popular belief the clan (*rid*) was an indivisible whole, consisting of the living, the dead, and the unborn. Death...did not sever the ties between the dead and the living. The ancestors participated in all the affairs of the family."

A similar yet somewhat different notion, depicted in medieval Germanic lore, is that the heroic dead dwell within mountains in a state of suspended animation and that they will be called back to life when they are most needed. Also somewhat similar is the belief that the dead dwell very near us, in an adjacent realm invisible to most (but not all) living persons; Gimbutas writes: "The Baltic *veles* go to live their family and village community lives, to a sandy hill, a hill of *veles*, where they have their houses…The hill of *veles* has gates through which the *veles* enter."

Many practitioners of earth-based traditions believed that the soul, part of it, or one of the souls journeyed to another world, typically a hell or paradise, depending on whether or not the person had lived a good life, and remained there. Whether to a hell or heaven, the journey was often an arduous one. Lithuanian *vëles* traveled by various means, including on the souls of horses, in invisible boats, on the ascending smoke of the funeral pyre, and in the form of birds. Indigenous Finns also believed that the soul traveled in a boat to the afterlife realm of Tuonela. Some Lithuanians and Slavs believed that the soul must climb a very steep hill of stone, glass, or iron in order to attain paradise. Those who had lived ethically and who had honored the gods successfully completed the climb; those who had not fell into the gaping jaws of a great dragon. Others believed that souls traversed the Milky Way, the "Birds' Way," to arrive at the Otherworld.

Germanic tradition describes a freezing, foggy hell to the far north, Niflheim, that commences with an inn at the end of a road, perhaps an ancient version of the Overlook in Stephen King's *The Shining*. But the paradise of Valhalla (or, Valhallar, Walhalla) awaits fearless warriors, including women warriors, who are welcomed by Odin and the Valkyries; while the joyful abodes of the goddesses Freyja, called Fôlkvângr, and Holda, occasionally depicted as a happy place reached by children who drown in wells, reminiscent of a *Twilight Zone* episode, "The Bewitchin' Pool," (1964). Fôlkvângr also – unlike the more well known Valhalla, also awaits those who have been farmers, artists, healers and others, those who don't relish the thought of eternal battle. Slavic and Baltic souls may reach an orchard paradise ruled by a goddess – in Slavic tradition, Zarya, in Baltic, the sun goddess Saulë – who sits beneath a sacred apple, birch, linden, or oak tree, upon a sacred rock, in the middle of a cosmic sea (perhaps resonant with the cosmic ocean in Stanislas Lem and Tarkovsky's *Solaris*). Or, as in Celtic tradition, the mortal may find his or her way neither to a hell or paradise per se but instead to the Realm of Faerie, the 'third' realm, which may lie beneath the earth, inside a hill, or beneath the sea.

In my view, one of the more intriguing beliefs held by Balts, although rooted in the common notion that the dead basically carry on as they have in mortal life, relates that the unmarried dead may marry in the afterlife. As one *daina* (sacred or folkloric song) goes, "My young brother is dead,/ He has taken a fiancée among the spirits."

George P. Fedotov, in *The Russian Religious Mind: Kievan Christianity* (1946), argues that the "core of Russian paganism was not the belief in great gods but the religious veneration of nature" and the "veneration of ancestors." He also observes that Russian "paganism…considered the individual only as a transient moment in the eternal life of the *rod* [ancestral cult] …This is the deepest religious root of Russian collectivism" and that in "pagan times all the dead became minor gods...The chief of the ancestors, or founder of the *rod*, became a particular patron of the house, who was, and still is, called by the general name of...*Domovoi*."

Some Europeans, for example, Latvians and Lithuanians, believed that funerals must take place before noon, when the "doors of the spirits" close. Funeral entertainments included horseracing, as practiced in Lithuania Minor. Funerals were typically followed by feasts. The dead were often fed special foods and beverages, including colored eggs (in the Ukraine) and wine. In Slavic and Baltic regions, one of the most significant foods given to the dead, called by various names including *kutia* and *kolyvo*, is comparable to today's oatmeal, Cream of Wheat, or rice pudding with raisins and honey. This custom of feeding the dead was linked to the veneration of ancestors, who were ritually fed both a year after death and then also on the occasion of certain seasonal festivals. Jan D³ugosz reported that in the fifteenth century, in allegedly Christianized Žemaitija, altars for the dead continued to appear in groves deemed sacred by practitioners of earth-based traditions: "Here are altars beside which stand tables made from cork-trees on which they set soft foods, such as cheese, while they pour mead over the altars,...thinking that the spirits of the dead they have buried there will come by night, eat the food, and drink the mead."

In Russia, a springtime feast was held for the dead in the bathhouse; at this time, the spirits of ancestors were believed to gather for a meal of meat, milk, butter, and eggs. This custom persisted into the nineteenth century.

Alleged witches were often thought to commune with, and occasionally spoke of themselves as communing with, the dead. Moreover, they were sometimes thought to be instructed in the arts of divination, magic, and healing by those who had passed before them; for example, in Scotland at the end of the sixteenth century, the alleged witch Alison Peirsoun (or, Alesoun, Allison; or, Pearson, Peirson) claimed to have learned the craft from the ghost of her cousin or uncle William Simpson (or, Sympson, Sympsoun).

In 1920s England, a "family of three daughters...spread a table with fruit, nuts, bread, butter, and a bowl of tea" for their deceased mother, while a "Devonshire woman sued the Paignton Urban District Council on the grounds that they wrongfully obstructed her deposit of food...in a vault."

Many continue to believe that the dead participate in the lives of the living and can occasionally assist them in bringing health, prosperity, and such. Padraic O'Farrell reports an Irish tradition which was in the recent past (being carried into Christianity) performed very shortly after a person's death: " 'Gather, gather, gather,' cried the woman of the house as she stirred the milk with the hand of the corpse. This was supposed to increase the butter yield."[72]

Chapter 8
Healing, Divination, and Magic

Remember, Mugwort, what you made known,
………………………………………..
You have power against poison and against infection . . .

   from an Anglo-Saxon healing charm[73]

Stroke me smooth and comb my head and thou shalt have some cockle-bread.

   from a love spell performed by women from the eleventh through (at least) the seventeenth centuries CE[74]

Healing

Many types of healing techniques existed in pagan cultures, frequently associated with healing different kinds of physical, emotional, and spiritual illness. Among the most common were fumigating the client with "burnt ingredients, healing by touch, …bathing parts of the body," having the client consume a medicinal beverage or food, and fashioning an amulet or talisman for the client to wear. Many of these practices continue to exist at present, although many have undergone partial Christianization, such as one finds in Mexican Curanderismo.

Many simple substances were used in traditional healing, including water, honey, and eggs. In traditional Russian medicine, for instance, bathing in pure water or rolling eggs over their bodies (a method also used at present by Latina *curanderas*) cleansed a person of evil beings or negative energy, while honey was used (also by Balts) as a preventative against winter illnesses.

Animals, animal parts, and substances from animals such as cow's milk and dung (called "witch's pancake" in the Fens of eastern England) were often used in traditional healing. For example, among persons living in the Fens, pig's tails, horse teeth, and hedgehog skulls were sometimes carried by persons, as garters made of dried eel skins were worn, to prevent and cure various illnesses including rheumatism and neuralgia. Roasted mice were eaten to cure whooping cough. Occasionally, cocks or hens to be sacrificed were passed over a person's body in order to facilitate healing, a practice presently common in the African-diasporic religion of Regla de Ocha (Lucumí, Santería).

Human substances including urine were also deployed. Sometimes metallic materia were also used by traditional healers. For example, pennies steeped in vinegar were believed to cure ulcers, whereas a penny bandaged to a sore and "left for a week or so, completely [healed] a wound." Alcohol, particularly whiskey and gin, were also used in traditional healing.

Perhaps the commonest form of healing, however, was that of herbal or plant medicine. This was typically performed in combination with invocations of deities and similar beings, although in Christianized Europe, such invocations became dangerous. The early ninth-century Spanish *Penitential of Silos*, the ninth-century *Penitential* of Halitgar (fl. *c.* 830 CE), and the eleventh-century *Corrector* of Burchard all prohibited the collecting of herbs when combined with earth-centered incantations rather than with the Credo or the Lord's Prayer. Church officials suspected "herbwives" or *herbaria*, women who collected herbs and who practiced herbal medicine of being witches. In German, these women were referred to as *Kräuterweiblein*, "Herb Women." Audrey L. Meaney writes in *Anglo-Saxon Amulets and Curing Stones* (1981): "It would have been exceedingly difficult...for anyone accustomed to using herbs with a certain incantation to have...abandoned [a pagan] incantation...to have given up that remedy altogether because it did not accord with Christian custom."

Acorns, feverfew, hemlock, hemp, horseradish, lavender, lily petals, mandrake, mint, parsley, poppies, rue (rue tea was called "witch broth" in the Fens), thyme, and wheat were among the many herbal, vegetable, and floral substances used in traditional healing. In traditional herbal or plant medicine, the association of healing and magic is noteworthy. For example, in or near 1603, the alleged Scottish witch James Reid "cured Sarah Borthwick of a grievous ailment by casting a certain quantity of wheat and salt about her bed."

One flowering plant that was especially esteemed by European wisewomen was the honeysuckle, or woodbine, deployed especially in childbirthing. In rites incorporating honeysuckle, the association of healing and magic is especially noticeable. Near 1600, the alleged witch Janet Stewart healed women "of the mysterious child-bed disorder *wedonymph*, by taking a garland of woodbine and putting them through it, afterwards cutting it into nine pieces, which she threw into the fire." According to Richard Folkard (1884), this rite included the recitation of "certain incantations and invocations." In Bulgaria, wisewomen-midwives brought dried honeysuckle, symbolic of a clenched fist, into the room of the woman who was having a difficult labor, where she would place it into a bowl of water so that it would open, which was meant to encourage the woman's birth canal to expand and the child to be released. Also during difficult labor, she would give the woman water in which honeysuckle had been seeped to drink.

Certain places were also thought to possess healing power, such as rooftops and crossroads. Both the tenth-century German *Ecclesiastical Discipline* attributed to the monk Regino of Prüm (d. 899/915) and the late twelfth-century Anglo-Norman *Penitential* of Bartholomew Iscanus prohibited the practice of placing a child on a roof or on an oven to heal the child, typically of a fever. Both Egbert (d. 839) and Aelfric of Eynsham (*c.* 955-*c.* 1010) condemned women who sought to heal their children by dragging them through the dirt at crossroads or who, perhaps in an effort to simulate rebirth, dug a small hole in the ground and then pulled sick children through it. Aelfric insisted that by way of such acts, women "commit[ted] themselves and their children to the devil," while Egbert condemned the actions as examples of "great paganism." In Burchard's penitential, we find: "Hast thou come to [a] crossroads, and there in reverence for the place lighted a candle or a torch or carried thither bread or any offering or eaten there or sought there any healing of body or mind? If thou hast done or consented to such things, thou shalt do penance for three years."

Needless to say, in regard to earth-centered/ indigenous traditions, from ancient offerings made to Hecate to those made at present to the African-diasporic deities of Vodou, the Regla de Ocha (Lucumí, Santería), and Candomblé, volumes might be written on crossroads and trivia. Solely in regard to Christian condemnations of works of healing at crossroads by medieval Europeans, four hundred years transpired between St. Eligius's seventh-century prohibition of crossroad healing rites – "Above all, should any infirmity occur, do not...use diabolic phylacteries [at] springs or groves or crossroads" – and Burchard's eleventh-century prohibition.

Traditional healers sometimes undertook practices that would at present be looked upon by many as extremely controversial, including performing abortions and actions meant to quicken the process of dying – practices that were seen by many who respected traditional healing and healers as humane, as opposed to permitting suffering to grow.

In the late sixteenth century, the alleged English witches Agnes and Jone Water-house and Elizabeth Frauncis, much of their practice focused on women's concerns (such as physical abuse by spouse), were charged, among other things, with using herbs to induce abortions.

In the Fens, into the early twentieth century, a certain rite known as "Snatching the Pillow," referring to a pillow "covered with black lace," was meant to make the dying more comfortable and to hasten death. Noteworthy is that a woman who also served as a midwife typically performed the rite. Enid Porter relates: "When an old person had been bedridden for months, or perhaps years, and there was no hope of recovery...the pillow would be sent for. As the nurse carried it through the village the inhabitants would go indoors and pull down the blinds, for they knew that soon they would be hearing the passing bell." Once the nurse arrived, she was served a "glass of fortifying gin." Then she put the special pillow behind the head of the dying person. "Then, crushing two opium pills, she would mix these with a strong dose of gin and spoon the mixture into the patient's mouth. Soon he would relapse into a coma." At this point, the nurse "snatched" the pillow away, the patient's "head would fall back with a jerk," and they died.

Traditional healers were concerned not only with the health of humans but also with that of animals. For instance, in Cambridgeshire, England, "mandrake root was widely used as a cure [for] sick horses." Other substances used in healing, and also in taming, horses included feverfew, hemlock, hemp, and rue.

Torun Zachrisson (2004) observes that there were three primary methods of healing among ancient Germanic peoples, all of which were associated with spirituality/

enspirited materiality: surgery, healing with herbs, and "healing through formulae and incantations." Of these, the third was considered the most effective. The aim of Germanic medicine, much like that of many indigenous healing systems, was to "restore the wholeness and well-being which had been upset by sickness or injury." Zachrisson relates that in Germanic healing practice, the "breath of the healer was perceived as curative." Odin was depicted as healing animals in this manner. Likewise, the healer's saliva was considered to possess healing power, as were his/her hands. Beyond the body of the healer, stones and soil were also used in healing, with stones being used to heal broken bones.

Not surprisingly, healing frequently involved invocation of deities and other beings. When Russians caught a cold, they believed that Žemyla, the Earth Mother, had given it to them because they had neglected her, so they would pray to her and make an offering: "Forgive me, Mother Earth! Mother Moisture! Here are groats for your meal." In Baltic medicine, numerous deities were invoked in healing incantations. In a charm included in *Lietuvos etnologia* (*Lithuanian Ethnography*, 1982), Pranò Dundulienò (1910-1991) draws our attention to a charm against fever, which invokes the sun goddess Saulë and the thunder god Perkûnas to take someone's, or an animal's, fever away.

A Germanic charm, written where the horses' fodder is kept, meant to protect horses from glanders, a contagious disease with symptoms including swelling beneath the jaw and discharge of mucous matter from the nostrils, invokes the elves as "Albo, Albuo, Alubo" to safeguard the horses.

In England and elsewhere, herbal medicine was associated with a great Goddess of Nature during the Middle Ages. In the late twelfth-century *Herbarius* of Apuleius Platonicus, the practitioner is told that in order to pick basil so that its powers are retained and perhaps enhanced, one should first bathe and dress in clean clothes. If female, one should pick basil when one is not menstruating. After dressing, one must locate the basil plant and then purify it by taking oak leaves, placing them in water, and then using the bunch of leaves to sprinkle over the basil plant. Then, before cutting the plant, one must offer a prayer to the "Holy Goddess Earth." Finally, before using the basil, one should place it on an altar with "gold, silver, ivory, boar's tusk, a bull's horn and...fruits." In perhaps the most well-known Anglo-Saxon charm, we find that the flora to be used in herbal medicine are considered as living beings possessing great powers:

> Remember, Mugwort, what you made known,
> What you arranged at the Great Proclamation.
> You were called Una, the oldest of herbs,
> You have power against three and against thirty,
> You have power against poison and against infection,
> You have power against the loathsome foe roving through the land.
> And you, Plantain, mother of herbs,
> Open from the east, mighty inside.

Over you chariots creaked, over you queens rode,
Over you brides cried out, over you bulls snorted...
: May you likewise withstand poison and infection...[75]

In the eighteenth century, Samuel Johnson reported that in spite of the passing of many earth-based concepts and practices in Scotland, he nevertheless learned there of a "great number of charms for the cure of different diseases."

Women versed in these practices, often called "white witches," continued to practice traditional healing into the nineteenth and twentieth centuries. In the last quarter of the nineteenth century, a Cornish woman whose knit work was prized was also known for her power to heal, such as "to staunch blood, etc., when doctors failed." This power included that of remote psychic healing: "It was not necessary for her to see the person; she could cure them by sitting by her fireside if they were miles away."

Enid M. Porter remarked in 1958 that traditional healing practices continued to be deployed into the twentieth century by persons living in the Fens of northeast England.

Divination

From penitentials and other fragmentary evidence, we know that many persons, especially women, continued to practice various forms of divination during the Middle Ages and thereafter, even when such practices were expressly forbidden by the Church as "custom[s] of the heathen[s]."

Two primary uses of divination were (and are) to foretell future events and to diagnose illness or misfortune. Divinatory readings were often undertaken at significant events such as seasonal celebrations and funerals. Certain places were considered centers of the divinatory arts and were visited by people journeying long distances; for example, during the eleventh century, the Curonian Spit, a long, sand-dune peninsula just to the west of Lithuania Minor, was known for its many "houses...of pagan soothsayers, diviners, and necromancers" and was visited by persons from as far away as Greece and Spain seeking divinatory counsel. This journeying and such centers suggest that a high level of cross-pollination may have occurred.

Particularly among non-elites and non-literate populations, divination often involved the use of common elements or entities including earth, blades of grass, "oat, wheat, and...reed," trees, stones, fire, water, grain and bread, animals, eggs, coins, and mirrors.

In Scotland, especially at Samhain/Hallowe'en, one type of divination made use of the furrows of ploughed fields. In "Scottish Lore of Earth, its Fruits, and the Plough," Mary MacLeod Banks explains that persons wishing to know their destiny would "enter the field from the west side, pass slowly over eleven ridges and stand at the centre of the twelfth where they listen for magic sounds." If they heard joyful music, this foretold a happy marriage, but if they heard weeping, this foretold death. She further speaks of young women of Aberdeen going to a field of barley and passing over "three ridges. Laying their hand in the furrow between the third and fourth rig they would hear sounds indicative of the occupation of a future husband: knocking betokened a carpenter, and so on."

In regard to stones, Slavic peoples sometimes divined by gazing at quartz, especially when placed in a glass of water; occasionally, silver coins were used instead of quartz. It was thought that one entered a trance state in this way. One of the simplest practices involving stones deployed by Western Europeans occurred when one visited the home of a sick person. Finding a stone near the dwelling, the visitor would turn it over to see if anything lay beneath it. If one found a "worm or a fly or an ant or anything that moves," then the ill person would soon recover. If nothing moved beneath the stone, the ill person was likely to die.

Simple forms of divination utilizing items from nature were employed by women (primarily) to learn about future mates. Young women wishing to know whom they might marry counted or otherwise divined with grass, grain, and other flora, saying, "Tinker, tailor, soldier, sailor, rich man, poor man, beggar man, thief." Frank Kmietowicz, in *Slavic Mythical Beliefs* (1982), notes that "pagan Slavs performed divination by listening to the sound of trees in sacred groves." Burchard speaks of simple divinations being performed by common people with barley. Grains were placed on the hearth; if they 'jumped' when heated, danger would ensue; if they remained still, "things [would] go well." Similarly, bread was also employed to foretell the future. MacLeod Banks relates that other materials used in Scottish divination included grains, especially corn, and fruits. She notes that on May 22, 1597, "Janet Wischert, spouse of John Leyis; Indytit [i.e., was indicted] for passing to the greyne growing corne [i.e., for practicing divination with corn] in May." For about twenty-two years, Wischert had paid very close attention to the way in which the corn was growing in order to divine whether the year would bring scarcity or abundance. Moreover, from closely watching the movements of kernels of corn placed on the hearth on January 1st, she could divine what sort of price the corn crop would command in the year that followed.

I'm reminded here of a passage in Indigenous American writer Linda Hogan's beautifully crafted *Dwellings: A Spiritual History of the Living World*, in which she speaks of the biologist Barbara McClintock, who "received a Nobel Prize for her work on gene transposition in corn plants. Her method was to listen to what corn had to say, to translate what the plants spoke into a human tongue. …She saw an alive world, a fire of life inside plants." It is highly likely that rather than receiving the Nobel Prize for her work, McClintock may well have been persecuted and perhaps even executed had she lived during the time of Janet Wischert.

MacLeod Banks also imparts that young persons in Scotland performed a type of amatory divination whereby winnowing corn in a barn three times was supposed to cause an apparition of one's future lover or spouse to manifest. During the harvest season, prophetic dreams were enhanced by placing three ears of corn or a corn doll or other representation of the Cailleach under one's pillow.

Divination was likewise performed using kale. MacLeod Banks relates: "Enquirers go forth after dark, and with eyes closed or blindfolded, to a neighbour's kail-yard [i.e., kale] and pull up the first plant their hand touches. Its shape and size foretell the appearance of future husband or wife."

In the late sixteenth century, Cesare Ripa (*c.* 1560- *c.* 1623), in *Iconologia* (*Iconology*, printed 1603) explained that the poppy was often used in love divination. To discover if one's love for another would be returned, she or he would place a poppy petal on a cupped hand and then slap the hand. If the petal popped, it meant that love would be returned. When young women wished to know whom they would marry, they would inscribe the names of the most likely candidates for future husband on several onions and then place the onions near the chimney. He would be her husband whose name was inscribed on the onion that sprouted first. Observing nuts set on the hearth or cast into the fire; eating an apple in front of a mirror; filling one's mouth with oats and walking to the gate; placing sprigs of gall or a sheaf of grain above the door; counting grains on a stalk; taking note of the color of straw; circling round a stack of barley; casting nine or ten pairs of beans, two of which were marked for the lover and beloved; and throwing a sickle into the air and noting the position of the hook on the ground were other forms of divination rooted in farming life, meant to predict such things as prosperity, one's future partner, and how many children a couple might have.

In Lithuania, if someone fell ill, she or he was placed near a bonfire. If their shadow fell directly behind them, they would probably recover shortly; if it fell to one side or the other, they most likely would not. Fire-gazing to divine the future was common among Slavs. Kmietowicz relates that women "in the Ukraine, Poland, and Czechoslovakia threw nine embers into a river. If more than half of them went down, it was a sign that the evil eye was the cause of the sickness."

Among Slavs, a "crowing hen meant death unless it was killed and a magic ritual performed upon it." The German Burchard, who regarded such things as superstitious, wrote: "When they make any journey, if a crow croaks from their left side to their right, they hope...to have a prosperous journey." The late twelfth-century *Penitential* of Bartholomew Iscanus condemned the belief "that anything comes out favorably or unfavorably because of the croaking of a young crow, or a raven." Spanish *curanderas* and Slavs numbered among those who diagnosed and foretold by means of examining eggs placed in water.

Women concerned with love and marriage undertook numerous forms of amatory divination including those with plants mentioned above. If they wished to know what sort of character their future husband might possess, they might draw sticks from piles of faggots. Should the stick be straight and smooth, that husband would be gentle; but should the stick be knotted and gnarled, that husband would be bad-tempered and boorish. Women might also circle a haystack and plunge a "black-handled knife into it in the name of the

Devil. They implicitly believed that the man who removed it would marry them." Or they might carry keys in a sieve and walk around haystacks, believing that the first man they encountered would be their future husband. Young Irish women living in Kerry hunted snails at Beltane: "The *druchtin* [i.e., the snail] so caught shall be placed on a plate of flour," said the instructions, "and the snail will move around the flour leaving in its trail the name off the one to whom the fair maid will be wed." In eighteenth-century Scotland, whoever would learn the name of her true love must at evening throw a ball of blue yarn – it must be blue – into a pot, then begin with a ply to wind a new ball from the old one. When a ply inevitably gets caught on something inside the pot, then she should demand who is holding the ply. She will then hear whispered the name of her true love.

During the nineteenth and early twentieth centuries, a form of love divination peculiar to leap years was practiced. A candle was pierced with twenty-seven pins in nine groups of three. It was then placed in a clay candlestick with the wrong end up and then lit and placed in the left-hand corner of the chimney. When the candle finished burning, the pins were placed in the petitioner's left shoe. Within nine nights, she would know who her future spouse would be.

Mirror-gazing, or scrying, known to us through the tale of "Snow White," was another popular method of divination, typically performed to discover a future mate. In "Circling as an Entrance to the Otherworld," Samuel Pyeatt Menefee describes yet another form of amatory divination, this one undertaken by both men and women, in eighteenth-century Scotland: "[G]irls in Breadalbane circled a house three times *deiseil* [or, *deosil*] (sunwise) with a drawn sword in one hand and a scabbard in the other. The future husband was supposed to take the sword from their hands and return it sheathed." Men, on the other hand, carried a distaff or spindle.

An ancient form of divination that was practiced in similar ways by Celts and Germanic peoples and which became hybridized and Christianized in medieval Scotland was called "*frith*." The term appears to have been derived from the Norse *frét*, "to inquire of the gods what the future might bring." Frith was employed for two primary purposes: to divine one's future; and to find lost persons, animals, and objects. Frith was performed on Mondays before sunrise at the doorstep of the house. The diviner beseeched the deity to reveal to him/her that which he/she desired to know. In its Christianized form, frith often depended upon responses from the Virgin Mary; as such, it became known as Frith Mhoire.

Among the most popular forms of divination in the Middle Ages was oneiromancy, dream divination. Dreams were typically considered to hail from another reality and were believed to be sent by deities or the dead. Practitioners of oneiromancy continued to consult Artemidorus's (fl. end of second-beginning of first cent. BCE) *Oneirokritika* (*The Interpretation of Dreams*) and Macrobius's (fl. 400 CE) *Commentary on the Dream of Scipio*. Texts on dream divination composed in the Middle Ages were also studied. Although Biblical tradition acknowledged dream divination, St. Augustine's branding of it as a form of idolatry caused it to be prohibited in Church capitularies dating from the eighth and ninth centuries. Among Germanic peoples, the ability to receive and interpret prophetic dreams was frequently thought to be hereditary. On occasion, the dreamer was believed to be visited by his tutelary genius or that of his/her family, the *fylgja* (or *aettarfylgja*), who told the dreamer of his/her destiny. Such dreamers were known as *draumspakrs*.

According to Saxo Grammaticus (*c.* 115-1220), some Wends practiced divination by throwing into the air three laths, painted black on the top and white on the bottom. They foretold future events by looking at how many laths turned up on the white sides and how many on their black sides. A very similar method of divination is performed in Yorùbá-diasporic traditions using pieces of coconuts, with the brown shell on one side and the white 'meat' on the other. A bit more complex form of this sort of divination included the casting of lots, after which they were covered with grass and a venerated horse was led over them. The horse's movements were carefully observed and contributed to the prediction. Wends also believed that when a period of war was imminent, a "great boar whose teeth are white and glistening with foam [would] emerge from [the]...lake and appear to many witnesses...with a terrible shaking."

Forms of sortilege, including divination utilizing such items as bones, stones, dice, runes, continued to be practiced during the Middle Ages and thereafter. Olaus Magnus reports that although Sweden had been officially Christianized for centuries, Swedes continued to practice divination by lots by "throwing two, three, or more spills" of "white, brown, [and] red" "wood into a vessel." In Greece, lekanomancy was practiced especially during the sixteenth and seventeenth centuries. In this form of bowl divination, a "bowl filled with water and various objects (a sheep's bone and a sprig of laurel) [was] left out overnight under the stars" prior to the act of divination.

More sophisticated systems of divination such as runes, palmistry and astrology also continued to be practiced in the Middle Ages and thereafter. As so much has already been written on these systems, I will only point out here that forecasting via runes as well as the carving of runes was often undertaken by women, and that although Paul and other early Christians had condemned astrology as pagan, it was increasingly appropriated by the Church. Astrology was employed in divination as well as in magic and medicine (via *melothesia*, "the assignment of various limbs or parts of the human body to different zodiacal signs or planets"). By the twelfth century, zodiac signs had come to be identified with Christian apostles and saints. A manuscript dated *c.* 1235 shows, for example, St. Paul standing above Pisces, while St. Andrew stands above Aries. Nevertheless, pagan deities also continued to be associated with astrology. As Kelly Kamborian observes in "Children of the Planets: Medieval Astronomical Imagery" (1987), "Once the pagan gods had established themselves in the sphere above, they remained unshakeable."

Divination, like other elements of the earth-centered worldview, has experienced innovation. For example, Marcu Beza points out that in 1800, one of the most common forms of amatory divination in Greece was apple divination, which had been practiced since antiquity. Young women would place apples in a vessel of water collected by a young man from a certain spring. After the apples were left in the water overnight, each woman would take an apple, "go out into the road," and listen for the first "name heard by chance," which would be that of her "future husband." "Nowadays," however, Beza, referring to Greek practice in the early twentieth century, noted that apples had been displaced by "rings, beads and the like."

Please note that (1) apple divination is traceable to pagan antiquity, and (2) its innovation has not been inspired by the New Testament.

One of the most significant innovations in divination occurred in or near the fifteenth century with the appearance of Tarot decks. Not surprisingly, the cards were attacked as thinly veiled Christian substitutes for "images of Idols and false Gods." The artwork and divinatory meanings of the early Tarot decks owed much to Classical paganism, including images of Apollo, Aphrodite/Venus, and the Muses. The Major Arcana of the Tarot may have been inspired in part by triumphal floats, or *trionfi*, of Italian Renaissance parades; these floats frequently depicted Classical deities. Another major innovation in divination during the Renaissance occurred with the introduction of dowsing, using dowsing rods, to the English by the Germans when Queen Elizabeth brought over German/Saxon miners to instruct the Cornish in mining. Dowsing was used not only to discover sources of water but also where mineral lodes were located.

Coscinomancy became increasingly popular in the sixteenth and seventeenth centuries in the British Isles, especially in Northumbria, although it was also popular among Slavs. This form of divination, now poorly understood, made use of a sieve and shears; it was commonly known as "turning the riddle" or "turning the riddle and shears." It also depended upon the recitation of words that would have seemed like nonsense to non-practitioners, and sometimes mixed earth-centered and Christian elements. Several women who were respected for their skill in the art of coscinomancy ended up being accused of witchcraft.

Scapulamancy refers to divining by the shoulder blade of a sacrificed sheep or other animal, usually by way of interpreting cracks in the roasted bone. This form of divination was practiced by the Chinese more than five thousand years ago; in Japan more than two thousand years ago; by Celts and Romans, who most probably introduced it to Scotland; and by Bulgarian gypsies in the sixteenth century. Scapulamancy appears to have been particularly prevalent in Russia, where it was called *lopatochnik*, and in Scotland, where it was called *sleing-nachd*. Thomas Pennant, traveling in Scotland, met a woman in 1769 on the island of Rhum (near Skye) who practiced scapulamancy with a "well scraped blade bone of mutton." It was practiced in Denbighshire in northeast Wales at least into the mid-nineteenth century, and in Macedonia until at least the end of that century.

In Lithuania Minor/East Prussia, many forms of divination, including austromancy (by the wind), ornithomancy, extispicy (via entrails), hydromancy, and coscinomancy, continued to be practiced in the seventeenth and eighteenth centuries.

Other forms of divination practiced from the Renaissance through the early twentieth century included: astrology; palmistry; Tarot; divining with plants and flowers including fern-seed, hempseed, ivy, onions, and bachelors' buttons; divining by dumb-cake (a cake made in silence); dowsing or using a divining rod; and reading coffee grounds. The early twentieth century witnessed an explosion of popular literature on divination, including books, pamphlets, and articles on astrology and numerology, with titles like *Consult the Oracle*, that were especially popular among women. This explosion of popular literature was due in no small part to the linking of divination, capitalism, and consumerism. The popularity of divination crossed boundaries of economic class not only when it came to diviners but also when it came to those seeking their services: "[T]he Society woman who visits the Bond Street clairvoyant, or palmist, or crystal-gazer has the same longing to divine the future as her East End sister for whom the greasy cards are turned over in the back street, or the leaves in the teacup are read by an old woman."

In 1908, English folklorists Edward Lovett and A. R. Wright noted that "[e]ven tea-leaf fortune-telling has been revived, and Spiers and Pond's, Hamley's, and other large stores have sold "The 'Nelros' Cup of Fortune" for that purpose." Moreover, advertising concerning, inspired by, or cashing in upon divination flourished, with ads like "Do you want to know what your Lucky Days are?" and "sandwichmen promenad[ing] London streets to invite all and sundry to visit Madam This or Madam That and be 'psychometrised.'" Wright in particular was extremely troubled by the "commercial exploitation" of divination, writing two decades later: "The professional fortune-teller of Mayfair and the back street, who works by cards, crystal-gazing, handwriting, palmistry, astrology, psychometry, or clairvoyance, has in great part displaced home practice of the old arts."

Magic

As with the healing and divinatory arts, we learn from penitentials and other fragmentary evidence that magic, even in the face of persecution, continued to be practiced in the Middle Ages and thereafter. I should point out that I have, on the whole, decided to avoid discussing magical practices generally classified as "ceremonial" or "ritual" magic, because these practices and the tradition(s) that congealed from them are not primarily earth-based, but rather predominantly monotheistic and patriarchal, drawing to a great extent upon Jewish, Gnostic, Christian, and Islamic traditions; "ceremonial" and "ritual magic" has been practiced since antiquity but may be said to have reached a pinnacle from the

Renaissance through the nineteenth century.

Magical practice of an earth-centered kind, especially when recorded in writing, offers evidence of the persistence of paganism in Christianized Europe. For example, in "Pagan Charms in Tenth-Century Saxony? The Function of the Merseburg Charms," Susan D. Fuller demonstrates that the Merseburg Charms – Merseburg being a town in the south of the German state of Saxony-Anhalt on the river Saale, – "were transmitted by means of a viable pagan oral tradition and committed to writing" by a Christian cleric who felt that, whether pagan or not, they were necessary to have access to during a time of great conflict with the Magyars and others. Fuller insists that the "Charms were still [in the tenth century CE] a part of a living oral tradition, and as such were transcribed from an oral performance – from memory or by dictation – not copied from an earlier manuscript which would have dated from before the Magyar invasions." "The Charms *do* represent a 'survival of German paganism,'" she writes, "but it is a survival that is not 'ancient'" but derives rather from a "living pagan oral tradition in the 10th century." This is extremely significant because it means that magic spells continued to be performed in tenth-century Saxony in the name of Freyja [as Friia], Wodan, Volla, and the Valkyries.

It's important to acknowledge that, with Christianization, many names of pagan deities and similar beings were removed from magic spells, leading to a misguided notion that magic and religion or spirituality belonged to entirely, or almost entirely, separate realms of spiritual practice, or else they were displaced by Biblical names – Jesus, Mary, the saints, etc. – leading to the equally misguided notion that in Christianized Europe, magic was no longer earth-centered but instead solely Christian. Anyone who is knowledgeable of African-diasporic religions/traditions like Vodou and Regla de Ocha (Lucumí, Santería) will immediately be suspicious of this latter simplistic and decidedly Christocentrically-motivated theory. The manipulation of earth-centered spells to appear Christian was part of an exceedingly conscious program of appropriation or, put differently, spiritual cannibalism. Felix Grendon (1909) points out that a "German manuscript of the thirteenth century contains specific directions to pastors for dealing with popular charm remedies and for altering names in invocations to the autochthonic gods." Grendon continues, "No longer were the wind-elves implored for succor in a storm; petitions were addressed to the saints, known in this capacity as *wazzer heilige*, that is, water-saints."

During the Early and High Middle Ages, some of the magical practices that most deeply concerned Church authorities were those deploying herbs, wool, and knotted pieces of fabric, often magical acts concerned with protecting livestock, bringing love, and influencing the weather, especially when these were combined with non-Christian incantations, or "diabolical formulae" [*carminae*, "charms"]. The manufacture of amulets and talismans was also viewed as a dangerous non-Christian practice (although many incorporated Christian[ized] symbols). One of the practices which intrigues me most is that of bathing "in reverse position," which bears an uncanny resemblance to ceremonial bathing in Vodou: when one is ridding the body of negativity or evil, one bathes from head to feet; whereas when one is seeking to beckon protection, health, and prosperity to oneself, one bathes oneself from feet to head. Magical rites were typically undertaken at certain places, such as crossroads and trivia, and at certain times, such as at the summer solstice. Not surprisingly, consulting practitioners of magic was forbidden by Church authorities.

In the Middle Ages, magical practices, particularly amatory magic, were generally more frequently associated with women than with men. One of the reasons for this association may have arisen from the association of magic and cooking, as in a cauldron, with cooking being more often associated with women than with men. Exemplary of the linking of women and magical practice is this notice in the so-called *Confessional of Egbert*: "If a woman works witchcraft [*dry-craeft*, {possibly} "Druid craft"] and enchantment [*galdor*] and uses magical philters [*unlibban*], she shall fast for twelve months." Julie Ann Smith, in *Ordering Women's Lives: Penitentials and Nunnery Rules in the Early Medieval West* (2001), observes that women often worked magic while spinning and weaving. "[W]omen were also believed to possess powers of creating binding- or loosing-magic through their looms and weaving tablets. Color was also an important element of textile-associated magic and healing charms regularly recommended the use of specifically colored threads or braids."

Other groups were, however, also associated more than others with magical practice, including "swineherds, ploughmen, and sometimes hunters" as well as beggars, vagabonds, minstrels, itinerant scholars, and immigrant populations, particularly the Romani (or "Gypsies").

Magic Involving Animals

Magic often involved animals, either by including them in spells or seeking to protect them or promote their productivity via magic. For example, snakes were considered sacred and employed in magic by Slavic peoples by so-called "snake magicians." An eleventh-century Anglo-Saxon beekeeper's spell to ensure that the bees he or she keeps will provide honey for him or her but not for others invokes "victorious women" who appear to refer to the bees themselves but who may also signify Germanic Norns or Valkyries: "Settle, victorious women, sink down to earth./ You must never fly wild to the wood./ Be...mindful of my welfare."

The late twelfth-century Anglo-Norman *Penitential* of Bartholomew Iscanus prohibited the practice of "mak[ing] magical knots or charms and hid[ing] them in the grass or in a tree or at a crossroads to free their animals from pestilence." Those who did so "must each do penance for two years."

Weather Magic

Because industries such as farming and maritime trade were so important to medieval and Renaissance cultures, weather magic became one of the most commonly practiced forms of magical practice. Much rested on maintaining calm weather and avoiding storms. Weather magic practitioners included *nephelote'chai*, rainmakers, and *tempestarii*, raisers of tempests. In the *Dicta* of Pirmin of Reichenau (d. 753), one finds: "Do not believe in weather-sorceresses;" and in the *Burgundian Penitential* of the same period, also directed toward inhabitants of Frankish territories: "If...anyone is a wizard...a conjuror-up of storms, he shall do penance for seven years." Christian converts of medieval Scandinavia associated practitioners of *seiðr* with witches – as *seiðkonur* – and more specifically with witches' creation of "magic storms." Witches often created storms by way of a magical object called a *veðbelgr*, a "weather bag."

Subsets of weather magic include wind and rain magic. Richard Perkins, in *Thor the Wind-Raiser* (2001), notes that there were several forms of wind magic, including: stirring a favorable wind to promote sailing; stilling a storm; and causing a storm to harm one's enemy. Reference to one of the most remarkable rainmaking ceremonies of the Middle Ages, regarded by Church authorities as a pagan rite punishable by penance, is recorded in Burchard's *Corrector* of the eleventh century. Therein, he describes a rite in which a young girl digs up a henbane plant, after which the other participants in the rite take her to a "nearby river and with these twigs sprinkle her with the water and thus they hope that by their charms they shall have rain." The completion of the rite entails the girl walking backward to the village.

Very similar rites were practiced by Greeks, Bulgarians, Romanians, and Russians and persisted into the recent past; in these rites, the young woman was typically called, and thought to embody, rain or thunder. In Russia, nude bathing *en masse* was also thought to evoke rain. Yet another magical method thought by Bulgarians to beckon rain was holding a funeral for a figure "with a phallus of clay," with women lamenting his death from lack of water; this rite persisted into the twentieth century. Slavs also whistled, yelled, banged pots and pans, etc., reminiscent of *charivari*, to ward off demonic beings who brought hailstorms; in the twentieth century, car horns joined the clamor.

Of wind magic and its medieval and later Hungarian practitioners, Eva Pócs observes in *Between the Living and the Dead* (1999) that a "wind magician," a "type of shamanistic fertility magician who was active on behalf of their community," after being initiated into a cult focused on the "dead – or, to be more specific, among the wind souls traveling in storm clouds," would "ensur[e] fertility...[by] regulating the weather." In or near the fifteenth century, women of the Isle of Man are said to have perfected the "art of selling wind;" they could "bind up the winds, or send forth tempests at will." In *The Hierarchy of the Blessed Angels* (1635), Thomas Heywood penned: "The Finns and Laplands [i.e., Sámi] are acquainted well/ With such-like Sp'rits, and Windes to Merchants sell."

In Normandy, the *meneurs de nuées*, "leaders of clouds," were believed to be extremely powerful in raising tempests. In doing so, they were able to ride over the earth enveloped in black clouds. Certain families were believed to promulgate *meneurs de nuées*. These practitioners have been documented from the Middle Ages into the nineteenth century.

In Romanian tradition, we read of "cloud-chasers" of the mid-seventeenth century that resonate with the "expellers of clouds" condemned a millennium earlier by the Council in Trullo. These 'cloud-chasers' were described as wild, vegetarian hermits with disheveled hair who lived in the wilderness. Also during the mid-seventeenth century, in the Scottish archipelago of Shetland, the alleged witch Marion Pardon is said to have practiced forms of wind magic, involving the deployment of knots and chants, rooted in Germanic practice. In this same area, around 1770, John Sutherland of Papa Stour practiced a similar form of wind magic, except that while Pardon's magic tended to be destructive, Sutherland was "in the habit of procuring a fair breeze for any boats that were wind-bound."

It is noteworthy that our term "gale," an extremely strong wind – and the surname of Dorothy who was swept up by a cyclone – appears to derive from the Norse terms *galen*, "angry, furious," *gala* or *galdra*, "to recite charms," *galdr*, the practice of witchcraft, and perhaps more particularly from *galdrahríð*, a "storm brought on by witchcraft."

Speaking of storms brought on by witchcraft, perhaps the most famous event of this kind concerned an attempt by the North Berwick witches – Agnes Sampson, John Fian, and company, whose trial was held in 1590 – to cause a storm at sea that would result in the shipwreck of the royal ship and death of King James VI/ I and his Queen.

Some alleged witches conjured storms by digging small holes in the dirt, filling them with water, and then stirring the water with one of their fingers until a thundering rain-cloud emerged from the water. Alleged witches of France burned black candles downward into bodies of water and then beat the water with black wands until a tempest arose. Some alleged witches were said to have raised themselves up onto the tops of oak trees or clouds in order to create storms from more advantageous locations.

Weather magic was gradually subjected to Christianization and resulted in hybrid pagano-Christian forms, which continued to be practiced in various places, including in Russia, into the early twentieth century.

Amatory Magic

Not surprisingly, many women – together with some men – practiced magic concerned with love and fertility. Indeed, so popular was love magic that during the seventeenth century, in Venice and other places in Italy, love magic was a factor in approximately 40% of witch trials. Unfortunately, since most spells of earth-centered magical traditions, as opposed to ceremonial magic, appear to have been transmitted orally, few have been preserved. Some are quite simple, as, for instance, women throwing dust collected in chapels into the air to provide favorable winds for sailors they loved.

Differing from healing magic, amatory magic encouraged people other than the practitioner of magic to sin.

The eighth-century *Indiculus superstitionem et paganiarum* (*Index of Superstitions and Paganism* prohibited "women command[ing] the moon that they may be able to take away the hearts of men, according to the pagans;" this indicates that the ancient practice of "drawing down the moon" was both widespread and long-lasting and that among its uses was to obtain lovers or spouses.

Love spells deployed many substances and activities, including the sprinkling of salt into a fire; "the tying of knots; the lighting of candles; the thrusting of a black handled dagger or nail in the floor, or in a flower pot;" and thrusting sticks into wax images made to resemble potential or straying partners.

Penitentials of the sixth through eleventh centuries indicate that women who sought to obtain or increase the desire of a man often drank "the man's blood or semen," "mix[ed] his semen with [their] food," or served the man a fish that they had previously placed in their vaginas or else food mixed with menstrual blood. In seventeenth-century Malta, Domenica Darmanin "recommended the mixing of menstrual blood with the lover's wine to ensure that he remain faithful."

Love spells including food mixed with menstrual blood, semen, or urine were traditional among Slavs, Greeks, and other peoples and have survived into the present; the performer of a Slavic love spell making use of menstrual blood asks, "May he return to my body,/ May he return to my desire."

Practitioners of love and other magics in seventeenth-century France utilized not only powdered menstrual blood but also "packets of nail clippings," "cauls, dried afterbirths, breast milk," and "dessicated umbilical cords." They also included bat's blood and hippomane and swore by Spanish fly.

Young Slavic women fed young men the hearts of moles wrapped in bread to "make them blind with love like the moles." Not surprisingly, the Church condemned such actions. The twelfth-century *Penitential* of Bartholomew Iscanus banned the making of philters, magical love potions. Such potions were particularly associated with the summer solstice. One of the most well-known love potions, or philters, in literature occurs in the tragic romance of *Tristan and Isolde*, told by numerous writers including Béroul (fl. 1190) and Gottfried von Strassburg (fl. 1210). Philippe Walter, in *La Mémoire du Temps: Fêtes et calendriers de Chrétien de Troyes à "la Mort Artu"* (1989), suggests that this potion may have been based on an actual beverage of wine mixed with herbs, herbs gathered during the moon's waxing, on or near Midsummer's Eve. Such potions are thought to have included millepertius/St. John's Wort and nutmeg, considered aphrodisiacs, artemisia, believed to promote women's fertility, and the blood of bats.

One of the most intriguing forms of love magic, a practice that persisted at least into the seventeenth century, involved the use of bread. Women desiring a lover or determined to maintain a faithful husband would strip, smear their bodies with honey – this is uncannily reminiscent of the Yòrubá orishá Oshún's – the goddess of sensuous love – deployment of honey in medicine and rites of love, would roll "to and fro often" on sheaves of wheat placed on a linen cloth, and "then carefully gather all the grains of wheat" which had clung to their bodies. From this, they would "grind it to flour; ...make bread from that flour and then give it to their husbands [or lovers] to eat, that on eating the bread they may...pine away."

It is noteworthy, especially in light of criticisms as to the lack of precedent as regards going naked or 'skyclad' in present-day Wiccan rites, that, according to Kmietowicz, in Slavic cultures, "[m]ost of the magical acts [were] performed in the nude. Not only witches, [but also] sorcerers and medicine-men were to be naked, but also spectators...[Later on, women] wore shirts but nothing else [and went] barefooted."

Carmel Cassar, in "Witchcraft Beliefs and Social Control in Seventeenth Century Malta," observes: "love magic was widely practiced by prostitutes...Love magic was mostly resorted to by desirable women referred to as 'courtesans' whose main intention was to reconcile with their 'carnal friend.'" Moreover, as Sally Scully points out in "Marriage or a Career?: Witchcraft as an Alternative in Seventeenth-Century Venice," the stereotypical association of prostitutes, love magic, and witchcraft sometimes manifested in the flesh, with courtesans practicing amatory magic as a way for independently-minded women to escape traditional marriage or the nunnery: "It was not unusual for prostitutes to supplement their incomes with love magic, and/or vice versa. Several named in [Venetian witch trials]... are identified as both *streghe* [witches, sorceresses] and as *meretrici* [prostitutes]."

A little explored aspect of love magic concerns stopping husbands and male lovers from abusing their wives or lovers. For example, in the late sixteenth century, alleged witch Margaret Clark stopped Walter Ronaldson from beating his wife by sewing pieces of paper together with threads of diverse colors and leaving these in their barn.

Among the earliest Christian condemnations of love magic is found in the mid-sixth century *Penitential of Finnian*; it is directed at Irish women and clerics performing amatory magic. Mary O'Neill, in "Magical Healing, Love Magic and the Inquisition in Late Sixteenth-Century Modena" (1987), points out that "the most extreme penalties handed out by the Modenese Inquisition [in Modena, Italy] are to be found not in trials against healers...but in the...sphere of love magic." It should be noted, however, that during the period of the witch trials, while amatory magic was frequently condemned as witchcraft, it tended not to be seen as dangerous as, or as heretical as, reverence of a goddess like Diana.

In 1930, many young women in London and in the English countryside continued to practice amatory magic. *Their spellwork, by the way, in no way emerged from their devout study of the New Testament.* They would cast dragon's blood or tormentil root into the fireplace on a Friday at midnight, chanting,

'Tis not this [dragon's] blood I mean to burn,
But my love's heart I wish to turn.
May he no pleasure nor profit see

Until that he comes back to me.[76]

Since at least the late 1960s, I have been told that when one is performing a love spell, one should never indulge in any sort of coercive magic, and most certainly none that involves cruelty. As you may have noticed, some of the spells we have recounted here radically depart from such a "New Age" notion, bearing much greater resemblance to spells found in the *Greek Magical Papyri*. In one such spell, a medieval Germanic one, a woman calls on nine wolves to pursue the man of her dreams "until in [his] heart [her] goodness [he] may never forget." In another such spell, this one from seventeenth-century Malta, a woman prays to "Stella della Crispa" – perhaps a star goddess from a particular location, or aligned with a particular plant – that she "Beat him, flog him,/ do not let him rest,/ [til he] come[s] for me."

Negative Sorcery and Combating It

Magical actions also include acts of negative sorcery and the removal or "sending back" of such. It is understandable why present-day Wiccans and others would wish to ignore, conceal, or condemn this dimension of magical practice, but the anti-historical aspect of the decision to do so troubles me. I think it is important to understand that not all those who have practiced magic, including alleged witches, have believed in "turning the other cheek," so to speak. I have no doubt that beyond the mean-spiritedness of some and the avenging spirit of others, a sense of powerlessness and a desire for justice may have led still others to perform acts of destructive magic.

Such spells included the bewitching of cattle (stealing their milk, causing them to fall ill, etc.) and harming the offspring of one's enemies and often involved sympathetic magic including plants, particularly their rotting. For example, as Padraic O'Farrell relates, in Ireland "an evil spell was sometimes put on a sheaf of corn which was then buried. As the sheaf rotted so would the person to whom death was wished."

Following the Tombland Fair of spring 1843 in Norfolk, England, a certain Mrs. Bell cursed a certain Mr. and Mrs. Curtis by lighting a candle and piercing it with pins, then mixing dragon's blood and water in an oyster shell and chanting an incantation over these items. This allegedly resulted in Mr. Curtis's becoming paralyzed. Whether he recovered or not remains a mystery.

On numerous occasions, the actions of ensorceling and curing bewitchment were coupled, so that a practitioner bestowing a curse might also be able to lift it. This is the case with an event that occurred in the early years of the nineteenth century, in Brandon Creek, Cambridgeshire, England. A woman suspected of being a witch, angered by a farmer's wife, told her that her "children would be born deformed." The farmer's wife's friends decided to drown the alleged witch. She promised, however, that if they let her live, she would remove the curse. She ordered a local blacksmith to "make a three-sided bottle...out of sheet iron." Arriving at the farmer's house, she undertook a rite that is uncannily resonant with certain practices undertaken in African and African-diasporic religions/traditions. She sacrificed a hen, cutting its throat "so that the blood ran into the bottle." She then placed the hen's intestines and tail feathers, together with fingernail and toenail clippings and urine of the farmer's wife and her husband, into the bottle. She dusted the farmer and his wife with chimney soot, wiped the wife's eyes with "[f]at from the gizzard," and bandaged the wife's eyes. She then placed the bottle in the fireplace; shortly thereafter, the bottle's stopper flew off, sending the contents up the chimney. The curse was thereby lifted. This, however, is not the end of the tale. The farmer, still infuriated with the alleged witch for having cursed his wife, "ordered the witch from the house and, retrieving with the tongs the red-hot bottle from the fire, flung it after her. … [T]wenty-five years later the farmer's daughter gave birth to a child with deformed hands."

Prosperity Magic

Another type of magical practice focuses on obtaining good fortune, prosperity, wealth, or riches. As so much has already been written on this, I will confine myself to one representative example which links magic with good fortune and the fairies. In 1926, on New Year's Eve, a Cornish maid placed all the coins in her possession on the ledge of her bedroom window so that they would be bathed in moonlight. On the following morning, she completed the spell by turning the coins over and kissing them, believing that this action would bring her good fortune in the year to come.

Magical Powers of Metamorphosis and Flight

Two of the most significant magical powers associated with many medieval, pagan ritual specialists were those of metamorphosis and flight, either of the ethereal or the physical body or both. Germanic priests and priestesses thought to have the power to metamorphose into the totemic animals of the deities they served; whereas those who served Odin were thought to be able to transform into wolves or werewolves, those who served Freyja were thought to transform into cats. Otherwise, priestesses and priests were believed to be capable of metamorphosing into birds (especially crows) and flying through the air. Certain terms such as *ütterbuck* ("uddered buck") also suggest transgender metamorphosis. Similarly, certain Slavic peoples were thought to possess the power of *mora*; they have been linked to spirits known as *kikimora*. These persons were able to send their souls out at night in the forms of butterflies, cats, snakes, and other animals to work magic. In the early eleventh century, Burchard prohibited Christians from believing in the possibility of metamorphosis of one being into another unless willed by the Christian God; Bartholomew Iscanus (d. 1184) reiterated this prohibition in the late twelfth century. Wisewomen/alleged witches of nineteenth-century Scotland were among those thought to possess the power of metamorphosis. One such woman, known to the writer Constance Gordon Cumming (1837-1924), was believed by her neighbors to "frequently assum[e] the form of a cat," a belief that was commonly held of alleged witches by others at that time.

Of belief in the power of flight, Burchard

found reprehensible the belief that "while thou art in bodily form thou canst go out by closed doors, and art able to cross the spaces of the world with others." Numerous women accused of being witches believed rhat they traveled through the air to attend gatherings, "sabbats," where they celebrated the goddess Diana. They "testified at their trials that by spreading an ointment on their bodies they were able to…fly."

In the early seventeenth century, according to the inquisitor Petrus Valderama (fl. *c.* 1610), it was not inconceivable that alleged witches were actually flying, since he believed that demonic beings (with whom he linked pagan goddesses and their devotees) were capable of transporting cities or whole provinces at will. Among numerous alleged witches believed to fly to the sabbat were Agnes Gerhardt, tried in 1596 and Ursula Kollarin, tried in 1661.

So were they flying? That depends, I suppose, on one's vision of reality. Do shamans journey to other realms, or only imagine that they do so? When we dream, does some part of us travel?

I'm reminded of the Broadway show *Wicked*, based on Gregory Maguire's marvelous 1995 novel, in which the most striking vision beheld by the citizens of Oz is that of the green-skinned witch Elphaba on her broom in flight. This scene and its accompanying song, "Defying Gravity," demonstrate brilliantly the association of witchcraft and magical flight.

In this light, have certain persons been abducted by aliens? If a certain culture consents to witness the magical, the miraculous, can it? Numerous divinities including Holda, Wanne Thekla, Isis, Inanna, Freyja and Nehalennia are thought to travel by way of a celestial steed or mount, chariot, boat, or ship.

Although it is not my intention here to equate divinities with aliens, nor to suggest that the existence of alien beings is peculiar to pagan traditions, I think it is nonetheless significant that many pagan divinities ride in celestial vehicles. (You'd never know that FEMALE deities numbered among them from watching *Ancient Aliens*!)

Manciocco and Manciocco (2006) compare the flights of goddesses and their devotees to shamanic flight among Indigenous Siberian shamans. A Sumerian poem in which Inanna "compares her vulva to…the Boat of Heaven" suggests that female, in contrast to male, deities may occasionally have been especially associated with flying crafts, as does a German expression for gathering storm clouds, perhaps in memory of a more otherworldly experience: *Muttergottesschiff*, that is, the Mother Goddess Ship. Might there not be a connection here with witches flying on broomsticks, if not with the "Mother Ship" of science fiction?

Of course, male beings are also thought to travel in or on such vehicles: Osiris, Thoth, Tammuz, Freyr (the Skiðblaðnir), Nokve (Germanic Moon god), and other deities. The dead are also sometimes said to travel in celestial or boats or ships.

In his illuminating article "Anchors in a Three-Decker World," Miceal Ross notes that in the *Annals of Ulster*, we find that "[s]hips with their crews were seen in the air" in Ireland in 748 CE. The *Book of Leinster* (compiled *c.* 1160) likewise records that during the mid-eighth century, three alien ships were sighted by the High King Domhnall and other persons attending the annual fair at Tailtiu, sacred to the goddess Tailtiu and major site of the festival of Lughnasa.

Agobard (779-840), the Archbishop of Lyon, France, was infuriated by the belief among many of his parishioners that there existed practitioners of wind-magic, *tempestatarii*, non-Christian ritual specialists who performed rites which beckoned alien visitors in cloud-ships to them. These visitors hailed from the land of Magonia, which may have suggested a "Land of Magic" or "Land of Magicians." Oddly, "Magonia" once referred to a gate of the city of Rome, apparently having to do with the "roar of oxen" entering the city, as well as to Mainz, Germany. The visitors arrived in a ship that seemed to be made of bronze. One of these aliens was thought to be a "lord of the weather." He caused a hailstorm to occur, with the assistance of the human practitioners of magic ("they are servants and assistants rather than originators of the storm"). The storm dislodged a goodly portion of grain, which the "conjurers [then sold] …to the aeronaut, [who] …carri[ed] it away." Apparently, it was believed that not all of the aliens had managed to escape. Agobard himself claimed to have encountered four of the aliens, "three men and a woman," and, moreover, to have freed them from chains just before an angry crowd was about to stone them. I find it fascinating, incidentally, that some of the more eccentric 'ancient alien theorists' who basically believe that all great monuments were constructed by aliens refuse to accept that the folk from Magonia were aliens or persons from another world or dimension.

Some have read into this account an early manifestation of "crop circles." The speculative writer Jacques Vallée makes an insightful point concerning the location of Magonia, which may enrich our understanding of medieval consciousness in relation to multidimensional reality: "The physical nature of Magonia…is quite noteworthy…[It may be] a remote country, an invisible island…a celestial country…[or] a sort of parallel universe, which coexists with our own."

In my view, one should be extremely careful when speaking of earth-centered traditions when one makes use of the term "transcendence," perhaps especially when one speaks of otherworldly locations; for what may seem like transcendence may in truth be a manifestation of invisible immanence, a peek into a parallel universe. To its inhabitants, Magonia is most likely as tangible as England is to its own, just as tangible as the Egyptian Otherworld was to those dwelling within it.

The English chronicler Gervase of Tilbury (*c.* 1150- c. 1220), in *Otia Imperialia* (*Recreation for an Emperor*, 1211), recounts an incident wherein Catholics leaving mass one morning witnessed a very strange event. They watched as an anchor dropped from a "cloud-ship" and was caught on a tombstone or pile of stones nearby. They continued to watch as one of the "cloud-sailors," a human-like being, exited the ship and attempted to free the anchor. As he struggled with it, he seemed to grow weaker and weaker. The villagers were powerless to help him, and he died in their arms, apparently due to the "gross air" of the earth. After "an hour's delay, [his "fellows above"] cut the cable, left their anchor, and sailed away."

Undoubtedly one of the most uncanny groups of aerial beings are the Planetniks, associated with Slavic paganism. These were depicted as humanoid but often much taller or shorter than humans. They sometimes dressed in black and wore big hats. Moreover, they often had black skin. They were thought to descend from and ascend to the heavens during storms; when on earth, they would sojourn among mortals for a time. They possessed the power to control the weather. Until recently, those who believed in and respected the Planetniks made offerings of flour and perhaps other substances as well to them. When baking bread, women in the Polish Carpathians used to throw a handful of flour into the fire, maintaining that the smoke would carry the flour to the clouds for the Planetniks.

In late nineteenth-century Connaught, Ireland, some described "fairy ships and boats" as "sail[ing] in the air...over Inishturk," Cliara, and elsewhere. These ships were outfitted with "magic lights" and they were sometimes seen floating over water and "sail[ing] against the wind." Occasionally, observers watched as fairies landed the ships and descended from them. Some believe that witches also travel in "cloudships" or "windships" (*vindflots*).

Were alleged coveners sharing lucid dreams, as Wilby suggests, or were they meeting in the flesh? Why was it so imperative that Church authorities deny the nocturnal gatherings of devotees of Diana while insisting upon the reality of women encountering Jesus after his death upon the cross? Did the night-traveling women master an alchemical magic, transform matter into energy and back into matter, as the cosmos-traveling crew of *Star Trek* has mastered science? What if, as the tales of the "third road" that leads not to Heaven or Hell but to Fairyland, the musical *Brigadoon*, films like *The Sixth Sense* and *The Others*, TV shows like *Fringe*, and string theory suggest, the Otherworld or – worlds lie/s parallel to, or occasionally even on top of or in the same, although (usually) invisible plane as our own? (I believe that the notion of "transcendence," incidentally, has led us to misinterpret the afterlives of many religions, such as the ancient Egyptian, as "transcendence" rather than what I refer to as "invisibly immanent.")

Several years ago, one of my students in California, a middle-aged Haitian woman who grew up in Haiti within a family that practices both Catholicism and Vodou, shared with me that one of the reasons she was glad she no longer lived in Brooklyn was that she no longer had to worry about *lougawous* flying around at night. In French, *loup-garou* refers to a werewolf, but in Vodou, a *lougawou* more often refers to a vampire. It can, however, refer as well to a woman who practices primarily destructive magic who flies in the skies at night. This is the sense in which my student used the term. When I asked her if she meant that the women she described were projecting themselves astrally, she responded, "No, they were *flying around at night.*" Whether one could see them or not was another matter. She could, and did. More recently, Mama Lola, a Haitian-American Vodou priestess in Brooklyn, concurred with my student. "Yes, they are flying in the sky at night. Don't mess with them."

The Material Culture of Magic
Earth, Stones, and Shells

Common substances such as dirt (such as "three clods of earth with grass on them [*devattis*]" deployed in Scottish witchcraft), stones, shells, and plants were often used in magic. Especially potent objects in Baltic tradition were the thunderstone and belemnite (a fossilized cylindrical shell), thought to be the thunderbolts or bullets of Perkûnas (or Perkons, as he was known to Livonians/Latvians). Thunderstones, incidentally, play a significant role in Haitian Vodou, wherein they are sacred to the gods Sobo and Shango. In Vodou, "they must be kept in oil, otherwise they lose their powers, which include whistling, talking, and moving from place to place. A spell to heal snakebite, brought to our attention by present-day Latvian folklorist Baiba Meistere, reads in part: "Three times nine times comes Perkunas' thunder from the sea/ Three times nine times bullets strike the swelling under the stone./ This man regains the health he enjoyed before!"

Amulets and talismans were also fashioned from cowry shells for fertility and for gentle and successful childbearing. In regard to cowries, Meaney draws our attention to the finding of cowry shells (or *cauris*, *kauris*; Portuguese, *buzios*) in at least eighteen Anglo-Saxon graves, mostly dating from the seventh century CE, at least sixteen of which are women's graves, including in containers such as wooden amulet-boxes and bags, at Marina Drive in Dunstable in Bedfordshire; Ellesborough in Buckinghamshire; Burwell and Shudy Camps in Cambridgeshire; Gloucestershire; Buckland, Kingston Down, and Sarre in Kent; Lechdale; Farthingdown in Surrey; and Driffield and Staxton in Yorkshire.

It is generally believed that cowries found in the Indian Ocean were found and disseminated to Asia Minor and Europe by Africans. They are also thought to have been carried by nomads from East to West Africa. As Maguy Vautier reports in *Le Chant des cauris* (*The Chant* [or *Song of the*] *Cowries*, 1999), cowries have been utilized in many parts of the world for three primary purposes: as money; for ornamenting works of art; and to communicate with deities and similar beings. Of course, as works of art often convey sacred meaning in indigenous/ earth-centered traditions, the second, aesthetic usage may be incorporated in the third, so that we arrive at two rather than three primary uses. According to Peter Mitchell in *African Connections: An Archaeological Perspective on Africa and the Wider World* (2005), the use of cowries as currency and as amulets has been widespread since the sixth millennium BCE.

The word "cowry" derives from Sanskrit; in ancient India, they were used to avert the evil eye and possibly also to promote fertility in women. Ancient Egyptians used cowries in amulets, while among the Baganda of the Sudan, one of the most important tools of magic is a leather strip on which are sown nine cowries. Ancient Chinese used cowries as money. They have been found in "many burials in numerous countries since prehistoric times," as, for example, in Mongolia, Italy, England, Scotland, and Hungary (as a necklace). Jan Hogendorn and Marion Johnson, in *The Shell Money of the Slave Trade* (1986), note that "the shells have [also] been found in Punic graves and the Carthagians possibly had some over-desert trading contact with black Africa. The Romans, too, had the cowrie, and posts deep in the Sahara." In the Middle Ages, Cairo became a "major market for cowries."

Hogendorn and Johnson also observe that "in Europe...cowries were used for...religious ritual...from prehistoric times." This observation is echoed by Ellen Ettlinger in "Documents of British Superstition in Oxford" (1943): "Since prehistoric times the supposition prevails in widely scattered localities that the spirit of fertility dwells in the cowries, and therefore they are looked upon as conferring the blessings of fertility on women and crops, as averting the evil eye, as harbingers of good luck." In Classical tradition, cowries were associated with Aphrodite/Venus, with their Latin name, *Cypraea moneta*, referring to Cyprus and its patron goddess, Aphrodite. As W. L. Hildburgh points out in "Cowrie Shells as Amulets in Europe" (1942), ancient Greeks and Romans, as well as, in more recent times, the French, Italians, Spaniards, Germans, Austrians, and others have employed cowries, wearing them individually or as necklaces, to promote fertility and/or to prevent the evil eye. Certain Anglo-Saxon graves indicate that some women continued to make use of cowrie shells as amulets after converting to Christianity, a practice that was most likely condemned by Church authorities.

Meaney especially draws our attention to an amulet bag containing cowrie shells found in one of the Anglo-Saxon women's graves; it is conceivable that this woman may have used them as a divinatory tool. Divination using cowries now seems generally limited to the Yorùbá, the Imazighen (also known as Berbers and Tuaregs), and a few other African peoples and their descendants in the diaspora. The Imazighen, who may have arrived in the British Isles over a millennium ago, have traditionally used cowries to communicate with the divine; they refer to divination via cowries as a kind of "writing." Cowries are thought to be living entities, and in order to serve as oracles, they must be fed with the blood of chickens, together with milk, honey, and grain, and they must be perfumed. The shells have a "feminine" and a "masculine" side; some are longer, shorter, thinner, or 'fatter' than others. They are interpreted according to their shapes as well as, primarily, how they fall onto a surface, typically a platter or mat. They are similarly deployed as *caracoles* in the Cuban-based Regla de Ocha (Lucumí, Santería) and as *búzios* in Brazilian-based Candomblé. All this leads one to wonder if somehow a divinatory art that was once practiced in the West was, over the centuries, lost, only to emerge again in African cultures, possibly due to cross-cultural influence.

Plants

In the mid-sixteenth century, in Pier Andrea Mattioli's (1500-1577) *Dei Discorsi* (*Discourses*, printed 1585), we learn that certain persons, mixing dandelion juice and oil, anointed their entire bodies with this mixture in order to obtain their desires, especially ones bestowed by powerful rulers. Florae were frequently employed in magical practice, one of the most well-known being fern-seed. Believed to be an attribute of the Fairy Queen and gathered on Midsummer Eve, fern-seed was "supposed to have the quality of rendering the possessor invisible at pleasure, and to be also of sovereign use in charms and incantations." Hawthorn, dog rose, blackthorn, and thistle were thought to protect one from evil. Slavs used the "smoke of nettle" to drive away demons. Among Slavs, however, when it came to protection against evil, there "was no plant more effective in magic than garlic." Sometimes onions were deployed in amatory magic. Longman and Loch note that in the nineteenth century, "[i]f a lover did not visit his sweetheart as often as she wished, she roasted an onion stuck full of…pins…The pins were supposed to prick his wandering heart and bring him to his lady's feet."

Animal and Human Body Parts

Sometimes animal hearts were used in amatory magic, including those of cows, sheep, and cocks; this type of practice came to be called "heart magic." Beyond their use in amatory and vengeful magic, animal hearts were sometimes deployed in binding curses, such as sticking pins in the heart of a bullock killed by sorcery in order to put an end to a curse placed by an alleged "black witch" (here meaning "negative," not "black skinned"), Paddy Goselin, on a farmer's livestock in South Devon circa 1860. Notably, the counter-spell was offered by a "white witch" nicknamed Mother Sunshine.

As for the deployment of human skulls and other bones, they have been deployed in magical practice as well as in traditional healing and in divination since antiquity, just as they continue to be deployed at present in the African-diasporic religion or tradition of Palo Monte Mayombe and in other present-day religions/traditions. Felix Grendon (1909) relates, "The dead were…worshipped by those who wished their aid, and parts of corpses were highly valued as amulets and periapts." In Egyptian, Greek, and Roman magic, skulls, especially of those who'd suffered untimely or violent deaths, were chiefly deployed in a specific form of necromancy called cephalomancy; in rituals including written texts, they would answer questions. Occasionally they were used to discover thieves and to "carry out binding curses." Grendon notes that the "canons of Edgar, and the penitentials of Egbert, expressly forbid sacrilege at the grave, and witchcraft [here meaning sorcery] by means of the dead." In Anglo-Saxon and later in Scottish traditional medico-magical practice, skulls and bones were ground to powder to effect various cures including of internal worms and epilepsy. At the 1612 trial of the so-called "Pendle Witches" of Lancaster and Salmesbury, England, several teeth were exhibited which had been allegedly used by two of the accused in magical practice.

Anne Chattox was said to have removed three skulls from graves at Newchurch in Lancashershire, taking eight teeth from the skulls, keeping four for herself and giving the rest to her comrade Old Demdyke (Elizabeth Sowtherns).

Fabric

Pieces of fabric were sometimes used in magical and healing practices. For example, pieces of white cloth were used by alleged witches to heal headaches; and a Scottish witch trial of 1596 includes description of a spell deploying what appears to be a swatch of Tartan plaid bearing the colors "green, red, and blue." Divinities and related beings, some of whom have metamorphosed into saints, continue to be offered bits of fabric at sacred wells in the British Isles in the hope that healing will come to those who offer them or else to their loved ones. Likewise, the *rusalki* were until recently, and may be still, offered strips of fabric in the hope that they will bring healing, fertility, and prosperity to those who remember(ed) them in this way.

Powders and Ointments

Alleged witches were often thought to be given, at the time of initiation, special powders and ointments with which to work magic. In other cases, such as that of Agnes Sampson (tried 1590), the making of enchanted powders appears to have been linked to associating with and perhaps learning from the dead, or as that of a wiseman of Yorkshire (tried 1593), whose magical powders had been bestowed by fairies. Similarly, in his *Description of the Shetland Islands*, Samuel Hibbert described a "good man" of Unst "who had an earthen-pot containing an unguent of infallible power" which he had received from the fairies.

These powders and ointments served numerous purposes, everything from inciting love or hatred to stirring tempests. They were often described in terms of colors, including white, yellow, red, black, grey, or green, or mixtures of these. Green and white preparations were used to heal. Grey preparations brought harm or illness, while black preparations were sometimes used to kill. Color signification appears, however, to have been localized to a certain degree. For example, the alleged French witches Jeanne Gallée and Alexée Drigie, both tried in 1586, claimed, respectively, that white and red ointments were deployed in many types of spells. They were usually stored, as familiars were housed, in clay pots. Although it was rare that powders and ointments were discovered by witch-finders, one German investigation of an alleged witch turned up two pots used to store powders and ointments, one of which contained a "hard, dry, black substance."

According to de Lancre, witches of the seventeenth century primarily used two sorts of ointments, one of which was supposed to induce an ecstatic trance state in which the practitioner would envision traveling – which we might refer to as astral travel – to a faraway place, the other of which was supposed to grant the power to *actually* travel in the flesh through the air to a non-Christian rite. Alleged ingredients of these ointments differ according to source and geographic location and remain controversial. Sometimes described as predominantly yellow in color, Western European ingredients may have included aconite, cinquefoil, cowbane, hemlock, henbane, deadly nightshade (belladonna, also called "moon shade"), mandrake, opium, poplar leaves, saffron, smallage, sweet flag (calamus), tobacco, and wolfsbane; whereas, in the Central Balkans, the ointment was believed to be made from the "excrement of black swine," "cooked toad," and "butter made from mare's milk."

Poppets

Poppets, very simple dolls, were frequently deployed in magical practice. According to Paul G. Brewster, writing of the use of poppets in twentieth-century magic of the American Ozarks (1950), "Of all the charms of witchcraft…the witch's doll is by all odds the most dreaded." Ancient Egyptians deployed poppets, usually made of wax or clay and called *shawabtis*, to perform work such as ploughing for them; destroy enemies; and assist the deceased in making his or her way to the afterlife. Greeks and Romans, referring to poppets as *kolossoi*, typically made them from wax, clay, and/or wood and most commonly used them to enhance erotic attraction, banish evil, or curse enemies. Poppet pairs bound together, called *symplegma*, were often deployed in amatory magic. In spells utilizing poppets, they were sometimes placed in jars together with written texts.

Poppets were sometimes used in the British Isles in connection with written spells of amatory – including anti-amatory – magic. As we have seen, one of the most powerful poppets is that made from mandrake (or, mandragora) root. Germanic cultures on the eve of Christianization frequently incorporated poppet-like images of deities. Poppets created in Europe and typically linked to witchcraft were made from various substances including "wood, wax, lead, rags, bone, and dough," as well as from butter. Sometimes toads stood in for poppets. Poppets were often "treated" by being "pierced with pins" or "slashed with knives." In Scotland, poppets (occasionally created from other materia) made of clay were called *corp criadh*. Sometimes the poppet looks very similar to the *paquet* used in Vodou, rather like a pin cushion topped by a doll's head; at others, like a gingerbread man or woman. When the poppet or *corp criadh* was made and ready to be stuck with pins, the practitioner said something like "From behind you are like a ram with an old fleece" and then commenced to recite the spell, something like "As you waste away, may she [or he] waste away. As this wounds you, may it wound her [or him]." Poppets made of clay were often placed into bodies of water; as they disintegrated, so would the body of the enemy. Brewster notes that "Neapolitan witches used (and perhaps still use) a green lemon, which they transfixed with nails and then suspended over a fire."

In 1479, over a dozen women and men were tried and executed for attempting to kill King James III (1451-1488; r. 1460-1488) of Scotland by way of a wax poppet. James III was an extremely unpopular monarch; one of those who sought to kill him through magic and died for his effort was his own brother, John Stewart, the Earl of Mar (d. 1479). In 1538, an unknown person sought to slay the infant Prince Edward by fashioning a wax poppet and piercing it with pins. In September 1578, "the English ambassador announced that three waxen images had been found buried in the mud bearing the names of the Queen of England and of others, and a courtier of Islington was suspected of it." A witch trial of 1612 describes the creation of a poppet, here called a "picture," of clay, "like unto the shape of the person whom they mean to kill." When the poppet has thoroughly dried, the practitioner is to "take a thorn or pin, and prick it in that part" of the poppet "you would so have to be ill." If one wishes to kill another person, the poppet should be burned. In the late seventeenth century, alleged witch Isobel Gowdie and accomplices supposedly sought to bring harm to the Laird of Parkis' son and his descendants via this method. Also during that time, "Sir George Maxwell of Pollok [c. 1688-1697][was] said to have been bewitched and tormented by means of waxen and clay images."

The German-born Princess, later Queen, Caroline "of Brunswick" (1768-1821), wife of George Prince of Wales, who later became King George IV (1762-1830; r. 1820-1830), is thought to have practiced poppet magic on her husband, who treated her disrespectfully and cruelly, even going so far as to forbid her to attend his coronation and to exile her. Her lady-in-waiting observed:

After dinner her Royal Highness made a wax figure as usual, and gave it an amiable addition of large horns; then took three pins out of her garment and stuck them through and through, and put the figure to roast and melt at the fire....[T]he Princess indulges in this amusement whenever there are no strangers at table, and she thinks her Royal Highness really has a superstitious belief that destroying the effigy of her husband will bring to pass the destruction of his Royal Person.[77]

In *Pins and Pincushions* (1911), Eleanor D. Longman and Sophy Loch draw our attention to a tradition found among the Flemish of Belgium circa 1840. They named the poppet made of wax or clay a *menikin*, a "dwarf," from which our word "mannequin" appears to derive. Typically deployed for the purpose of revenge, the "name of the person...should be written upon the breast of the image."

In 1960, a poppet and accompanying spell were discovered in Herefordshire. They were created in the late nineteenth century by someone placing a curse on Mary Ann Ward: "I act this spell upon you from my holl heart wishing you never rest nor eat nor sleep the rest part of your life I hope your flesh will waste away and I hope you will never spend another penny I ought to have Wishing this from my whole heart." Sometimes poppets took the form of cloth hearts (or, occasionally, hearts of animals) and as such were stabbed with pins. This image may have drawn upon both earth-centered and Christian iconography, with the latter inspiration reflecting Our Lady of the Sorrows stabbed by swords. In or near 1897, a spell of this sort was performed by a jilted lover; it included the verse,

> May each pin
> Thus stuck in
> This poor heart

In hers go
  Who hurts me so
    Till she departs.[78]

A similar spell from 1920 or thereabouts included this rhyme: "With this pin I thee prick,/ My enemy's heart I hope to stick." These spells are far more reminiscent of those found in the ancient *Greek Magical Papyri* than in present-day, New Age-influenced Wiccan texts.

In 1900, a "pin-studded wax figure of President William McKinley was burned on the steps of the American embassy in London." A poppet was also deployed in the infamous 1928 "hex murder" of Nelson Rehmeyer, a Pennsylvania "witch doctor." In 1929 in England, an alleged "witch in [living in] Norwich… ma[de] images of candle wax. At midnight she sticks pins into the image and says incantations." The making of poppets and such has continued into our own century; today, such images are often sold at occult shops.

Amulets, Talismans, Jewelry

Prohibitions listed by church councils, penitentials, and other gatherings and documents indicate that persons continued to manufacture and use pagan-inspired amulets, talismans, and jewelry in medieval and post-medieval Europe; although some of these mixed earth-centered and Christian elements, they were nonetheless earth-based in terms of origin and were, as noted, often condemned by Church officials.

Amulets and talismans employed in medieval England, France, Austria, Switzerland, Denmark, Iceland, and elsewhere, which appear to have served healing, divinatory or magical purposes included: amulets fashioned from "copper, bronze or iron;" "amulets [made] of grass" and various dried herbs; amulets made of stones and gems such as jet (such as a medieval Germanic spindle-whorl invoking Vár, the goddess of marriage), quartz crystal, amethyst, and as well as of amber; talismans of boar, fox, horse (to journey to the otherworld), ox, or wolf teeth (for protection and success in hunting); the "right shank [bone] of a…black dog;" beads made of animal bones; hair contained in a ball of wax; and rings made of stag antlers (against snakebite and in amatory magic).

Amulets and talismans were worn not only by humans but also by animals. In Ireland, for example, cows were given necklaces of holed stones to protect them from evil beings.

In the *Life of Eligius* of the seventh century, we learn that the wearing of amber necklaces by women came to be viewed as a sign of paganism: "Let no woman hang amber around her neck…or have recourse … to enchanters … or …[makers of] amulets." The wearing of such necklaces may have been linked to dyeing and weaving and to reverence of Minerva or a kindred goddess of weaving.

The Thor's Hammer, or Mjöllnir, a metallic, miniature hammer that was worn around the neck, became extremely popular in Scandinavia and Britain during the tenth century. Representations of this hammer were used not only as weapons but also to bless weddings and the births of children. Both Meaney and Perkins suggest that this amulet, especially due to its rise in popularity during the tenth century, may have signified pagan resistance against Christianization; in Meaney's words, "Could the English models have originated from the same cause – a desire by pagans to imitate and even counteract the wearing of a cross?"

Some persons in France were said to believe in the magical efficacy of serpents' tongues suspended from necklaces; and Anglo-Saxons similarly swore by spider amulets, with spiders being placed in nutshells, wrapped in silk, and worn around the neck to protect from illness. Amulets and talismans were also fashioned from coins and from braided thread, often of various colors, to be worn around the wrist or neck to avert the evil eye. Many amulets and talismans were made to attract love and marriage; for example, in the late sixteenth century, in the British Isles, a small pouch containing red wax and a bent penny was worn around the neck to attract a potential husband.

Perkins speaks of "wind-amulets" made of three knots, sold by wind-magicians from near the Arctic to Scots, the first of which "should be untied for a light wind, the second for a strong one; but the third should never be undone as this would produce a violent storm."

Amulets and talismans were also fashioned in diverse shapes. Some were shaped like the moon, often from silver or gold; Meaney suggests that these were "connected with moon worship, with the ever changing shape of the moon, or with its function as an attribute of divinities such as Diana." Others, like ex-votos or Hispanic *milagros*, made of metal, were shaped into miniatures of human body parts, tools, weapons, and other figures, as well as representations of deities. Still other talismans were "pieces of wood, metal, stone, fabric, or parchment covered with symbols" such as Greek "characters" and runes.

Amulets and talismans have persisted and undergone innovation over the course of time and continue to be worn today by many. Mandrake amulets were so popular in fifteenth-century France that Friar Richard, a controversial Franciscan priest best known for believing that Joan of Arc did in fact hear the voice of God and that the world was going to end in 1430, "furiously denounced" the wearing of them and was responsible for the burning of "vast numbers" of the amulets. In spite of religious zealotry, "bits" of mandrake were being "worn by the young men and maidens of Greece [in 1885] to bring them fortune in their love-affairs." Moreover, mandrake root was "carried as an amulet" during World War I by a soldier in the East London Regiment.

Amulets and talismans experienced another dramatic rise in popularity during plagues, especially those of the seventeenth and eighteenth centuries. Dried toads and "plague cakes," amulet bags filled with arsenic, were placed next to the skin and over the heart.

British soldiers during World War I carried not only mandrake but also other amulets including holed stones, thunderstones, and "sea beans" and/or "drift seeds" thought to have washed upon their shores from places as far away as Africa and the West Indies. Likewise in the early twentieth century, an East End,

London physician "estimated that forty percent of the children at the schools which he attended [wore] some sort of [protective] amulet," such as a necklace of blue beads, "under their clothes."

Furthermore, the first decades of the twentieth century witnessed innovation of, and a dramatic rise in, the popularity of amulets. Texts on gemstones as amulets were especially popular. The rise in popularity of amulets was due in part to their being dubbed "mascots," a seemingly less troubling term in the view of "moderns" than "amulet," "fetish," "talisman," and the like. If "mascot" seemed more modern, however, its origin was no less pagan, for anyone who dared to explore its etymology. Popularized circa 1880 by way of a comic opera, *La Mascotte*, "mascot"'s roots lay in medieval Latin and Provençal. In those tongues, it signified "mask" "specter," "witch," "sorcery," and "fetish." Moving from these tongues into the *patois* of Marseille, in late nineteenth- and early twentieth-century French, it came to mean a "sorcerer's charm." At first primarily popular among "bridge-players, actors, sportsmen, motorists, gamblers," "mascots" soon became all the rage among the general public.

Together with "rheumatism rings, 'electropathic' belts," and other eccentric inventions, those in the know sported necklaces bearing Maori gods in "lucky jade" (paunamu greenstone). These were joined by items made in Japan, including animal amulets, such as ones depicting lucky cats, and others depicting the *tomoe*, a swirling symbol of "the revolution of the universe" connected to samurai and Shinto. Amulets made in Africa, including rings made in West Africa and "bangles" of wire and beads made by the Zulu, also became popular.

"Rag-doll and metal mascots for fixing to the cap of the radiator," including one representing a policeman, with the words "Propitiate the Fates!" written on it, to keep cops who would ticket drivers away, sold as "novelties in jewelry," but daring drivers knew better. Slogans linked to mascots proliferated. For instance, "Never Despair! A silver sixpence may be your mascot" meant that sixpence could buy you a packet of Dr. Tibbles' Vi-Cocoa, which would work like a charm. Not only amulets, by the way, became "mascots"; black cats and some young men involved in sports also came to be called "mascots." British folklorist A. R. Wright wrote:

> There is even a London manufacturer of talismans, designed on astrological lines. At the height of the craze, about 1922-1925, the chosen mascots were put on nearly everything feminine: handbags, handker-chiefs, scarves, umbrella handles, bathing caps, and hats, and even "undies" were marked with the mascot instead of the monogram. The fashion affects both sexes, and mascots are poured as lucky gifts upon candidates, …flying men, and football and cricket teams. Few motor-cars are now without [them]…Will's issued cards of "lucky charms" with their cigarettes. The Great Western Railway Company in 1922 took advantage of the craze and distributed to its staff 50,000 copies of a small metal "charm against accidents"…and

expected them to be carried.[79]

This kaleidoscopic array of innovative amulets and talismans was joined by traditional ones, ancient, medieval, and Renaissance items including: holed stones (sometimes carried by chauffeurs); thunderstones (or, "thunderbolts"); precious stones; cowries; amanita muscaria mushrooms; amulets bearing images of pigs; animal claws, hooves, bones, and skins (although a dramatic rise in the popularity of the rabbit's foot was attributed to recent African-diasporic influence in the U.S. South); horseshoes with seven nail heads; knotted charms; and talismans utilizing red fabric. While all of these were rooted in earth-centered traditions, even more specifically pagan were the ankh, the caduceus, the Thor's Hammer, and rings engraved with astrological signs. Early twentieth-century amulet-making also included innovation of ancient, medieval, and Renaissance items, such as "Charmides" sachets bearing astrological symbols, fashioned in corresponding colors and bearing corresponding scents.

Despite the proliferation in amulets, or "mascots," however, Wright points out that when shopkeepers were asked about such amulets by persons unknown to them, they would typically say that the amulets were "just for fun." When he confronted one of them regarding shell necklaces made for many years by fishermen in Southport, remarking that they were not "just for fun" but were in fact meant to bring prosperity, the shopkeeper replied, "Who told you that? ...[T]hat was silly."

During World War II, a Basque boy came to the attention of British authorities when it was discovered that in his baggage was underwear embroiderd with what appeared to be a swastika. It was not a Nazi swastika, but rather a Basque *tetraskele* ("four human legs bent by the knees and joined together at the base of the thighs"), similar to the Italian (etc.) *triskele*, sewn there as a talisman to provide protection.

Today, amulets and talismans are sold in profusion at occult shops, botanicas, and the like.

Amulet Bags and Similar Collections

More complex amulets and talismans (evidenced especially by findings in Anglo-Saxon women's graves but found in others as well) included: miniature work-boxes (also called thread-boxes, relic-boxes) which have been linked to women's weaving magic and which included needles and thread (red, yellow, blue, black, and green) and fragments of woven textiles as well as seeds, garnet, and calcite; and "amulet bags" (sometimes made of leather and worn at the waist) which included such items as thread, falcon claws, boars' teeth, stags' antlers, snakes' tails, cowrie shells (of which we have spoken above), bits of colored glass, discs of iron, bronze, and bone, and "something at least one hundred years old." Such bags may date from the Bronze Age in Scandinavia. In ancient Greek magical practice, the "skutária raptá [*skutaria rapta*] are little leather amulet-bags to be hung around the neck or shoulders."

In the seventh century CE, it appears that a majority of Anglo-Saxons possessing such bags were women. Meaney suggests that "these collections of diverse objects were used in divination" and/or in healing rituals and that "the women who possessed them were the 'cunning women' of the tribe." Meaney suggests that an amulet bag allegedly discovered among the personal effects of Adam de Stratton, Chancellor of the Exchequer, who was arrested in 1289 on charges of forgery and sorcery, indicates that such bags continued to be employed by practitioners of magic into at least the late thirteenth century. This bag contained nail pairings, human hair, parts of animals, and other objects. A Basque combination of the seventeenth century might include "mole bones, bat wings, stones removed from the heads of toads, the wood of the gallows, a needle that touched the clothing of a dead person, powder taken from the skull of the head of a thief just hanged." Another example of a bag deployed by a wisewoman of premodern Europe to heal headaches was comprised of seeds, snake bones, and other items gathered up in a piece of white cloth. Beyond the bounds of Europe, in the early twentieth century, "small bags taken from the necks of child-patients in a hospital in Egypt were found to contain such oddments as the dried head of a hoopoe, a dried chameleon, the cast [off] skin of a snake, other [substances of] vegetable or animal origin, pebbles, etc." Similarly, in sixteenth- through twentieth-century Greece, a typical combination of materials might include candles, honey, and a skull wrapped in red cloth. General Makrygíannis (1983) describes such an object that he discovered that his wife and a friend had put together that was supposed to cure her of several illnesses allegedly brought on by negative sorcery, including insomnia, skin rash, and the withering of her breasts during pregnancy. The "cloth parcel bound with much string …[contained] three long nails, many needles, mercury, ash, human bones, and pieces of both Makrygíannis's and his wife's clothing."

These bags and their contents bear a striking resemblance to bags known as *gris-gris* in Vodou, *mojo* in Hoodoo, and *resguardos* in La Regla de Ocha (Lucumí, Santería); and their contents, when taken together, resonate profoundly with the "add-on," "assemblage" sacred aesthetic that governs West African-diasporic religions/traditions.

Intriguingly, such "grab-bags" are uncannily reminiscent of items that were spewed out by persons being cured of negative sorcery. For example, one observer of a sixteenth-century European ritual wrote that he had "seen woolen rags, iron nails…, iron and brass pins, [and] needles …sometimes wrapped in a cloth and tied" coughed up by ensorcelled patients.

Texts

The later Middle Ages witnessed the dramatic rise of ceremonial magic, a generally elite, male system of magic heavily influenced by Abrahamic religions. Exemplary of ceremonial magic are the works of Heinrich Cornelius Agrippa von Nettesheim (1486?- 1535). However, the texts of this tradition often also include earth-centered elements. Intriguingly, however, these elements are typically ignored by scholars wishing to stress Abrahamic and/or Neoplatonic and

Hermetic influences. Nevertheless, one frequently finds in such texts, sometimes called grimoires, spells in which the practitioner must invoke, for instance, Immanuel and Jehovah as well as "Fairies, Nymphs, and Satyrs." In a spell meant to "raise up the Ghost of one that hath hanged himself," one may need to call upon Hecate as well as the "Savior of the World" (i.e., Jesus Christ).

Some texts, however, were not heavily influenced by Abrahamic faiths. For example, in laying the foundation of St. Alban's Church at St. Albans in southern Hertfordshire, England during the tenth century, some magical texts were allegedly discovered. Included were invocations of Phoebus Apollo, Mercury, Diana, and Neptune (or their Germanic counterparts). The texts were, not surprisingly, burned.

One of the most well-known texts of ceremonial magic is the *Ghâya*, or *Picatrix* (its Latin title, perhaps alluding to Hippocrates), an Arabic manual composed in the tenth century and translated into Spanish during the reign of Alfonso X (1221-1284, r. 1252-1284). Although this text is heavily Abrahamic, it also embraces Greco-Roman pagan concepts and practices. This is especially evidenced by its invocations of planetary deities. It is important in our context to stress that these invocations do not rely only upon knowledge of astrology; they also rely upon belief in the deity and upon the formulaic structure of earth-centered invocation (which is strikingly similar to the structure of the praise-hymn of the Yorùbá and Yorùbá-diasporic and other West African-based religions), which is inclusive of: a salute, a naming of manifestations, a listing of attributes, and a plea for that which the suppliant desires. For example, the invocation of Saturn includes salutes (sometimes blended with manifestations and attributes) such as: "O Master of sublime name and great power, supreme Master;" a naming of manifestations: "Thou, the Cold, the Sterile, the Mournful...the Sage...the Impenetrable;" a listing of attributes: "Thou, whose promises are kept...Thou, the old and cunning ...deceitful, wise, and judicious; Thou who bringest prosperity or ruin, and makest men to be happy or unhappy;" and a supplication: "I conjure Thee, O Supreme Father, by Thy great benevolence and Thy generous bounty, to do for me what I ask." In *The Survival of the Pagan Gods*, Jean Seznec exclaims, "[H]ow amazing to think that such prayers were now being raised to the skies in Christian Europe!"

Texts of divination and magic mixing ceremonial and earth-centered traditions proliferated in medieval and post-medieval Europe. In Russia, for example, such texts were particularly popular among *koludny*; by the seventeenth century, however, they were becoming increasingly popular among the wider Russian population. The *brontologion* predicted thunderstorms, while the *seismologion* predicted earthquakes; the *lopatochnik*, concerning scapulamancy; and the *trepetnik*, divination based upon involuntary movements of the human body. Other texts focused on alchemy, astrology, geomancy, divination by the moon and dreams, and magic spells (*zagovory*). Texts focusing on blessing and healing were called *lechebniki*, deriving from *lechit*, 'to cure;'

while texts focusing on poisoning and cursing were called *travniki*, after *travit*, 'to poison.'

In the early seventeenth century, Leonora Galigaï allegedly deployed not only wax figures and amulets but also texts "inscribed with magical characters" in bewitching Marie de Medicis (1575-1642).

In 1685, a little book was published which insisted that it would do "no harm" but would instruct young women and men to find mates: *Mother Bunch's Closet*. The name "Mother Bunch" appears in a 1604 collection titled *Pasquil's Jests, mixed with Mother Bunch's Merriments*. During the seventeenth and eighteenth centuries, "Mother Bunch" became a recognized archetypal figure not unlike Mother Goose. In the 1685 publication, "Mother Bunch" may have been employed as a pseudonym for a particular individual or may have signified a composite portrait. It may also have functioned as a fictional vehicle to convey information about magical and divinatory practices primarily linked to romance. If, however, "Mother Bunch" was at least loosely based on a person living in the seventeenth century, then we are told several things about her. She lived in western England, in the countryside. She loved "to walk abroad in the fields, to take [in] the air." She married and, outliving her husband, became a widow; but she did not wish to live as a spinster, and so practiced the love magic her grandmother had taught her and that she had learned from magical texts. "When I was young," she tells the writer who recounts her life and recipes, "reading over some histories, I found out the art to know him that should be my husband, and what color of hair he should be." Finding the magical practice successful, she "took [it] upon her[self] to teach other maidens" and apparently some young men as well. She insisted that her practice of magic was accomplished "without the help of the Devil." Her practice was accomplished, however, by combining oral tradition and transmission, by way of her grandmother, with literary tradition, via magical texts attributed to Hermes Trismegistus, Cornelius Agrippa, and the "Twelve Sibyls." This mixing of oral and literary traditions is significant because it demonstrates that there was no impenetrable barrier between these, such as has been continually stressed in studies of witchcraft and magic that offer stereotypical portraits of intellectual, male practitioners of constructive ceremonial magic versus illiterate, female practitioners of primarily destructive witchcraft. A love spell to be undertaken on St. Agnes' Eve demonstrates a pagano-Christian amalgamation typical of magical receipts of this period. Performed on an ostensibly Christian holiday, the spell includes a pagan invocation to Cupid or Eros: "Now the god of love send me my desires." It is, however, the case that during this period, one rarely encounters direct references to pagan deities in magical texts. The spell is reminiscent of others, such as that undertaken by young women from the eleventh century (or before) through the seventeenth century involving the making of bread in love magic. Kneading dough with the buttocks into croissant-like cockle-bread to attract lovers, they would chant, "Stroke me smooth and comb my head and thou shalt have some cocklebread."

Sometimes texts were themselves considered as living entities and/or as possessing magical powers. Among magical practices undertaken in the Renaissance (reported *c.* 1500 CE), a common one was the placement of scrolls of magic in doorways as well as in fields, groves, and vineyards to promote fertility and prosperity. In nineteenth-century Brittany, it was commonly held that magical texts were alive; this aliveness was indicated by certain events, as when a person gave away a copy of such a text and it returned to his home, and when another tried to burn such a text, but the text refused to comply.

There are of course reasons why we possess so few divinatory and magical texts from earlier periods, including, not least, their burning. Moreover, many persons have guarded systems of divination and magic as sacred and secret mysteries not to be publicly shared, and many have not been literate and so have passed down traditions orally. Many have believed, like Mary Colling, an early nineteenth-century commoner of Devonshire, England, that "once these charms get...into a printed book, all their efficacy will be for ever destroyed."

Before leaving the subject of texts, I would like to say just a word about mysterious words that occur in magical and non-Abrahamic spiritual contexts. I think that while we need to avoid indulging in fanciful etymology – for example, that "gay," here meaning "homosexual," derives from the goddess Gaia – I also think that we need to avoid chalking up mysterious words to mere "nonsense" or "gibberish." Doing so, in my view, preempts further research.

For example, in 1597 the alleged witch Andro Man of Scotland claimed that at the end of a rite, in bidding farewell to the "Devil," one should say the word "*Maikpeblis.*" Although I have not discovered an exact etymology for "*Maikpeblis,*" I have found that both "*maik*" and "*peblis*" are Scottish words. "*Maik*" is a multivalent term which may signify "match," "pair," "equal," "mate," or "halfpenny." "*Peblis*" is thought to originate in a term meaning "tents" used by an ancient tribe of Scotland. Beginning perhaps as "*pebyll,*" the term later transformed into "*peblis,*" then into "Peebles," a surname and town, and "Peeblesshire," a county in Scotland. Although at first I am uncertain as to what "*Maik*" signifies in "*Maikpeblis,*" and while "*-peblis,*" although on the surface, except for being a Scottish term, seems unrelated to the case of Andro Man, a bit more searching unearths an intriguing possibility as to the meaning of the term.

When Andro Man spoke of 'laying' "the Devil" by means of the term, he was most probably not referring to Satan, but rather to the Queen of Elfland or Fairy or her male counterpart Christsonday, both of whom he encountered. On digging a bit more deeply, I believe that "*Maikpeblis*" may well be related to the Queen of Elfland or Fairy and her "*maik,*" that is, her "mate," with "*Maik-*" referring either to Christsonday, Andro Man, or both. I say this because of the centuries-old association of "*peblis,*" that is, Peebles and Peeblesshire, with the indigenous feast of Beltane and its Queen, and because of the appearance of the term "maik" in the context of the poem.

Not only are Peebles and Peeblesshire rich in earth-centered history, home to standing stones, Roman ruins, and Saxon influence, not to mention the alleged "burial-place of the great enchanter Merlin," but also Peebles has been celebrated for its feast of Beltane since at least the early fifteenth century, when Scottish King James I (1394-1437) observed or took part in the festivities. A fifteenth-century satirical lyric often attributed to James I, "Peblis to the Play," points to the importance of Beltane at Peebles. It begins:

> At Beltane, quhen ilk bodie bownis [when each person sets forth]
> To Peblis to the play [To Peebles, to the festivities],
> To heir [hear] the singin' and the soundis,
> The solace, suth to say;
> Be firth [From outlands] and forrest furth they found [went],
> Thay grayhit [clad] them full gay;
> God wait that wald they do that stound [on this occasion],
> For it was thair feist day [feast-day]...[80]

We join a crowd that is gathering from far and wide, gaily dressed, making its way to Peebles. We are led by a man who plays the bagpipe and another who wears a hat of birch or decorated with birch ["*ane birken hat*"] who leads us in a bawdy song ["*ane hie ruf sang*"]. We haven't even reached Peebles when a sort of madness comes upon us ["*quhen the madinis come upon thame;*" "*We ar all in ane trance*"]. We notice a young couple including a bawdy young woman, who says to the young man, "What need do you have to play the mate?" ["*Quhat neidis you to maik it sua*"], in which the term "*maik*" appears in the context of coupling. Shortly thereafter we are told, possibly of the young woman of this couple, "Some say the Queen of May has come!" ["*Sum said the Quene of May/ Was cumit*"].

The poem continues, becoming increasingly like a brew of slapstick, a Bruegel painting, and Lorca's *Blood Wedding*. It has been treated to an illuminating analysis by George Fenwick Jones (1953), in which he draws our attention to a host of earth-centered elements and concludes that the poem reflects a "pagan rite." Thus, in Andro Man's time, we can fairly safely say that Peebles was widely associated with the celebration of Beltane, and that the festival included a significant appearance of the Queen of May (Fairy, Elfland) and a ritualized coupling of the Queen – a *maik*-ing – with a male partner, hence, perhaps: *Maikpeblis!*

Incidentally, in the fifty years following Andro Man's trial, Peebles and Peeblesshire became increasingly known for its alleged witches, and in 2009, Peebles continues to boast of its Beltane celebration.

These sorts of complex, indirect collections of signs requiring semiotic 'detective work' may prove to be "phrases" or "sentences" in a kind of code of subjugated knowledge or anti-hegemonic discourse/counterdiscourse, such as Ida Nelson has discovered in the French burlesque *sotties*, that may ultimately shed greater light on the persistence and innovation of pagan concepts and practices than more direct and simpler statements.[81]

Notes

Chapter 1
Block quotations:
1 See Carmichael, Watson, and Matheson, eds., *Carmina Gadelica*, vol. 2, p. 45; I have used the translation by Noragh Jones, Power of Raven, p. 152.
2 Linton, *Witch Stories*, p. 82.
3 Holmqvist, *Swedish Vikings on Helgo and Birka*. page 60.
4, Baudelaire, *Fleurs du mal*, 13 (my translation).
5 Other main sources for Chapter 1: Abram, *Spell of the Sensuous*, 103; Biese, *Development of the Feeling*, 1; Brøndsted, *Vikings*, 42, 150-154; Clifton, "Nature Religion for Real," 336-338; Cornford, *From Religion to Philosophy*, 201-204; Fedotov, *Russian Religious Mind*, 9; Gimbutas, *Balts*, 193; Glosecki, *Shamanism and Old English*, 8; Gutierrez, "Ancient Imagination," 178; Harvey, *Animism: Respecting the Living*, xi, xvii, 3. 17, 38, 55, 167; Magoun, Jr., "On Some Survivals," 34-37; Merchant, *Death of Nature*, 1-2, 8-20, 127-128, 132-143; Obenga, *Philosophie Africaine*, 47-49; Rio, *Arbre philosophal*, 10, 14-15, 18-19; Skrbina, *Panpsychism in the West*, 24-31, 43-46, 58; Sundqvist, *Freyr's Offspring*, 97, 100, 102, 107, 123, 128-130, 132-134.

Sources for Chapter 2:
6 Block quotations: Bray, *Borders of the Tamar*, 56.
7 Denham, *Denham Tracts*, 18.
8 or, Old Cambus. Denham, *Denham Tracts*, 150.
9 Denham, *Denham Tracts*, 129, 143, 150;
10 Ó Tuathail, Excellence of Ancient Word (website).
11 Denham, *Denham Tracts*, 197-198. Other main sources for Chapter 2: Awolalu, *Yoruba Beliefs*, 115, 117; Chambers, *Domestic Annals*, vol. I, chap. 9; Denham, *Denham Tracts*, 19, 197-198; Harvey, *Animism: Respecting*, 37; Henderson, *Survivals in Belief*, 190-199; Meaden, *Goddess of the Stones*, 110-126, 135; Menefee, "Circling as an Entrance," 14; Miller, *Myth and Magic*, 109-123; Mohen, *Megaliths: Stones of Memory*, 17-19, 118-119, 161-163; Murphy, *Santería: An African Religion*, 41; Narby, *Intelligence in Nature*, 32-2 Slupecki, *Slavonic Pagan Sanctuaries*, 198; Vaitkevicius, *Senosios Lietuvos*, 1: 736-739; Vaitkevicius, *Studies into the Balts*, 50-61; Velius, *World Outlook*, 29-32, 45.

Sources for Chapter 3:
12 Block quotations: Porteous, *Forest Folklore*, 178-179.
13 Oisteanu, *Cosmos vs. Chaos*, 144.
14 Oisteanu, *Cosmos vs. Chaos*, 149-150.
15 Porteous, *Forest Folklore*, 178-179.
16 Other main sources for Chapter 3: Audin, "Eaux saintes," 416; Dalyell, *Darker Superstitions*, 403-404; Davidson, *Gods and Myths*, 165-166; Gifford, *Wisdom of Trees*, 12-13, 29, 58, 131-132, 139-140, 147, 153-155; Gimbutas, *Balts*, 190-194; Gimbutas, *Language of the Goddess*, 255, 319-320; Graves, *White Goddess*, 30, 49, 124, 227, 244, 281, 291, 340; Hageneder, *Spirit of*

Trees, 19, 97, 100-102, 113, 120-121, 138, 140, 167, 175, 192-193, 221, 237; Harvey, *Animism: Respecting the Living*, 37; Hull, *Folklore of the British*, 241-244; Kuršite, "Baltic Sanctuaries," *Encyclopedia of Religion*, 2: 774; Mac Coitir, *Irish Trees*, 24-30; Markale, *Celts*, 29, 62, 226, 231, 237-251, 257; Matthews, *Taliesin: The Last Celtic*, 22, 52, 174, 198, 211, 224-246, 253, 256, 296-301; Schama, *Landscape and Memory*, 84-85; Müller-Ebeling, Rätsch, and Storl, *Witchcraft Medicine*, 6, 13, 43-44; Narby, *Intelligence in Nature*, 32-33; Nikov, *Holidays of the Bulgarians*, 11-12; Oisteanu, *Cosmos vs. Chaos*, 119-136; Polomé, "Germanic Religion," *Encyclopedia of Religion*, 5: 524-525; Porteous, *Forest Folklore*, 85-8, 93, 109, 161, 166, 181-189, 258-290; Porter, *Cambridgeshire Customs*, 61; Rio, *Arbre philosophal*, 184-187; Roskos, "Cathedral Forests," *Encyclopedia of Religion and Nature*, 1: 274; Slupecki, *Slavonic Pagan Sanctuaries*, 16, 160-163; Sundqvist, *Freyr's Offspring*, 128-131; Vaitkevicius, *Senosios Lietuvos*, 1:732; Vaitkevicius, *Studies into the Balts'*, 20, 52-54; Velius, *World Outlook*, 194-215.

Sources for Chapter 4:

17. Block quotations: Narby, *Intelligence in Nature*, 6.
18. Kirk, *Secret Commonwealth*, 78.
19. Katzenelenbogen, ed., *Daina: An Anthology*, 4.
20. As cited by Abram, *Spell of the Sensuous*, 87.
21. Leather, *Folk-Lore of Herefordshire*, 23, 28, 123.
22. 101 Ogrodowska, *Polskii Obrzedy Doroczne*, 61.
23. Other main sources for Chapter 4: Biedermann, *Dictionary of Symbolism*, 32-33, 92, 97-98, 164-165, 178, 280-281, 310-311; Cato, in Cato and Varro, *On Agriculture*, CXXXIV, p. 115, etc.; Cranston, ed., *Reincarnation: The Phoenix Fire*, 14; Davidson, *Myths and Symbols*, 51, 57; Grimm, *Teutonic Mythology*, 1: 184, 212; 2: 663-669, 687, 844; 3: 997, 1045, 1126; 4: 1347; Henderson, *Norse Influence*, 101-10; Henderson, *Survivals in Belief*, 53-55, 79, 81, 88-93, 117, 170-173, 271; Hull, *Folklore of the British*, 157-158; Kmietowicz, *Slavic Mythical Beliefs*, 189; Kuršite, "Changing Borderland Identity," 78; Layard, *Lady of the Hare*, 170, 182-183; Merrifield, *Archaeology of Ritual*, 107, 117-118, 128-131; Narby, *Intelligence in Nature*, 15, 47, 52; Oinas, *Essays on Russian Folklore*, 78-80; Siikala, *Mythic Images*, 233; Thiselton Dyer, *Folk-Lore of Shakespeare*, 156-159; Wilson, *Magical Universe*, 17, 41.

Sources for Chapter 5:

24. Block quotations: Grimm, *Teutonic Mythology*, 2: 705.
25. Hole, *Thaumaturgia*, 78.
26. Hole, *Thaumaturgia*, 79.
27. Bray, *Traditions, Legends, Superstitions*, 36.
28. Chambers, and Chambers, *Book of Days* (website).
29. Hibbert, *Description of the Shetland*, 566.
30. Hibbert, *Description of the Shetland*, 566.
31. As cited by Waddell, *Wandering Scholars*, 160.
32. Beza, *Paganism in Roumanian*, 21-22.
33. Other main sources for Chapter 5: Andrews, *Dictionary of Nature Myths*, 4, 10, 20-29, 72, 74, 101, 112, 125, 128, 134, 138-139, 145, 148, 162, 165, 169, 189,

196, 198, 201, 214, 220, 230; Aubrey, *Three Prose Works* (*Remaines of Gentilisme*), 241; Beza, "Pagan Remnants," 394-395; Beza, "Roumanian Legends," 360, 361 (my lining); Blum, and Blum, *Dangerous Hour*, 112-113; Boyer, Art, Myth and Magic, 40, 43; Brown, "Folklore of Devon," 150; Burton, *Anatomy of Melancholy*, 180, 186-187, 191-193; Chesnel de la Charbouclais, *Dictionnaire des superstitions*, 398, 678; Clifton, "Nature Religion for Real," 336-338; Davidson, *Gods and Myths*, 79; Davidson, *Roles of the Northern*, 9, 133-136; Denham, *Denham Tracts*, 77-80; Douce, *Illustrations of Shakespeare*, 84, 240; Filotas, *Pagan Survivals*, 124-140; Gimbutas, *Balts*, 193-198, 203-204; Gimbutas, *Living Goddesses*, 174, 194, 205; Grimm, *Teutonic Mythology*, 1: 257, 267-268, 431-432; 2: 484, 488, 492, 588, 592, 612-613, 618, 620-624, 627, 631-632, 641-643, 713-733, 882-890; 3: 1052-1053; 4: 1310, 1341, 1405; Hallberg, "Elements of Imagery," 59, 61, 67-70; Hartnup, *"On the Beliefs,"* 280-285, 308-315; Henderson, *Norse Influence*, 85-89, 98-99; Jobes, and Jobes, *Outer Space*, 97-100, 144, 176, 266; Johnson, and Boswell, *Journey to the Western*, 110; Jones, "Irish Folklore," 319; Jouet, *Religion et mythologie*, 126; Katzenelenbogen, ed., *Daina: An Anthology*, 4, 89, 91; Kmietowicz, *Slavic Mythical Beliefs*, 17, 168-178, 188, 200-201, 206; Krupp, *Beyond the Blue*, 230-231; Kuršite, "Baltic Sanctuaries," *Encyclopedia of Religion*, 2: 774-775; Lavonen, "On the Beliefs," 245-247; Lecouteux, "Le Radeau des vents," 195-198, 203-207; Lecouteux, *Au-delà du merveilleux*, 53-54, 163; MacCulloch, "Lycanthropy," 207; Máchal, "Slavic Mythology," 41-42, 46-48, 52-53; Markale, "L'éntrée ouverte," 248-249; McCrickard, *Eclipse of the Sun*, 74, 105, 121; McNeill, and Gamer, *Medieval Handbooks*, 321-322, 329-330, 420-421; Miller, *Myth and Magic*, 29, 32-45; Monaghan, *Book of Goddesses*, 256-257, 303; Paper, "Chinese Religion," 120-122; Porteous, *Forest Folklore*, 90-96, 105-106, 110; Quitzmann, *Die Heidnische Religion*, 266; Ralston, *Songs of the Russian*, 145; Rattue, *Living Stream*, 23, 28, 37, 41-42, 57; Richer, "Spirits of the Elements," *Mythologies*, 2: 772; Rodd, *Customs and Lore*, 107, 174-177; Sinclair, *Statistical Account*, 2: 556; Sirvaitis, "Religious Folkways," 115; Skrbina, *Panpsychism in the West*, 24-31; Stewart, *Demons and the Devil*, 4-5, 73, 97, 106, 110, 117, 130, 148, 152, 156, 160-163, 170-176, 181, 190, 229, 279, n. 181; Thorpe, *Northern Mythology*, 1: 211, 246-251, 2: 71, 170-171; Vaitkevicius, *Senosios Lietuvos*, 1: 733-735; Vaitkevicius, *Studies into the Balts'*, 37, 39, 41, 43, 44-46, 54; Velius, *World Outlook*, 44, 53, 78, 213, 227-228, 273.

Sources for Chapter 6

34. Block quotations: Bray, *Borders of the Tamar*, 283.
35 Forster, *Perennial Calendar*, 14-15.
36 Forster, *Perennial Calendar*, 124.
37 Haliburton, *Festival*, 38.
38 Ditchfield, *Old English Customs*, 73-74.
39 Stewart, *Popular Superstitions and Festive Amusements*, 259.
40 Stow, *Survey of London*, 124; Brand, *Observations on the Popular*, 1: 215.
41 Stubbes, *Anatomie of Abuses*, 209-210.
42 Spenser, "Shepherd's Calendar," Eclogue 5.

43 Swift, in Reeves and Seymour-Smith, *New Canon* 172-173.
44 Swift, in Reeves and Seymour-Smith, *New Canon* 172-173.
45 Hampson, *Medii Aevi Kalendarium*, 233.
46 Brady, *Clavis Calendaria*, 330.
47 Brand, *Observations on the Popular*, 1: 219.
48 Brand, *Observations on the Popular*, 1: 230-231.
49 Gordon Cumming, *In the Hebrides*, 232.
50 Aubrey, *Three Prose Works* (*Miscellanies*), 83.
51 Laroque, *Shakespeare's Festive World*, 158.
52 Aubrey, *Three Prose Works* (*Remaines of Gentilisme*), 143.
53 Aubrey, *Three Prose Works* (*Remaines of Gentilisme*), 199.
54 Hutchinson, quoted in Frazer, *New Golden* 478.
55 Bray, *Traditions, Legends, Superstitions*, 330.
56 Ditchfield, *Old English Customs*, 153.
57 Gordon Cumming, *In the Hebrides*, 220.
58 As cited by Ralston, "Forest and Field," 35.
59 Warmstry, as cited by Forster, *Perennial Calendar*, 736.
60 Brand, *Observations on the Popular*, 1: 524-525.
61 Janvier, *Christmas Kalends*, 15-17.
62 Gordon Cumming, *In the Hebrides*, 222.
63 Ditchfield, *Old English Customs*, 47.
64 Forbes-Leslie, *Early Races*, 169.
65 Forster, *Perennial Calendar*, 7.
66 Callcott, *Three Months Passed*, 276.
67 Forster, *Perennial Calendar*, 6-7.
68 Hampson, *Medii Aevi Kalendarium*, 144-145.
69 Other main sources for Chapter 6: Aubrey, *Three Prose Works* (*Remaines of Gentilisme*), 139-140; Baltrušaitis, *Moyen Âge*, 187-188; Barnum, ed., *Dives and Pauper*, 2: 63, explanatory notes on 157/6-7; Billington, *Midsummer: A Cultural Sub-Text*, 6-8, 21, 42-43; Brand, *Observations on the Popular*, 1: 218-232, 377-379, 399-402; Brasey, *Fées et elfes*, 61; Braudel, *Structures of Everyday Life*, 486-487; Bray, *Traditions, Legends, Superstitions*, 329-332; Dexter, *Pagan Origin*, 11; Filotas, *Pagan Survivals*, 84, 153-154, 173-175; Haliburton, *Festival*, 39; Harden, "Liberty Caps," 66-71, 73; Homans, *English Villagers*, 380; Iannella, "Fêtes de la Saint-Jean," 173-177; Kahk, "Estonia II," 279-280; Kirchmaier, *Popish Kingdom* (1877 ed.), 329-330; Laroque, *Shakespeare's Festive World*, 144, 158; Lecouteux, *Au-delà du merveilleux*, 173-174; Levi D'Ancona, *Botticelli's "Primavera,"* 14, 40-43; Lloyd, *Folk Song*, 96-97; MacNeill, *Festival of Lughnasa*, 418-429; Mannhardt, *Götterwelt der Deutschen*, 200, 231-232; Maury, *Croyances et légendes*, 375; Meslin, *Fête des kalendes*, 80-88; Muchembled, *Popular Culture*, 50-53, 58, 305; Panzer, *Beitrag zur deutschen Mythologie*, 1: 16, 63, 98, 198 ff., 260; Russ, *German Festivals*, 56; Rybakov, *Kievan Rus'*, 161; Sokolov, *Russian Folklore*, 193; Spalding Club, *Miscellany*, 1: 97, 165, 167; Spears, "Boar's Head Carol," 194-197; Stewart, *Popular Superstitions and Festive Amusements*, 259; Trinkunas, ed. *Of Gods and Holidays*, 118, 131-135; Trottein, *Enfants de Vénus*, 42, 74, 79, 125 fig. 50; Valdivieso, *Religiosidad Antigua*, 86-87; Velius, *World Outlook*, 167-176; Walter, *Mémoire du Temps*, 135-136, 272-273; Warner, and Kustovskii, *Russian Traditional Folksong*, 28-34; Westropp, "Marriages of

the Gods," 111, 121; Wilde, *Legends, Charms*, 109; Wimberly, *Folklore*, 189-190.

Sources for Chapter 7

70, Block quotations: Uminska and Kennedy, *Chopin: The Child*, 54

71. Kennedy, "Polish Peasant Coutship," 55.

72. Other main sources for Chapter 7: Ammianus Marcellinus, *Later Roman Empire*, Book 31, sec. 9, p. 427; Aristotle, *Politics*, II. 9, p. 68; Athenaeus, *Deipnosophists*, vol. 6, Book 13. 603 a, p. 251; Bindokiene, *Lietuviu Paprociai ir Tradicijos*, 270, 318.; Velius, *World Outlook*, 28, 204-205; Binkley, "Liner Notes," *Robin et Marion* (CD); Boase, *Origin and Meaning*, 86-89; Bogatyrëv, *Vampires in the Carpathians*, 16, 101, 103; Boswell, *Christianity, Social Tolerance, and Homosexuality*, and Boswell, *Same-Sex Unions in Premodern Europe*; Brand, *Observations on the Popular*, 2: 102, 115, 137; Bremmer, "Enigmatic Indo-European Rite," 279-293; Canadian Institute of Ukrainian Studies, "Korovai," *Encyclopedia of Ukraine* (website); Christiansen, *Northern Crusades*, 138; Davidson, *Gods and Myths*, 80, 89, 102, 111-112, 119, 120-121, 156, 195; Davidson, *Roles of the Northern*, 85, 123, 127, 134, 145, 147, 148, 152-153, 174-175; Diodorus Sicilus, *Works*, vol. III, Book 5, sec. 32.7, pp. 183 and 185; D³ugosz, *Annals of Jan D³ugosz*, 414; Fedotov, *Russian Religious Mind*, 16-19, 350-351; Filotas, *Pagan Survivals*, 337; Gimbutas, *Balts*, 184-191; Gimbutas, *Language of the Goddess*, 209-210; Gimbutas, *Living Goddesses*, 194, 204-206; Gordon Cumming, *In the Hebrides*, 266; Grimm, *Teutonic Mythology*, 2: 773, 801, 803, 818-824, 836, 841; Hartland, *Science of Fairy Tales*, 100-101; Henderson, *Notes on the Folklore*, 100-101; Henderson, *Survivals in Belief*, 23-24; Herberger, *Batfeld und das Burgfeld*, LXXXIV (Roman numeral pagination); Herrmann, *Deutsche Mythologie*, 305; Hogan, *Dwellings: A Spiritual*, 109-110; Hopkins, *Book of Courtly Love*, 11; Hull, "Pagan Baptism," 410-418; Hull, *Folklore of the British*, 215; Ivanits, "Three Instances," 71; Jouet, *Religion et mythologie*, 171-172; Kappelhoff, *Geburt und Taufe* and *Verlobung* (website); Karras, "Pagan Survivals," 564; Kennedy, "Polish Peasant Coutship," 54-61; Kmietowicz, *Slavic Mythical Beliefs*, 27, 31, 122-123, 143-144, 210; Knab, *Polish Customs*, 173-174, 235-236, 239, 249, 255-258; Knowlson, *Origins of Popular*, 98; Kravchenko, *World of the Russian*, 36; Law, *Memorialls; or, the Memorable*, xxxviii; Lecouteux, *Au-delà du merveilleux*, 51; Lewis, *Allegory of Love*, 9, 20-22; Lindahl, McNamara, and Lindow, eds., *Medieval Folklore*, 257; Máchal, "Slavic Mythology," 40-41; Markale, *Courtly Love*, 2, 5, 7, 12, 16-17, 21, 147, 155, 159, 182-183, 206-210; Marwick, *Folklore of Orkney*, 82, 92; McNeill, and Gamer, *Medieval Handbooks*, 103, 172-173, 185, 226, 246, 250, 252, 254, 274, 302, 335, 355; Miller, *Myth and Magic*, 112; Motz, *Faces of the Goddess*, 80-82; Müller-Ebeling, Rätsch, and Storl, *Witchcraft Medicine*, 8, 61-70; Mushynka, "Paganism," *Encyclopedia of Ukraine* (website); Newman, ed., *Meaning of Courtly Love*, 92; O'Connor, "Saying 'I Do,'" 48; O'Farrell, *Superstitions of the Irish*, 77; Odarchenko, "Ancestor Worship," "Burial Rites," "Folk Customs," *Encyclopedia of Ukraine* (website); Ogrodowska, *Polskii Obrzedy Doroczne*, 90; Polish Culture, eds.,

"Sinking of Marzanna" (website); Porter, "Some Folk Beliefs," 114; Read, "Some Characteristics," 270; Rybakov, *Kievan Rus'*, 25; Sextus Empiricus, *Outlines of Pyrrhonism*, vol. I, Book 3, sec. 199-200, p. 461; Siikala, *Mythic Images*, 129, 139, 145; Silverstein, "Guenevere, or the Uses," 84; Singleton, "Dante: Within Courtly Love," 48; Sokolov, *Russian Folklore*, 203, 205-207, 211-223; Suziedelis, ed., "Wedding Customs," *Encyclopedia Lituanica*, 6: 240-241; Thiselton Dyer, *Folk-Lore of Shakespeare*, 313-315, 337-338; Thorpe, *Northern Mythology*, 1: 286-292; Trottein, *Enfants de Vénus*, 35, 203; Tucker, "Childbirth," *Medieval Folklore*, 75; Vaitkevicius, *Studies into the Balts'*, 56; Warner, and Kustovskii, *Russian Traditional Folksong*, 36, 43-44; Watts, *Religion in Late Roman*, 82-88; Welsford, "Old Prussians," *Encyclopædia of Religion and Ethics*, 9: 487-490; Westermarck, *History of Human Marriage*, 2: 269, 437, 452-466, 469-470, 475, 479, 480, 489, 497, 505-508, 510-515, 569; Wilde, *Legends, Charms*, 115-117; Wilson, *Anglo-Saxon Paganism*, 140-141; Wilson, *Magical Universe*, 129-131, 134, 197, 203-206; Wood-Martin, *Elder Faiths*, 1: 331; Wright, *English Folklore*, 34.

Sources for Chapter 8

73 Block quotations: Brooke, *History of Early*, 338-339; Baker, "Nine Herbs Charm" (website).
74 Wilson, *Magical Universe*, 145; *OED* "cockle-bread."
75 Brooke, *History of Early*, 338-339; Baker, "Nine Herbs Charm" (website).
76 Wright, *English Folklore*, 104-105.
77 Bury, ed., *Court of the English*, vol. 1, p. 162.
78 As cited by Kittredge, *Witchcraft in Old*, 98.
79 Wright, *English Folklore*, 110.
80 Eyre-Todd, ed., *Scottish Poetry*, 159, ll. 1-10.
81 Other main sources for Chapter 8: Agobard, *Ecclesiae Lugdunensis Opera*, 140; Anon., 'Folk-Lore of Drayton, Part III," 368-369; Araquistáin, "Some Survivals," 34; Banks, "Scottish Lore," 18-23, 29-30; Bassett, *Wander-Ships*, 31; Beza, "Pagan Remnants," 388-389; Brand, *Observations on the Popular*, 1: 314-315, 330, 387-388; 3: 329-360; Budge, *Chapters of Coming Forth*, 105; Cassar, "Witchcraft Beliefs," 229-232; Cavendish, *Tarot*, 15; Chambers, *Domestic Annals (Reign of James VI, 1591-1603)*; Ciruelo, *Treatise Reproving All Superstitions*, 193-197; Cote, ed., *Wicked: The Grimmerie*; Courtney, "Cornish Folk-lore," 198; Dalyell, *Darker Superstitions*, 515, 517; Doering-Manteuffel, "Dissemination of Magical Knowledge," 187-206; Duerr, *Dreamtime*, 1-2; Ettlinger, "British Amulets," 152-157; Ettlinger, "Documents of British," 236-237; Fuller, "Function of the Merseburg," 162-168; Gomme, ed., *Mother Bunch's Closet*, I, 1-3, 17, 20; Grendon, "Anglo-Saxon Charms," 123, 135-136, 148; Hildburgh, "Cowrie Shells," 178-195; Hogan, *Dwellings: A Spiritual*, 48; Hogendorn, and Johnson, *Shell Money*, 5, 12-15; Kaplan, *Tarot Classic*, 25; Kmietowicz, *Slavic Mythical Beliefs*, 25-39, 146, 150, 156-157; Law, *Memorialls, or the Memorable*, xxxviii; Lea, *Materials Toward*, 2: 605, 611, 3: 1076-1077, 1098, 1105; 3: 1098, 1105, 1138; Lecouteux, *Au-delà du merveilleux*, 57; Linton, *Witch Stories*, 6, 43-

44, 121; Longman, and Loch, *Pins and Pincushions*, 31-41; Maguire, Gregory, *Wicked: The Life*; Manciocco, and Manciocco, *L'Incanto e l'arcano*, 162, 170; Mcleod, and Mees, *Runic Amulets*, 2, 50-51; McNeill, and Gamer, *Medieval Handbooks*, 90, 196, 229, 246, 275, 288-289, 305-306, 329-331, 338-339, 340-341, 349-350, 419, 421; Meaney, *Anglo-Saxon Amulets*, 7, 10-17, 28, 30-32, 67-77, 98, 122-130, 131-191, 249-259; Menefee, "Circling as an Entrance," 13, 17, n. 65; Meyer, *Germanische Mythologie*, 90; Mitchell, *African Connections*, 72; Mollenauer, *Strange Revelations*, 20, 44, 87, 88-89; O'Neil, "Magical Healing," 98, 100; Ogden, *Greek and Roman Necromancy*, 166, 204, 208-213; Palmer, *Herefordshire Folklore*, 111-112; Perkins, *Thor the Wind-Raiser*, 10-12, 55-60; Pócs, *Between the Living*, 127; Pollack, *Complete Illustrated Guide*, 26; Porter, "Some Folk Beliefs," 116, 119; Potts, *Wonderfull Discoverie*, 184; Pressel, *Hexen und Hexenmeister*, 88; Remy, *Demonolatry*, Book I, chap. 2, p. 3, chap. 4, p. 7; Ross, "Anchors in a Three-Decker World," 63-64; Ryan, "Magic and Divination," 38-55; Schade, *Die Sage con der heiligen Ursula*, 98-99; Scot, *Discoverie of Witchcraft*, 471-474; Scully, "Marriage or a Career," 859; Smith, *Ordering Women's Lives*, 96; Spalding Club, *Miscellany*, 1: 91; Stewart, *Demons and the Devil*, 225-226, 289; Storms, *Anglo-Saxon Magic*, 133; Stuart, ed., *Miscellany of the Spalding*, vol. I, part 3, pp. 119-121; Vallée, *Passport to Magonia*, 102; Vautier, *Chant des cauris*, 5, 7; Vukanoviæ, "Witchcraft," 12-13; Walter, *Mémoire du Temps*, 269-270; Wilson, *Anglo-Saxon Paganism*, 103-107; Wright, and Lovett, "Specimens of Modern," 288-300; Young, *Women Who Fly*, 167; Zachrisson, "Holiness of Helgö," 157-158.

Index

A

Abundance
    Prosperity 30, 37, 42, 43, 56, 61, 62, 64, 65, 78, 82, 83, 89, 98, 99, 107, 108, 142, 144, 146, 147, 148, 149, 150, 153, 161, 174, 181, 187, 193, 200, 206, 208, 210
    Treasures 31, 32, 85, 99, 122
    Wealth 95, 140, 180
African and African-diasporic religions
    La Regla de Ocha 9, 207
    Palo Monte 199
    Vodou 61, 158, 177, 186, 187, 196, 197, 201, 207
Altered states of consciousness
    Ecstasy 46, 200
    Trance 180, 200, 211
Ancestral spirits 61, 70, 123, 136, 141, 143, 144, 160, 172, 173, 174
Animals
    Bat 190, 207
    Bear 12, 55
    Bee 32, 55, 56, 67, 68, 70, 144, 172, 187
        Honey 88
        Telling the bees of a farmer's death 67
    Boar 56, 69, 71, 77, 106, 141, 153, 168, 178, 183, 203
    Bull 51, 53, 57, 63, 64, 130, 142, 178
    Butterfly 57, 58, 70, 71, 72, 172, 193
    Cat 9, 20, 26, 58, 63, 65, 66, 67, 68, 70, 158, 193, 205
    Cattle 39, 42, 46, 55, 57, 59, 64, 65, 66, 67, 71, 79, 93, 94, 96, 120, 128, 133, 139, 143, 145, 149, 175, 192
    Chicken 58, 59, 64, 65, 66, 162, 198
    Crow 24, 61, 71, 157, 181
    Cuckoo 70, 71, 104, 111
    Deer 49, 54, 59, 65, 66, 67, 71, 132, 133
    Dog 9, 20, 49, 52, 53, 59, 63, 64, 65, 70, 96, 169, 199, 203
    Eel 88, 175
    Falcon 70, 206
    Goat 20, 60, 64, 65, 66, 142, 145, 148
    Hare 60
    Hedgehog 175
    Horse 12, 53, 54, 60, 61, 64, 65, 67, 69, 70, 83, 88, 89, 96, 120, 142, 143, 149, 153, 171, 173, 175, 177, 178, 183, 203
        Telling the horse/s of the death of their master 67
    Lark 108, 109
    Magpie 71
    Mouse 53, 63, 70, 172, 175
    Owl 31
    Pig 88, 142
    Rabbit 60, 63, 156, 162
    Ram 45, 53, 64, 66, 76, 201
    Raven 47, 53, 54, 61, 70, 71, 142, 158, 181
        Huginn 61
        Muninn 61
    Reindeer 148
    Rooster 58, 59, 66
        Fjalar 59
        Gullinkambi 59
        Salgófnir 59
        Viðofnir 59
    Serpent 12, 25, 36, 47, 53, 54, 55, 61, 62, 66, 67, 69, 70, 71, 74, 78, 125, 172, 187, 193, 204, 206, 207
        Serpentine 61
    Stag 53, 55, 59, 68, 142, 146, 203
    Toad 54, 70, 172, 201
    Wolf 62, 63, 66, 68, 69, 70, 71, 79, 93, 139, 142, 143, 157, 192, 193, 203
        Fenrir 62
Arthurian legends
    Guinevere 27, 166, 167
    King Arthur 27
    Lady of the Lake 122
    Merlin 42, 44, 122, 211
Astrology
    Zodiac 95, 160, 183
Avatar and hypostasis 7, 50, 55, 58, 59, 61, 89, 111, 129, 142, 152

B

Beverages

Beer 40, 41, 48, 49, 67, 80, 112, 120, 131, 139, 144, 159, 163, 172
Gin 175, 177
May wine 113
Mead 172, 174
Whiskey 120, 134, 153, 175
Wine 22, 32, 64, 103, 105, 113, 119, 121, 126, 137, 139, 147, 153, 156, 158, 162, 163, 174, 190

Boats and ships
　Alien ships 195
　Fairy ships 196
　Muttergottesschiff 194
　Navigium Isidis 107

Broom, staff, wand
　Broom 35, 40, 42, 48, 60, 109, 158, 194
　Staff 39, 61, 161
　Wand 39, 40, 42, 48, 119, 121, 189

C

Celestial bodies
　Aurora Borealis 99
　Caer Arianrhod 99
　Cassiopeia 99
　Children of Luna 97
　Corona Borealis 99
　Eridanus 99
　Milky Way 99, 100, 173
　Moon 8, 32, 46, 52, 55, 87, 95, 96, 97, 98, 99, 100, 109, 143, 152, 190, 201, 204, 208
　Orion 99
　Path of ghosts 99
　Pleiades 100, 103, 112
　Road of the dead 99
　Sirius 20
　Sun 8, 12, 17, 32, 33, 36, 41, 44, 59, 60, 62, 73, 77, 84, 92, 95, 96, 104, 109, 111, 119, 124, 130, 142, 143, 144, 152, 153, 154, 160, 170, 172, 173, 178
　Ursa Major 99, 100
　Way of Birds 99

Chant, music, and dance
　Abbots Bromley Horn Dance 133, 148
　Benevento wedding 47
　Caroles 122, 126
　Caroling 140, 144, 145
　Chanting 135, 159, 191, 192
　Chorus 164
　Daina 65, 96, 173
　Dancing 46, 66, 85, 90, 91, 115, 116, 117, 119, 121, 122, 123, 127, 130, 135, 147, 164, 165
　Drumming 132
　Flute 78
　Keening 170
　Koliaduvannia 144
　Opera 205
　Singing 27, 90, 115, 116, 117, 121, 122, 123, 132, 135, 147, 152, 159, 162
　Troubadour 114, 164
　Trumpet 92
　Vesnyanki 128

Christian Penitentials
　Burgundian Penitential 168, 188
　Halitgar 176
　Indiculus 83, 92, 97, 190
　Iscanus 50, 146, 176, 181, 187, 190, 193
　Penitential of Theodore 167, 168
　Silos 176

Christianization
　Baptism 88
　Burning of their homes, crops, and domestic anima 175, 179, 183, 205, 206
　Crusades 94, 115
　Deicide 19
　Demonization 32, 146
　Inquisition 191
　Massacre 123
　Missionaries 171
　Penance 95, 167, 177, 187, 188

Church authorities
　Atto of Vercelli 111, 124
　Augustine 126, 183
　Bede 168
　Benedict XIV 155
　Burchard 83, 95, 148, 168, 176, 177, 180, 181, 188, 193
　Columban 168
　Eligius 80, 113, 177, 203
　Eugenius III 51
　Jan D³ugosz 174
　Lactantius 126
　Martynas Mazvydas 84
　Merkelis Giedraitis 62
　Petrus Valderama 84, 92, 194

Pirmin of Reichenau 188
Pope Gelasius I 155
Regino of Prüm 176
Thietmar 51, 77, 83, 154
Church councils and synods
Trullo 107, 189
Clans and families
Connolly 69
Donnachaidh, or, Robertson 69
Flaherty 87
Hennessy 87
Iver/Maciver 69
Lee 69
Mac Cuill 11
Macc Dara 11
MacCodrum 69, 88
MacCulloch 69
MacLeod 69
Matheson/MacMhathain/Macmaghan 69
Crossroads and trivia
Crossroads 22, 23, 68, 176, 177, 187
Trivia 137, 177, 187
Cults of the Virgin Mary and the saints
St. Barbara 145

D

Days of the week
Monday 102, 153
Tuesday 63, 102, 106, 75
Wednesday 40, 102, 107
Thursday 97, 142
Friday 18, 55, 102, 110, 145, 191
Sunday 45
Death
Funeral rites 38, 42, 44, 46, 68, 70, 130, 169, 173, 188
Death and rebirth
Burial 25, 27, 29, 38, 68, 169, 170, 172, 198, 211
Cremation 93, 170, 171
Metempsychosis 69, 172
Regeneration 34, 58, 59, 108, 145, 167
Reincarnation 61, 69, 70, 170, 172
Transmigration 11, 13, 60, 61, 69, 70, 170
Deities
Goddess of Liberty 120
Deities, African and African-diasporic
Ogún 93

Orishá 24, 158, 190
Oshún 23, 190
Yemayá 23
Deities, Baltic
Žemepatis 144
Gabija 93, 94
Giltine 169
Laima 43, 60, 65, 81, 100, 156, 157, 158, 160
Medeina 36, 60
Menulis 32, 95, 96
Patrimpas 62
Perkûnas 26, 27, 32, 44, 45, 59, 60, 62, 65, 81, 83, 93, 130, 133, 136, 178, 197
Ragana 59, 81, 83, 96, 169
Saulë 32, 33, 60, 76, 95, 124, 144, 173, 178
Vejopatis 59
Velnias 35, 81, 83
Deities, Basque
Eguski Amandrea 95
Mari 96
Deities, Celtic and Celto-Roman
Aengus 32, 33, 42, 57
Aeracura 31, 33
Arduinna 36, 56
Arianrhod 31
Badb 61
Belenus 51, 113, 119, 123, 161
Blodeuwedd 31, 40, 41
Brigid 32, 40, 56, 57, 81, 82, 92, 153
Cailleach 28, 58, 134, 140, 181
Cernunnos 55, 59, 61, 132
Dagda 32, 44
Danu 48, 58, 99, 140, 166
Epona 59, 60
Gwydion 31, 49, 99
Lleu Llaw Gyffes 31, 44
Lugh 31, 40, 95, 130
Macha 60
Matronae 32, 78, 140
Medb 57
Mórrígán 57
Rhiannon 60, 61
Rosmerta 31
Sirona 81
Sulis 81
Tailtiu 130, 195
Tuatha Dé Danaan 46, 99, 113
Deities, Earth and/or Mother Goddess 26, 75, 166,

172, 178, 194
Anima Mundi 14
Žemyna 57, 130, 131, 139, 144, 156, 158, 160, 172
Nature/Natura 15, 16, 178
Tellus 132
Terra Mater 76
Deities, Egyptian
Isis 16, 47, 58, 77, 107, 147, 194
Osiris 58, 77, 194
Sekhmet 58
Serapis 147
Thoth 74, 194
Deities, Finno-Ugric
Tapio 37
Deities, Germanic
Dísir 21, 141
Freyja 26, 31, 32, 33, 40, 43, 57, 58, 59, 60, 64, 93, 102, 106, 111, 113, 129, 134, 141, 152, 156, 158, 160, 173, 186, 193, 194
Freyr 21, 32, 50, 57, 64, 66, 81, 106, 113, 141, 152, 153, 156, 160, 194, 212, 213
Frigga 26, 40, 99, 102, 129, 156, 160
Loki 59, 93, 141
Njörð 81, 142
Norns 62, 158, 187
Odin 21, 26, 27, 29, 33, 39, 40, 42, 48, 50, 55, 60, 61, 62, 64, 76, 81, 89, 91, 94, 99, 100, 102, 113, 130, 134, 138, 142, 156, 159, 160, 162, 173, 178, 193
Ostara/Eostre 31, 40, 60, 111
Thor 21, 26, 33, 39, 40, 42, 44, 46, 55, 57, 59, 64, 76, 81, 82, 91, 92, 94, 99, 102, 112, 113, 138, 142, 154, 158, 159, 160, 188, 203, 206, 218
Urðr 35
Valkyries 92, 99, 100, 173, 186, 187
Vanir 106
Vár 203
Deities, Greek and Roman
Aphrodite/Venus 18, 23, 26, 31, 32, 40, 55, 60, 91, 100, 103, 111, 114, 115, 117, 126, 155, 163, 166, 184, 198
Apollo 23, 61, 62, 64, 74, 81, 95, 103, 114, 118, 129, 184, 208
Ares/Mars 102, 103, 107, 115, 147, 183
Artemis/Diana 32, 36, 41, 44, 46, 47, 55, 57, 58, 59, 60, 67, 84, 96, 103, 107, 109, 110, 122, 129, 132, 136, 140, 147, 152, 156, 191, 194, 196, 204, 208
Asclepius 148
Attis 108
Cupid 155, 166
Cybele 108, 165, 166
Demeter/Ceres 107, 149, 152, 153, 163
Dionysus/Bacchus 106, 107, 147, 162
Pan 22, 23, 32, 45, 59
Ares/Mars 58, 60, 62, 64
Asclepius 59, 61
Attis 45, 57
Boreas 90
Cupid 209
Cybele 31, 32, 45, 55, 58, 66, 112, 127
Demeter/Ceres 31, 44, 45, 55, 56, 64, 84, 92, 103, 120, 127, 131, 132, 134, 139
Dionysus/Bacchus 31, 32, 46, 57, 64, 78, 111, 120, 138, 139, 140, 152
Eros 60, 161, 209
Euros 90
Flora 31, 41, 113, 114, 115, 117, 118, 120
Ganymede 58
Hecate 22, 23, 31, 48, 58, 59, 60, 177, 208
Helios 12, 17
Hephaestus/Vulcan 23, 103, 163
Hera/Juno 32, 61, 64, 103, 107, 111, 114, 154, 155
Hermes/Mercury 15, 23, 24, 59, 61, 74, 97, 112, 209
Hesperides 32, 114
Hestia/Vesta 32, 92, 103, 147
Iris 100
Janus 41, 64, 147
Maia 112, 120, 165
Minerva 82, 103, 107, 203
Mithra 57, 140
Morpheus 31
Muses 31, 55, 184
Notos 90
Pales 92, 112, 113
Pan 102, 153, 155
Persephone/Proserpina 32, 45, 47, 57, 64, 107, 108, 149, 153
Pomona 32, 136
Poseidon/Neptune 12, 17, 20, 39, 89, 103, 208
Priapus 32, 36

Prometheus 92
Robigo 112
Robigus 112
Saturn 102, 140, 147, 150, 208
Tyche/Fortuna 122, 124, 125, 126, 140
Zephyrus 90
Zeus 44, 57, 58, 114
Zeus/Jupiter 102, 103
Deities, Indigenous American
   La Llorona 169
Deities, Mesopotamian
   Baal 113
Deities, Sami
   Baiwe 95
   Sáráhkká 59
Deities, Slavic
   Baba Yaga 59, 169
   Borute 46, 51
   Ciza 130, 134, 158
   Dazhbog 95
   Dziewanna 46, 109, 110
   Žemlya 111
   Ileana Sânziana 129, 143
   Kolyada 95, 143, 144
   Kupala 126, 127
   Kupalo 123, 124, 126, 128, 129
   Lada 108, 143, 149, 161, 162
   Lelum 161
   Malanka 149
   Marzanna 109, 110
   Maslenitsa 108, 109
   Morena 110, 126, 169
   Radegast 69
   Rozhanytsi 26
   Stribog 91
   Svantovit 60, 130
   Svarog 93
   Svyetlaya 111
   Volos 55, 59, 62
   Yarilo 31, 127
   Zorya 90, 100
Deities, witchcraft and/or Winter
   Chlungeri 146
   Gruagach 27
   Grýla 146
   Habundia 84
   Herodias 91, 136
   Holda 31, 91, 111, 134, 136, 146, 194
   La Befana 146, 150
   Nicneven 89, 136
   Perchta 94, 146, 159
   Pharaildis 99
   Rupfa 146
   Saelde 146
   Tante Arie 146
   Wanne Thekla 194
Destiny and fate 26, 28, 35, 37, 42, 43, 47, 49, 77, 84, 111, 125, 158, 160
   The Fates 146, 205
Divination
   Amatory divination 129, 180, 181, 182, 184
   Astrology 183, 205
   Coscinomancy 184, 185
   Frith 182
   Grains, especially corn 180
   Lekanomancy 183
   Lots 183
   Oneiromancy 182
   Palmistry 183, 185
   Pyromancy 94
   Runes 39, 40, 42, 183, 204
   Scapulamancy 157, 184, 208
   Scrying 136, 182
   Sortilege 183
   Tarot 97, 184, 185, 217
Drama
   Masques 132, 147
   Sotties 211
   William Shakespeare
      Groundlings 105, 127
Dreams 23, 71, 128, 129, 182, 183, 194
   Nightmare 57

E

Earth-centered beliefs and practices
   Specific traditions
      Animism 10, 11, 18, 73
      Hylozoism 12
      Pantheism 16, 17, 18
      Shamanism 12
Earth-centered worldview 5, 6, 8, 9, 10, 11, 12, 14, 15, 16, 17, 18, 19, 26, 27, 39, 54, 55, 57, 67, 73, 82, 83, 95, 184
Elementals
   Elementals of air
      Sylphs 75, 92

Elementals of earth 77
   Bush grandmothers 77
   Forest nymphs 77
   Gnomes 75
   Moss women 77
   Wild women of the woods 77
   Wood-wives 77, 146
Elementals of fire
   Perelesnyk 94
   Salamander 75, 94
   Tan-we(d) 94
Elementals of water
   Dracae 88
   Nickers 89
   Nymphs 83
   Ondines 75
Elves and dwarves
   Álfablót 142
   Dwarves 26, 27, 43, 91, 156
   Elves 31, 37, 43, 57, 71, 75, 91, 141, 142, 146, 178, 186
Embodiment, possession 7, 10, 49, 117, 147, 158, 193

F

Fairies 7, 8, 17, 27, 28, 33, 35, 41, 42, 43, 54, 57, 59, 75, 77, 78, 82, 83, 84, 85, 111, 117, 120, 124, 129, 130, 135, 136, 146, 147, 150, 158, 159, 169, 193, 196, 200
   Cleena 120
   Esterelle 156
   Fairy Queen 82, 120, 124, 129, 134, 199
   Laumës 35, 81, 83, 100
   Nibelungen 91, 99
   Queen Maeve/Mab 57, 82
   Sleeping Beauty 143, 158
   Snow White 32
   The Snow Queen 79
Fire
   Bonfires 44, 93, 111, 116, 119, 121, 124, 125, 130, 136, 151
   Hearth 92, 93, 136, 149, 163, 180, 181
   Need-fires 93
   Panike 93
   Uguns mate 93
   šventaragiai 93
Flowers 31, 116, 119
   Aconite 33, 201
   Arnica 33
   Bachelors buttons 185
   Cowslip 31
   Dandelion 199
   Lavender 36, 176
   Lilies 36
   Lily of the valley 31
   Periwinkle 161
   Poppies 176
   Rose 12, 18, 28, 31, 32, 36, 71, 72, 81, 122, 126, 139, 143, 155, 158, 165, 199
   Sânziene 129
   Violet 108, 153
   Woodbine 176
   Woodruff 113, 156
   Yarrow 33
Folk figures and local divinities
   Aitvaras 59
   Žaltys 46
   Brownie 27, 30
   Christsonday 210
   Dick-a-Tuesday 75
   Dimstipatis 59
   Faun 59, 77, 146, 164
   Fru Gaue 130
   Green Man 111, 120
   Gruagach 27, 30
   Harvest Queen 134
   Jack-in-the-Wad 75
   Jenny Greenteeth 89
   Jinny-burnt-tail 75
   Kaukai 41
   Kikimora 59, 160
   Leshy 59, 79, 80
   Maid Marian 148
   Malanka 149
   Maulkin 121
   Mavka 78
   Mermaid 27, 86, 87, 90
   Merman 86, 87
   Mother Goose 150, 209
   Mourie 66, 136
   Muma Padura 79
   Nanny Powler 89
   Nymph 32, 164
   Ovinnik 59
   Peg Powler 89
   Polevik 59

Puck 82, 136
Robin Artisson 58
Robin Goodfellow 75
Robin Hood 44, 58, 75, 77, 139, 146
Satyr 59, 77, 146, 164
Scrat 146
Selkies 69, 87, 88
Shony 136
Snegurochka 79, 108
Swan maiden 87
Trolls 33, 77
Vodny Muz 88
Werewolf 78, 79, 97, 193, 196

Foods
  Bairin breac 154
  Bannock 119
  Boars head 66, 141
  Bread 30, 41, 43, 78, 79, 82, 83, 84, 89, 90, 92, 98, 110, 130, 131, 133, 139, 142, 143, 145, 146, 153, 154, 158, 161, 162, 174, 175, 177, 179, 180, 190, 191, 196, 209, 210, 217
  Butter 43, 84, 90, 108, 119, 130, 154, 162, 174, 201
  Cabbage rolls 144
  Cake 41, 61, 64, 83, 97, 110, 111, 119, 120, 133, 138, 141, 147, 149, 150, 151, 162, 163, 204
    Cakes shaped like animals 66
  Cranberry pudding 145
  Feast 23, 64, 86, 104, 106, 111, 112, 114, 116, 122, 123, 129, 132, 133, 135, 136, 138, 140, 141, 143, 145, 151, 152, 153, 154, 157, 159, 162, 163, 164, 174, 210, 211
  Gingerbread 201
  Herring 145
  Honey 56, 85, 88, 108, 109, 144, 145, 146, 147, 148, 158, 162, 174, 175, 187, 190, 198, 207
  Hot cross buns 110, 111
  Korowaj 97
  Kutia 143, 144, 145, 149, 174
  Mushroom dumplings 145
  Pancakes 79, 90, 109, 144, 146
  Poppy seed cookies 145
  Potatoes mashed with garlic 144
  Pyrohy [pirogies] 144
  Salad 145
  Stewed fruit 144

Fruits
  Apple 32, 33, 37, 44, 136, 138, 141, 144, 147, 162, 173, 181, 184
  Cranberries 32
  Figs 32, 147, 148
  Fruits 31, 32, 36, 47, 84, 112, 116, 129, 132, 135, 143, 156, 178, 180
  Pomegranates 32
  Strawberries 20

G

Gender diversity
  Ceremonial cross-dressing or mixed gender attire 107, 113, 115, 120, 152
  Change of sex 100
  Effect of the rainbow upon 100
  Effect of water upon 80
  Hermaphrodite or intersex 16
  Personae
    Junius 127
    Mad Moll 121
    Malanka 149
    Marmselle Molliowski 121
    Qinter 120
  Transgender metamorphosis 193

H

Healing 5, 27, 30, 41, 42, 46, 48, 53, 59, 77, 78, 82, 83, 85, 91, 96, 100, 122, 128, 156, 174, 175, 176, 177, 178, 179, 185, 187, 189, 199, 200, 203, 207, 208
  Eggs 175
  Epilepsy 63, 66, 124, 199
  Fever 28, 85, 176, 178
  Fumigation 175
  Glanders 178
  Rheumatism 28, 175, 205
  Snakebite 59, 197, 203
  Staunching blood 179
  Toothache 26
  Tuberculosis 28, 66
Herbal medicine
  Basil 83, 178
  Feverfew 176, 177
  Herbal medicine 78, 176, 178
  Mugwort 33, 156, 158

Plantain 128
Herbs 33, 116, 217
    Rosemary 112, 161
    Rue 36, 53, 161, 176, 177
    Thyme 36, 158, 161, 176
Heroes
    Cú Chulainn 59, 61, 166
Hills and mountains
    Bobkalniai 76
    Brocken 76, 121
    Donnersberg 76
    Harz Mountains 76, 121
    Hills 75, 76, 77, 93, 116, 124, 135
    Hörselberg 76
    Kalnai 76
    Mergakalniai 76
    Mountain 6, 7, 19, 77, 79, 91
    Mountains of Connacht 113
    Rambynas 25, 43, 76
    Sleza 77
    Szatria 76
    Wuotansberg 76

I

Incantation, invocation, praise-hymn
    Incantation 106, 137, 176, 178, 186, 199, 203
    Invocation 43, 80, 85, 128, 135, 137, 144, 147, 148, 156, 157, 160, 170, 176, 178, 186, 208, 209
    Invoke 27, 50, 79, 80, 95, 109, 147, 149, 161, 162, 208
    Praise-hymn 133, 208
Incense and perfume
    Incense 64, 85, 93, 149, 150, 152, 171
    Perfume 64, 152, 198
Indigeneity 5, 6, 8, 16, 18, 19, 21, 22, 24, 31, 34, 39, 53, 55, 64, 65, 73, 75, 80, 82, 84, 85, 93, 94, 95, 98, 101, 133, 171, 177, 178, 197, 210

L

Literature, 20th and 21st centuries
    William Butler Yeats 33
Literature, ancient
    Apuleius 178
    Athenaeus 168, 169
    Homer 22
    Ovid 126

Literature, medieval
    Geoffrey of Monmouth 122
    Giovanni Boccaccio 125
    Mabinogion 44
    Prose Edda 64
    Taliesin 49, 213
    Tristan and Isolde 190
Love, sexuality, marriage
    Amatory magic 113, 116, 187, 189, 191, 199, 201, 203
    Aphrodisiac 28, 160
    Bride 161, 162, 163, 164
    Courtesan 113, 117, 126, 191
    Erotic mysticism 166
    Eroticism 107, 122, 127, 128, 147, 163, 167, 168, 169
    Finamor 164, 166, 167
    Groom 161, 162, 163, 164
    Handfasting 29, 160
    Hieros gamos 16
    Love 10, 13, 14, 16, 18, 29, 31, 32, 33, 37, 40, 42, 43, 46, 57, 60, 75, 78, 84, 85, 87, 89, 90, 96, 97, 113, 114, 115, 116, 122, 125, 127, 129, 136, 137, 138, 149, 153, 159, 160, 161, 162, 163, 164, 165, 166, 167, 171, 175, 181, 182, 186, 189, 190, 191, 192, 200, 204, 209
    Lovemaking 113, 116, 117, 123, 129, 130, 160, 162, 167
    Marriage 16, 34, 36, 42, 49, 81, 100, 111, 114, 128, 130, 136, 144, 145, 149, 159, 160, 161, 162, 163, 164, 166, 167, 179, 181, 191, 203, 204
    Nuptial chamber 163
    Prostitute 117, 191
    Same-sex intimacy 58, 167, 168, 169
        Celts 168
        Christian "particular friendships" 169
        Germanic peoples 168
        In Christianity, punishable by death 169
        Initiatory same-sex eroticism among Greeks 169
    Threshold 81, 163
    Wedding 37, 40, 68, 81, 84, 97, 149, 156, 159, 160, 161, 162, 163, 203

M

Magic
    Bewitching 192, 209

Charm 40, 175, 178, 186, 205
Curse 91, 144, 192, 193, 199, 201, 202
Galdr 189
Love magic 33, 97, 189, 190, 191, 209
Love potion 113
Magic circle 148
Magical practice 43, 62, 92, 129, 187, 192, 193, 199, 201, 206, 209
Meneurs de nuées 188, 189
Merseburg Charms 186
Rainmaking 188
Seiðr 142, 158, 160, 188
Weather magic 188, 189
Wind magic 188, 189

Magical practice
Magical flight 170, 193, 194, 196

Materials used in pagan practices
Amulet 59, 125, 175, 197, 198, 203, 204, 206
Amulet bags 206
Bits of colored glass 206
Bottle 192, 193
Cauldron 65, 187
Chalice 47
Charmides sachets bearing astrological symbols 206
Corp criadh 201
Cowries 197, 198
Dirt 176, 189, 197
Dragons blood 191, 192
Fetish 205
Greek Magical Papyri 192, 203
Gris-gris 207
Gunpowder 85
Hair 159
Knotted charms 206
Mandrake 176, 177, 201, 204
Menstrual blood 113, 190
Mirror 165, 181
Necklace of blue beads 205
Ointment 200
Poppet 201, 202
Powder 54, 159, 199, 207
Rags 42
Sea beans 204
Shells 197, 198, 206
Talisman 161
Wax figure 202, 203

Metamorphosis 55, 57, 58, 59, 69, 74, 108, 142, 193. *See also* See gender diversity
Shapeshifting 79, 87, 88
Theriomorphic 69

Music and dance
Charivari 127, 162, 164, 188
Dance 40, 46, 47, 77, 78, 84, 96, 106, 115, 116, 117, 118, 119, 121, 122, 123, 124, 125, 126, 127, 129, 133, 135, 148, 154, 155, 162, 165
Morris dance 115, 116

O

Offerings and sacrifice
Cake 30, 98, 127, 130, 142, 147, 150, 151, 154, 161, 162, 185

Offerings and sacrifices
Bears 50
Black sows 88
Boar 66
Candles 43, 92, 128, 143, 144, 150, 151, 153, 154, 163, 189, 190, 207
Chicken 58
Human figure made of wax 128
Milk 62
Rooster 58, 66
Sacrifice of boars 64
Sacrifice of bulls 64
Sacrifice of dogs 64
Sacrifice of goats 64
Sheep 20, 64, 65, 68, 83, 88, 90, 120, 149, 157, 162, 184, 199
Sow 142
White male goat 90

Otherworlds and afterlife locations
Avalon 33, 92
Bouyan 90
Dvergasteinn 27
Fôlkvângr 173
Magonia 195, 218
Niflheim 91, 173
Tír na nÓg 123
Tuonela 173
Valhalla 57, 59, 99, 100, 173

P

Pagan rebellion
Magyars 186

Philosophers and related
Democritus 14

Empedocles 13, 75
Leo Allatios 74
Plato 14, 15, 74
Pythagoras 13, 74
Robert Burton 74
Socrates 14, 15, 74
Thales 12, 13, 80
Voltaire 114
Zeno 13
Procreation, pregnancy, childbirth
  Bathhouse 157
  Childbirth 26, 28, 33, 37, 109, 111, 143, 156, 157, 158, 176, 203
    Birthing ceremony 159
    Caul 159
    Changeling 159
    Umbilical cord 158, 159
  Labor 157, 176
  Pregnancy 28, 41, 66, 109, 156, 157, 207
  Procreation 156
Professions
  Weaver 118
Psychic abilities 159
  Clairvoyance 185

R

Rainbow 95, 100
Ritual specialists
  Druid 6, 39, 44, 46, 48, 52, 92, 140, 187
  Hexenmeister 218
  Kräuterweiblein, Herb Women" 176
  Krive 51, 52
  Persons
    Agnes and Jone Waterhouse 177
    Alexée Drigie 200
    Alice Kyteler 58
    Alison Peirsoun 174
    Andro Man 210, 211
    Anne Chattox 200
    Circe 97
    Domenica Darmanin 190
    Elizabeth Frauncis 177
    Isobel Gowdie 202
    James Reid 29, 176
    Janet Wischert 180
    Jeanne Gallée 200
    John Fian 189
    John Sutherland 189
    Jonet Anderson 118
    Kusti Ihalainen 62
    Margaret Aiken 118
    Margaret Clark 191
    Marion Pardon 61, 189
    Mother Sunshine 199
    North Berwick witches 189
    Old Demdyke (Elizabeth Sowtherns 200
    Pendle Witches 199
    Thomas Leyis 137
  Priestess 47, 55, 58, 62, 90, 128, 158, 160, 193, 197
  Seiðkonur 188
  Sorceress 57
  Spakona 143
  Streghe 191
  Tietäjä 62
  Völva 58
  Wisewomen 39, 40, 43, 44, 48, 78, 85, 160, 170, 176
Rulers and nobles
  Caroline of Brunswick 202
  Charlemagne 106, 171
  Constantine the Great 112
  Empress Helena 89
  Gediminas 25
  Grand Duke Algirdas 171
  Harald Hardrada 20
  James VI/ I 67, 91, 189
  King Cnut 95
  Queen Elizabeth I 184
  Queen of Sheba 84

S

Sacred energy or force
  Ashé 7, 9
  Aurr 7
  Chi 7
  Chi-sei 7
  Élan vital 7, 35
  Mana 7, 35
  Máttr 7
  Navala 7
  Seite 7
  Teotl 7
  Toradh 7
  šventas 7
Sacred hybridity 18, 86, 130, 141

Pagano-Christian 89, 111, 124, 128, 150, 151, 169, 171, 189, 209
Societies and communities
   Walpurgis Society 121
Stones, gemstones, metals
   Amber (fossilized resin) 203
   Gemstones 26
      Amethyst 26, 203
      Carnelian 26
      Jet 203
      Ruby 26
      Sapphire 26
   Metals
      Bronze 20, 111, 195, 203, 206
      Copper 44, 83, 203
      Gold 47, 52, 78, 109, 141, 146, 160, 161, 178, 204
      Iron 20, 23, 44, 93, 137, 143, 170, 173, 192, 203, 206, 207
      Silver 44, 80, 98, 124, 141, 158, 161, 178, 180, 204, 205
   Named stones
      Baba stones 26
      Fairy stones (laumiø akmenys) 25
      Lia Fail 28
      Menhir of Kerloas at Plouarzel 29
      Mermaids Stone 25
      Stonehenge 24, 123
      Stones of Stenness 29
   Quartz 28, 29, 171, 180, 203
   Sacred stones 22, 24, 25, 26, 29, 30, 43, 51, 66, 119, 122, 126, 160
   Stones as living beings 24
   Types of stone structures
      Dolmen 25, 29
      Megalith 25, 122
      Menhir 24, 25, 29, 66
   Veneration of stones 9, 25, 29

T

Tasks and professions
   Beekeeper 67, 68, 187
   Blacksmith 56, 192
   Farmer 8, 46, 90, 98, 127, 128, 131, 133, 135, 139, 145, 173
   Fisher folk 87, 88, 206
   Maritime trader 187
   Midwife 156, 157, 158, 159, 176
   Miner 184
   Shepherd 79, 112, 116
   Spinner 26, 78, 90, 146, 187
      Distaff 99, 182
   Vintner 105
   Weaver 20, 78, 89, 187, 203, 206
The Devil and kindred beings
   Beelzebub 74
   Devils Grandmother 32
   Lucifer
      Luciferan cult 58
The soul 13, 29, 38, 40, 43, 44, 45, 46, 56, 57, 58, 70, 71, 90, 136, 146, 156, 170, 172, 173
   Hugr 172
   Siela 38, 70, 172
Theisms
   Deism 17
   Henotheism. *See* See pantheism, panpsychism
   Monotheism 36, 185
   Polytheism 27, 36
Theoretical concepts
   Archetypal perspective 15, 209
   Bricolage 39, 55, 138
   Cartesian paradigm 18
   Counterdiscourse 211
   Enspirited materiality 8, 115, 178
   Fluidity 97
   Hegemonic discourse 211
   Holistic perspective 52
   Invisible immanence 17, 195
   Liminality 42
   Multidimensional reality 17, 69, 172, 195
   Parallel universe 195
   String theory 196
   Theory of correspondences 16, 18, 52, 94
   Vernacular theory 132
Trees
   Alder 34, 39, 49
   Ash 35, 39, 40
   Beech 35, 38, 40, 50, 51
   Birch 9, 34, 35, 37, 40, 42, 46, 49, 50, 79, 90, 104, 113, 116, 156, 158, 173, 211
   Blackthorn 199
   Bo-träd 37
   Cornel 36
   Covin-trees 37
   Elder 38, 41

Fir tree 38, 46
Hawthorn 41, 42, 163, 164
Hazel 11, 34, 37, 42, 49, 50, 82, 156
Irminsul 7, 35
Juniper 37, 43, 112, 149
Linden 36, 37, 43, 44, 54, 56, 60, 104, 158, 173
Maple 31, 37, 38, 82
Oak 11, 20, 31, 35, 36, 37, 39, 40, 43, 44, 45, 48, 49, 50, 52, 54, 56, 78, 82, 120, 133, 140, 151, 158, 173, 178, 189
Pine 35, 36, 37, 45, 61, 110, 160, 161, 191
Poplar 36, 120, 201
Rowan 34, 37, 45, 46, 158
Sacred groves 8, 21, 49, 50, 51, 58, 65, 170, 171, 180
   Gaj (enclosed space) 51
   Romuva 44, 51, 52
   Sœlundr 50
   Swiety Bor 51
   šventa giria 51
Spruce 36, 37, 46, 110
Walnut 46, 47
Willow 50, 82, 90, 119, 121
World-tree 7, 36, 40, 43, 59, 156
Yew 34, 37, 39, 44, 47, 48
Yggdrasil 39, 59, 81, 100

V

Vegetables
   Beet 163
   Corn 7, 15, 40, 59, 70, 93, 98, 100, 125, 127, 130, 131, 132, 133, 134, 135, 153, 158, 163, 172, 180, 192

W

War, warriors, weapons
   Axe 57
   Battle 27, 28, 40, 49, 56, 61, 62, 92, 99, 100, 108, 120, 167, 173
   Berserkr 55
   Helmet 56
   Shield 39
   Spear 81, 170
   Sword 182, 202
   Ulfserkr 62
   War 51, 56, 100, 130, 183
   Warrior 40, 41, 55, 56, 57, 59, 62, 91, 99, 142, 166, 170, 171, 173
   Warriorship 44
Water, bodies of water, and water rites
   šaltiniai 81
   Baptism 80, 159
   Bathing rites 117
   Ežerai 81
   Fountain 80, 84, 117, 137
   Loch Shiant 82
   May bathing 117
   Raganines 84
   Sacred lake 81, 82
   Sauna 117, 145
   Spring 77
   Spring of Glomac 83
   Thors Well 82
   Upes 81
Wheel of the Year
   Autumn
      Harvest Home 131, 132, 135
      Harvest rites 130, 131, 134, 135
      Samhain (Halloween) 33, 42, 43, 82, 84, 103, 106, 107, 123, 135, 136, 137, 154, 160, 179
   Spring
      Beltane 40, 42, 43, 49, 66, 82, 83, 94, 105, 112, 113, 114, 118, 119, 120, 123, 166, 182, 210, 211
      Calendimaggio (Feast of the Kalends of May) 114
      Floralia 112, 113, 114, 119
      May Day (May 1) 103, 119
      Navigium Isidis 107
      Parilia 92, 112, 113
      Robigalia 112
      Rosalia 122
      Spring equinox 43, 55, 60, 66, 70, 72, 79, 94, 104, 106, 107, 108, 109, 110, 111, 149, 153, 165, 166, 167, 192
      Velykos 109
      Walpurgisnacht 112, 113
   Summer
      Kupalo 123
      Lughnasa/Lammas 105, 130, 132, 160
      Midsummer rites 122, 124, 127, 128
      Summer solstice 47, 77, 103, 122, 123, 124, 125, 126, 187, 190
   Summer and autumn
      Harvest rites 60

Winter
  Bacchanalia 152, 155
  Carnival 63, 106, 107, 115, 149
  Feast of Fools 106, 151, 152
  Imbolc/Candlemas 105, 153, 154, 160
  Kolyada 143
  Lupercalia 102, 107, 153, 154, 155
  Matronalia 107
  Modranicht 141
  Samborios 139
  Saturnalia 107, 139, 140
  Solstice 24, 66, 69, 78, 95, 140, 142, 143, 146, 153
  Twelfth Night 150, 151, 152
  Vilci Prazdnici, Wolf Holidays' 143
  Wassailing 33, 49, 147, 151
  Wild Hunt 142, 146, 170
  Yule 40, 46, 66, 93, 103, 106, 139, 140, 142, 145, 146, 153

www.ingramcontent.com/pod-product-compliance
Lightning Source LLC
Chambersburg PA
CBHW080410230426
43662CB00016B/2365

The Pagan Heart of the West

by
Randy P. Conner Ph.D.

Vol. II
Nature and Rites